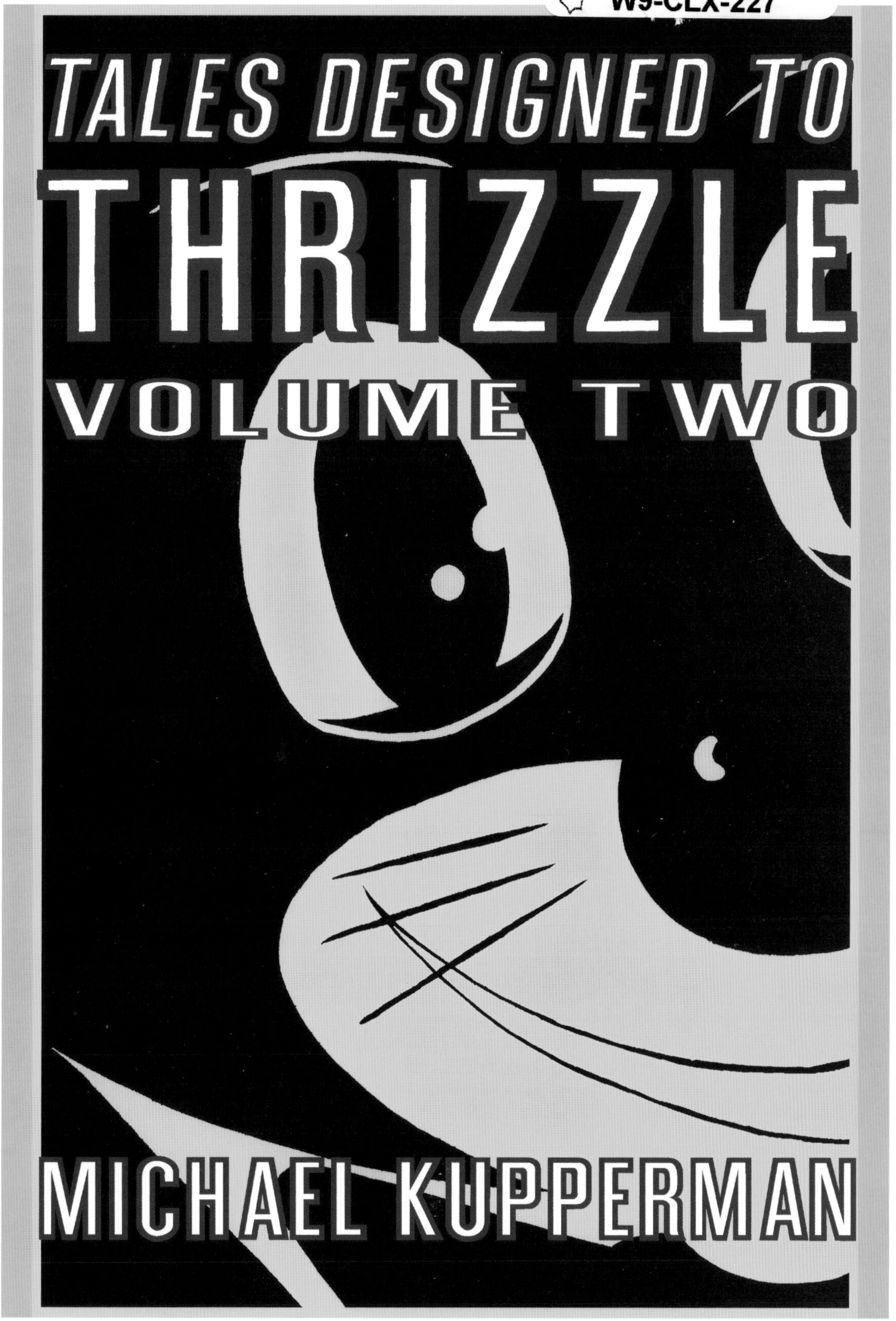
TALES DESIGNED TO
THRIZZLE
VOLUME TWO
MICHAEL KUPPERMAN

FANTAGRAPHICS
7563 LAKE CITY WAY
SEATTLE, WA 98115

ASSOCIATE EDITOR:
ERIC REYNOLDS PRODUCTION
ASSISTANCE BY PAUL BARESH
PUBLISHERS: GARY GROTH AND KIM
THOMPSON

DISTRIBUTED IN THE U.S. BY W.W. NORTON AND COMPANY, INC (800-233-4830)
DISTRIBUTED IN THE U.K. BY TURNAROUND DISTRIBUTION (20-8829-3002)

VISIT THE FANTAGRAPHICS WEBSITE AT WWW. FANTAGRAPHICS.COM

PHOTOCOMIC ACTORS: JULIE KLAUSNER, NEIL CASEY AND KATE HAMBRECHT
SPECIAL THANKS TO BIANCA D'SOUZA SOME COMICS IN THIS BOOK HAVE APPEARED IN THE
SEATTLE STRANGER, THE OXFORD AMERICAN AND THE NEW YORKER

FIRST PRINTING: NOVEMBER, 2012 ISBN: 978-1-60699-615-7 PRINTED IN CHINA

DEDICATED TO THE SPIRIT OF MANKIND

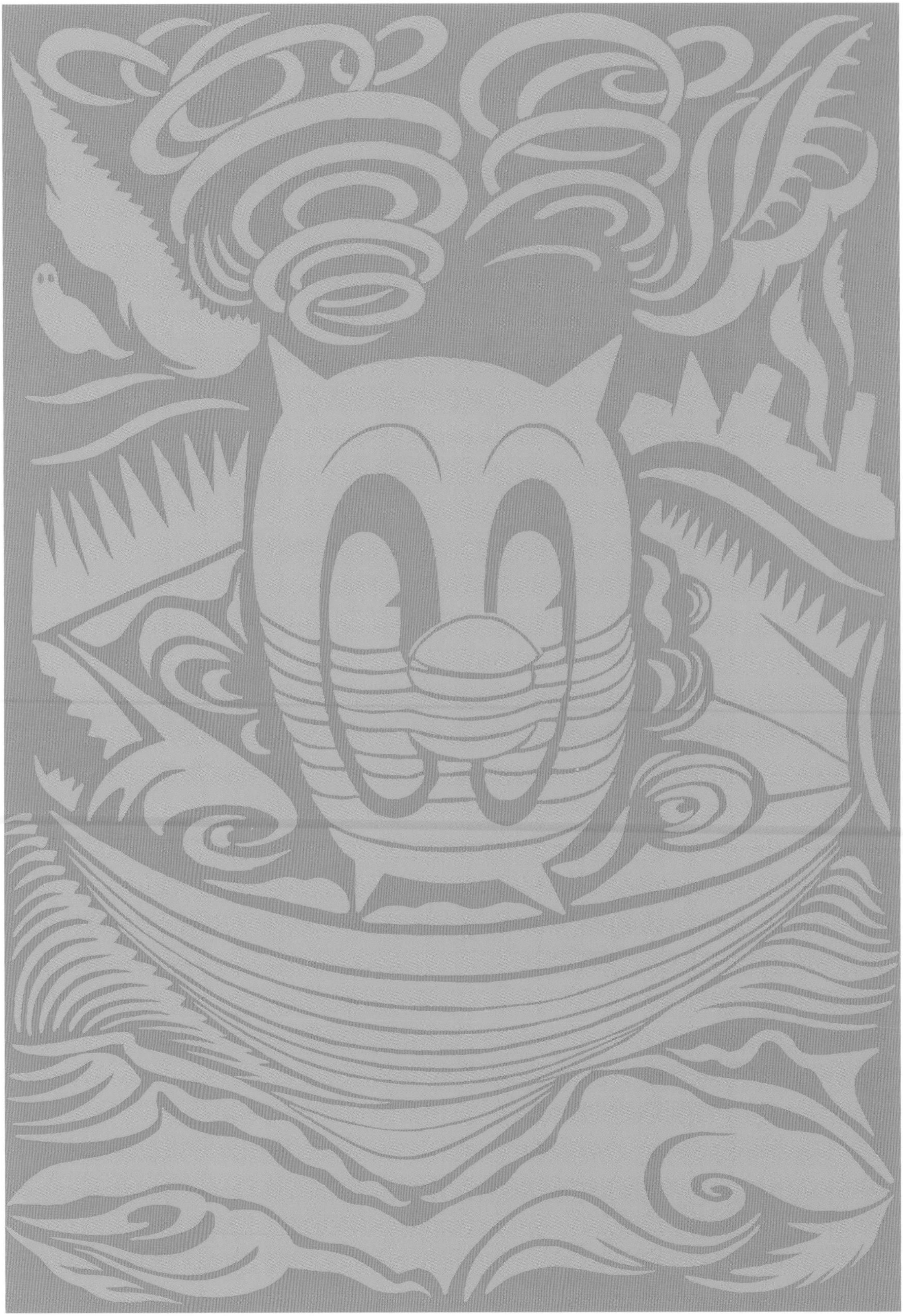

MANDATE *the* MAGICIAN

MANDATE IS PERFORMING IN VEGAS

WHAT IS YOUR NAME, MISS?

JANICE

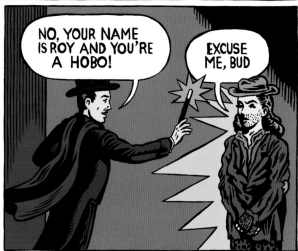

NO, YOUR NAME IS ROY AND YOU'RE A HOBO!

EXCUSE ME, BUD

NOW YOU'RE BEGGING ON THE MOON!

SPARE CHANGE?

TIME TO REJOIN US, JANICE! HAS YOUR EXPERIENCE TAUGHT YOU ANYTHING?

YES, I NOW KNOW WHAT IT'S LIKE TO BE HOMELESS & IN SPACE!

YOU'VE BEEN A TERRIFIC CROWD — THANK YOU AND GOODNIGHT!

HE DIDN'T REMIND THE AUDIENCE TO TIP US!

THAT'S NOT LIKE HIM!

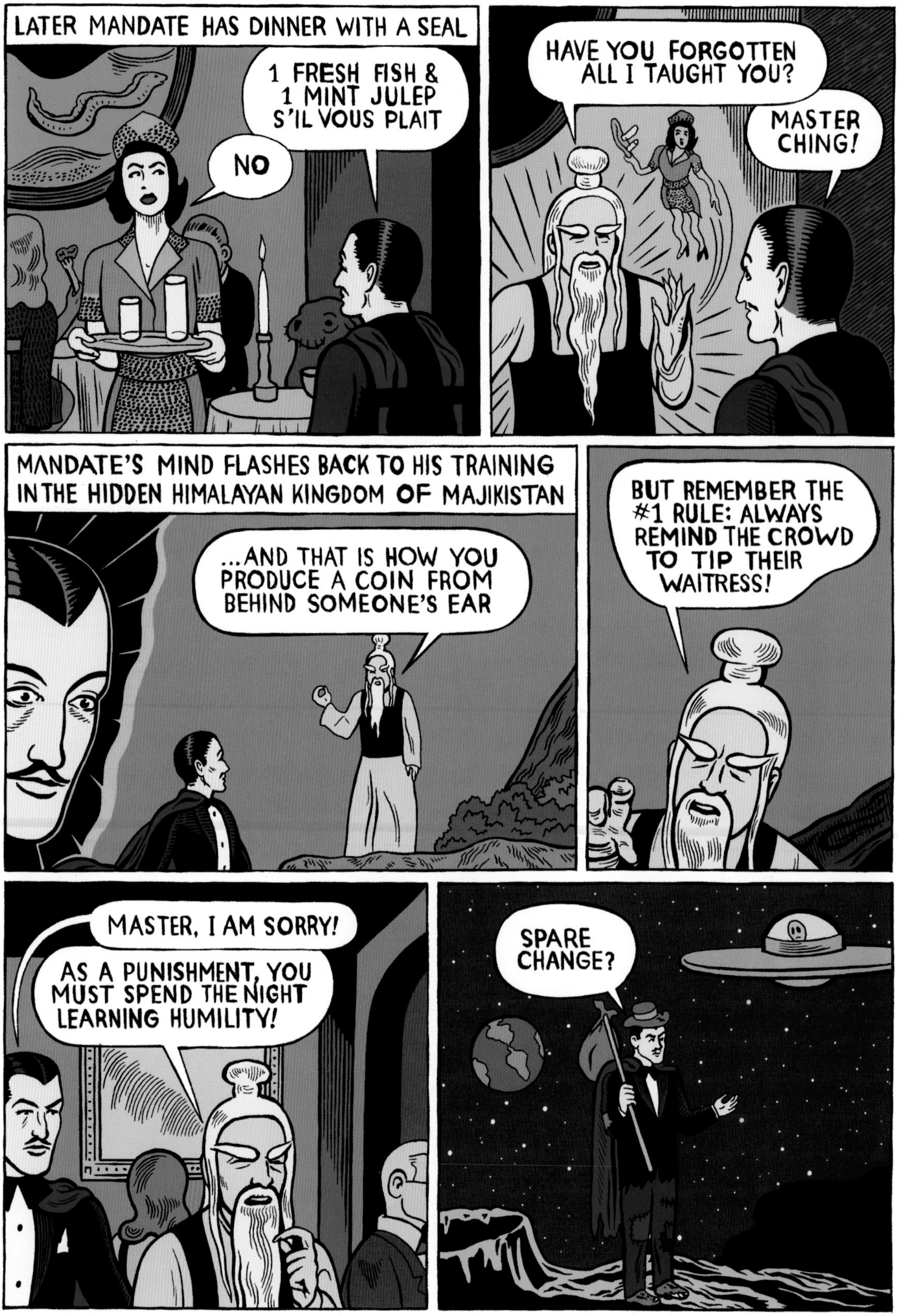
LATER MANDATE HAS DINNER WITH A SEAL
1 FRESH FISH & 1 MINT JULEP S'IL VOUS PLAIT
NO
HAVE YOU FORGOTTEN ALL I TAUGHT YOU?
MASTER CHING!
MANDATE'S MIND FLASHES BACK TO HIS TRAINING IN THE HIDDEN HIMALAYAN KINGDOM OF MAJIKISTAN
...AND THAT IS HOW YOU PRODUCE A COIN FROM BEHIND SOMEONE'S EAR
BUT REMEMBER THE #1 RULE: ALWAYS REMIND THE CROWD TO TIP THEIR WAITRESS!
MASTER, I AM SORRY!
AS A PUNISHMENT, YOU MUST SPEND THE NIGHT LEARNING HUMILITY!
SPARE CHANGE?

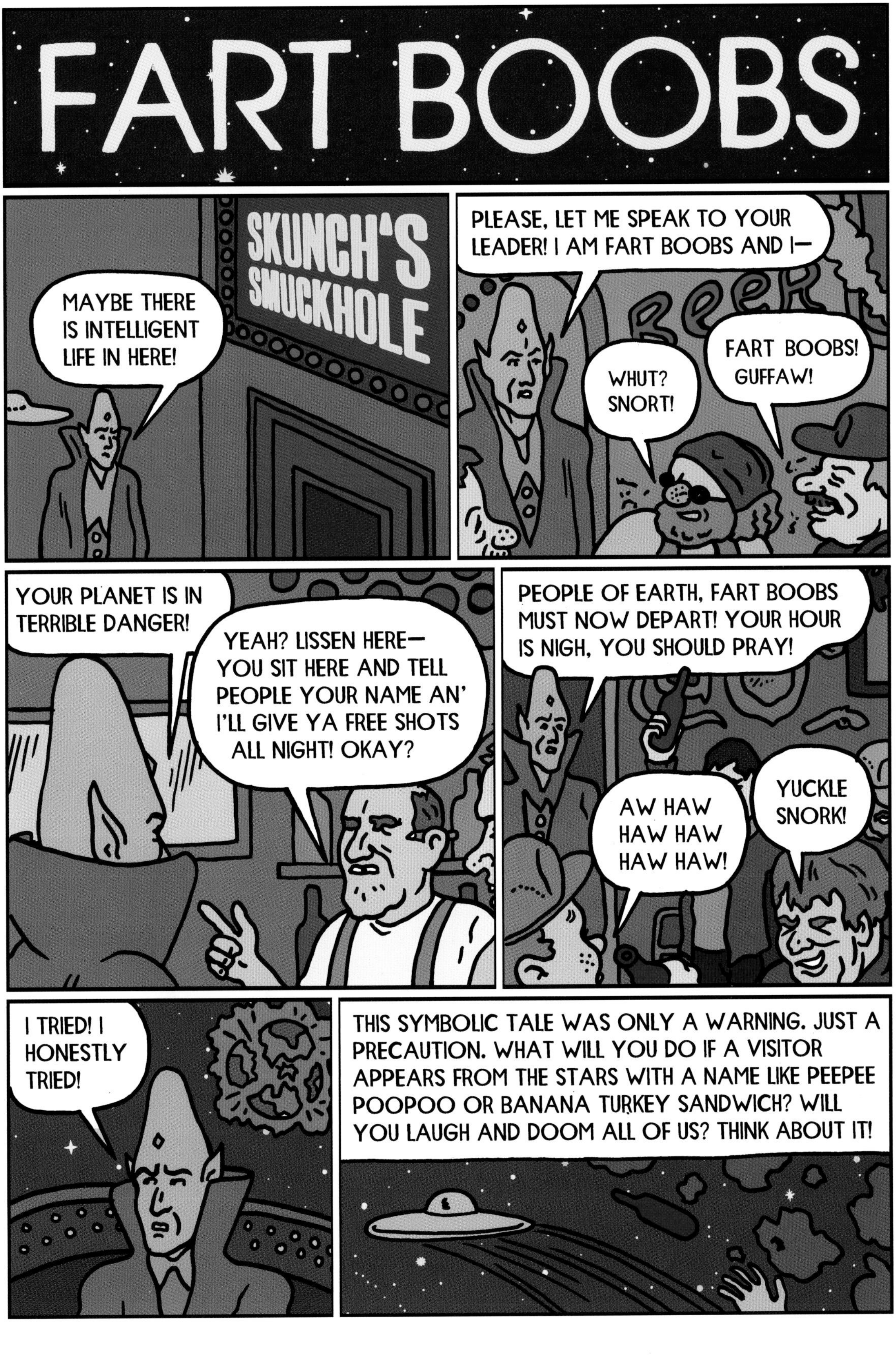
FART BOOBS
SKUNCH'S SMUCKHOLE
MAYBE THERE IS INTELLIGENT LIFE IN HERE!
PLEASE, LET ME SPEAK TO YOUR LEADER! I AM FART BOOBS AND I—
BEER
WHUT? SNORT!
FART BOOBS! GUFFAW!
YOUR PLANET IS IN TERRIBLE DANGER!
YEAH? LISSEN HERE— YOU SIT HERE AND TELL PEOPLE YOUR NAME AN' I'LL GIVE YA FREE SHOTS ALL NIGHT! OKAY?
PEOPLE OF EARTH, FART BOOBS MUST NOW DEPART! YOUR HOUR IS NIGH, YOU SHOULD PRAY!
AW HAW HAW HAW HAW HAW!
YUCKLE SNORK!
I TRIED! I HONESTLY TRIED!
THIS SYMBOLIC TALE WAS ONLY A WARNING. JUST A PRECAUTION. WHAT WILL YOU DO IF A VISITOR APPEARS FROM THE STARS WITH A NAME LIKE PEEPEE POOPOO OR BANANA TURKEY SANDWICH? WILL YOU LAUGH AND DOOM ALL OF US? THINK ABOUT IT!

JOURNEY INTO ADVENTURE

I'M *BAMBIFFPOW JACKSON* — THERE'S A FISTFIGHT IN MY VERY NAME!

YES, I KNOW. YOU WERE HERE BEFORE, AND WERE ASKED NOT TO RETURN.

MY SUBSTANTIALITY IS THREATENED BY A POSSIBLE LAW SUIT BY THE MAKERS OF THE 1987 FILM "ACTION JACKSON!" HEEEEEELP ME!

UH-HUH.

MAYBE WHAT YOU NEED IS A FRESH START IN A NEW CITY, FAR AWAY.

I'M FADING... FADING...

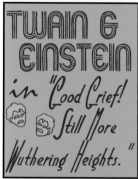

TWAIN & EINSTEIN in "Good Grief! Still More Wuthering Heights."

UGH! THESE HEIGHTS ARE WUTHERING!

GET WITH IT, AL! HEIGHTS ARE "IN" RIGHT NOW! KIDS ARE TALKING ABOUT THEM RIGHT NOW, I THINK.

PRINCETON

LOOK! THERE'S HEATHCLIFF!

WHO'S HEATHCLIFF?

PRINCETON

HE'S THE PEPSI TO GARFIELD'S COKE! YOU DON'T SEE HIM MUCH ANYMORE!

LET'S NOT SEE HIM NOW!

PRINCE
END

THE LIBRARIAN IN THE TUNA CASSEROLE

OH MY GOODNESS — THERE'S SOMEONE IN OUR TUNA CASSEROLE!

IT'S OUR SCHOOL LIBRARIAN, MOM, MR. MORALES!

PLEASE, MISTER! GET OUT OF OUR TUNA CASSEROLE!

NO, I WON'T!

NOT UNTIL BILLY RETURNS HIS OVERDUE BOOKS!

The HOARDY BOYS

I THINK THE SMUGGLERS CAME THROUGH HERE — THIS CIGAR BUTT LOOKS FOREIGN!

EVERYTHING HERE COULD BE EVIDENCE — LET'S BAG AND TAG IT ALL!

THAT CAN HAS CLEARLY BEEN HERE A LONG TIME!

I JUST LIKE THE LABEL — GONNA ADD IT TO MY COLLECTION!

LATER —

I CAN HARDLY MOVE IN HERE, THANKS TO ALL THE EVIDENCE!

WE SHOULD TRY AND SOLVE SOME OF THESE CRIMES! CAN'T GET RID OF ANY EVIDENCE UNTIL WE DO!

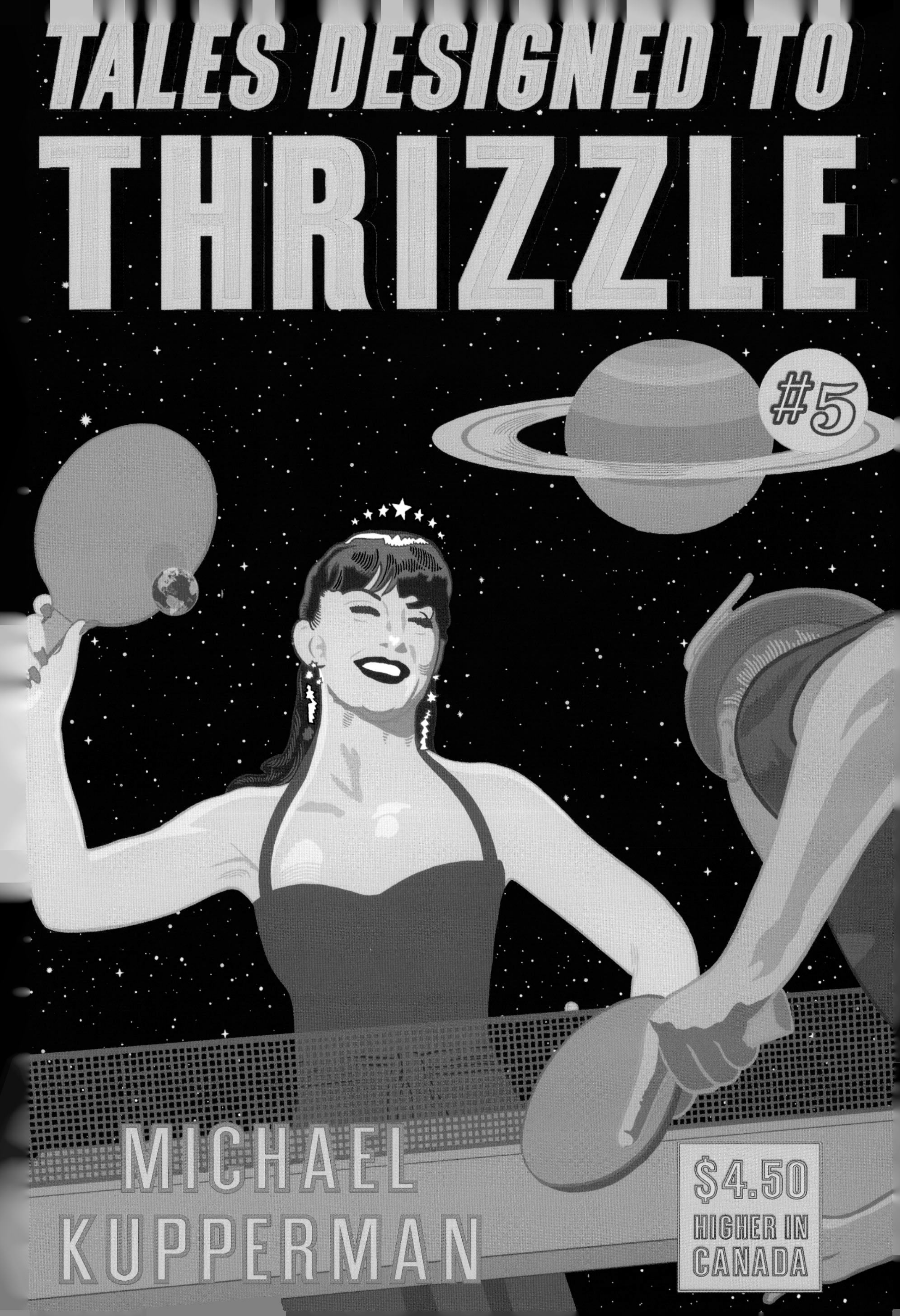
TALES DESIGNED TO
THRIZZLE
#5
MICHAEL
KUPPERMAN
$4.50
HIGHER IN
CANADA

#5 is The OLD PEOPLE'S ISSUE!

Dedicated to the Greatiest Generations.

TALES DESIGNED TO
THRIZZLE

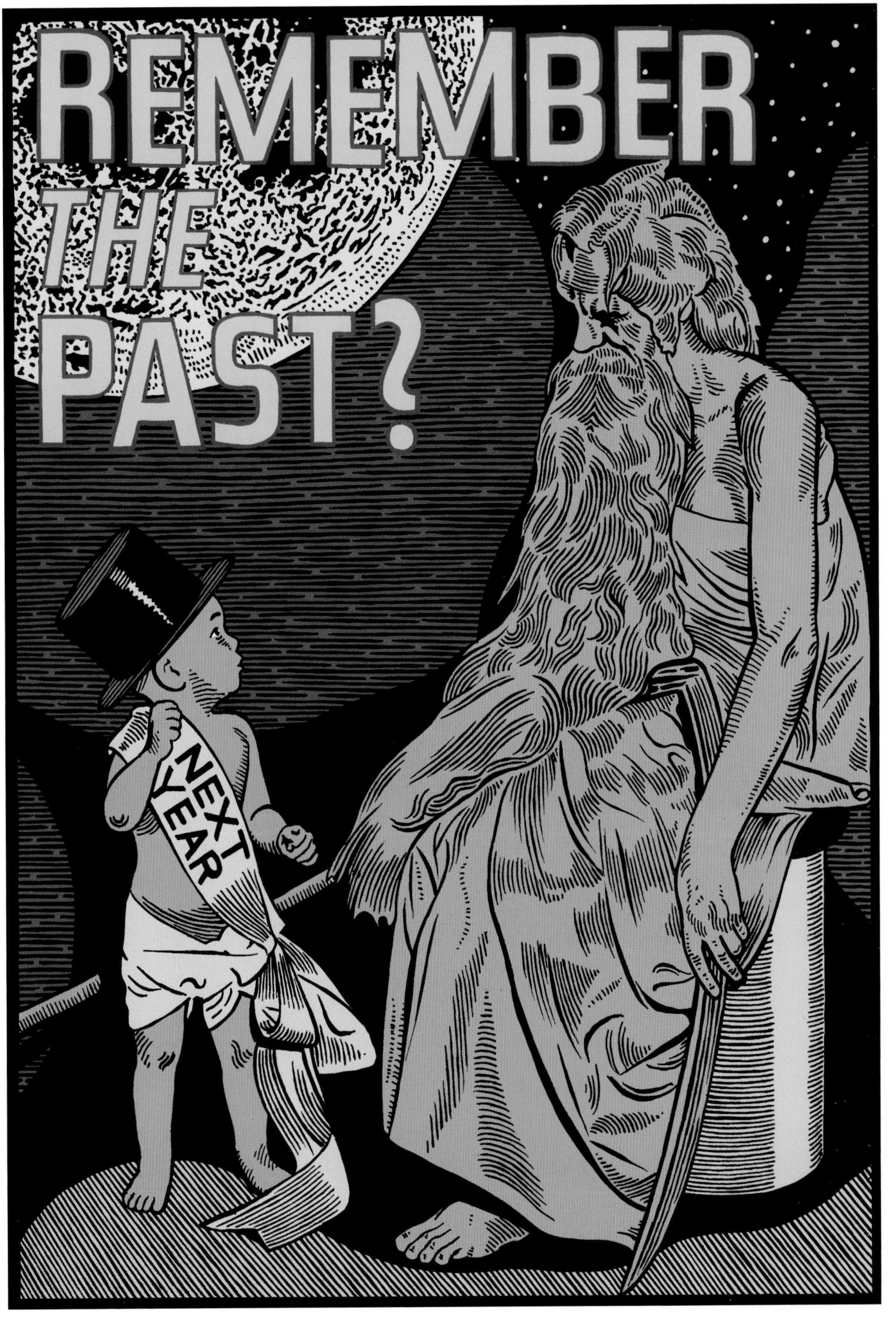
REMEMBER
THE
PAST?
NEXT
YEAR

REMEMBER THEM?

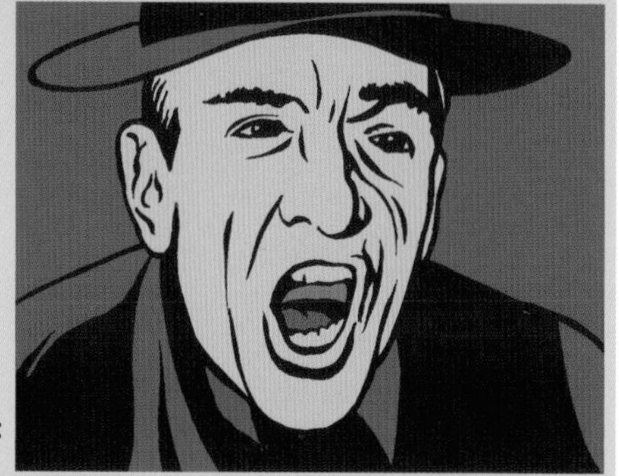

TEODORE "SHOUTY" JACKSON During the early days of talking pictures, the sound was terrible. The whirr of the camera, the rattle of the sound equipment, the heavy fans needed to cool the cameras- all these factors conspired to make the dialogue nearly inaudible. What the movies needed was actors who could be heard, and one man fit the bill: Teodore "Shouty" Jackson. "His bellowing is so loud, yet so clearly enunciated" raved the Cleveland Plain Dealer. Jackson quickly became the number one male lead, appearing in thirty-seven movies in a year and a half. Whatever the part he played, the acting style was the same: feet firmly planted and fists clenched, Teodore would shout his lines exactly as he had issued orders as a Marine drill instructor. Usually he would also summarize the plot in his speeches, so that audiences could keep up:

Jackson: YOLANDA, I HAVE BEEN FAITHFUL AND TRUE! BUT YOU HAVE BETRAYED ME REPEATEDLY WITH THAT WEASELY FELLOW WHO I TUSSLED WITH IN THE LAST SCENE! I BEG OF YOU, TELL ME WHY!
Yolanda: ?mumble mumble? to the safari ?mumble inaudible?
Jackson: YOU HAVE BEEN BLACKMAILED? BY A BALD MAN WHO IS EVEN NOW ESCAPING IN A LOCOMOTIVE?

This exchange comes from I'm *Hollering, You Betcha!* Other hits include *Shut Up, You Louse!*, *I Ain't Deaf*, *Let Me Explain*, *Rackets Are For Mugs*, and *Dames Sure Is Sensitive*, which co-starred the other major loudmouth star of 1931... a young actor named Jamesington (later Jimmy) Cagney. As sound technology improved, Jackson's star waned. He retired from showbusiness in 1953, only to return twenty years later for the bizarre, made-in-the-Philippines *Shouty's Big-Ass Score*. He died a year later yelling at a waiter.

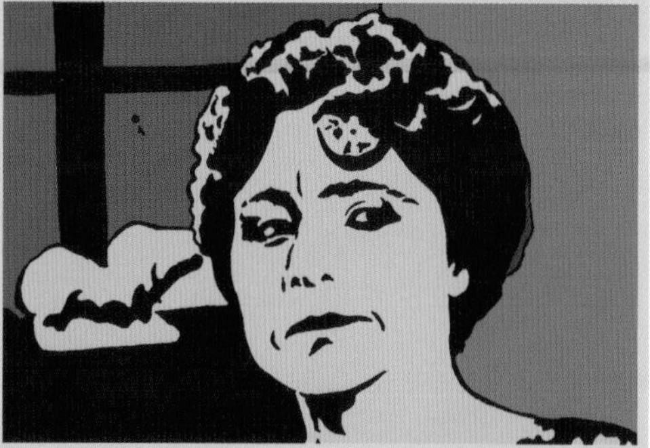

MATRICIA WAMBAUGH is familiar to comedy fans from her portrayal of a wealthy society matron in films featuring The Two Chumps, Burton and Taylor, The Dribbling Idiots, and many, many others. Invariably the comedy team disrupts her banquet/gala/political rally when they screw up the plumbing/painting/wall repair. *Spare Me Your Nonsense* with Horgan and Dooler features a fairly typical exchange:

Horgan: You're a well-padded lady, you oughtta be called sofa.
Lady Doodlesnicker (Matricia): You, you horrible little man! Leave my house immediately.
Horgan: What I'm saying is that I love you and I want to marry you.

Following fifty-seven appearances in films such as *Pardon My Yanking* and *Mail Me Soup, Moron*, Legitimate Pictures apparently felt it owed her something and allowed her to make *Matricia Has It Her Way*. The film features scenes like this one:

Repairman: The kitchen is completely fixed, Mam.
Matricia: Why thank you, that's excellent! Your workmen have been so quiet and courteous, my gala wasn't disturbed at all!

The film was not a hit. Later Matricia played the Noisy Toilet Woman in the Parker House Margerine Spread commercials.

THEODORE EDWARD RUSSELL, a.k.a. "Professor Anus"
A brilliant mathematician, he made the mistake of moving into
a colorful working-class neighborhood; from there he charted
an unusual path to fame. "Because I was known locally as a
man of some intelligence, drunken characters began
showing up at my door late at night and asking me to remove
items which had become lodged in their anuses! At first I was
appalled at their impertinence, but felt I had no choice but to
accede to their demands." As these visits by various individuals
continued, Russell began to amass an impressive collection of
items harvested from the anuses, and eventually went on tour
with them. His first foray into radio, "What Came Out of Your
Anus?" was an immediate smash success and stayed on the

Dumont network for 17 years. But the first episode of his 1953 television show, *Anus Treasure Hunt*,
resulted in America finally realizing what an anus actually was. After the resulting outcry, Russell
and his odd avocation quickly faded from memory, and his death in 1967 of a "salad bar mishap" was
barely noticed.

GERALD ST. VINCENT MUTLEY served in World War I,
where he was stationed in a trench. He enjoyed the experience
so much he dug trenches in his property when he got home to
Indiana, and started a society to promulgate the "trench lifestyle."
His brochure explains his philosophy: "A man appreciates life a
little more when the ground is at eye level. Brings privacy and
intrigue into everyday life, and the kids love it too."
The craze reached even to Washington, where President
Roosevelt explained why he couldn't use a trench. Mutley
appeared on the cover of *Life* magazine, peering out of one of
his company's deluxe trenches. Then World War II happened.

When it was over, the American public had lost interest in trenches, and foxholes too. After being
evicted from his house Mutley moved into one of his trenches, but drowned during a particularly
heavy rainfall.

OSCAR WILDE III burst onto the scene in 1947 claiming to be the grandson of Oscar Wilde.
"My grandfather was not a homosexual. That is a desperate smear by the pervert sector." He threatened to sue anyone who said otherwise, and even produced a movie starring Errol Flynn (*The Skirt-
Chasing Antics of Oscar Wilde*). In reality, he was probably Mack Buchalsitzky, son of a Pittsburgh
steelworker.
Wilde III, trading on the strength of his assumed name, became a radio gossip columnist. His program "Stars In the Gutter: The Gossip Program for Dreary Housewives" sported the slogan
"Remember we're all filth, but some of us are in the gutter, and some of us are in the sewer." Here
are some lines from a typical program:

*William Bendix was spotted looking tiresome on Franklin
and Vine yesterday evening... don't be tiresome, William,
don't be tiresome.*
*And speaking of big apes, I went by the zoo yesterday, and
that same tiresome baboon was up to his same tiresome
tricks, swinging from a tree branch and munching on a
banana as if his life depended on it. What a depressing
sight! The Aesthete in me despairs at the sight of such a
thing... etc.*

Wilde III died in 1953, choking to death on a tuna fish sandwich while giving a demonstration at the Y on how not to
choke to death on a tuna fish sandwich.

EVER-APPROACHING GRANDPA

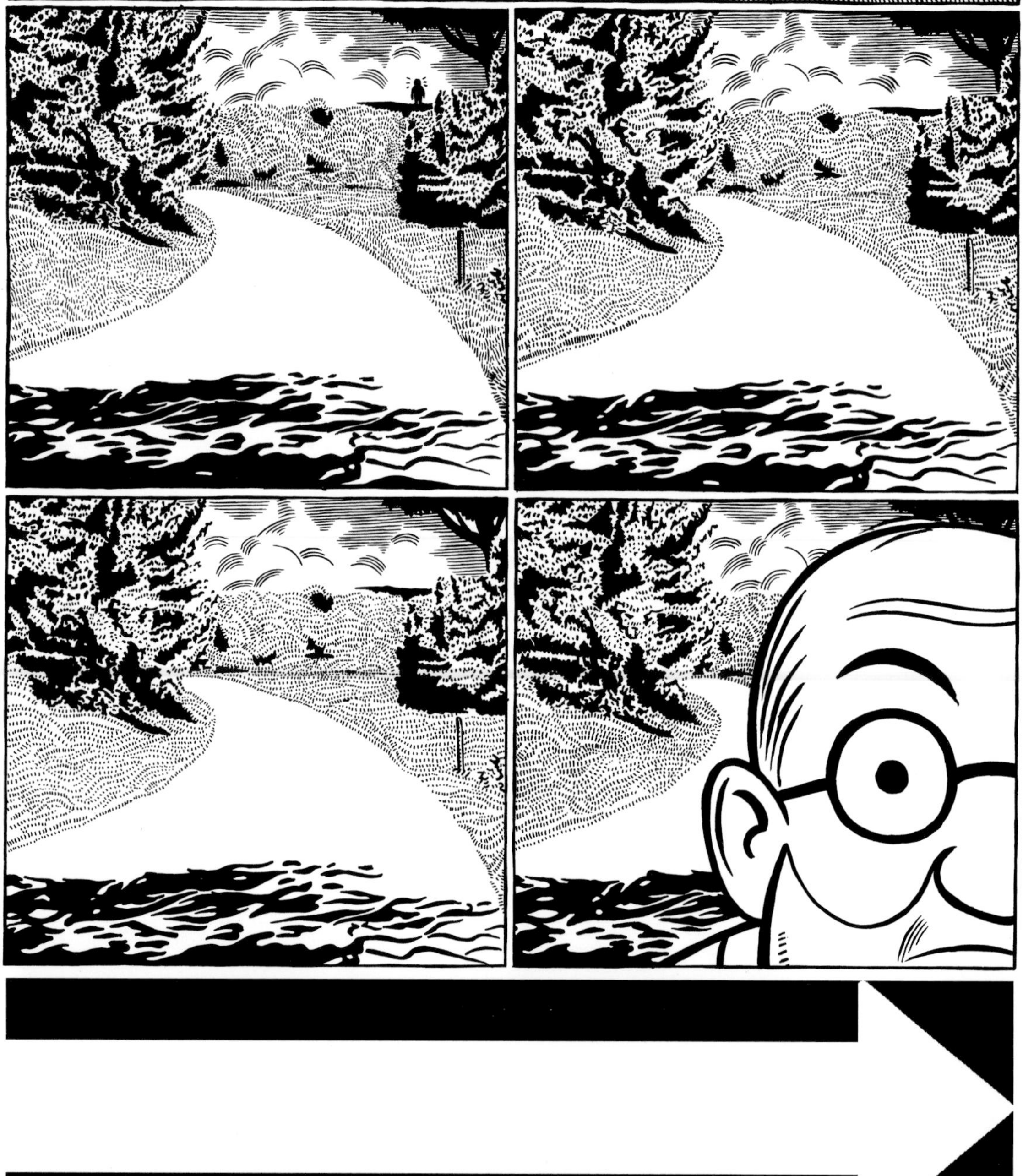

SHERLOCK HOLMES
VERSUS
JUNGLE BOY

MAR
30¢

JUNGLE BOY'S THUMBS... CRUSHING MY WINDPIPE! I HAVE TO HIT HIM... WITH MY VIOLIN!

MAR. TALES OF THE
INTESTINAL
SUBMARINE

1$

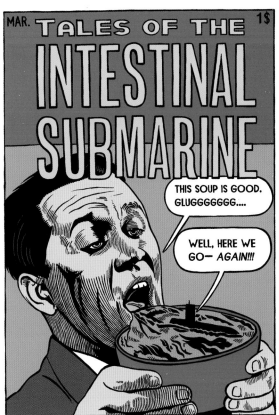

THIS SOUP IS GOOD. GLUGGGGGGG....

WELL, HERE WE GO— *AGAIN!!!*

#15 JOHNNY
EXPOSITION

MAR
30¢

PERHAPS I SHOULD EXPLAIN, DOCTOR KNUDSEN! PROFESSOR SNELL AND VICE-SUPERINTENDENT MCELROY COULDN'T STAND TO SEE THEIR FUNDING CUT. HOW THEY SEETHED AND SEETHED! THEN THEY HIT UPON AN IDEA: WHY NOT SIT UPON EACH OTHER'S SHOULDERS? THAT WAY, THEY'D RESEMBLE THE SEVEN FOOT-TALL FOUR ARMED BLETCHLEY MONSTER, IF SEEN IN THE DARK! AND WHO WOULD SUSPECT? NOT YOU, MISS VIOLET MONTAGUE; YOU WERE COMPLETELY TAKEN IN BY THEM, AND EVEN BELIEVED THAT YOUR UNCLE HAD COMMITTED SUICIDE, ALTHOUGH AS WE KNOW NOW THERE WERE OTHER FACTORS AT PLAY. BESIDES YOU WERE BEING BLACKMAILED, AND YOUR EFFORTS TO LEAD THE POLICE ASTRAY RESULTED IN YOU DOING THE AMUSING "OCTOPUS DANCE" AT THE COUNTY CARNIVAL. YOU'D BEEN LED IN THIS DIRECTION BY SHIFTY DANIELS, WHO (ETC., ETC.)

FEBRUARY
25¢

SHOW ME YOUR
WEINER!

SHOW ME YOUR *WEINER!*

HERE IT IS, DEAR CHAP! I HAVEN'T EATEN IT, AS I PROMISED...

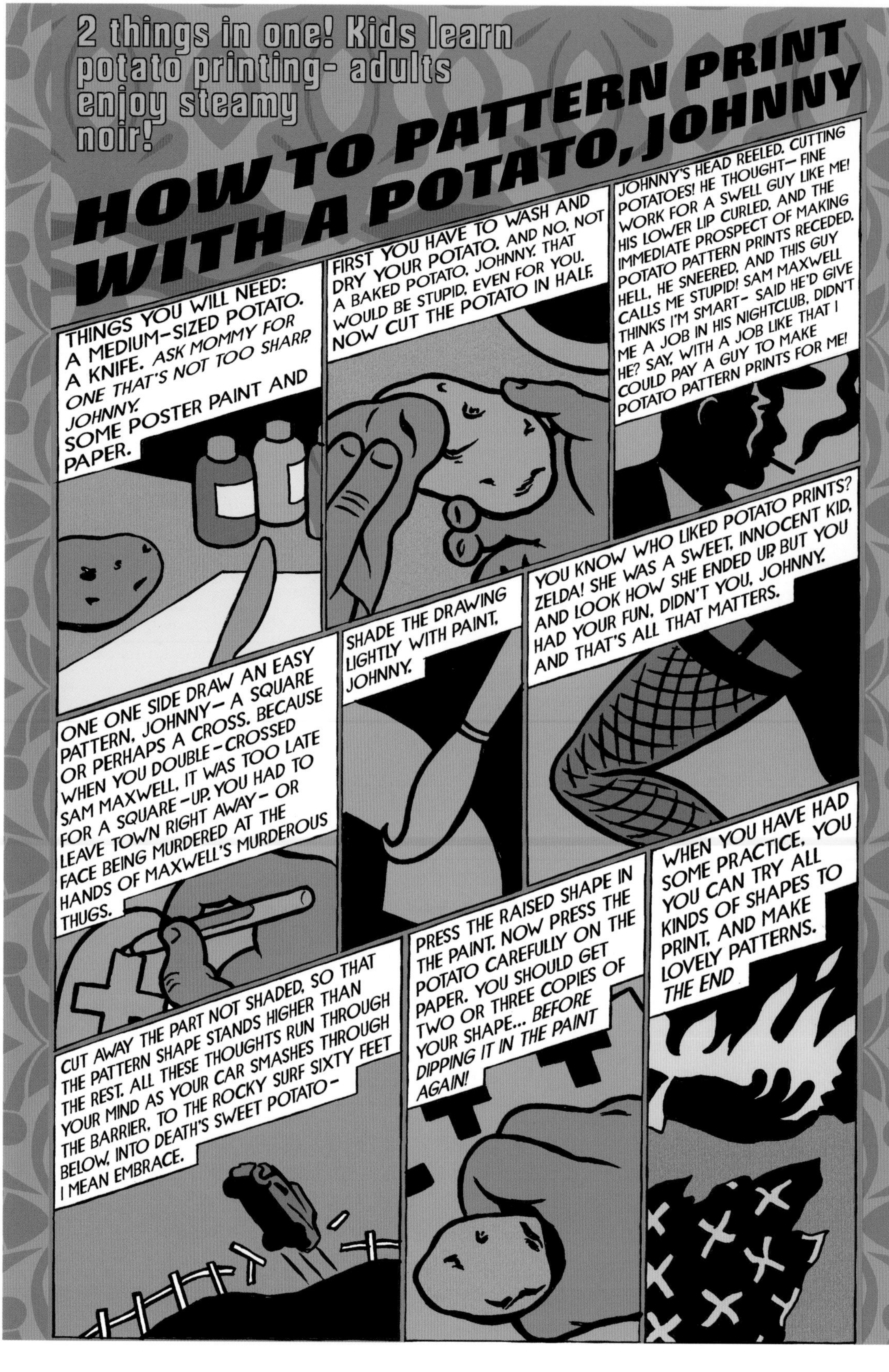
2 things in one! Kids learn potato printing- adults enjoy steamy noir!
HOW TO PATTERN PRINT WITH A POTATO, JOHNNY
THINGS YOU WILL NEED: A MEDIUM-SIZED POTATO. A KNIFE. ASK MOMMY FOR ONE THAT'S NOT TOO SHARP, JOHNNY. SOME POSTER PAINT AND PAPER.
FIRST YOU HAVE TO WASH AND DRY YOUR POTATO. AND NO, NOT A BAKED POTATO, JOHNNY. THAT WOULD BE STUPID, EVEN FOR YOU. NOW CUT THE POTATO IN HALF.
JOHNNY'S HEAD REELED. CUTTING POTATOES! HE THOUGHT- FINE WORK FOR A SWELL GUY LIKE ME! HIS LOWER LIP CURLED, AND THE IMMEDIATE PROSPECT OF MAKING POTATO PATTERN PRINTS RECEDED. HELL, HE SNEERED, AND THIS GUY CALLS ME STUPID! SAM MAXWELL THINKS I'M SMART- SAID HE'D GIVE ME A JOB IN HIS NIGHTCLUB, DIDN'T HE? SAY, WITH A JOB LIKE THAT I COULD PAY A GUY TO MAKE POTATO PATTERN PRINTS FOR ME!
ONE ONE SIDE DRAW AN EASY PATTERN, JOHNNY- A SQUARE OR PERHAPS A CROSS. BECAUSE WHEN YOU DOUBLE-CROSSED SAM MAXWELL, IT WAS TOO LATE FOR A SQUARE-UP. YOU HAD TO LEAVE TOWN RIGHT AWAY- OR FACE BEING MURDERED AT THE HANDS OF MAXWELL'S MURDEROUS THUGS.
SHADE THE DRAWING LIGHTLY WITH PAINT, JOHNNY.
YOU KNOW WHO LIKED POTATO PRINTS? ZELDA! SHE WAS A SWEET, INNOCENT KID, AND LOOK HOW SHE ENDED UP. BUT YOU HAD YOUR FUN, DIDN'T YOU, JOHNNY. AND THAT'S ALL THAT MATTERS.
CUT AWAY THE PART NOT SHADED, SO THAT THE PATTERN SHAPE STANDS HIGHER THAN THE REST. ALL THESE THOUGHTS RUN THROUGH YOUR MIND AS YOUR CAR SMASHES THROUGH THE BARRIER, TO THE ROCKY SURF SIXTY FEET BELOW, INTO DEATH'S SWEET POTATO- I MEAN EMBRACE.
PRESS THE RAISED SHAPE IN THE PAINT. NOW PRESS THE POTATO CAREFULLY ON THE PAPER. YOU SHOULD GET TWO OR THREE COPIES OF YOUR SHAPE... BEFORE DIPPING IT IN THE PAINT AGAIN!
WHEN YOU HAVE HAD SOME PRACTICE, YOU CAN TRY ALL KINDS OF SHAPES TO PRINT, AND MAKE LOVELY PATTERNS.
THE END

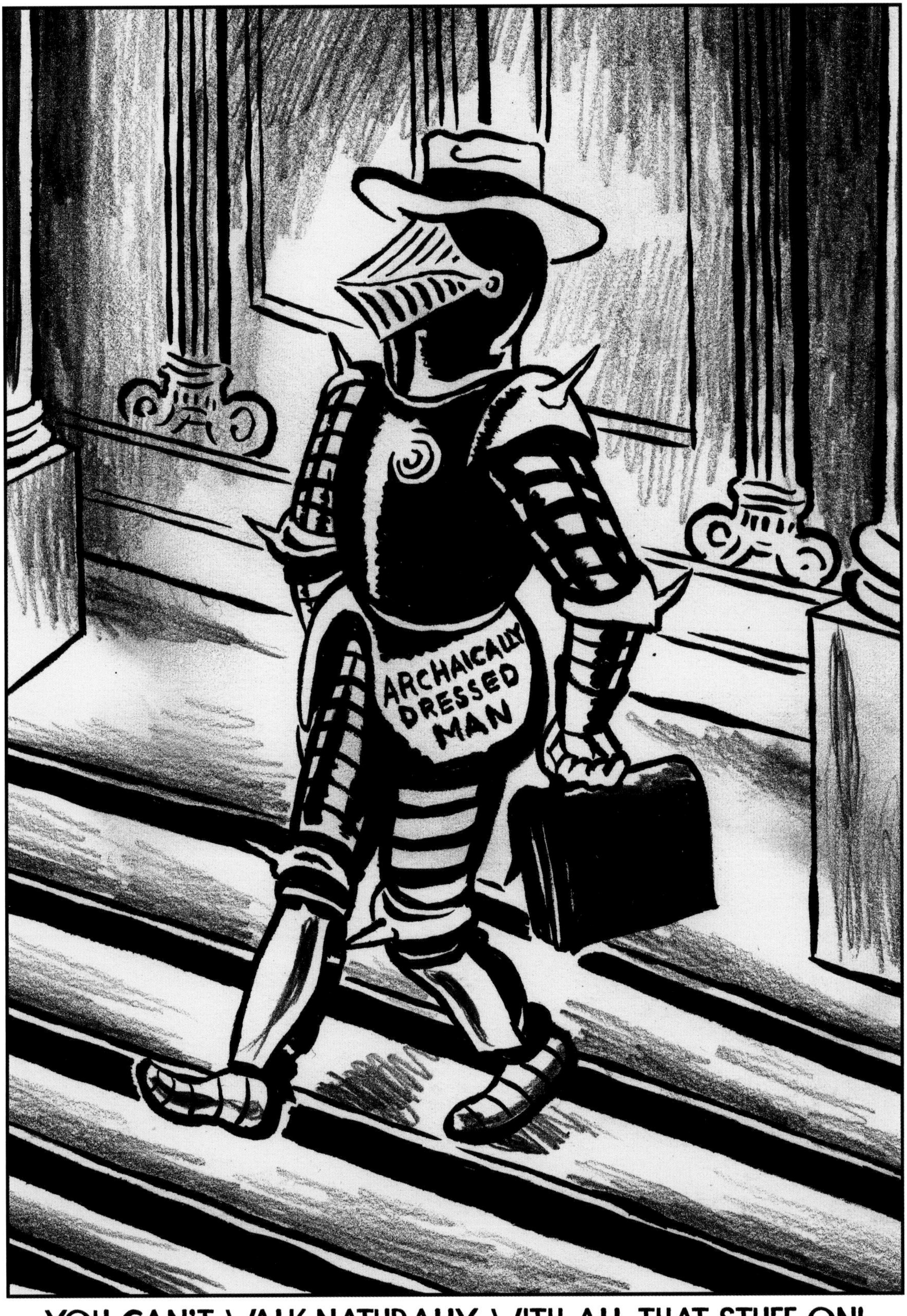
ARCHAICALLY DRESSED MAN

YOU CAN'T WALK NATURALLY WITH ALL THAT STUFF ON!

Hum Along With your Grandkids-
OLD TUNE FAVORITES!
The only page where we remembered to use large type.

"When Squirrel Met the Ant"
This simple tune contains an amazing story.
Bum-da-bumm bum, waaah wah wah buumm bum bum mmmm... ba bump ba bump ba bump, waaaah! (Repeat)

"Dribble Glass" by Pompiavelli
This more complicated piece is not for beginners... you will need to make tooting "horn" noises as well as humming ones!
Doo-doodoo-doo doo-wheee- proot proot doo prouple bom ba mmmmmmmm...vheet vheet vheet whee vheet vheet primble mmmmm.... waaah wah wah bom (repeat)

Charlie Chan, Hercules and Johnny Yuma
Kids love humming along to the theme song of their favorite show.
Bah bum be dum pa mmmmmm, mmmmm.... mmmmm... wah wah wah wah hmmmmm.... mmmmmm wah bom mmm pa.... mmmmm.... mmmmm... wah wah wah mmm hmmmmm.... (repeat)

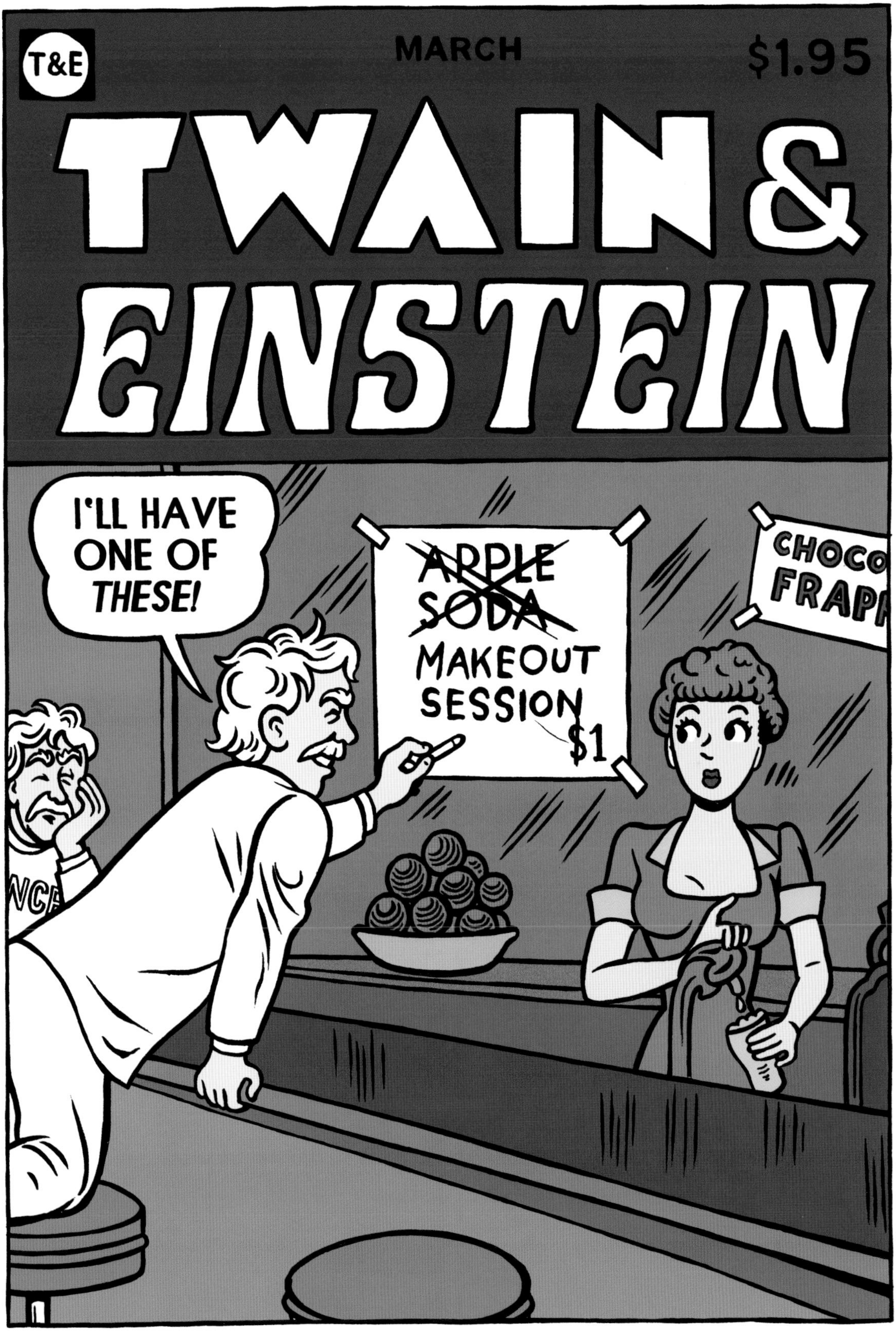
T&E
MARCH
$1.95
TWAIN & EINSTEIN
I'LL HAVE ONE OF THESE!
APPLE SODA
MAKEOUT SESSION
$1
CHOCO
FRAPP
NCE

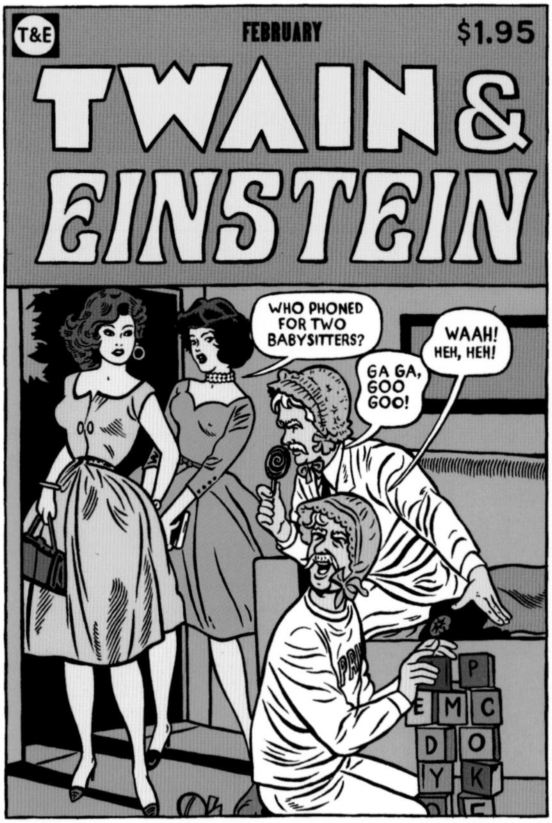
T&E
FEBRUARY
$1.95
TWAIN &
EINSTEIN
WHO PHONED FOR TWO BABYSITTERS?
GA GA, GOO GOO!
WAAH! HEH, HEH!

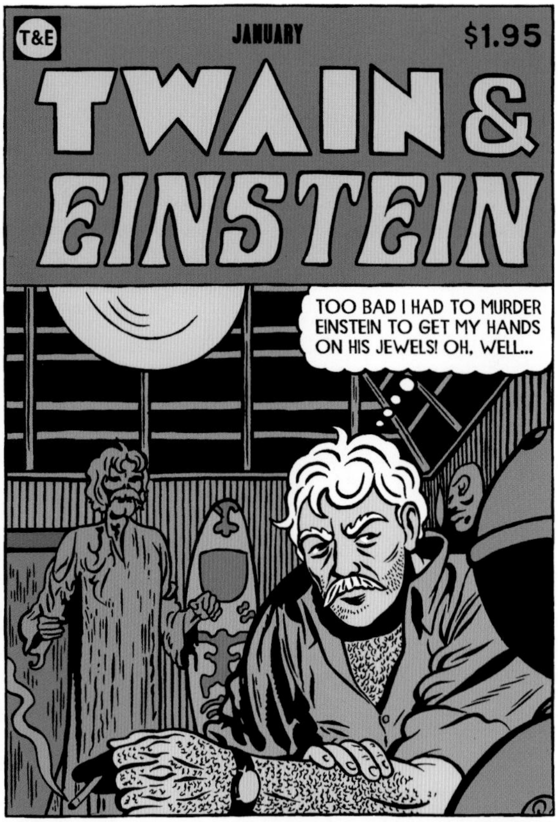
T&E
JANUARY
$1.95
TWAIN &
EINSTEIN
TOO BAD I HAD TO MURDER EINSTEIN TO GET MY HANDS ON HIS JEWELS! OH, WELL...

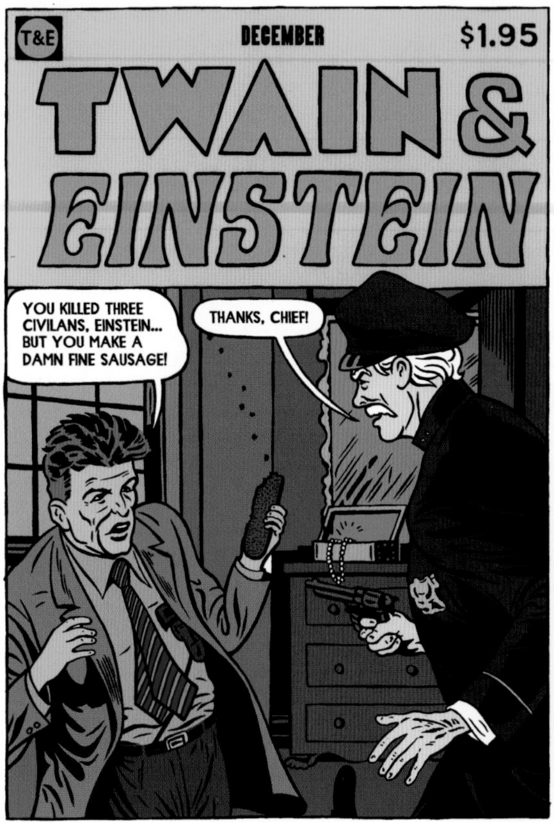
T&E
DECEMBER
$1.95
TWAIN &
EINSTEIN
YOU KILLED THREE CIVILANS, EINSTEIN... BUT YOU MAKE A DAMN FINE SAUSAGE!
THANKS, CHIEF!

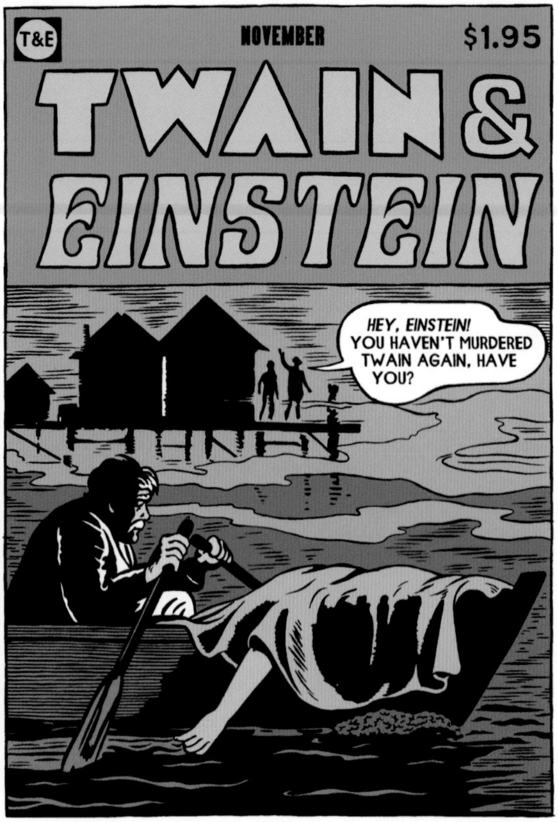
T&E
NOVEMBER
$1.95
TWAIN &
EINSTEIN
HEY, EINSTEIN! YOU HAVEN'T MURDERED TWAIN AGAIN, HAVE YOU?

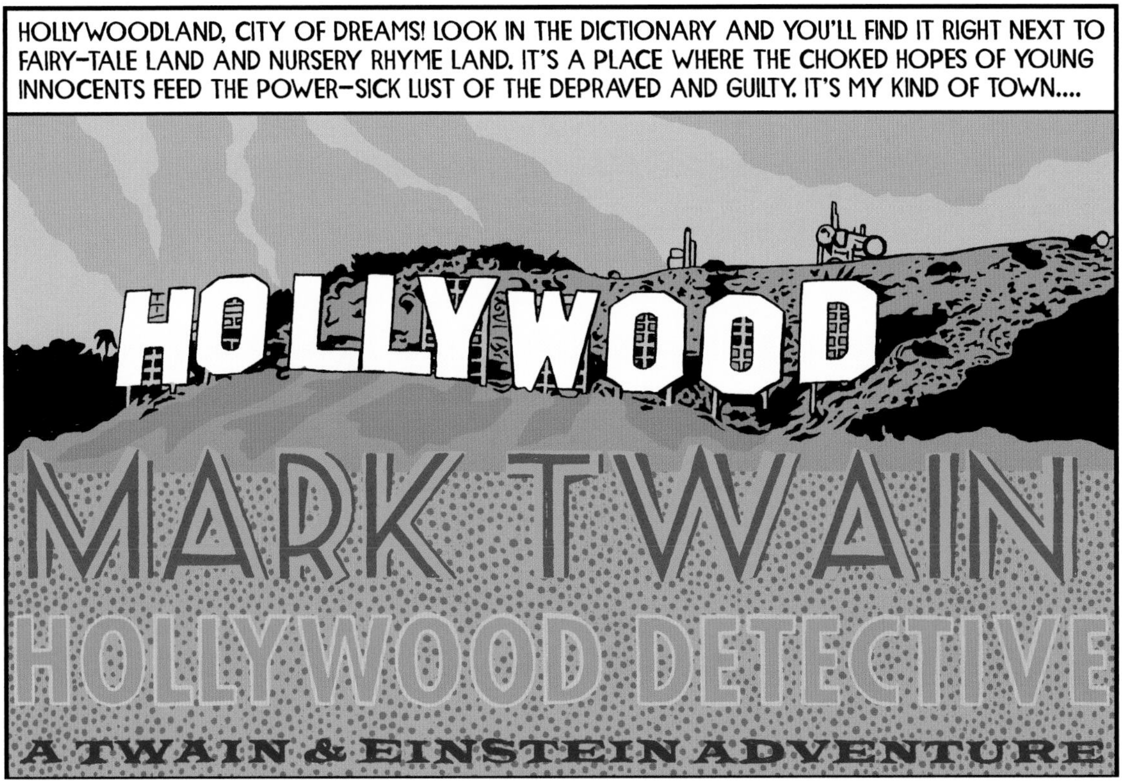
HOLLYWOODLAND, CITY OF DREAMS! LOOK IN THE DICTIONARY AND YOU'LL FIND IT RIGHT NEXT TO FAIRY-TALE LAND AND NURSERY RHYME LAND. IT'S A PLACE WHERE THE CHOKED HOPES OF YOUNG INNOCENTS FEED THE POWER-SICK LUST OF THE DEPRAVED AND GUILTY. IT'S MY KIND OF TOWN....
HOLLYWOOD
MARK TWAIN
HOLLYWOOD DETECTIVE
A TWAIN & EINSTEIN ADVENTURE

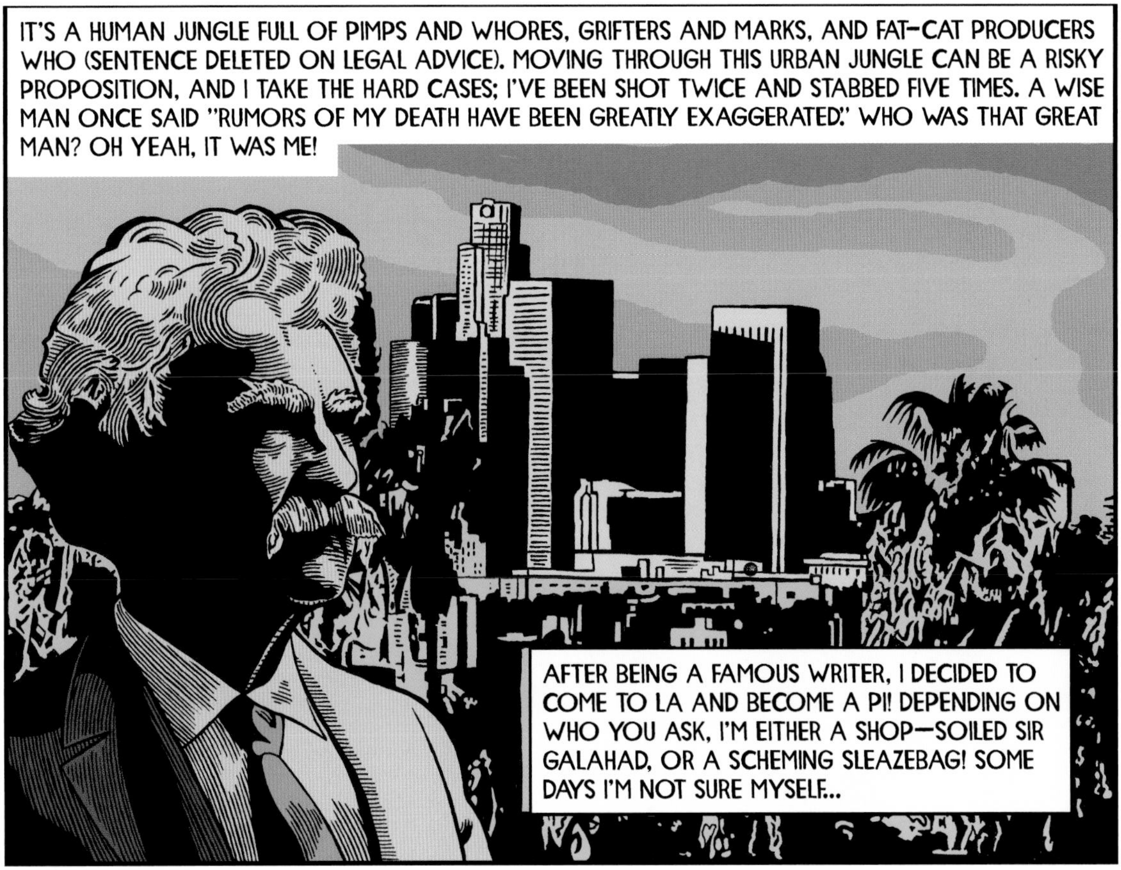
IT'S A HUMAN JUNGLE FULL OF PIMPS AND WHORES, GRIFTERS AND MARKS, AND FAT-CAT PRODUCERS WHO (SENTENCE DELETED ON LEGAL ADVICE). MOVING THROUGH THIS URBAN JUNGLE CAN BE A RISKY PROPOSITION, AND I TAKE THE HARD CASES; I'VE BEEN SHOT TWICE AND STABBED FIVE TIMES. A WISE MAN ONCE SAID "RUMORS OF MY DEATH HAVE BEEN GREATLY EXAGGERATED." WHO WAS THAT GREAT MAN? OH YEAH, IT WAS ME!
AFTER BEING A FAMOUS WRITER, I DECIDED TO COME TO LA AND BECOME A PI! DEPENDING ON WHO YOU ASK, I'M EITHER A SHOP-SOILED SIR GALAHAD, OR A SCHEMING SLEAZEBAG! SOME DAYS I'M NOT SURE MYSELF...

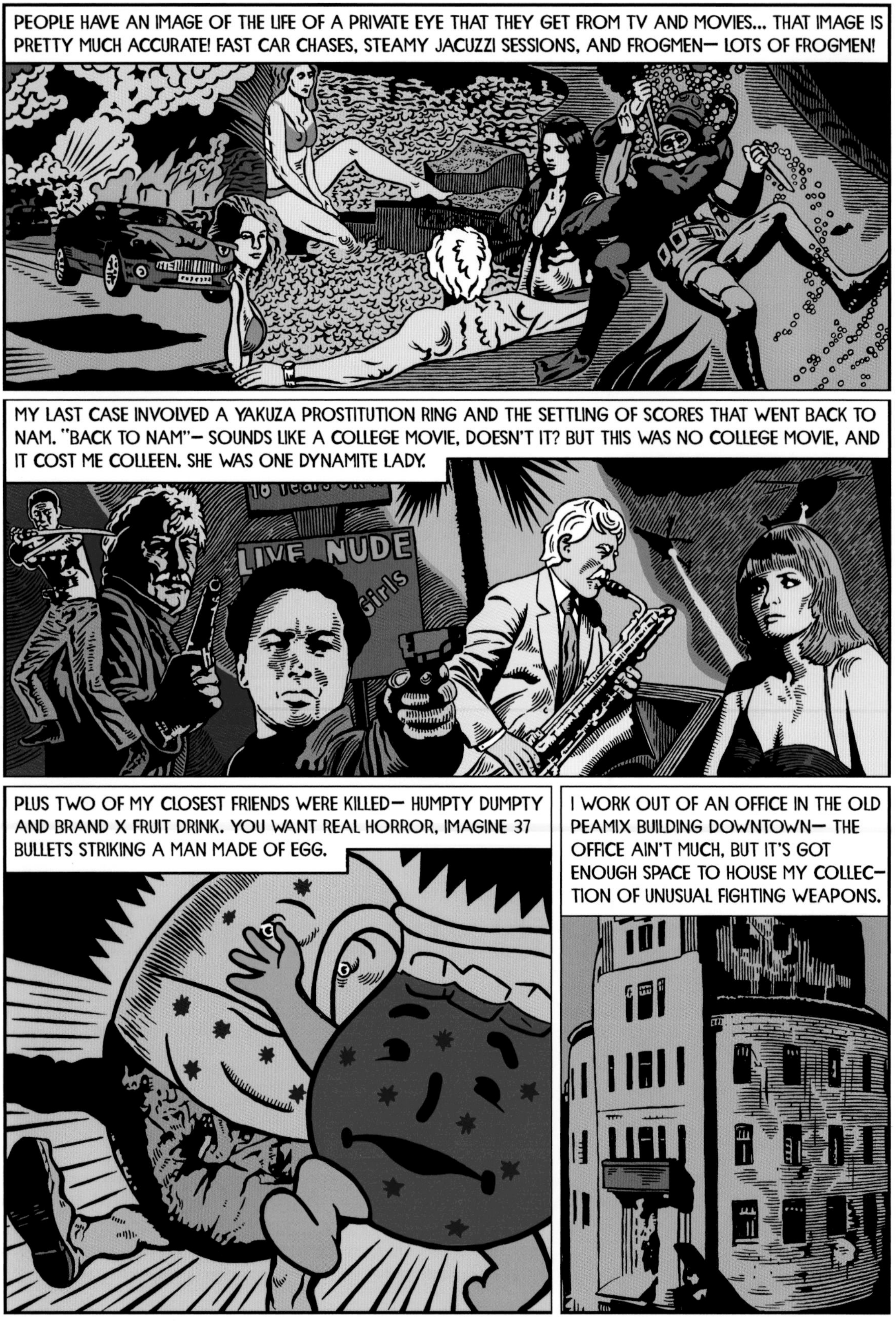
PEOPLE HAVE AN IMAGE OF THE LIFE OF A PRIVATE EYE THAT THEY GET FROM TV AND MOVIES... THAT IMAGE IS PRETTY MUCH ACCURATE! FAST CAR CHASES, STEAMY JACUZZI SESSIONS, AND FROGMEN— LOTS OF FROGMEN!
MY LAST CASE INVOLVED A YAKUZA PROSTITUTION RING AND THE SETTLING OF SCORES THAT WENT BACK TO NAM. "BACK TO NAM"— SOUNDS LIKE A COLLEGE MOVIE, DOESN'T IT? BUT THIS WAS NO COLLEGE MOVIE, AND IT COST ME COLLEEN. SHE WAS ONE DYNAMITE LADY.
LIVE NUDE
Girls
PLUS TWO OF MY CLOSEST FRIENDS WERE KILLED— HUMPTY DUMPTY AND BRAND X FRUIT DRINK. YOU WANT REAL HORROR, IMAGINE 37 BULLETS STRIKING A MAN MADE OF EGG.
I WORK OUT OF AN OFFICE IN THE OLD PEAMIX BUILDING DOWNTOWN— THE OFFICE AIN'T MUCH, BUT IT'S GOT ENOUGH SPACE TO HOUSE MY COLLECTION OF UNUSUAL FIGHTING WEAPONS.

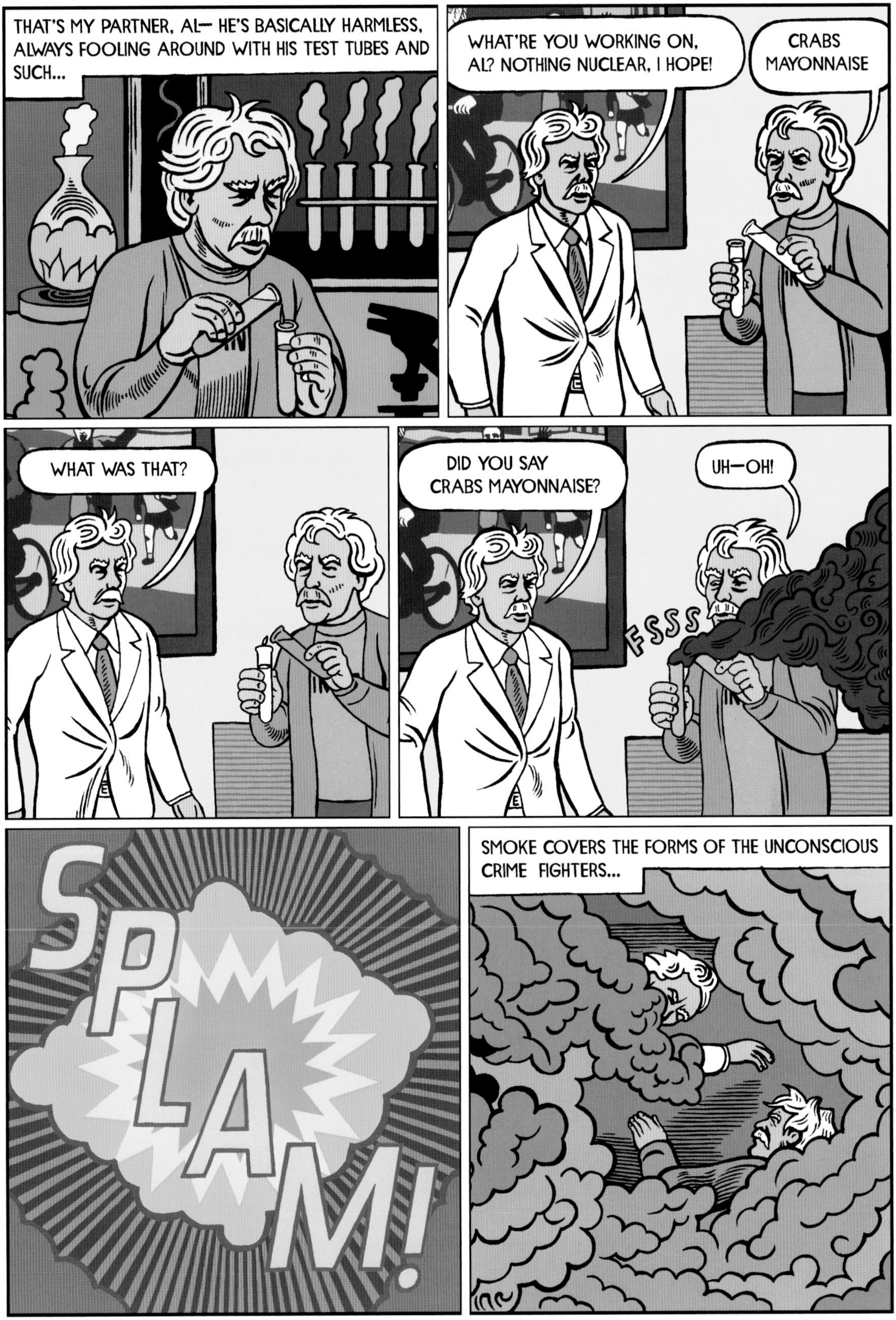
THAT'S MY PARTNER, AL— HE'S BASICALLY HARMLESS, ALWAYS FOOLING AROUND WITH HIS TEST TUBES AND SUCH...
WHAT'RE YOU WORKING ON, AL? NOTHING NUCLEAR, I HOPE!
CRABS MAYONNAISE
WHAT WAS THAT?
DID YOU SAY CRABS MAYONNAISE?
UH—OH!
FSSS
SPLAM!
SMOKE COVERS THE FORMS OF THE UNCONSCIOUS CRIME FIGHTERS...

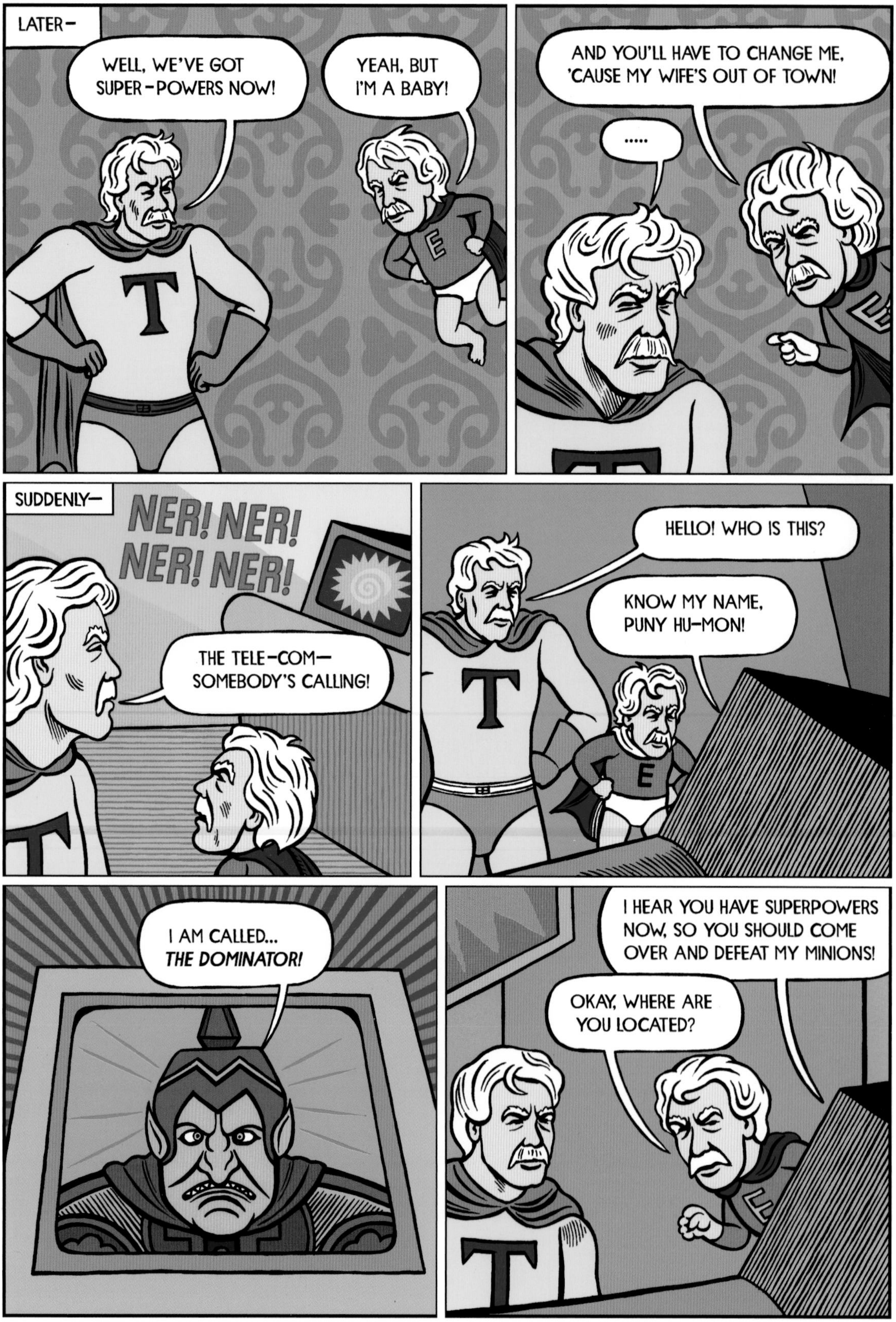
LATER—
WELL, WE'VE GOT SUPER-POWERS NOW!
YEAH, BUT I'M A BABY!
AND YOU'LL HAVE TO CHANGE ME, 'CAUSE MY WIFE'S OUT OF TOWN!
.....
SUDDENLY—
NER! NER! NER! NER!
THE TELE-COM— SOMEBODY'S CALLING!
HELLO! WHO IS THIS?
KNOW MY NAME, PUNY HU-MON!
I AM CALLED... *THE DOMINATOR!*
I HEAR YOU HAVE SUPERPOWERS NOW, SO YOU SHOULD COME OVER AND DEFEAT MY MINIONS!
OKAY, WHERE ARE YOU LOCATED?

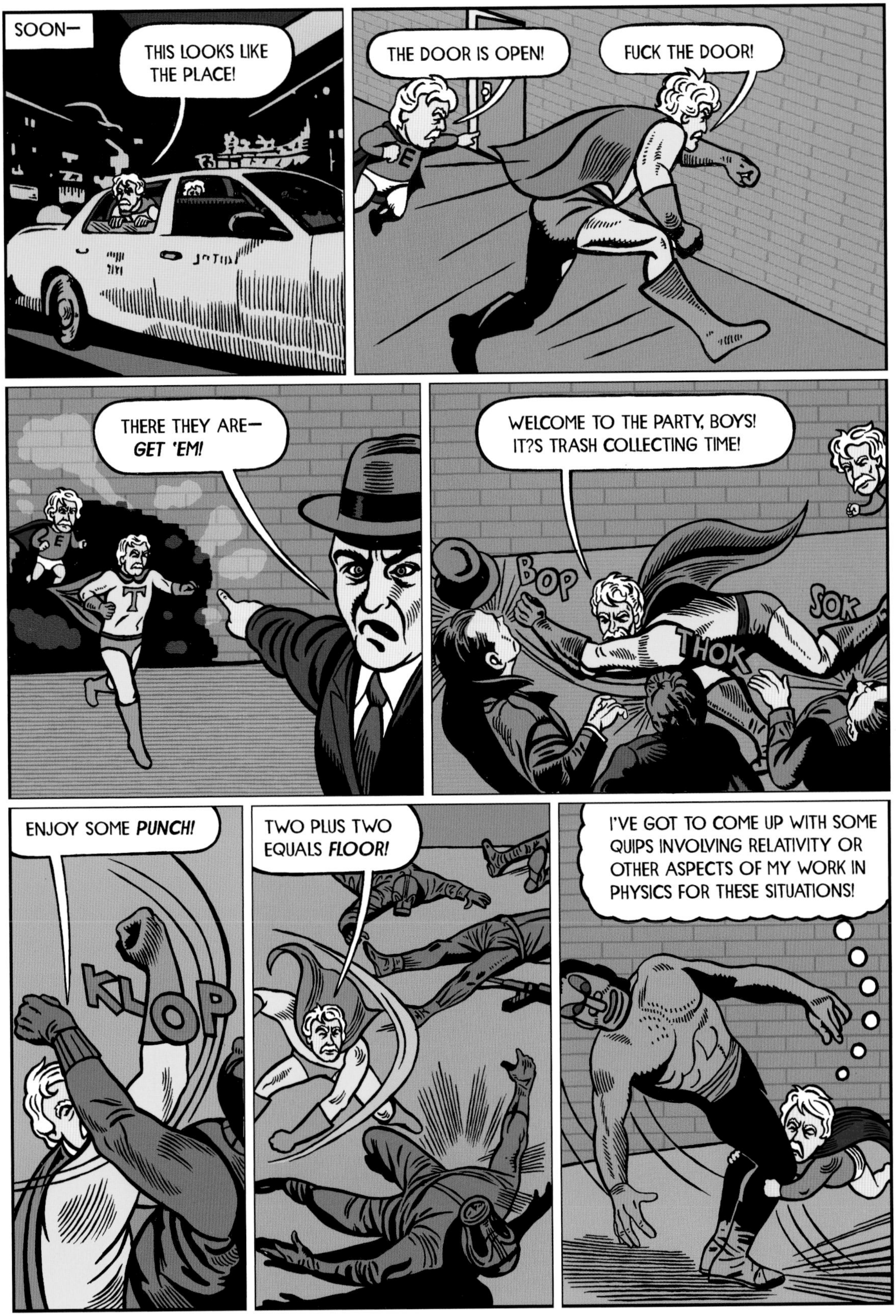
SOON—
THIS LOOKS LIKE THE PLACE!
THE DOOR IS OPEN!
FUCK THE DOOR!
THERE THEY ARE— GET 'EM!
WELCOME TO THE PARTY, BOYS! IT?S TRASH COLLECTING TIME!
BOP
SOK
THOK
ENJOY SOME PUNCH!
KLOP
TWO PLUS TWO EQUALS FLOOR!
I'VE GOT TO COME UP WITH SOME QUIPS INVOLVING RELATIVITY OR OTHER ASPECTS OF MY WORK IN PHYSICS FOR THESE SITUATIONS!

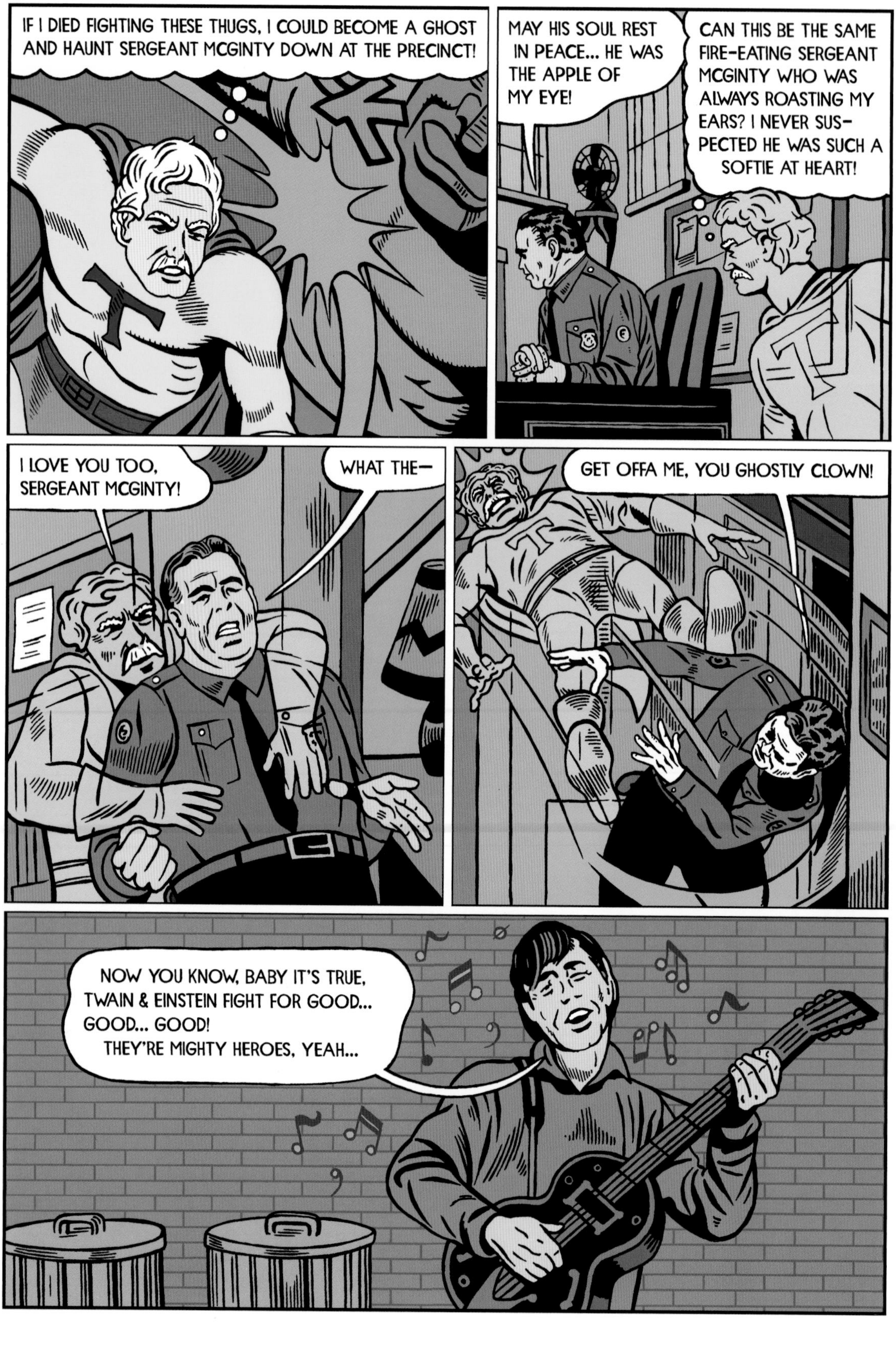
IF I DIED FIGHTING THESE THUGS, I COULD BECOME A GHOST AND HAUNT SERGEANT MCGINTY DOWN AT THE PRECINCT!
MAY HIS SOUL REST IN PEACE... HE WAS THE APPLE OF MY EYE!
CAN THIS BE THE SAME FIRE-EATING SERGEANT MCGINTY WHO WAS ALWAYS ROASTING MY EARS? I NEVER SUS-PECTED HE WAS SUCH A SOFTIE AT HEART!
I LOVE YOU TOO, SERGEANT MCGINTY!
WHAT THE—
GET OFFA ME, YOU GHOSTLY CLOWN!
NOW YOU KNOW, BABY IT'S TRUE, TWAIN & EINSTEIN FIGHT FOR GOOD... GOOD... GOOD! THEY'RE MIGHTY HEROES, YEAH...

TWAIN & EINSTEIN LETTERS PAGE

DEAR MR. EINSTEIN,
WHAT IS THE PRECISE AMOUNT OF SPINNING NEUTRONS IN YOUR GRAVITY BOX?
YOUR FAN,
JIMMY POPEIL

DEAR JIMMY,
48 HOURS AGO I WAS A SIMPLE COUNTRY LAWYER. THAT WAS BEFORE I DISCOVERED... *THE TRENTAGON CONSPIRACY!* NEVER BEFORE HAD A CYBORG BRAIN CHOSEN TO UNLEASH PURE FORCE IN A DEADLY TEST OF WITS. A CRAZY, ROLLER-COASTER RIDE OF PURE HIGH-OCTANE THRILLS.
WHEN THE DANGER STOPS, THERE'S TIME TO GET NAKED. *THE TRENTAGON CONSPIRACY—* RATED R.
MARK TWAIN

DEAR MR. EINSTEIN,
WHY, WHEN I WRITE TO YOU WITH A SCIENTIFIC QUESTION, DO I GET A REPLY FROM YOUR PARTNER THAT READS LIKE THE ANNOUNCER'S COPY FOR A B-MOVIE TRAILER?
JIMMY POPEIL

DEAR JIMMY,
THE POPE COULDN'T STOP HIM! THE WHITE HOUSE COULDN'T BLACKMAIL HIM. AND NO-ONE COULD HOPE TO STAND AGAINST MARK TWAIN AND HIS FISTS OF STEEL. HE'S GOING TO PUNCH AND KARATE CHOP HIS WAY TO THE TRUTH. BECAUSE HE CAN'T STAND *LUMPY GRAVY. LUMPY GRAVY.* WHEN A MAN IS PUSHED TO THE EDGE, HE'S GOT TO RESPOND WITH EXTREME MEASURES. (SFX: EXPLOSION) *LUMPY GRAVY*, RATED R. *LUUUMPY GRAAAVYYYYY!*
MARK TWAIN

DEAR MR. TWAIN,
I WAS LISTENING TO THE RADIO RECENTLY, AND HEARD WHAT SOUNDED LIKE YOUR VOICE DOING AN AD FOR AN UPCOMING MOVIE! WAS IT REALLY YOU?
PAUL MOSER

DEAR PAUL,
MAX TWAIN NEVER COULD 'KICK IT' WITH THE LADIES! *WOMAN'S VOICE:* "GET LOST, NERD!" BUT ON NOVEMBER 17TH, ALL THAT'S GOING TO CHANGE! BECAUSE WHEN HE TRIES A NEW EXPERIMENTAL COLOGNE, HE'LL FIND THAT HE *CAN'T STOP THE PLEASING! YOUNG MAN'S VOICE:* "I NEVER— THAT IS TO SAY I— UH— I MEAN I—" *WOMAN'S VOICE:* "OHHHH, MAX!" *CAN'T STOP THE PLEASING! OLDER MAN'S VOICE:* "TWAIIIN! YOUR MEDULLA OBLONGATA HAS GONE AND BEEN WHERE IT OUGHTN'T OUGHTA!" AND MAYHEM ENSUES WHEN MAX'S FAMOUS UNCLE MARK COMES TO VISIT! *MARK TWAIN'S VOICE:* "HELLO, GIRLS!" *CAN'T STOP THE PLEASING!* RATED R. *CAN'T STOP THE PLEASING!* COMING SOON.
MARK TWAIN

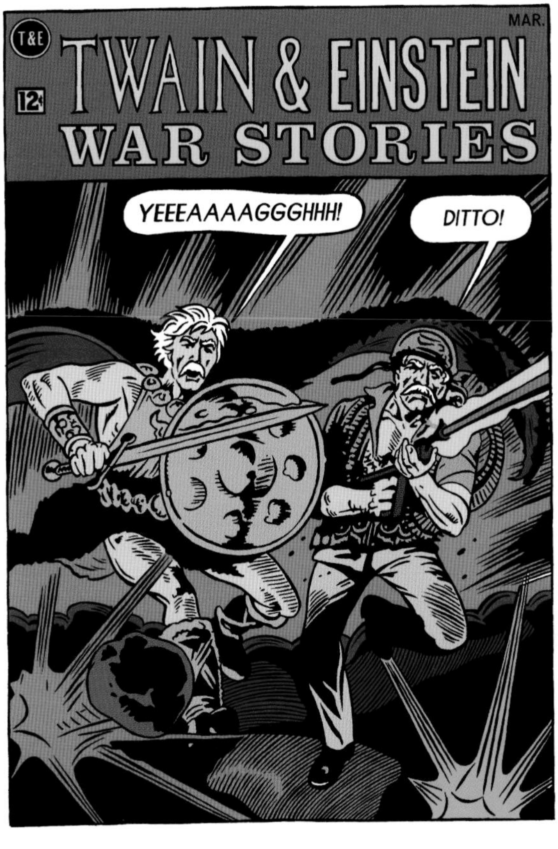
T&E
MAR.
12¢
TWAIN & EINSTEIN
WAR STORIES
YEEEAAAAGGGHHH!
DITTO!

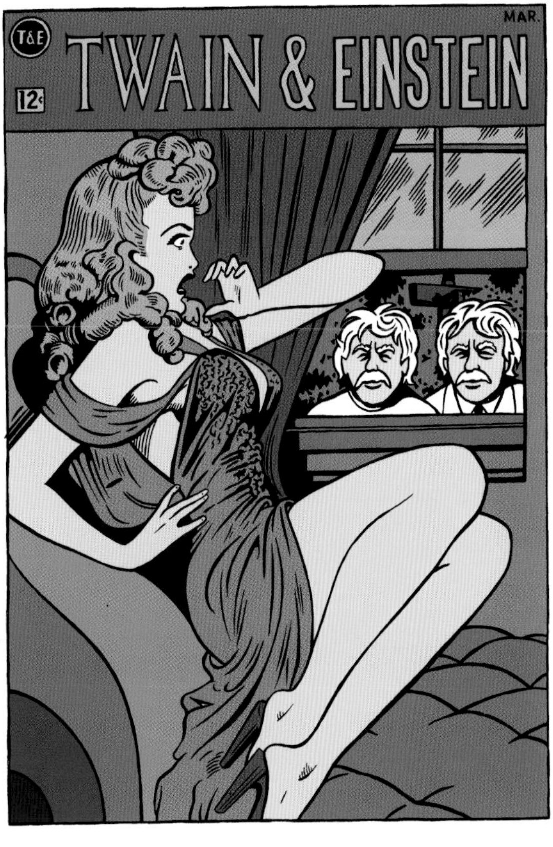
T&E
MAR.
12¢
TWAIN & EINSTEIN

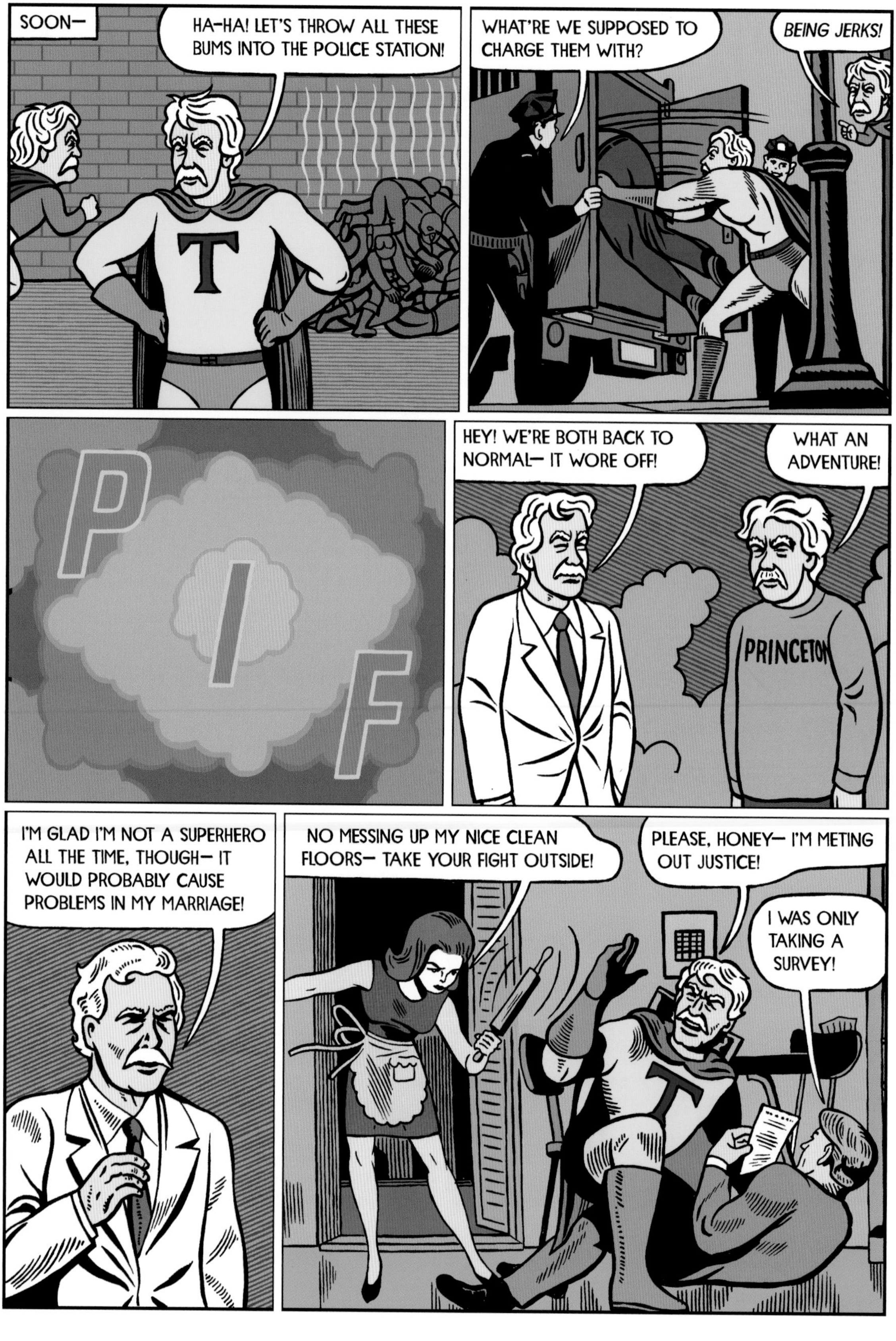
SOON—
HA-HA! LET'S THROW ALL THESE BUMS INTO THE POLICE STATION!
WHAT'RE WE SUPPOSED TO CHARGE THEM WITH?
BEING JERKS!
P I F
HEY! WE'RE BOTH BACK TO NORMAL— IT WORE OFF!
WHAT AN ADVENTURE!
PRINCETON
I'M GLAD I'M NOT A SUPERHERO ALL THE TIME, THOUGH— IT WOULD PROBABLY CAUSE PROBLEMS IN MY MARRIAGE!
NO MESSING UP MY NICE CLEAN FLOORS— TAKE YOUR FIGHT OUTSIDE!
PLEASE, HONEY— I'M METING OUT JUSTICE!
I WAS ONLY TAKING A SURVEY!

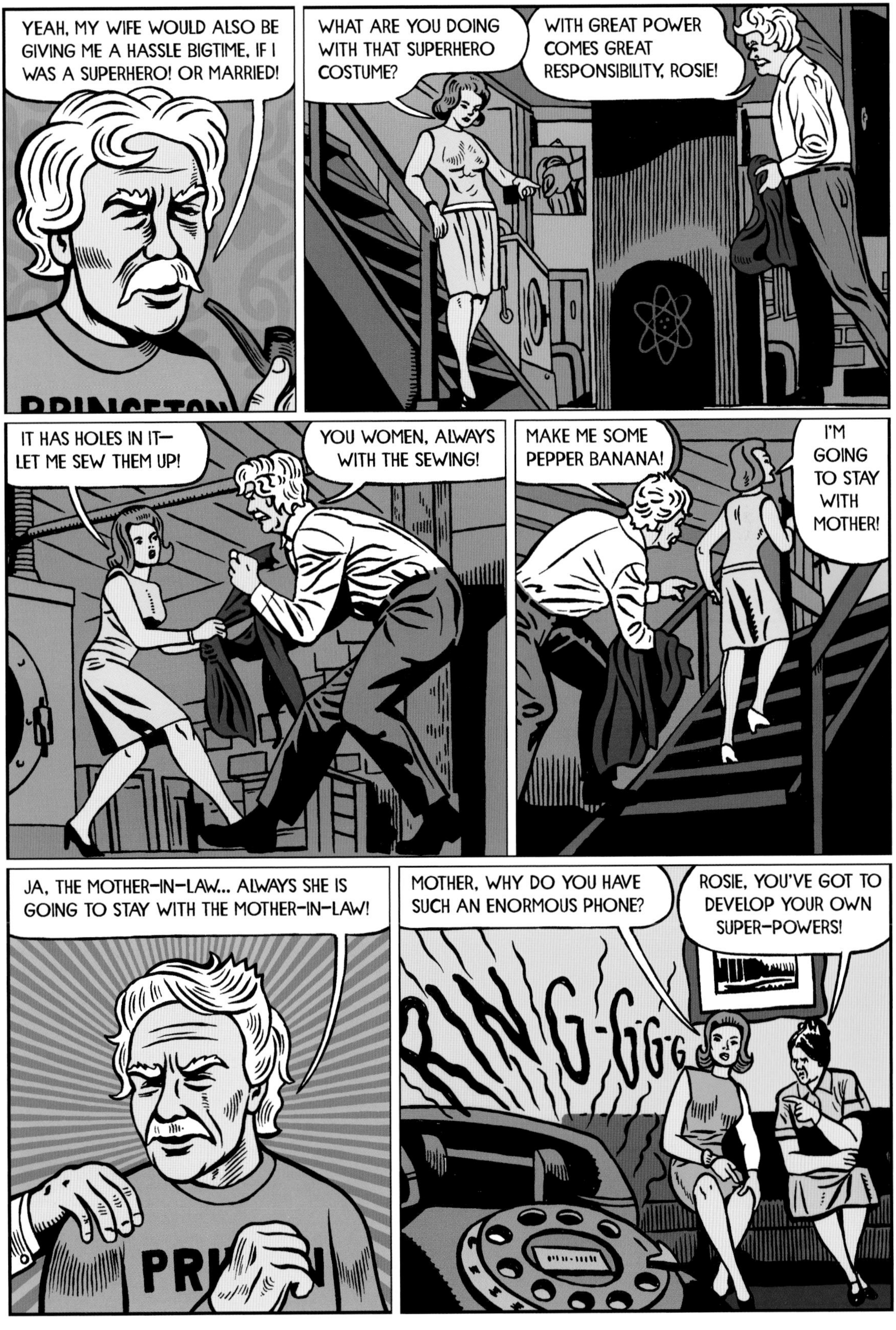
YEAH, MY WIFE WOULD ALSO BE GIVING ME A HASSLE BIGTIME, IF I WAS A SUPERHERO! OR MARRIED!
WHAT ARE YOU DOING WITH THAT SUPERHERO COSTUME?
WITH GREAT POWER COMES GREAT RESPONSIBILITY, ROSIE!
IT HAS HOLES IN IT— LET ME SEW THEM UP!
YOU WOMEN, ALWAYS WITH THE SEWING!
MAKE ME SOME PEPPER BANANA!
I'M GOING TO STAY WITH MOTHER!
JA, THE MOTHER-IN-LAW... ALWAYS SHE IS GOING TO STAY WITH THE MOTHER-IN-LAW!
MOTHER, WHY DO YOU HAVE SUCH AN ENORMOUS PHONE?
ROSIE, YOU'VE GOT TO DEVELOP YOUR OWN SUPER-POWERS!
RING-G-G-G

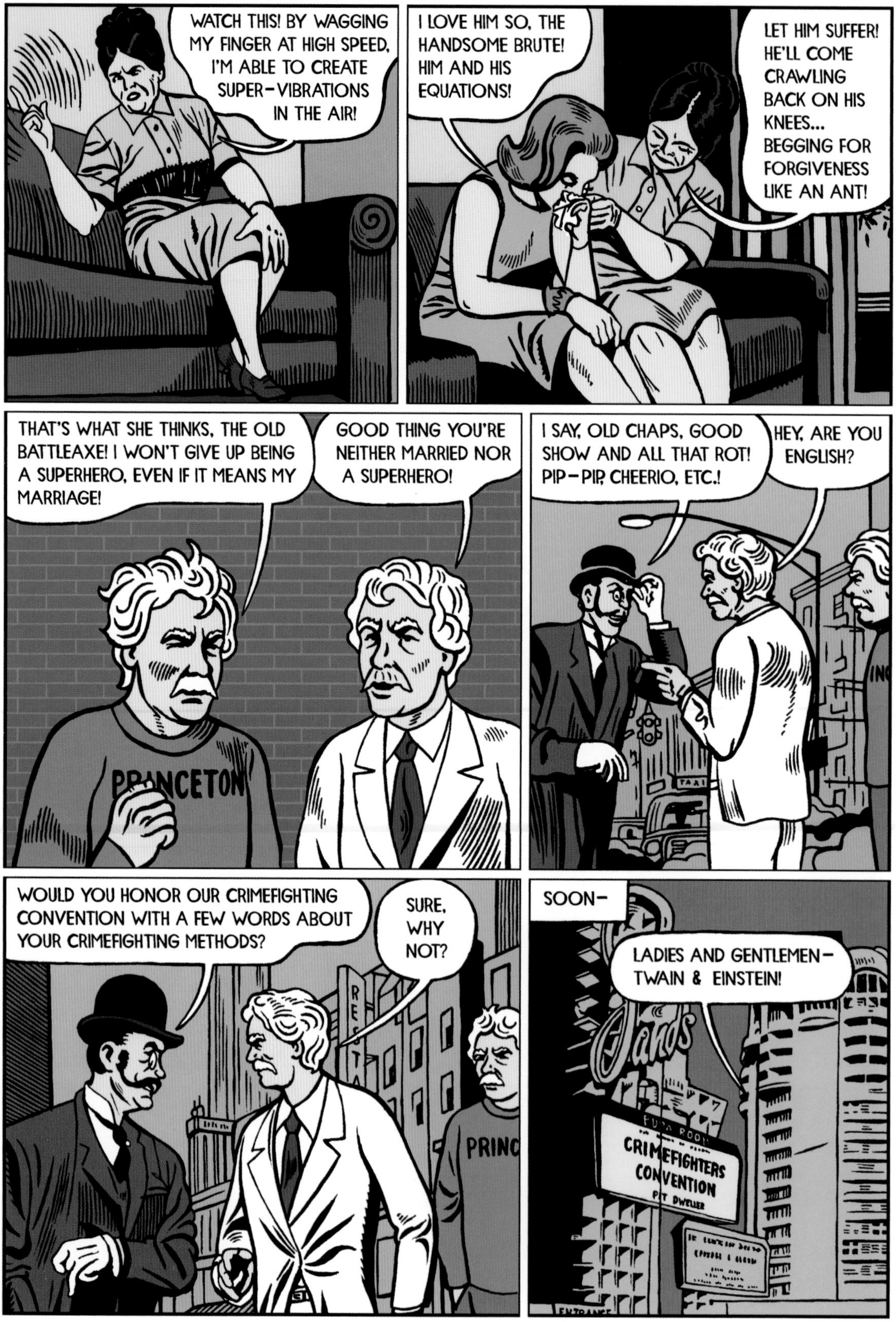
WATCH THIS! BY WAGGING MY FINGER AT HIGH SPEED, I'M ABLE TO CREATE SUPER-VIBRATIONS IN THE AIR!
I LOVE HIM SO, THE HANDSOME BRUTE! HIM AND HIS EQUATIONS!
LET HIM SUFFER! HE'LL COME CRAWLING BACK ON HIS KNEES... BEGGING FOR FORGIVENESS LIKE AN ANT!
THAT'S WHAT SHE THINKS, THE OLD BATTLEAXE! I WON'T GIVE UP BEING A SUPERHERO, EVEN IF IT MEANS MY MARRIAGE!
GOOD THING YOU'RE NEITHER MARRIED NOR A SUPERHERO!
PRINCETON
I SAY, OLD CHAPS, GOOD SHOW AND ALL THAT ROT! PIP-PIP, CHEERIO, ETC.!
HEY, ARE YOU ENGLISH?
WOULD YOU HONOR OUR CRIMEFIGHTING CONVENTION WITH A FEW WORDS ABOUT YOUR CRIMEFIGHTING METHODS?
SURE, WHY NOT?
PRINC
SOON-
LADIES AND GENTLEMEN-TWAIN & EINSTEIN!
CRIMEFIGHTERS CONVENTION

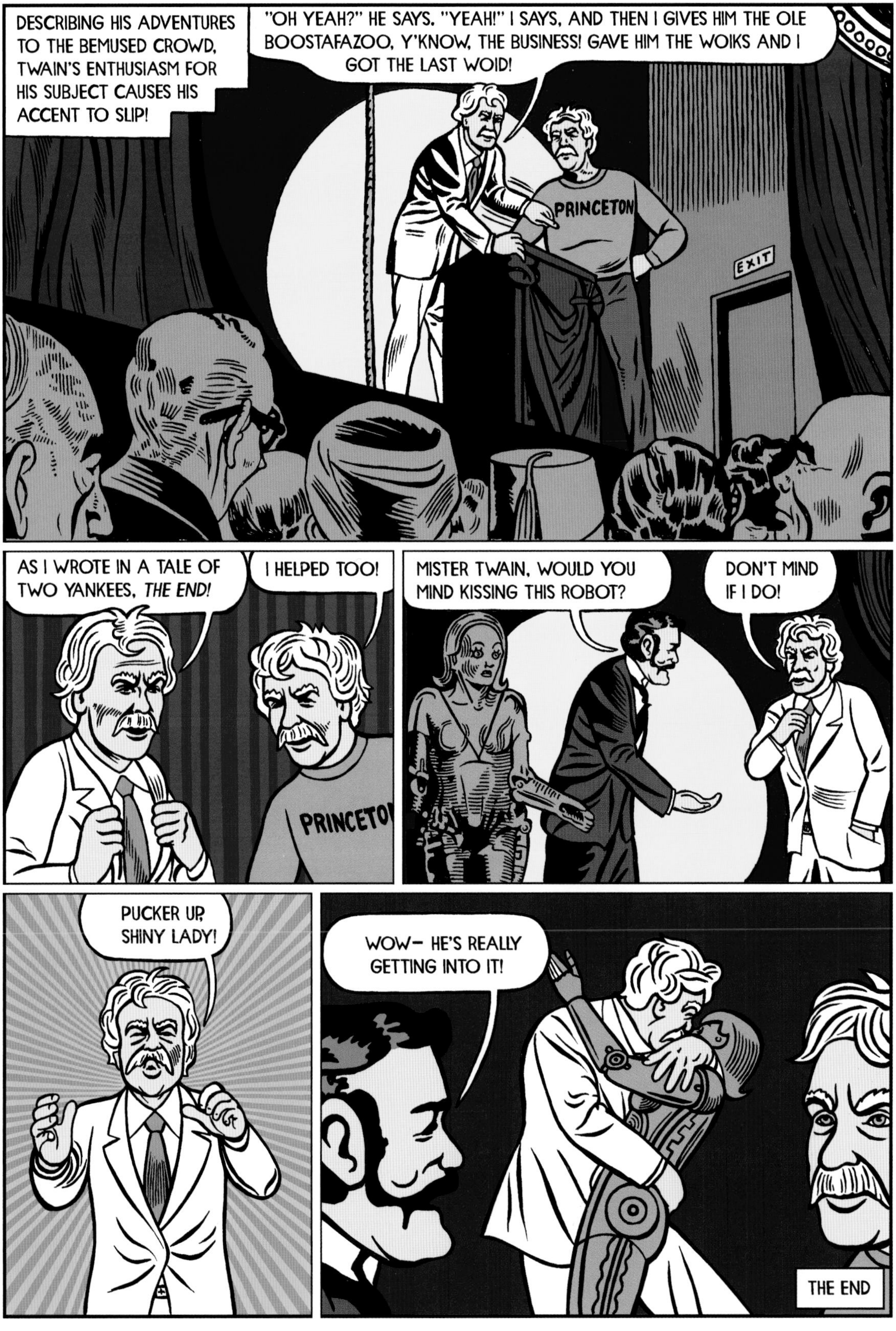
DESCRIBING HIS ADVENTURES TO THE BEMUSED CROWD, TWAIN'S ENTHUSIASM FOR HIS SUBJECT CAUSES HIS ACCENT TO SLIP!
"OH YEAH?" HE SAYS. "YEAH!" I SAYS, AND THEN I GIVES HIM THE OLE BOOSTAFAZOO, Y'KNOW, THE BUSINESS! GAVE HIM THE WOIKS AND I GOT THE LAST WOID!
PRINCETON
EXIT
AS I WROTE IN A TALE OF TWO YANKEES, *THE END!*
I HELPED TOO!
PRINCETON
MISTER TWAIN, WOULD YOU MIND KISSING THIS ROBOT?
DON'T MIND IF I DO!
PUCKER UP, SHINY LADY!
WOW— HE'S REALLY GETTING INTO IT!
THE END

THE TWAIN FILES: 1975

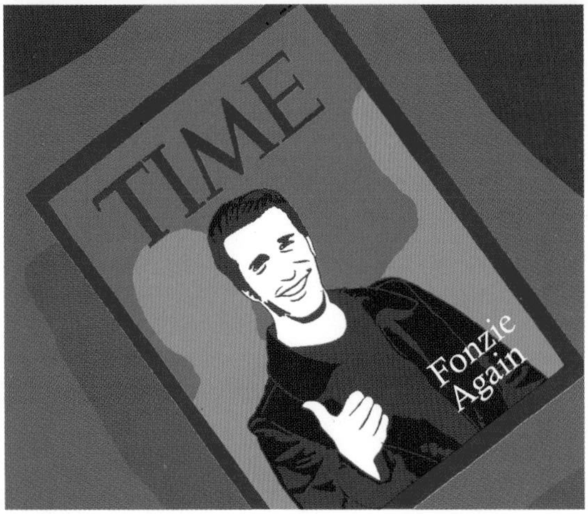
TIME
Fonzie Again

The year 1975 was an exciting one. Fonzie was on the cover of Time magazine 37 times in a row.

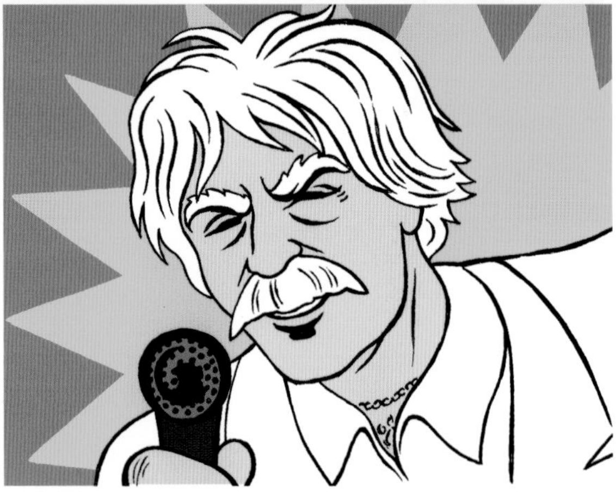

America was having a love affair– a love affair with mustachioed sexy reporters! And Mark Twain was one of the sexiest and mustachiest.

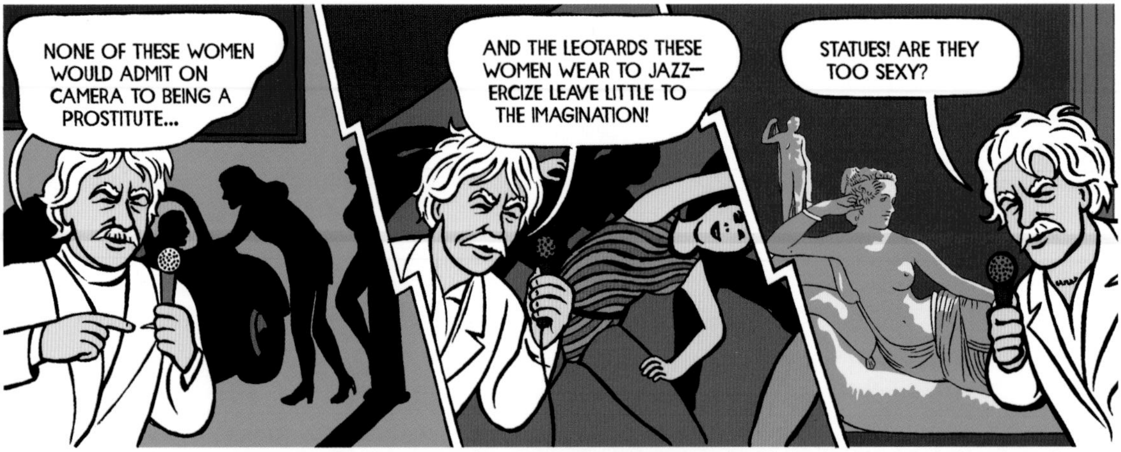
NONE OF THESE WOMEN WOULD ADMIT ON CAMERA TO BEING A PROSTITUTE...
AND THE LEOTARDS THESE WOMEN WEAR TO JAZZ–ERCIZE LEAVE LITTLE TO THE IMAGINATION!
STATUES! ARE THEY TOO SEXY?

But unbeknownst to everyone, he was secretly taking "Sexy Reporter" pills he had smuggled in from Japan.

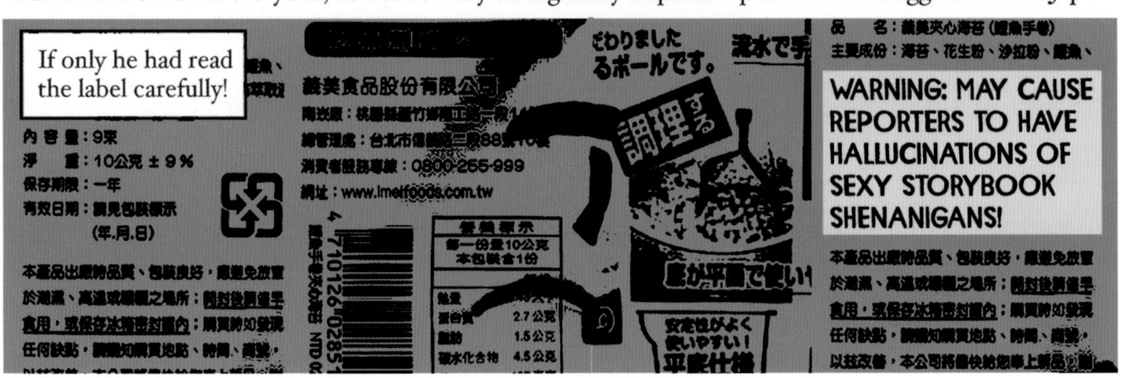
If only he had read the label carefully!
義美食品股份有限公司
消費者服務專線：0800-255-999
網址：www.imeifoods.com.tw
調理する
WARNING: MAY CAUSE REPORTERS TO HAVE HALLUCINATIONS OF SEXY STORYBOOK SHENANIGANS!

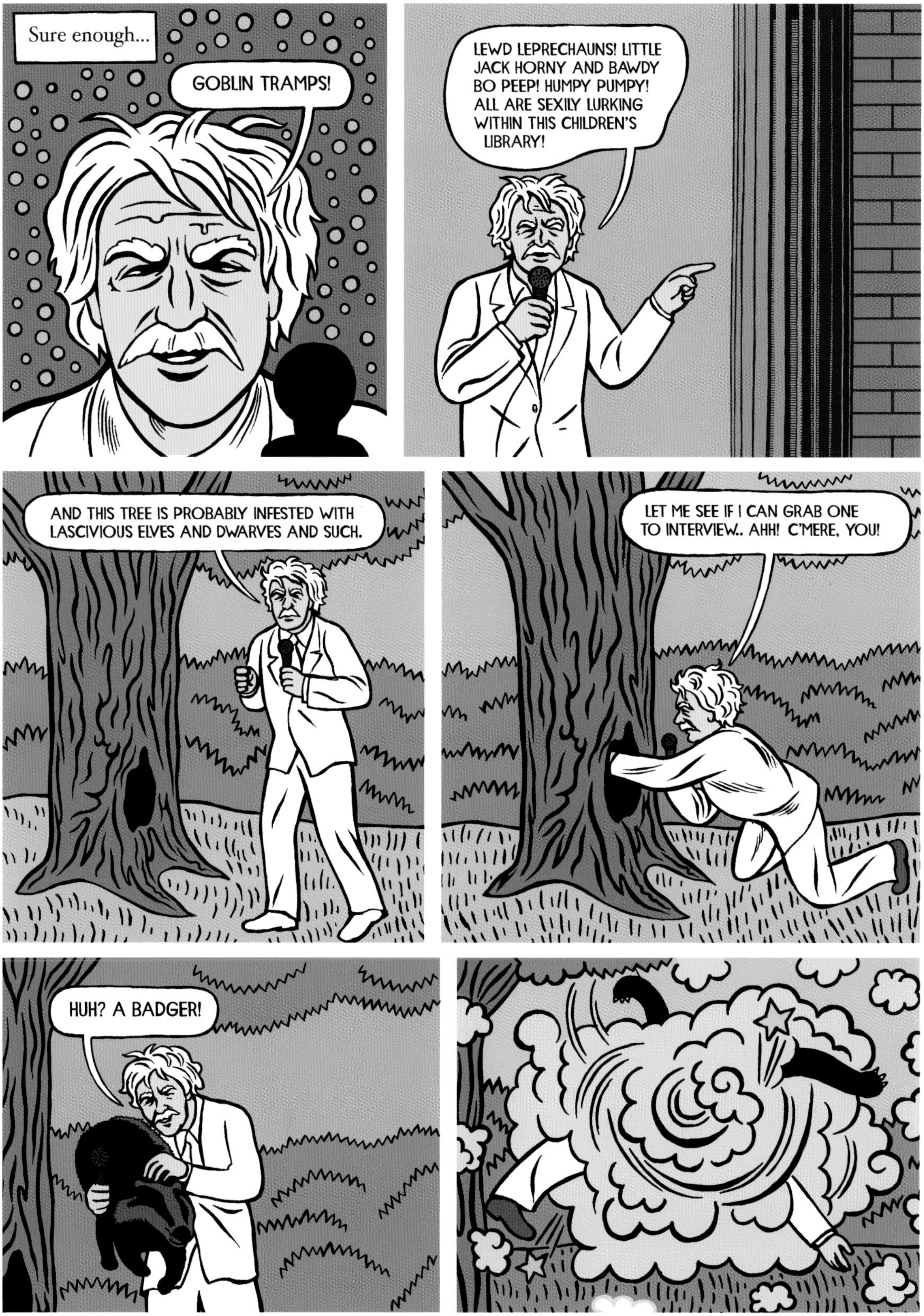
Sure enough...
GOBLIN TRAMPS!
LEWD LEPRECHAUNS! LITTLE JACK HORNY AND BAWDY BO PEEP! HUMPY PUMPY! ALL ARE SEXILY LURKING WITHIN THIS CHILDREN'S LIBRARY!
AND THIS TREE IS PROBABLY INFESTED WITH LASCIVIOUS ELVES AND DWARVES AND SUCH.
LET ME SEE IF I CAN GRAB ONE TO INTERVIEW.. AHH! C'MERE, YOU!
HUH? A BADGER!

Following this incident, Twain was hospitalized for two months, suffering from rabies, withdrawal, and numerous bites and lacerations. His sexy reporting days, sadly, were at an end. THE END

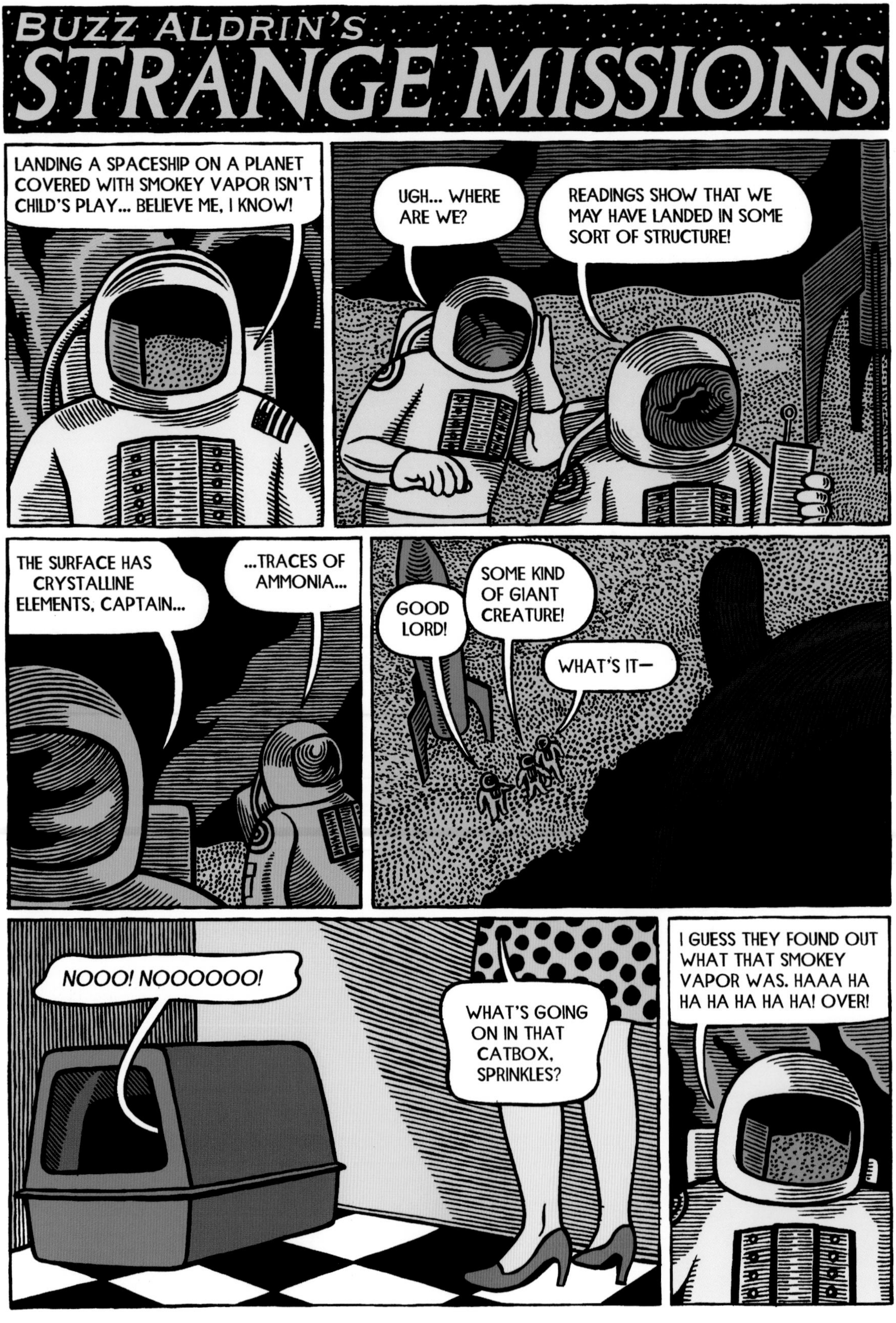
BUZZ ALDRIN'S
STRANGE MISSIONS
LANDING A SPACESHIP ON A PLANET COVERED WITH SMOKEY VAPOR ISN'T CHILD'S PLAY... BELIEVE ME, I KNOW!
UGH... WHERE ARE WE?
READINGS SHOW THAT WE MAY HAVE LANDED IN SOME SORT OF STRUCTURE!
THE SURFACE HAS CRYSTALLINE ELEMENTS, CAPTAIN...
...TRACES OF AMMONIA...
GOOD LORD!
SOME KIND OF GIANT CREATURE!
WHAT'S IT—
NOOO! NOOOOOO!
WHAT'S GOING ON IN THAT CATBOX, SPRINKLES?
I GUESS THEY FOUND OUT WHAT THAT SMOKEY VAPOR WAS. HAAA HA HA HA HA HA HA! OVER!

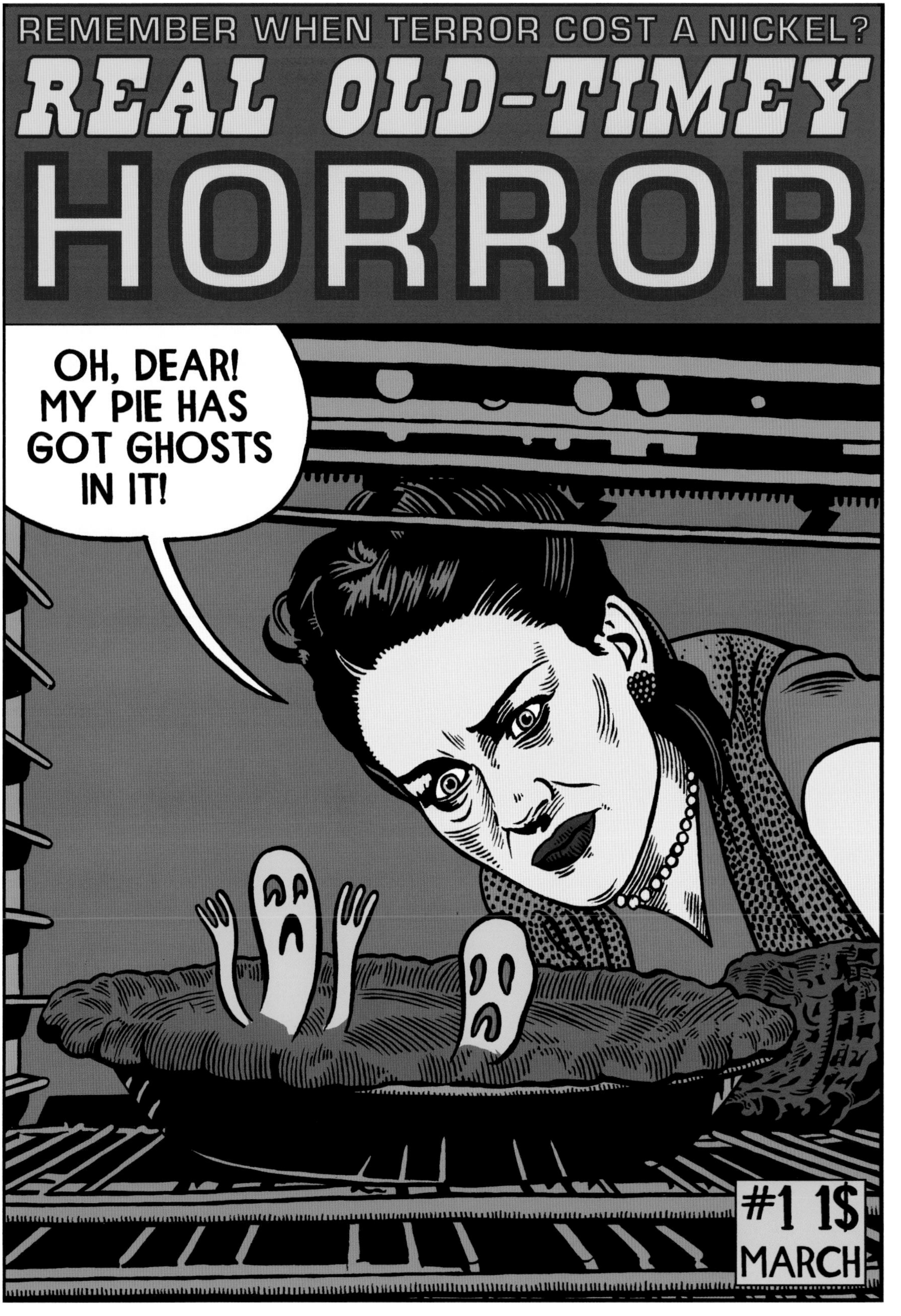
REMEMBER WHEN TERROR COST A NICKEL?
REAL OLD-TIMEY
HORROR
OH, DEAR! MY PIE HAS GOT GHOSTS IN IT!
#1 1$
MARCH

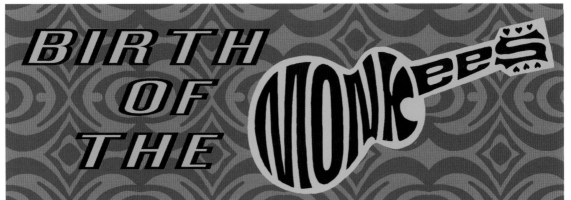

BIRTH OF THE MONKEES

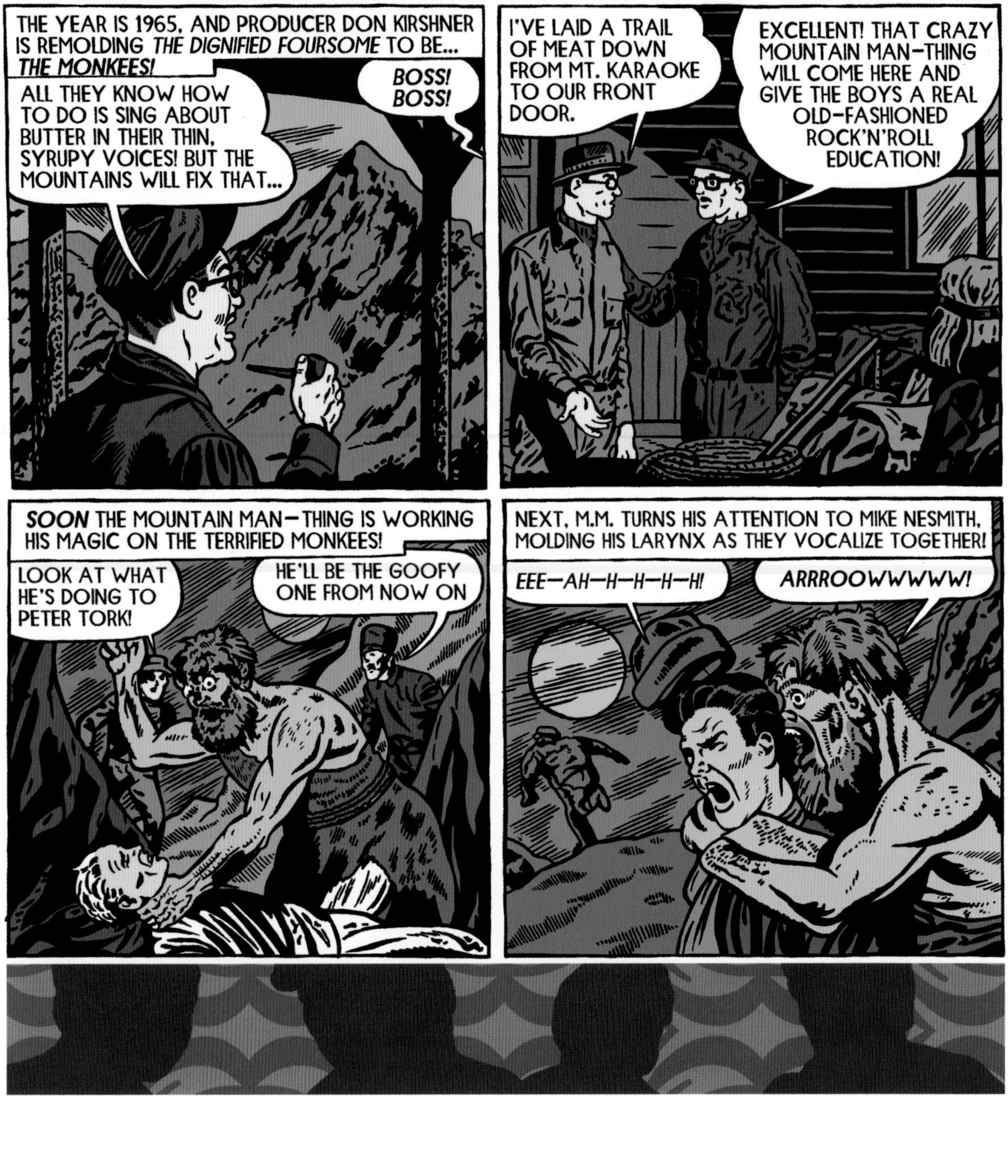
THE YEAR IS 1965, AND PRODUCER DON KIRSHNER IS REMOLDING *THE DIGNIFIED FOURSOME* TO BE... ***THE MONKEES!***
ALL THEY KNOW HOW TO DO IS SING ABOUT BUTTER IN THEIR THIN, SYRUPY VOICES! BUT THE MOUNTAINS WILL FIX THAT...
BOSS! BOSS!
I'VE LAID A TRAIL OF MEAT DOWN FROM MT. KARAOKE TO OUR FRONT DOOR.
EXCELLENT! THAT CRAZY MOUNTAIN MAN—THING WILL COME HERE AND GIVE THE BOYS A REAL OLD—FASHIONED ROCK'N'ROLL EDUCATION!
SOON THE MOUNTAIN MAN—THING IS WORKING HIS MAGIC ON THE TERRIFIED MONKEES!
LOOK AT WHAT HE'S DOING TO PETER TORK!
HE'LL BE THE GOOFY ONE FROM NOW ON
NEXT, M.M. TURNS HIS ATTENTION TO MIKE NESMITH, MOLDING HIS LARYNX AS THEY VOCALIZE TOGETHER!
EEE—AH—H—H—H—H!
ARRROOWWWWW!

YOU'VE ENTERED THE RIGHT CAVE, MY FRIEND! WE KNOW WHAT YOU'VE BEEN THROUGH! HOW YOU BECAME SO CONFUSED AND FRIGHTENED...WHY YOU RAN AWAY... AND HOW EXACTLY IT IS YOU GOT YOURSELF A PAIR OF

LEGS TO DIE FOR!

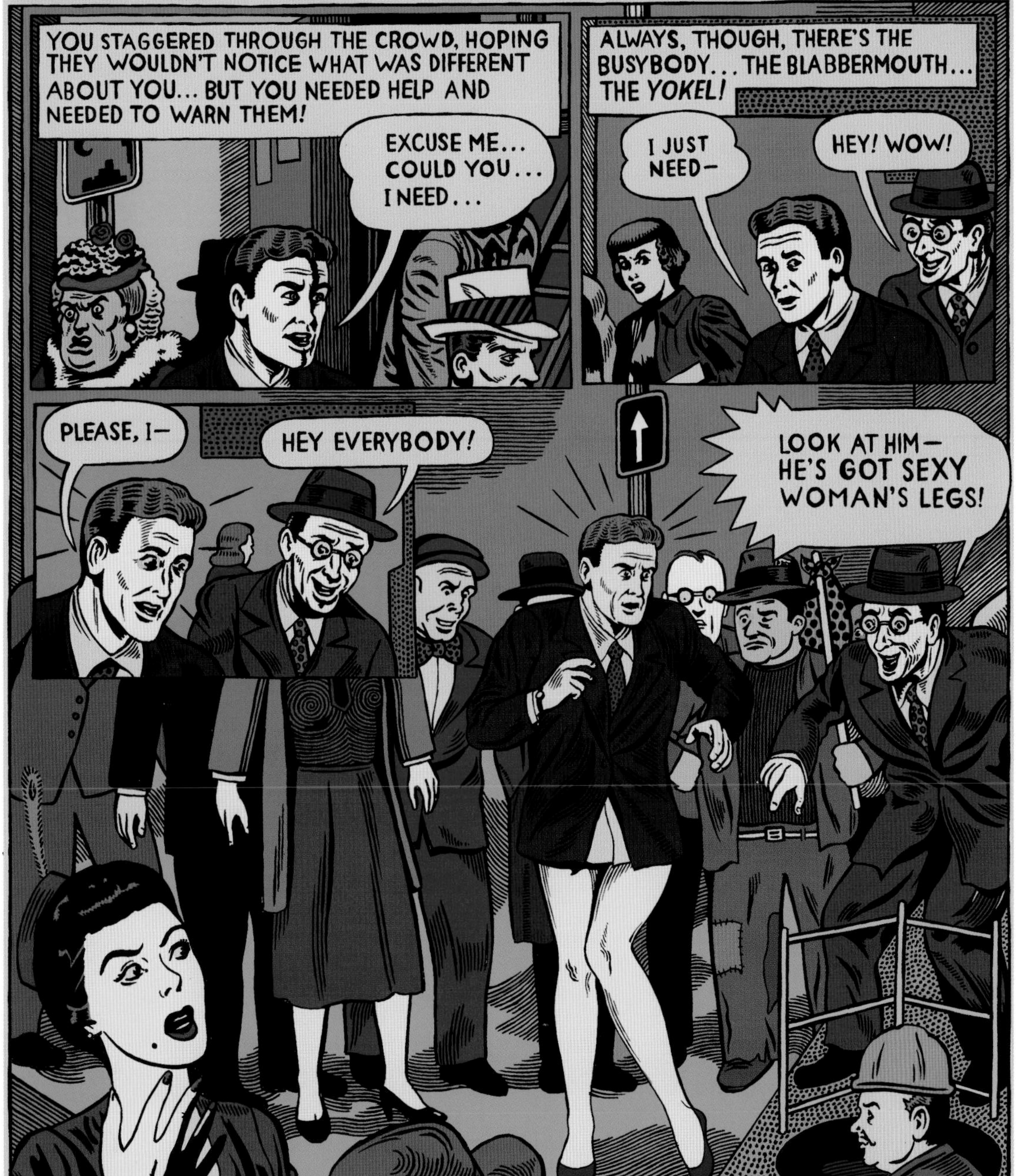

YOU STAGGERED THROUGH THE CROWD, HOPING THEY WOULDN'T NOTICE WHAT WAS DIFFERENT ABOUT YOU... BUT YOU NEEDED HELP AND NEEDED TO WARN THEM!
EXCUSE ME... COULD YOU... I NEED...
ALWAYS, THOUGH, THERE'S THE BUSYBODY... THE BLABBERMOUTH... THE *YOKEL!*
I JUST NEED—
HEY! WOW!
PLEASE, I—
HEY EVERYBODY!
LOOK AT HIM— HE'S GOT SEXY WOMAN'S LEGS!

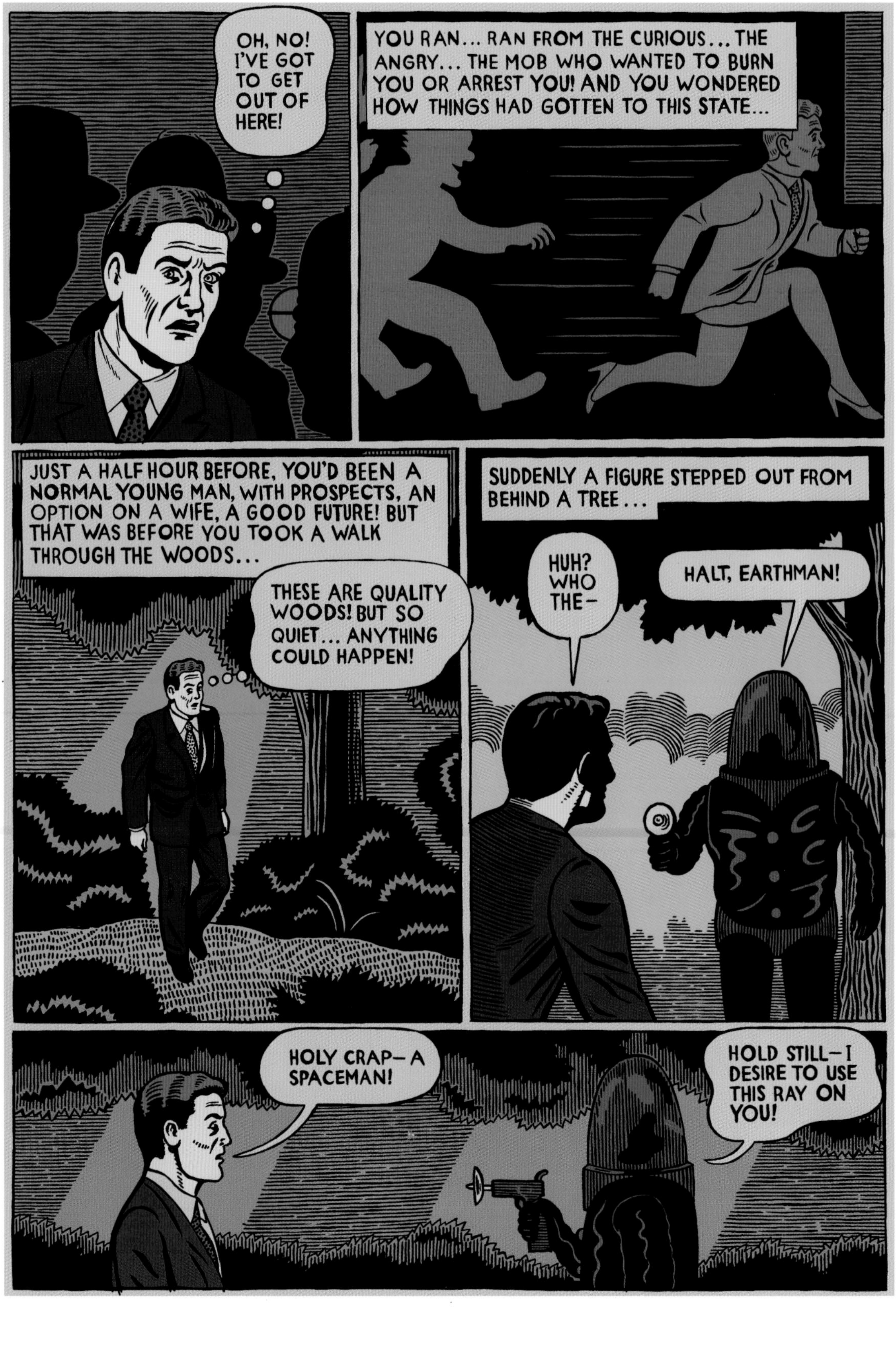
OH, NO! I'VE GOT TO GET OUT OF HERE!
YOU RAN... RAN FROM THE CURIOUS... THE ANGRY... THE MOB WHO WANTED TO BURN YOU OR ARREST YOU! AND YOU WONDERED HOW THINGS HAD GOTTEN TO THIS STATE...
JUST A HALF HOUR BEFORE, YOU'D BEEN A NORMAL YOUNG MAN, WITH PROSPECTS, AN OPTION ON A WIFE, A GOOD FUTURE! BUT THAT WAS BEFORE YOU TOOK A WALK THROUGH THE WOODS...
THESE ARE QUALITY WOODS! BUT SO QUIET... ANYTHING COULD HAPPEN!
SUDDENLY A FIGURE STEPPED OUT FROM BEHIND A TREE...
HUH? WHO THE—
HALT, EARTHMAN!
HOLY CRAP— A SPACEMAN!
HOLD STILL—I DESIRE TO USE THIS RAY ON YOU!

THE ALIEN'S RAY BATHED OVER YOU... AND YOU FELT IT BEGINNING TO HAPPEN...

YOUR LEGS BEGAN TO TRANSFORM... BEGAN TO BECOME...

SEXY WOMAN'S LEGS!

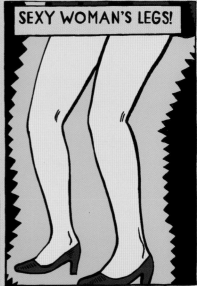

WHEN HE SAW WHAT HAD HAPPENED, THE ALIEN ENTERED SOME DATA IN SOME KIND OF SPACE NOTEBOOK...

THEN HE TURNED AND WALKED AWAY!

YOU WENT TO TOWN TO LOOK FOR HELP... BUT WE KNOW HOW THAT WORKED OUT! YOU OUTRAN THE YOKELS, UNTIL YOU CAME TO THIS CAVE!

YOU SCANNED THE MURKY INTERIOR... THEN YOU ENTERED!

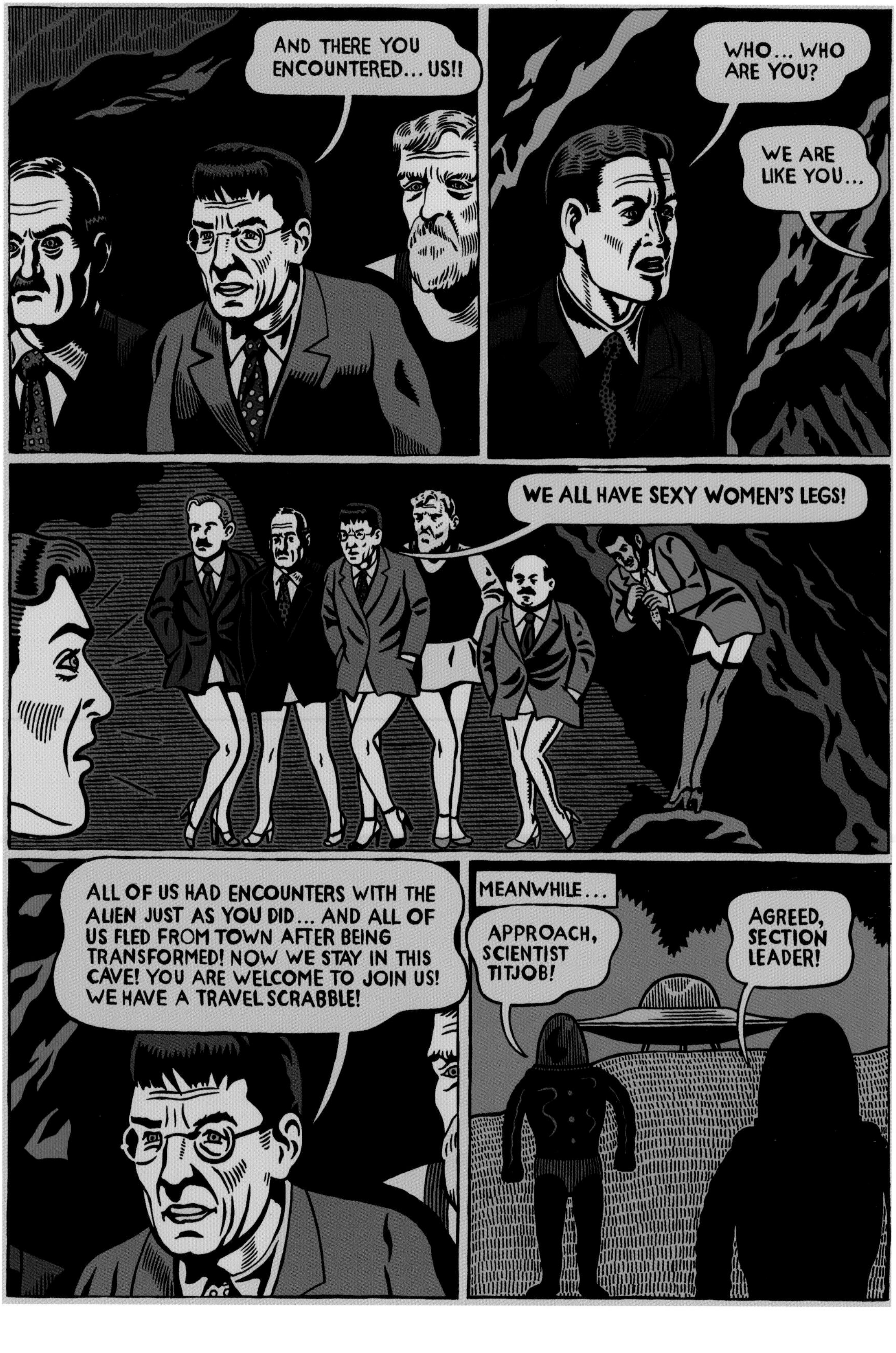
AND THERE YOU ENCOUNTERED... US!!
WHO... WHO ARE YOU?
WE ARE LIKE YOU...
WE ALL HAVE SEXY WOMEN'S LEGS!
ALL OF US HAD ENCOUNTERS WITH THE ALIEN JUST AS YOU DID... AND ALL OF US FLED FROM TOWN AFTER BEING TRANSFORMED! NOW WE STAY IN THIS CAVE! YOU ARE WELCOME TO JOIN US! WE HAVE A TRAVEL SCRABBLE!
MEANWHILE...
APPROACH, SCIENTIST TITJOB!
AGREED, SECTION LEADER!

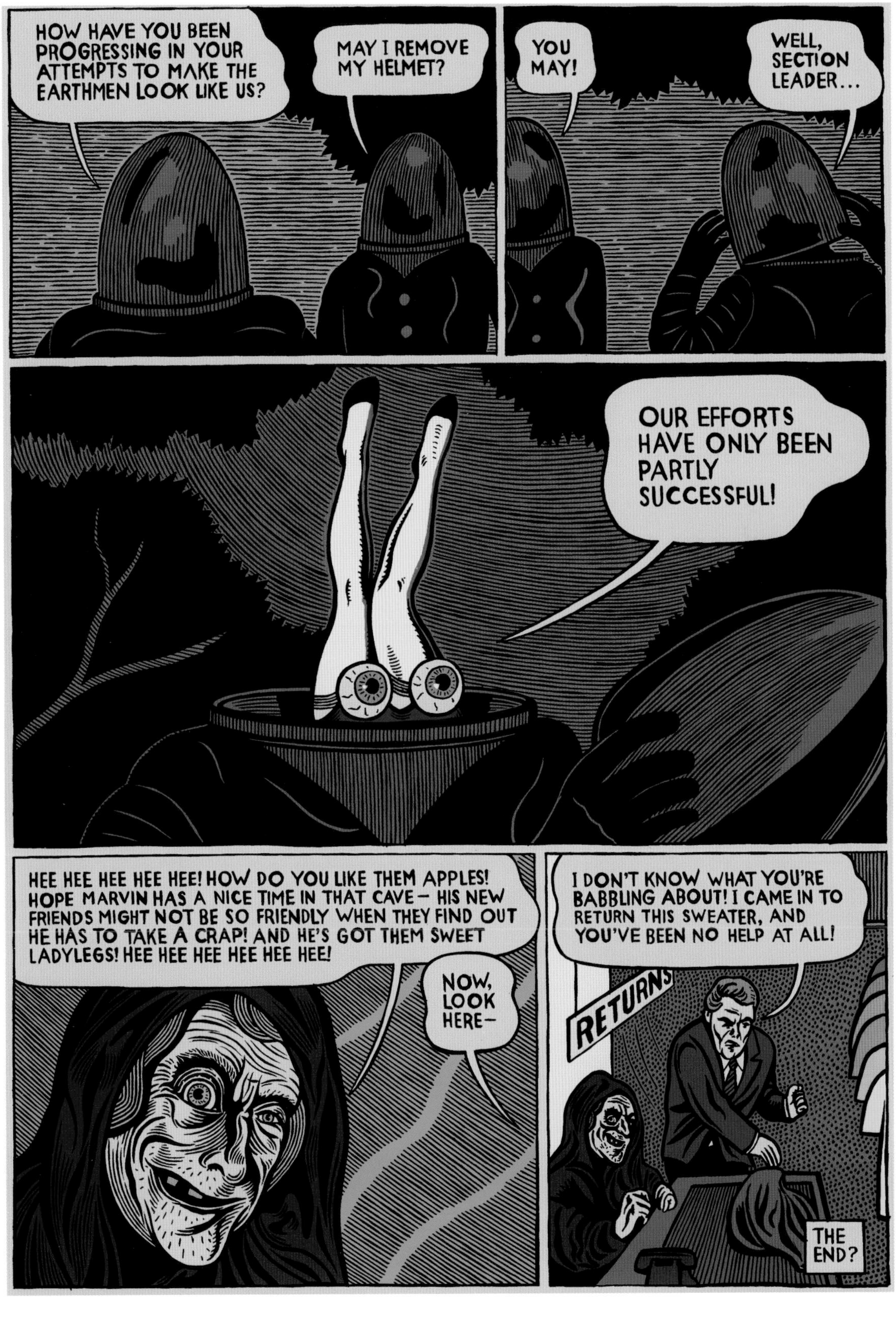
HOW HAVE YOU BEEN PROGRESSING IN YOUR ATTEMPTS TO MAKE THE EARTHMEN LOOK LIKE US?
MAY I REMOVE MY HELMET?
YOU MAY!
WELL, SECTION LEADER...
OUR EFFORTS HAVE ONLY BEEN PARTLY SUCCESSFUL!
HEE HEE HEE HEE HEE! HOW DO YOU LIKE THEM APPLES! HOPE MARVIN HAS A NICE TIME IN THAT CAVE— HIS NEW FRIENDS MIGHT NOT BE SO FRIENDLY WHEN THEY FIND OUT HE HAS TO TAKE A CRAP! AND HE'S GOT THEM SWEET LADYLEGS! HEE HEE HEE HEE HEE HEE!
NOW, LOOK HERE—
I DON'T KNOW WHAT YOU'RE BABBLING ABOUT! I CAME IN TO RETURN THIS SWEATER, AND YOU'VE BEEN NO HELP AT ALL!
RETURNS
THE END?

A Short Work of Speculative Fiction

ALBERT EINSTEIN'S FLASHBACK SCHEME

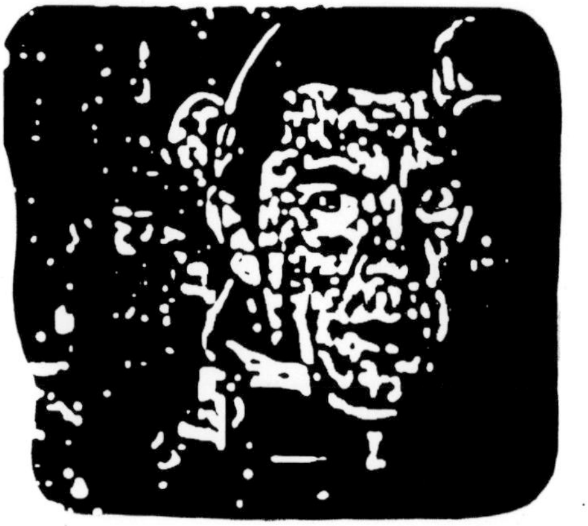

"I'll tell you one thing, Al," murmured Mark Twain. "I never thought we would end up on a game show hosted by Count Dracula!"

Albert Einstein nodded his assent. For it was Friday night in Transylvania and they had ended up on a game show hosted by Count Dracula. As Frankenstein's monster spun the giant wheel, Einstein's mind drifted back... back to that hazy day in lower Manhattan when he had listened to Twain negotiate the unfortunate return of a consignment of talking Gordon Ramsay underpants. The underpants had the TV chef and restaurateur's face on them, speaking one of six phrases upon removal– an effort, in Twain's words, to bring some "humor and spirit" to lovemaking. The phrases, taken from Ramsay's TV shows, included "Oh, dear," "You've got to be fucking kidding me," "This is a disgrace" and three more. A large department store chain had accepted an order based on the understanding that Ramsay had given his approval; but all Twain had was a verbal exchange outside a nightclub, and he wasn't even sure that guy was Ramsay. Hence the desperation in his voice.

"Don't send 'em back," he begged. "I'll change 'em so it's C-3PO from Star Wars." But the caller had hung up. Twain slammed the receiver down. "Well, Al, Twain and Einstein Import and Export is officially a bust."

"Don't worry," observed Einstein, busy ogling the stars in a new astronomy catalogue. "Something else will come along. It always does."

"We could start the old vaudeville act," began Twain, but luckily then a messenger came running in.

"Telegram! Special delivery for Albert Einstein," he barked. Einstein slid the kid a nickel, and slid off his stool to examine the telegram under a stronger light. "Judging by the type of paper, this telegram comes from Egypt," he observed as he rubbed it with his fingers. "Other than that, I can deduce nothing." He dropped it on the floor, and went back to smoking his pipe.

Twain grabbed for the crumpled telegram. "Have you tried reading it?" he barked. He cleared his throat and began. "Dearest Albert– Have found Yeti in pyramids– stop– am in great danger– stop-stop– stop– no– aiiieeee." he finished. "Guess something attacked her before she could finish the telegram," he said solemnly.

Einstein was baffled. "What makes you think it was a lady?" he demanded.

"Something you, with your rational scientist's mind, missed, Al," mused Twain. He held out the telegram. "The scent of violets."

"Katrina!" gasped Einstein. So, she was in trouble again. His mind flashed back to the first time he had met her. He and Twain had been working as bodyguards then, and had been hired to guard The California Raisins.

Twain had been disgusted. "How in hell are we supposed to guard a bunch of raisins that don't exist?" he demanded of his partner. They were sitting in Lou's diner, eating a greasy Fatboy special.

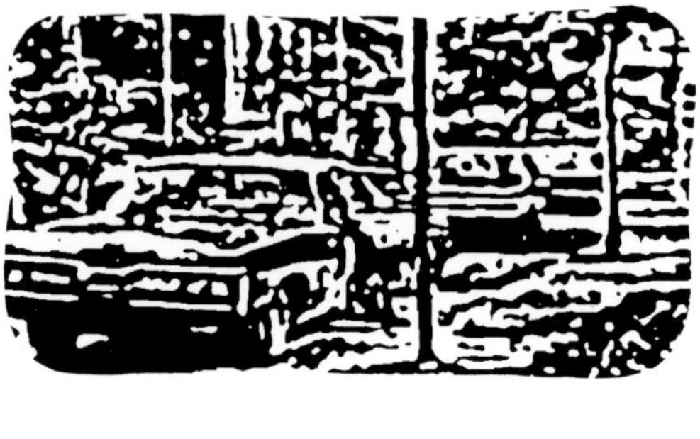

"It's symbolic, I guess," replied Einstein, feeding coins into his clams casino. "I got one of those mini boxes of raisins in my pocket, and I'm keeping it safe."

"All so they can claim the publicity" grouched Twain, wolfing down purloin strips. Just then their police radio rang.

"Attention car 23" it squawked. "There's a disturbance in progress at the corner of Jeeves and Wooster.

Please advise."

"Another lunch ruined," groused Twain, but Einstein noted the change from grouching to grousing. Throwing away their lunches, they jumped in the car and drove over to the disturbance.

It was quite a scene. An elegant silver spaceship was floating right over the street. All the cars were stopped and people craned their necks, and Twain and Einstein pushed and shoved their way onto the scene. "Now then, what's all this then?" they challenged.

A figure appeared on the rim of the spaceship. "People of Earth!" it started, but Twain and Einstein had their guns out and were already firing. Bullets pinged around the street and a plate glass window shattered. A car tire deflated with a sudden hiss as it was punctured. "You shall never know what knowledge I could have given your race!" were the alien's final words as it jumped back into its spaceship. Bullets zinging off its hull, it shot out towards the stars.

Twain turned to Einstein. "That was some mighty good shooting, partner," he said. "Between us, I'd say we saved the people of this planet from being possibly annoyed. And that, my friend, leads me to the real reason we're here tonight... to steal the Frenchman's gold."

A buzz went around the room. Buzz Aldrin was the first to speak.

"I'm just an astronaut, Twain," he said. "I want no part of this." And with that he left with his wife, Lola Falana.

"Does anyone else have any objections?" asked Twain. "No? Good. I have invited you all here because you all have certain specialties necessary to complete the mission. Khuran, you know how to haggle. Find me those bargains! Mesmero, you shout at the alarms. Johnny Pablum, you dress as a sexy female Triffid in case there are Triffid guards that need distracting." Here he paused, and his tone turned serious. "But the pleasure of killing The California Raisins will be mine alone."

Einstein gasped as the implications of this triple-cross hit him. They had been hired to kill the very imaginary clients that they had been hired to protect. His knowledge of the precedents extended to an old cartoon where talking pastries put a sleeping bug on trial. Now he had to honor the assignment, or face The Commission. And nobody faced The Commission and came back alive, unless they wanted to pay a substantial fine. He felt in his pocket– the box of raisins was gone!

Later, after they had stolen the Frenchman's gold, Einstein went to see his mistress. "How you doing, baby," he lilted, and from his pocket he brought the Vienna brooch. "Here it is... a lot of good people died for this." She snatched it from his hand. A smile played at Einstein's lips, and he went over to the piano, pouring himself three fingers of whiskey as he went. Tossing it down, he started to play The Relativity Rag. "You know, that patrolman had three kids."

She turned, her nostril flaring. "What's this crap? I thought you were supposed to be the tough hard guy, and here you are, acting like a weepy little girl." Einstein jumped up, his face clenched. But she was ready for him.

"Face it, Johnny Ultrafresh (for this was the name he had given her), face it, you can't dabble in murder. Either you're in you're out. But you can't escape history."

Phantoms appeared behind Einstein– the ghosts of historical figures. His mouth opened to scream, but already Ben Franklin and Allen Funt were pulling him back, taking him to the shack behind the pizza hut.

Then he woke up. He was bathed in sweat.

"And your next question is in Botany," said Dracula.

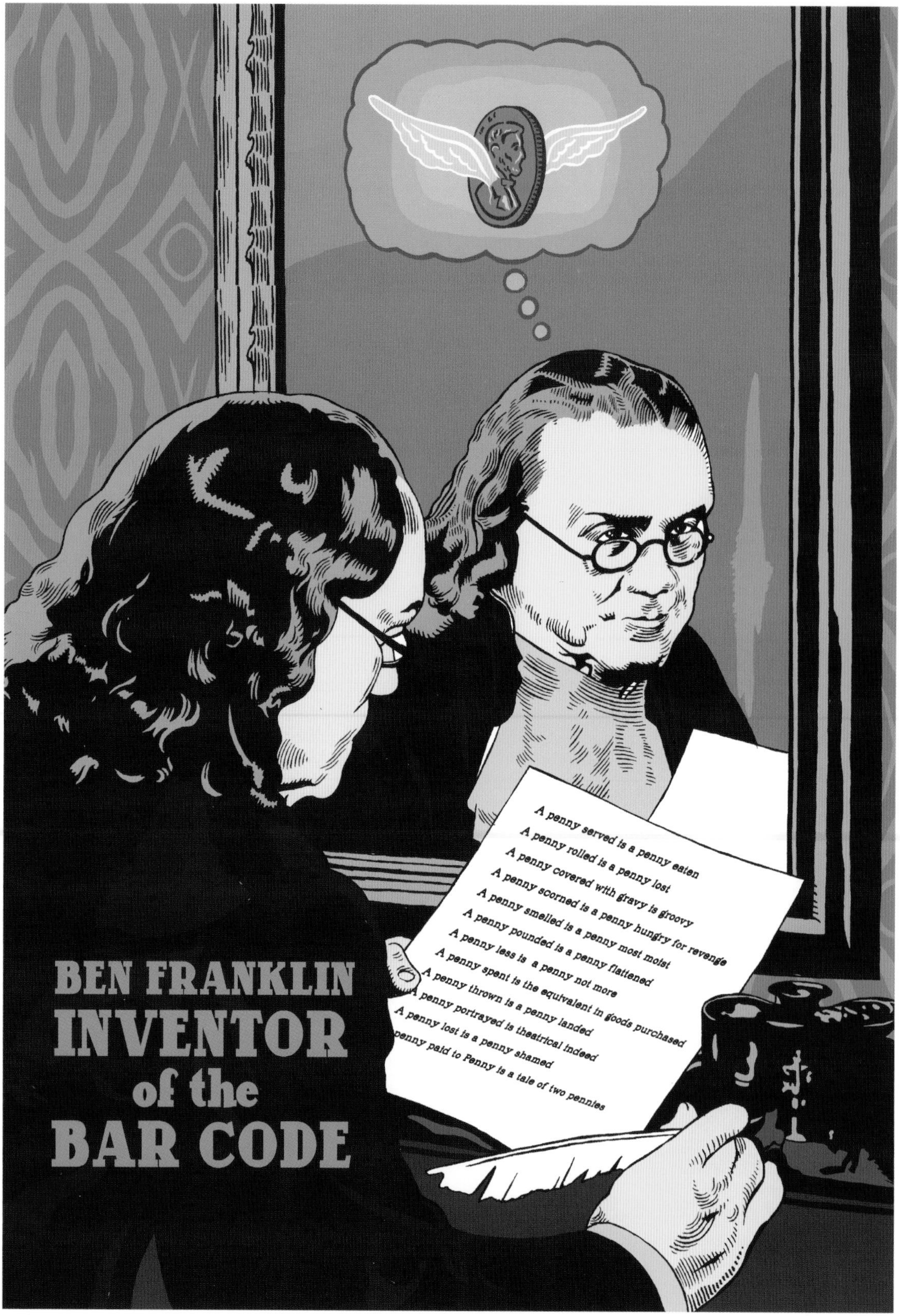

A penny served is a penny eaten
A penny rolled is a penny lost
A penny covered with gravy is groovy
A penny scorned is a penny hungry for revenge
A penny smelled is a penny most moist
A penny pounded is a penny flattened
A penny less is a penny not more
A penny spent is the equivalent in goods purchased
A penny thrown is a penny landed
A penny portrayed is theatrical indeed
A penny lost is a penny shamed
penny paid to Penny is a tale of two pennies
BEN FRANKLIN
INVENTOR
of the
BAR CODE

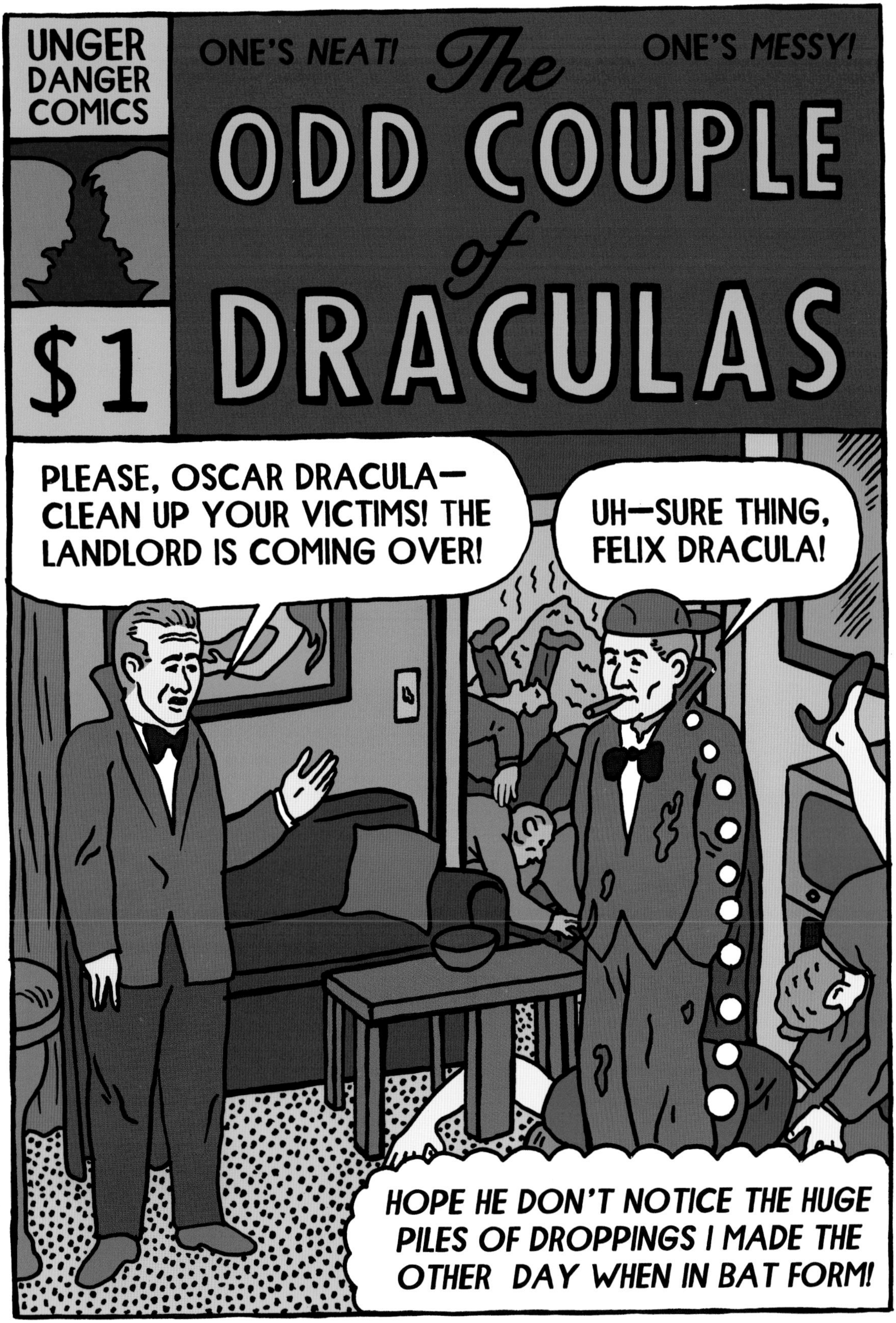
UNGER DANGER COMICS
$1
ONE'S NEAT!
ONE'S MESSY!
The ODD COUPLE of DRACULAS
PLEASE, OSCAR DRACULA— CLEAN UP YOUR VICTIMS! THE LANDLORD IS COMING OVER!
UH—SURE THING, FELIX DRACULA!
HOPE HE DON'T NOTICE THE HUGE PILES OF DROPPINGS I MADE THE OTHER DAY WHEN IN BAT FORM!

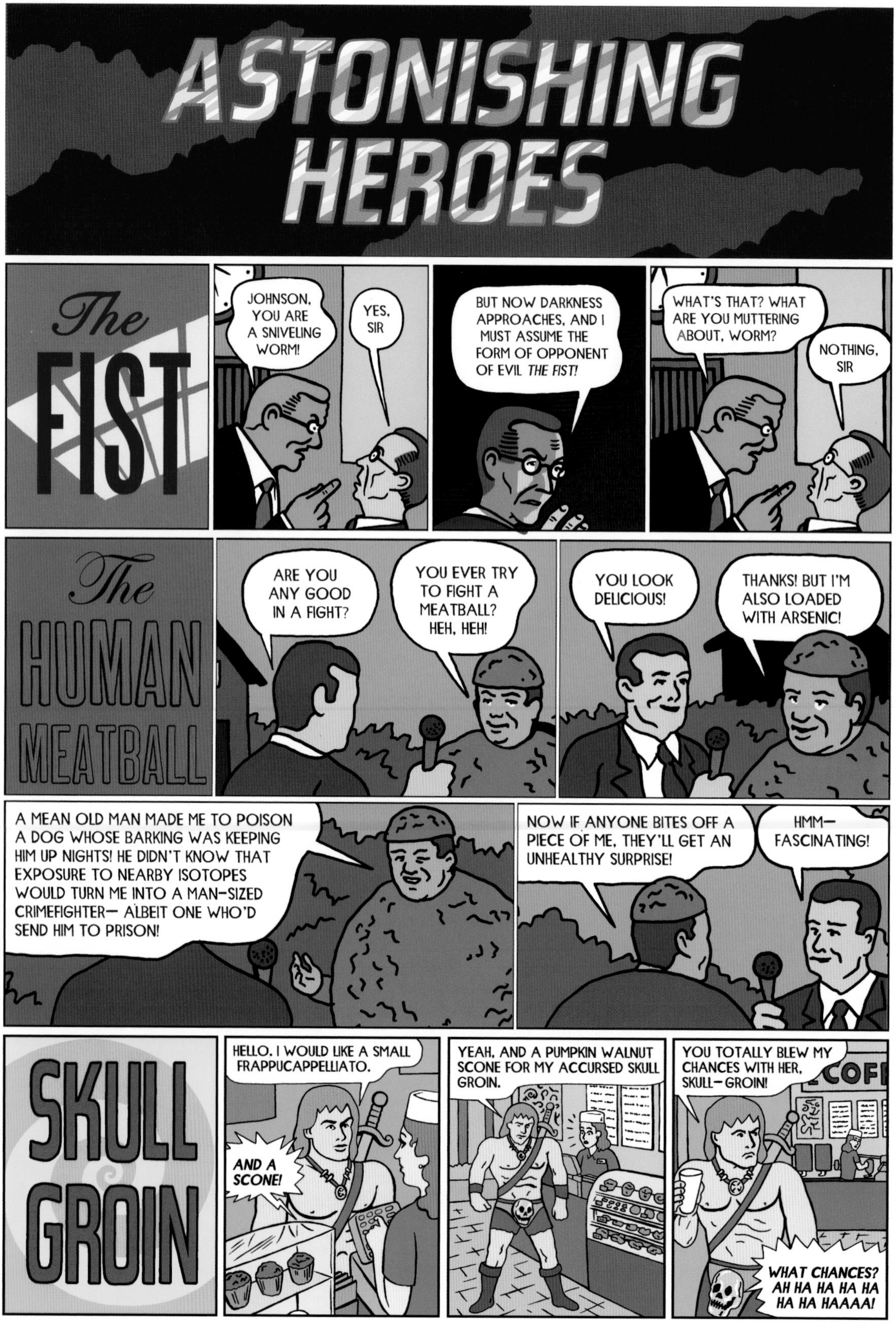
ASTONISHING HEROES
The FIST
JOHNSON, YOU ARE A SNIVELING WORM!
YES, SIR
BUT NOW DARKNESS APPROACHES, AND I MUST ASSUME THE FORM OF OPPONENT OF EVIL THE FIST!
WHAT'S THAT? WHAT ARE YOU MUTTERING ABOUT, WORM?
NOTHING, SIR
The HUMAN MEATBALL
ARE YOU ANY GOOD IN A FIGHT?
YOU EVER TRY TO FIGHT A MEATBALL? HEH, HEH!
YOU LOOK DELICIOUS!
THANKS! BUT I'M ALSO LOADED WITH ARSENIC!
A MEAN OLD MAN MADE ME TO POISON A DOG WHOSE BARKING WAS KEEPING HIM UP NIGHTS! HE DIDN'T KNOW THAT EXPOSURE TO NEARBY ISOTOPES WOULD TURN ME INTO A MAN-SIZED CRIMEFIGHTER— ALBEIT ONE WHO'D SEND HIM TO PRISON!
NOW IF ANYONE BITES OFF A PIECE OF ME, THEY'LL GET AN UNHEALTHY SURPRISE!
HMM— FASCINATING!
SKULL GROIN
HELLO. I WOULD LIKE A SMALL FRAPPUCAPPELLIATO.
AND A SCONE!
YEAH, AND A PUMPKIN WALNUT SCONE FOR MY ACCURSED SKULL GROIN.
YOU TOTALLY BLEW MY CHANCES WITH HER, SKULL-GROIN!
WHAT CHANCES? AH HA HA HA HA HA HA HAAAA!

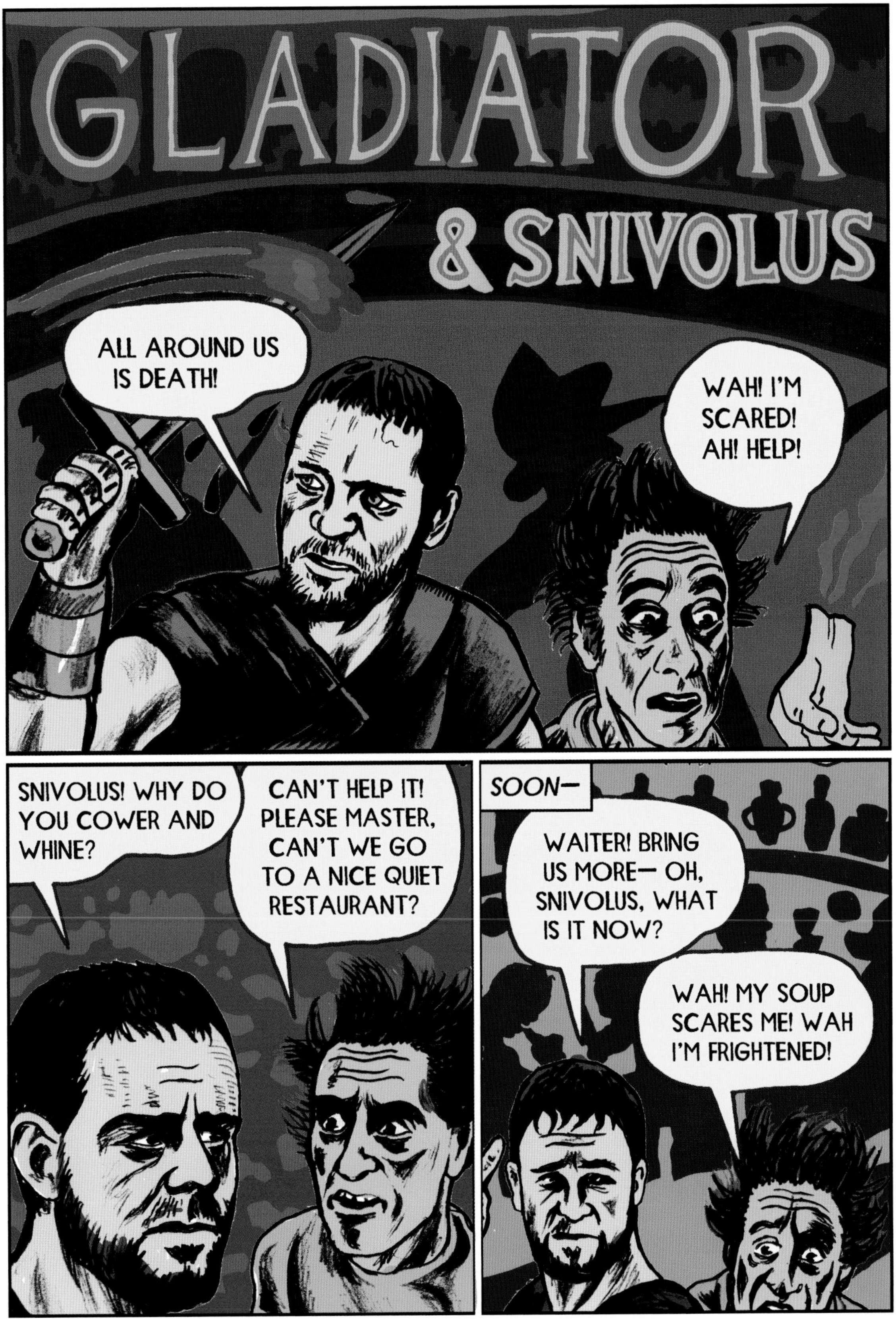
GLADIATOR
& SNIVOLUS
ALL AROUND US IS DEATH!
WAH! I'M SCARED! AH! HELP!
SNIVOLUS! WHY DO YOU COWER AND WHINE?
CAN'T HELP IT! PLEASE MASTER, CAN'T WE GO TO A NICE QUIET RESTAURANT?
SOON—
WAITER! BRING US MORE— OH, SNIVOLUS, WHAT IS IT NOW?
WAH! MY SOUP SCARES ME! WAH I'M FRIGHTENED!

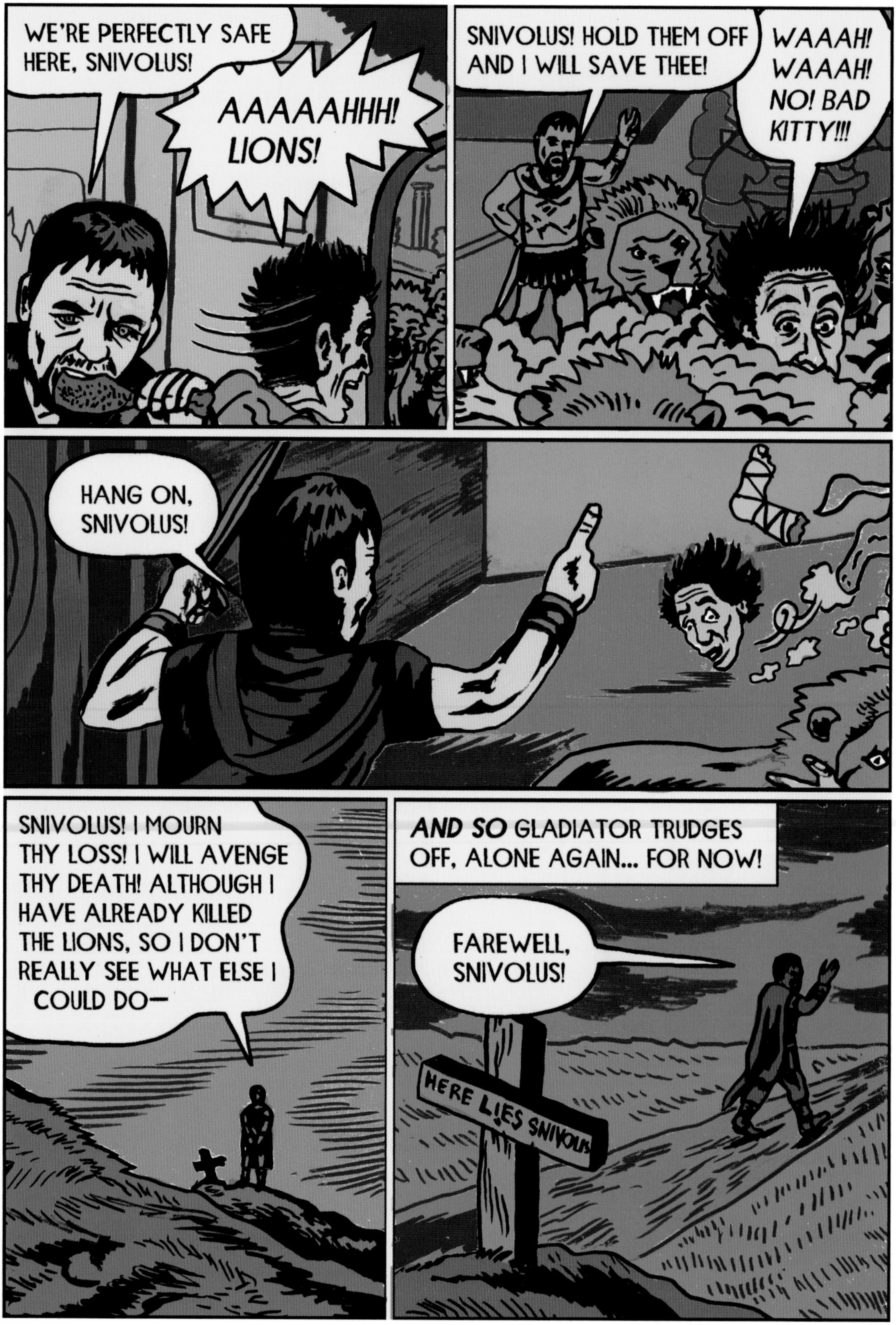
WE'RE PERFECTLY SAFE HERE, SNIVOLUS!
AAAAAHHH! LIONS!
SNIVOLUS! HOLD THEM OFF AND I WILL SAVE THEE!
WAAAH! WAAAH! NO! BAD KITTY!!!
HANG ON, SNIVOLUS!
SNIVOLUS! I MOURN THY LOSS! I WILL AVENGE THY DEATH! ALTHOUGH I HAVE ALREADY KILLED THE LIONS, SO I DON'T REALLY SEE WHAT ELSE I COULD DO—
AND SO GLADIATOR TRUDGES OFF, ALONE AGAIN... FOR NOW!
FAREWELL, SNIVOLUS!
HERE LIES SNIVOLUS

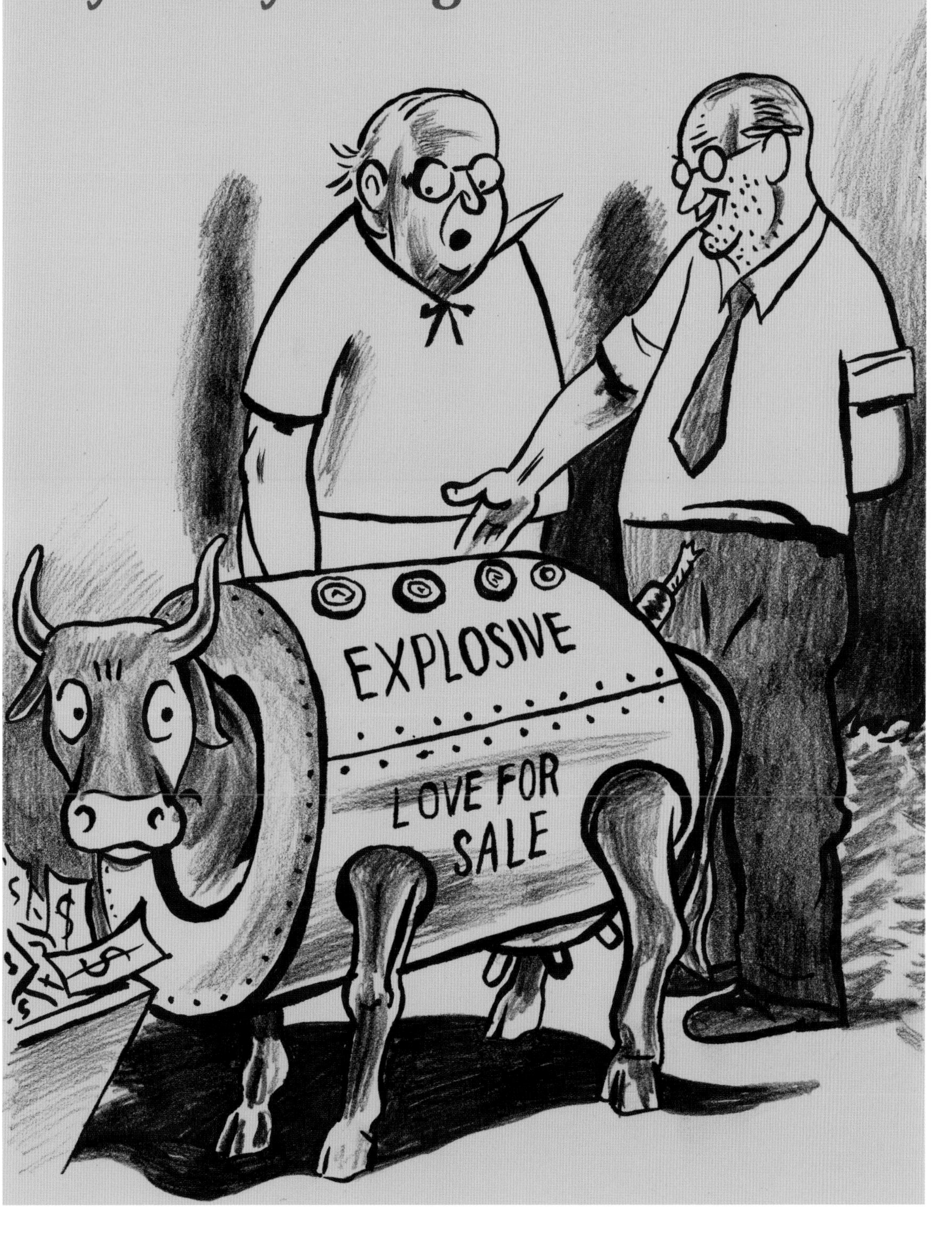
EXPLOSIVE
LOVE FOR SALE

"They said I was crazy, but look at my money-eating cow-whorebomb!"

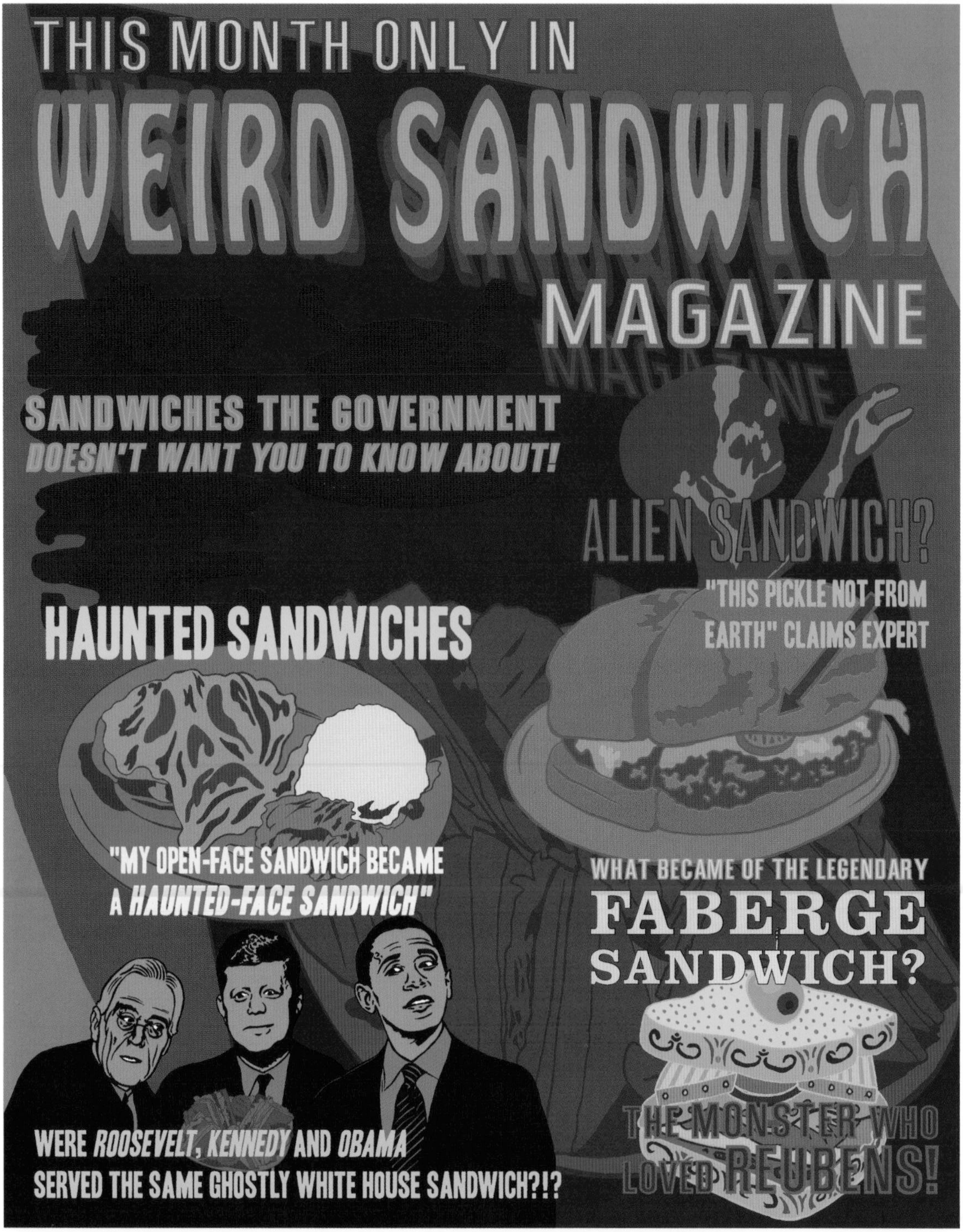
THIS MONTH ONLY IN
WEIRD SANDWICH
MAGAZINE
SANDWICHES THE GOVERNMENT
DOESN'T WANT YOU TO KNOW ABOUT!
ALIEN SANDWICH?
"THIS PICKLE NOT FROM
EARTH" CLAIMS EXPERT
HAUNTED SANDWICHES
"MY OPEN-FACE SANDWICH BECAME
A HAUNTED-FACE SANDWICH"
WHAT BECAME OF THE LEGENDARY
FABERGE
SANDWICH?
WERE ROOSEVELT, KENNEDY AND OBAMA
SERVED THE SAME GHOSTLY WHITE HOUSE SANDWICH?!?
THE MONSTER WHO
LOVED REUBENS!

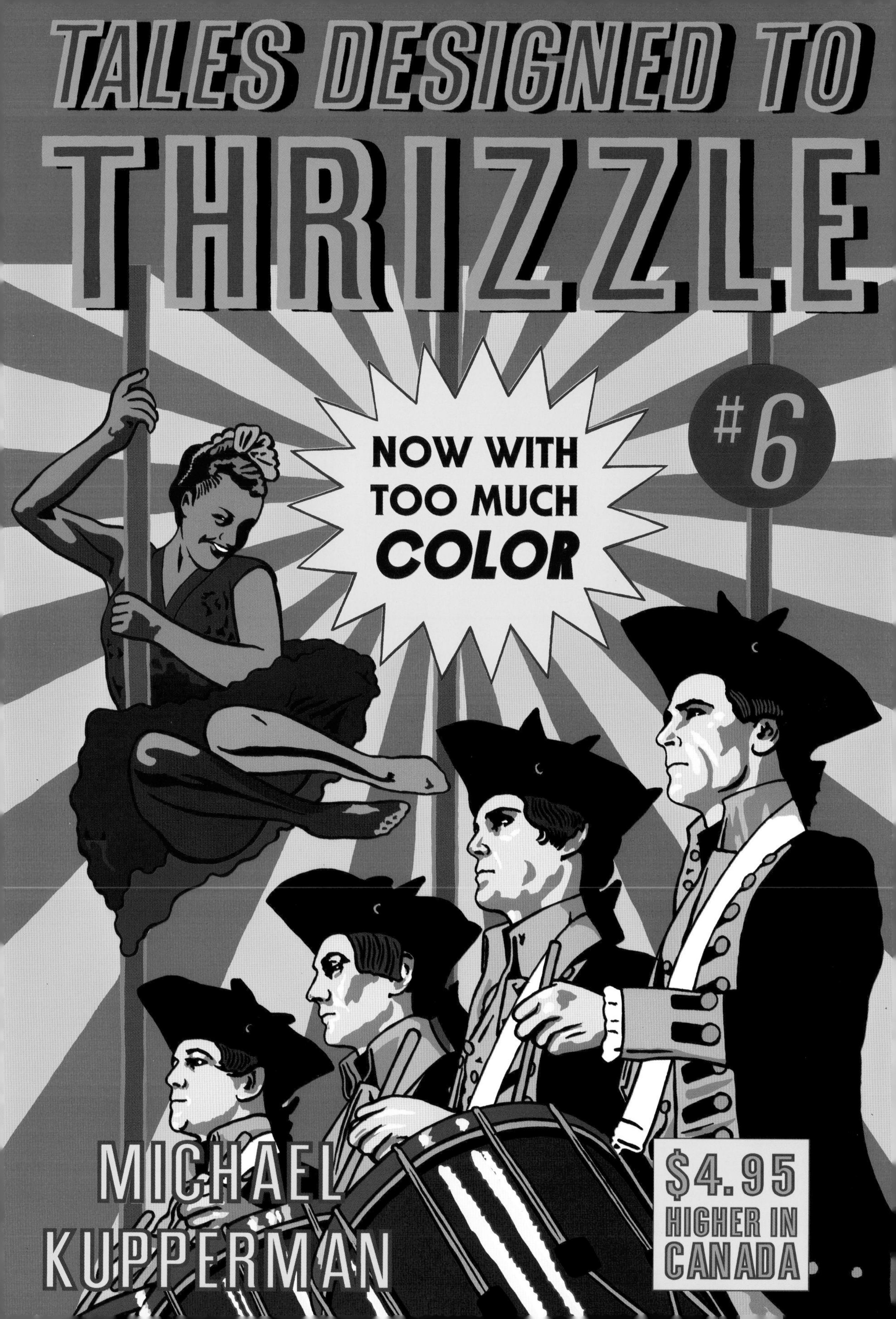

TALES DESIGNED TO
THRIZZLE
NOW WITH TOO MUCH COLOR
#6
MICHAEL KUPPERMAN
$4.95 HIGHER IN CANADA

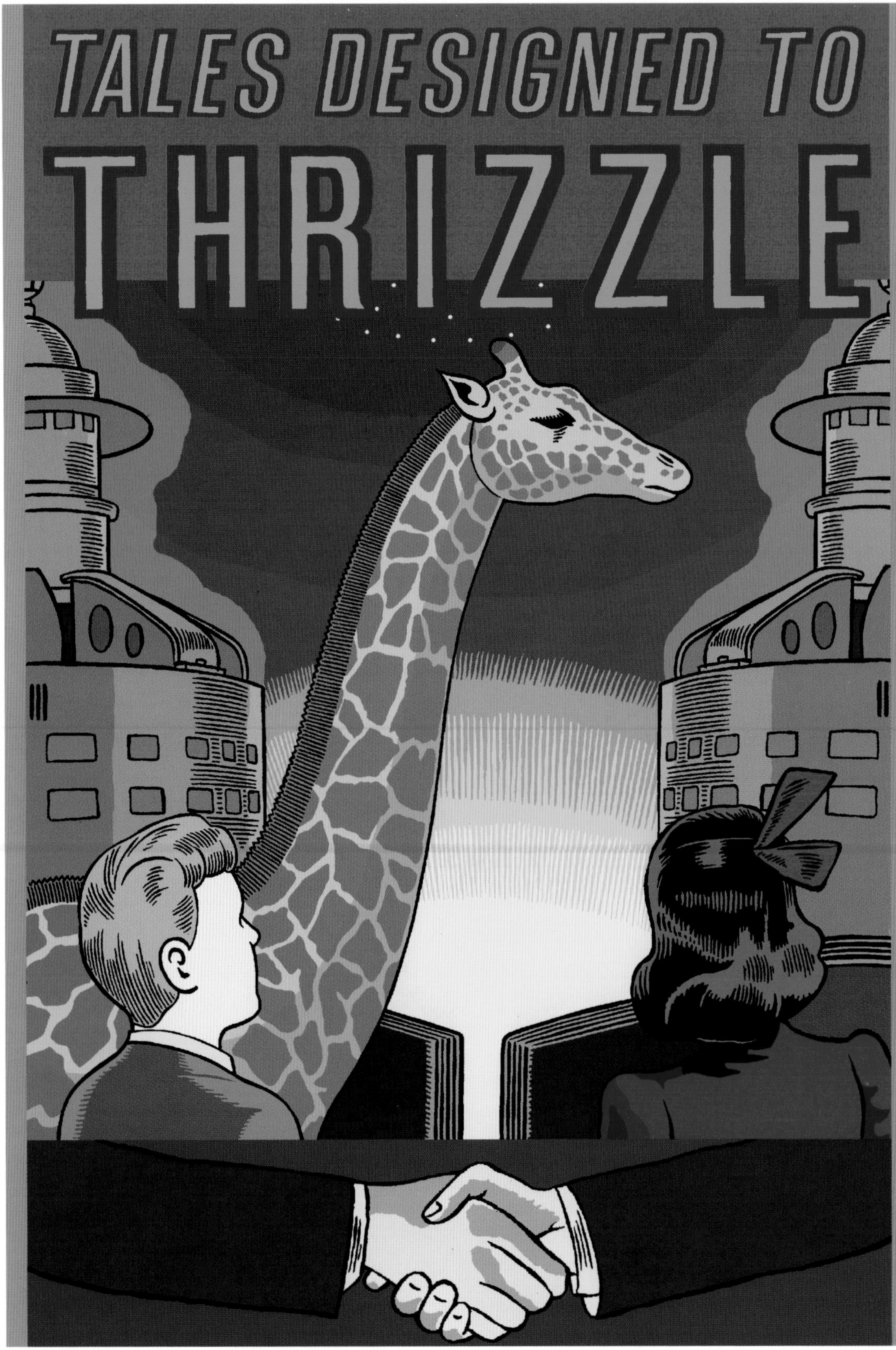
TALES DESIGNED TO
THRIZZLE

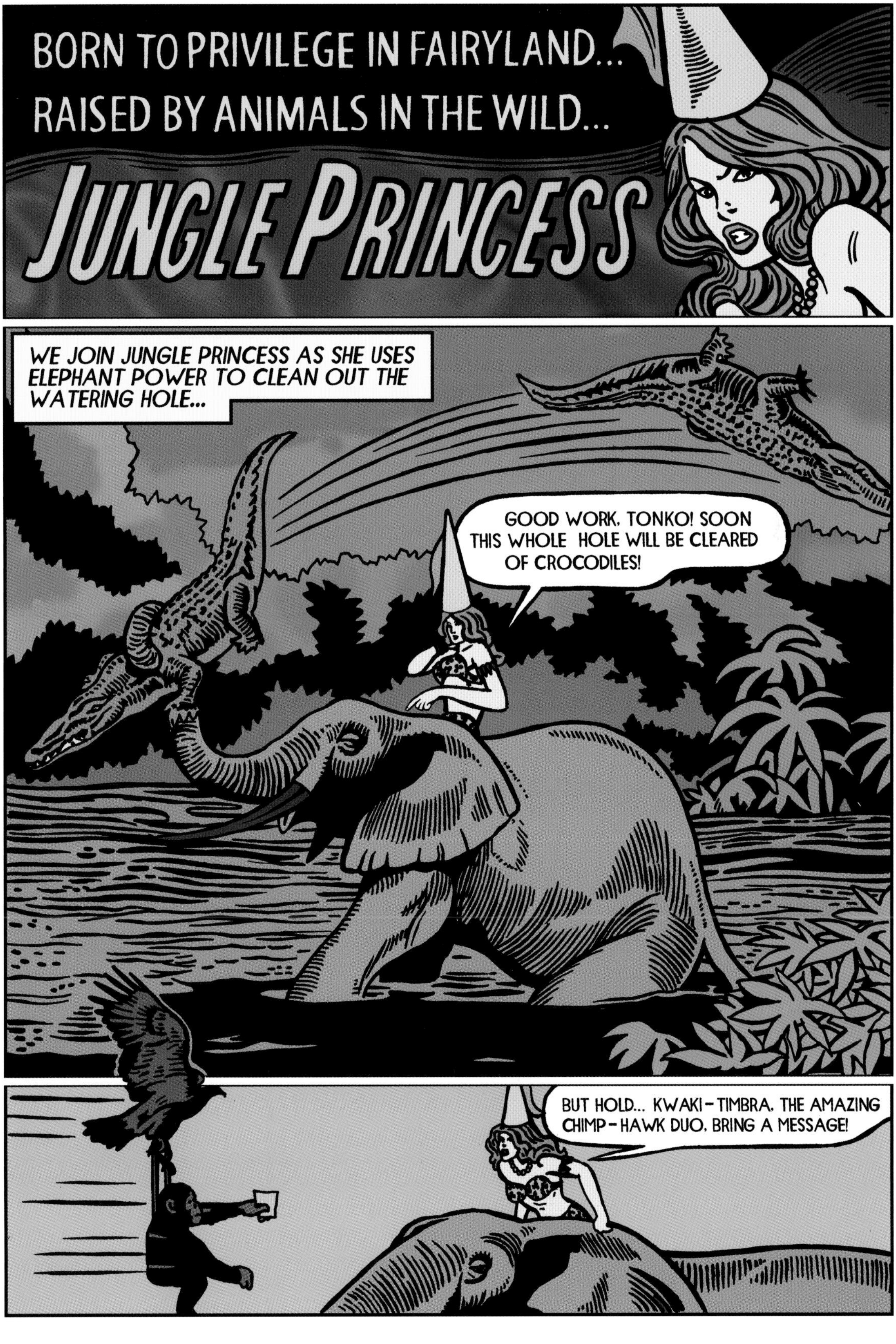
BORN TO PRIVILEGE IN FAIRYLAND...
RAISED BY ANIMALS IN THE WILD...
JUNGLE PRINCESS
WE JOIN JUNGLE PRINCESS AS SHE USES ELEPHANT POWER TO CLEAN OUT THE WATERING HOLE...
GOOD WORK, TONKO! SOON THIS WHOLE HOLE WILL BE CLEARED OF CROCODILES!
BUT HOLD... KWAKI-TIMBRA, THE AMAZING CHIMP-HAWK DUO, BRING A MESSAGE!

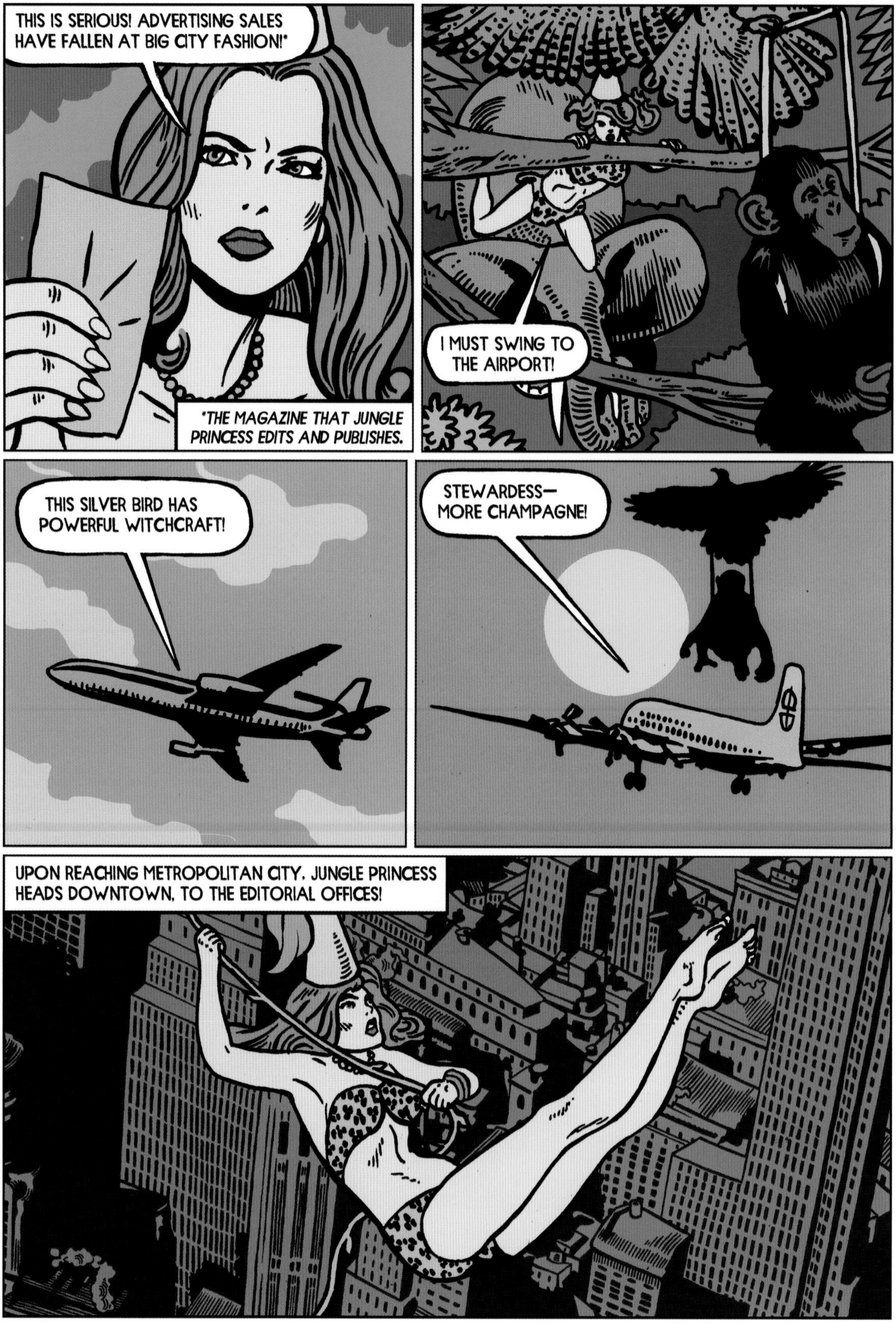
THIS IS SERIOUS! ADVERTISING SALES HAVE FALLEN AT BIG CITY FASHION!*
*THE MAGAZINE THAT JUNGLE PRINCESS EDITS AND PUBLISHES.
I MUST SWING TO THE AIRPORT!
THIS SILVER BIRD HAS POWERFUL WITCHCRAFT!
STEWARDESS— MORE CHAMPAGNE!
UPON REACHING METROPOLITAN CITY, JUNGLE PRINCESS HEADS DOWNTOWN, TO THE EDITORIAL OFFICES!

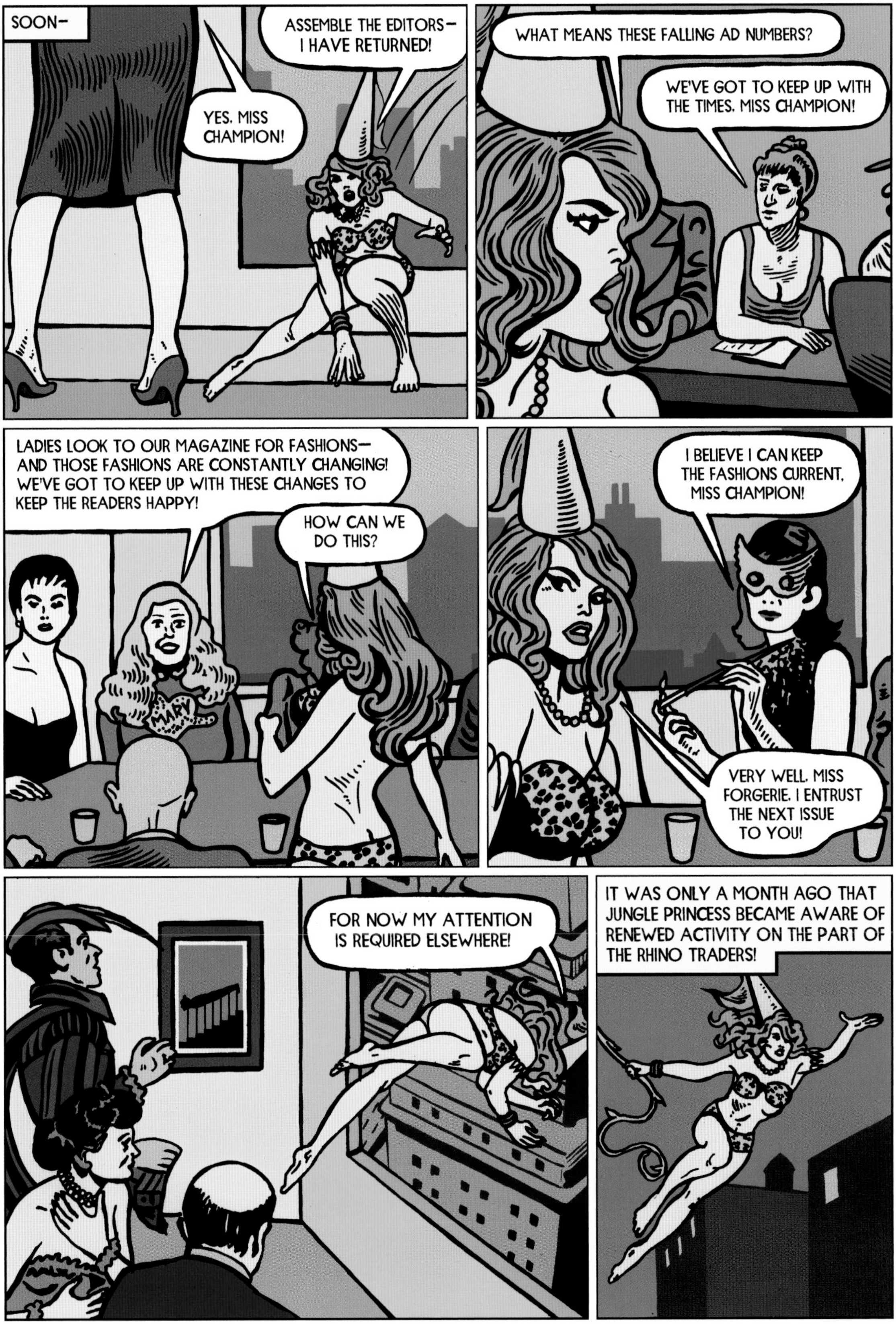
SOON—
YES, MISS CHAMPION!
ASSEMBLE THE EDITORS— I HAVE RETURNED!
WHAT MEANS THESE FALLING AD NUMBERS?
WE'VE GOT TO KEEP UP WITH THE TIMES, MISS CHAMPION!
LADIES LOOK TO OUR MAGAZINE FOR FASHIONS— AND THOSE FASHIONS ARE CONSTANTLY CHANGING! WE'VE GOT TO KEEP UP WITH THESE CHANGES TO KEEP THE READERS HAPPY!
HOW CAN WE DO THIS?
MARY
I BELIEVE I CAN KEEP THE FASHIONS CURRENT, MISS CHAMPION!
VERY WELL, MISS FORGERIE. I ENTRUST THE NEXT ISSUE TO YOU!
FOR NOW MY ATTENTION IS REQUIRED ELSEWHERE!
IT WAS ONLY A MONTH AGO THAT JUNGLE PRINCESS BECAME AWARE OF RENEWED ACTIVITY ON THE PART OF THE RHINO TRADERS!

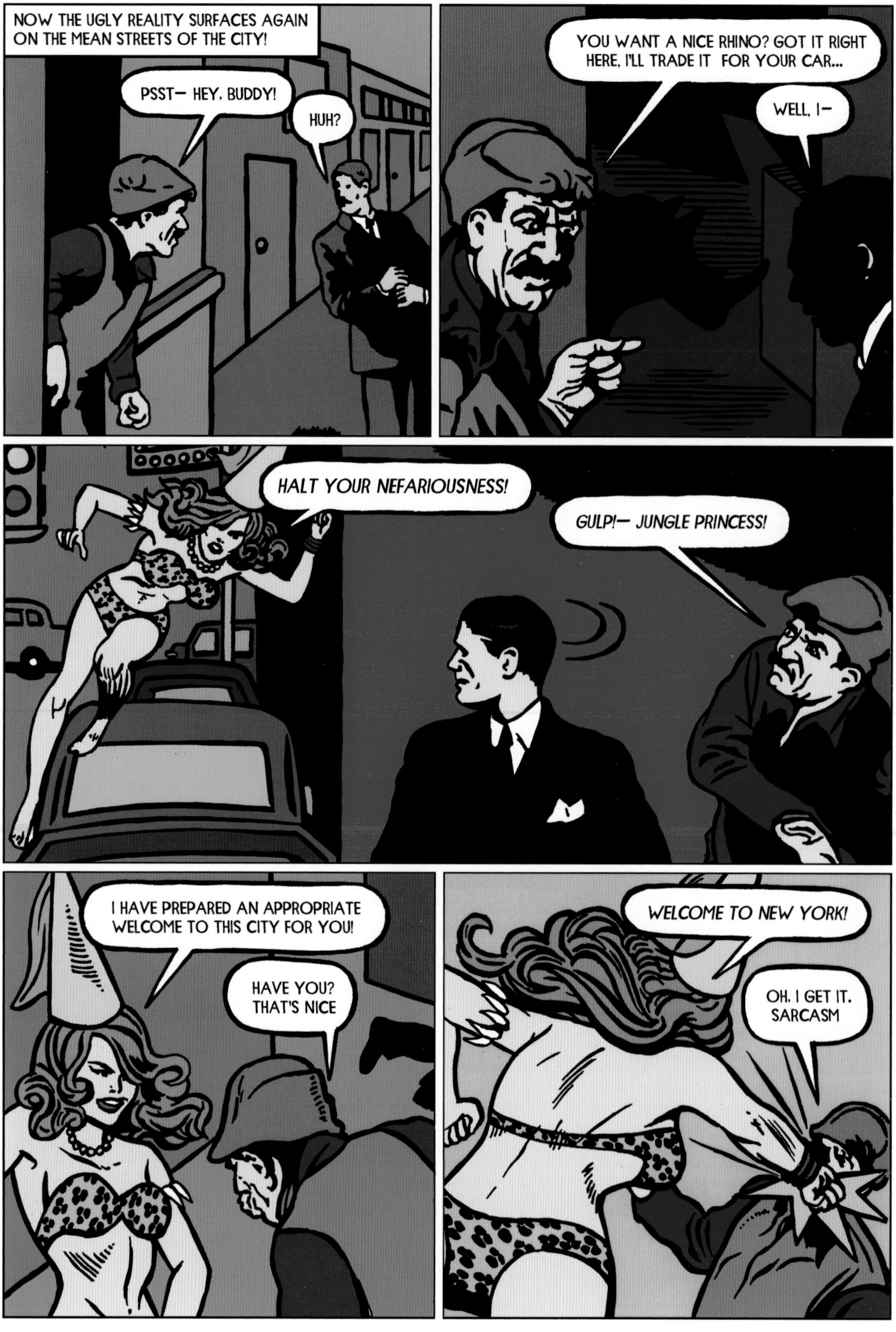
NOW THE UGLY REALITY SURFACES AGAIN ON THE MEAN STREETS OF THE CITY!
PSST— HEY, BUDDY!
HUH?
YOU WANT A NICE RHINO? GOT IT RIGHT HERE, I'LL TRADE IT FOR YOUR CAR...
WELL, I—
HALT YOUR NEFARIOUSNESS!
GULP!— JUNGLE PRINCESS!
I HAVE PREPARED AN APPROPRIATE WELCOME TO THIS CITY FOR YOU!
HAVE YOU? THAT'S NICE
WELCOME TO NEW YORK!
OH, I GET IT. SARCASM

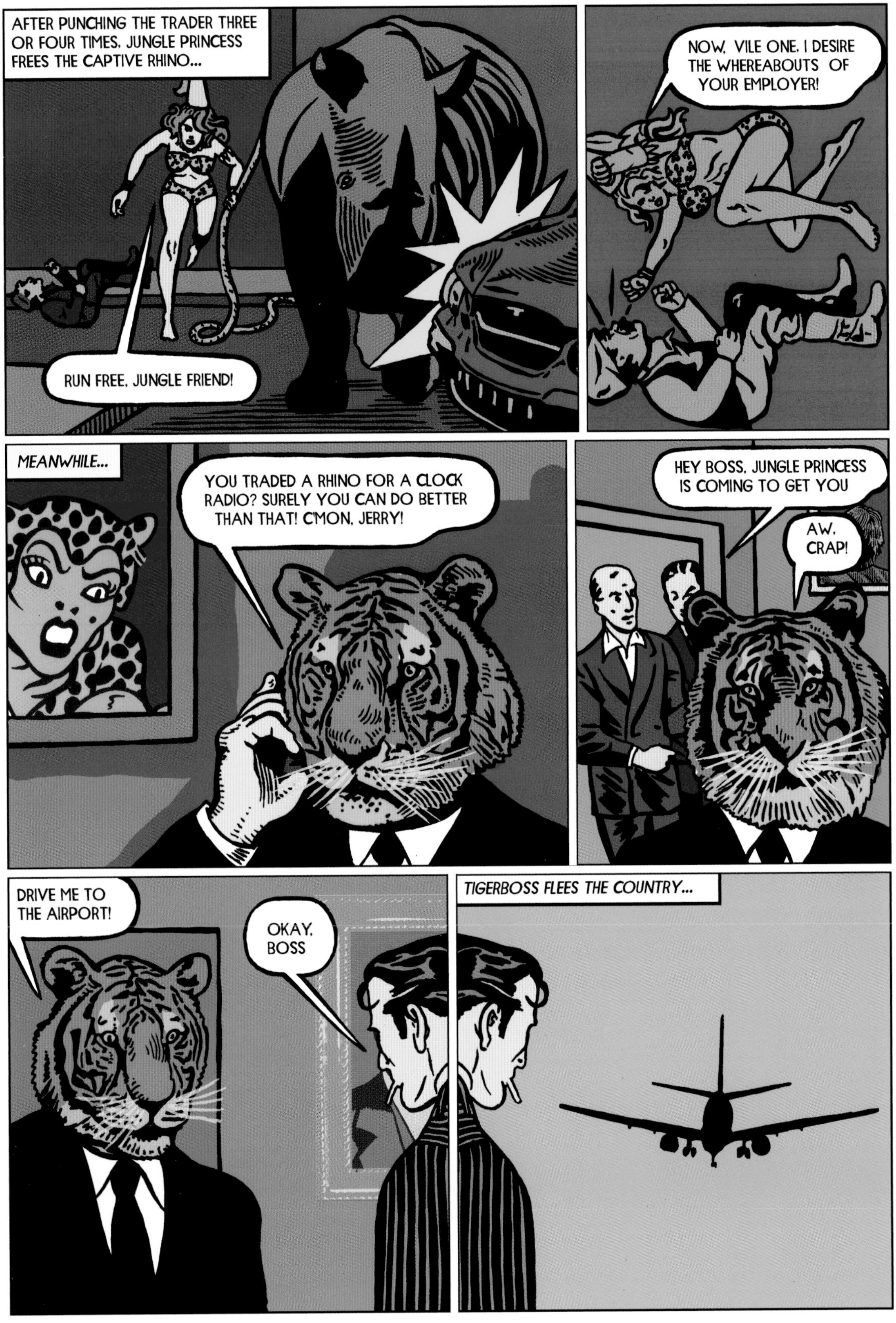
AFTER PUNCHING THE TRADER THREE OR FOUR TIMES, JUNGLE PRINCESS FREES THE CAPTIVE RHINO...
RUN FREE, JUNGLE FRIEND!
NOW, VILE ONE, I DESIRE THE WHEREABOUTS OF YOUR EMPLOYER!
MEANWHILE...
YOU TRADED A RHINO FOR A CLOCK RADIO? SURELY YOU CAN DO BETTER THAN THAT! C'MON, JERRY!
HEY BOSS, JUNGLE PRINCESS IS COMING TO GET YOU
AW, CRAP!
DRIVE ME TO THE AIRPORT!
OKAY, BOSS
TIGERBOSS FLEES THE COUNTRY...

AND JUNGLE PRINCESS FOLLOWS!

TIGERBOSS SWITCHES FLIGHTS!

SO DOES JUNGLE PRINCESS!

THE GAME CONTINUES!

CIRCLING THE GLOBE, TIGERBOSS AND JUNGLE PRINCESS ENGAGE IN A DEADLY GAME OF CAT AND MOUSE!

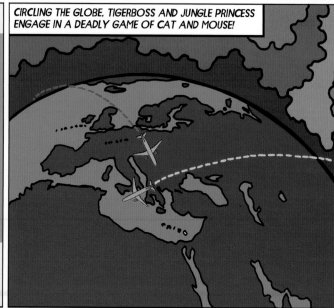

FINALLY, THE CHASE ENDS ON AN ISLAND IN THE PACIFIC!

AT LEAST I'LL BE ABLE TO SEE HER COMING...

BUT FOR NOW I'LL... WHAT'S THAT NOISE?

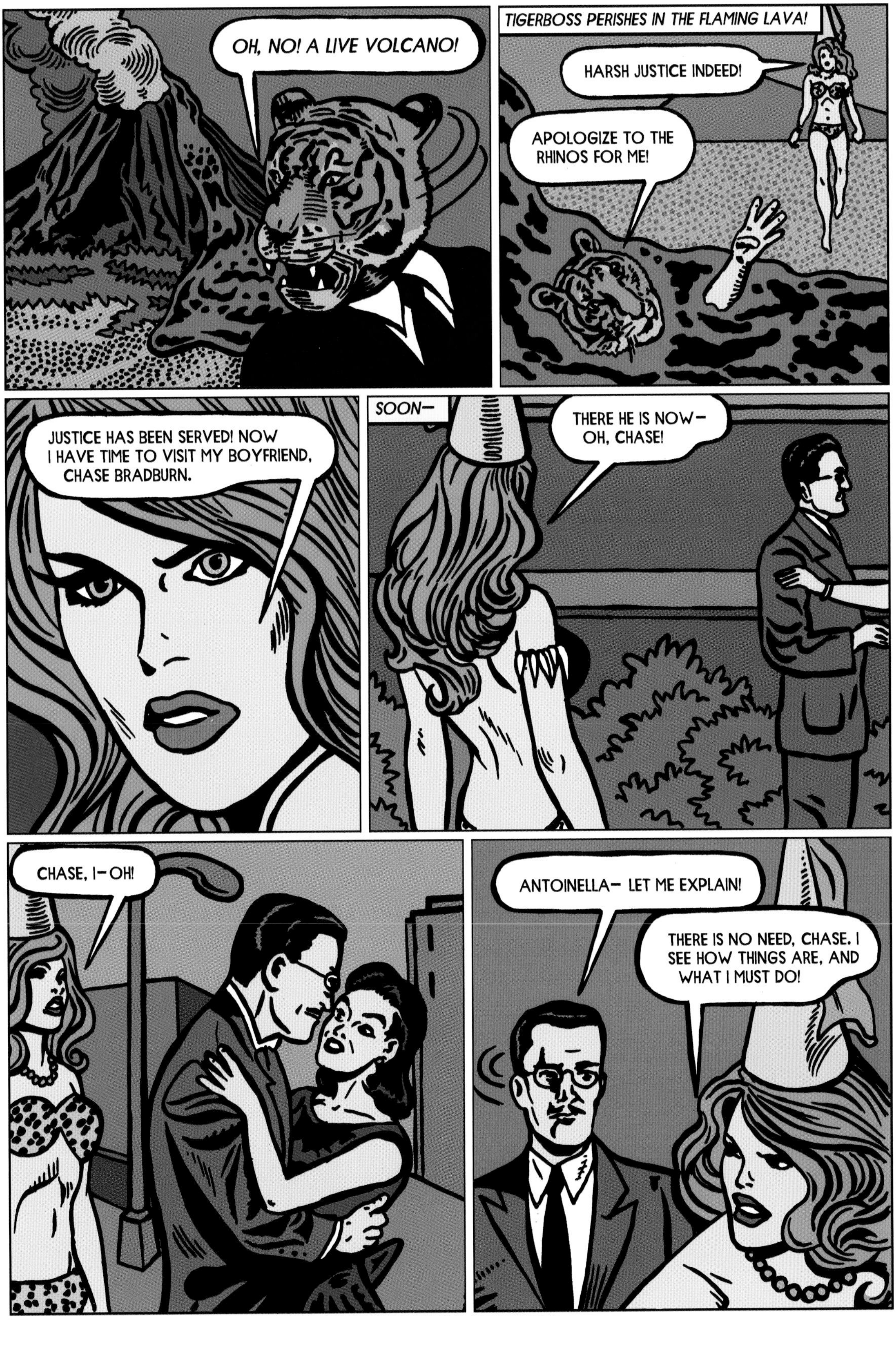
OH, NO! A LIVE VOLCANO!
TIGERBOSS PERISHES IN THE FLAMING LAVA!
HARSH JUSTICE INDEED!
APOLOGIZE TO THE RHINOS FOR ME!
JUSTICE HAS BEEN SERVED! NOW I HAVE TIME TO VISIT MY BOYFRIEND, CHASE BRADBURN.
SOON—
THERE HE IS NOW— OH, CHASE!
CHASE, I—OH!
ANTOINELLA— LET ME EXPLAIN!
THERE IS NO NEED, CHASE. I SEE HOW THINGS ARE, AND WHAT I MUST DO!

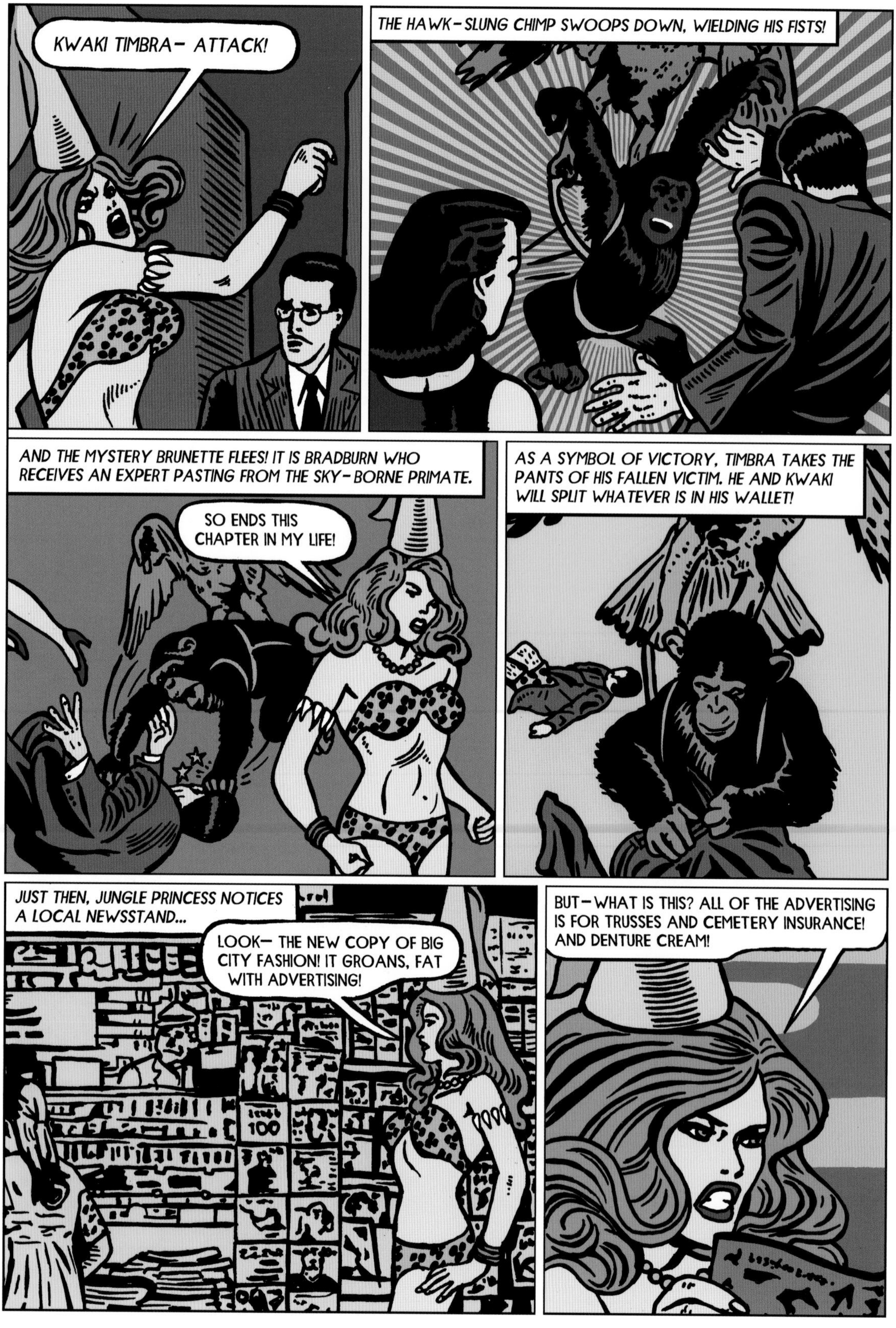
KWAKI TIMBRA— ATTACK!
THE HAWK—SLUNG CHIMP SWOOPS DOWN, WIELDING HIS FISTS!
AND THE MYSTERY BRUNETTE FLEES! IT IS BRADBURN WHO RECEIVES AN EXPERT PASTING FROM THE SKY—BORNE PRIMATE.
SO ENDS THIS CHAPTER IN MY LIFE!
AS A SYMBOL OF VICTORY, TIMBRA TAKES THE PANTS OF HIS FALLEN VICTIM. HE AND KWAKI WILL SPLIT WHATEVER IS IN HIS WALLET!
JUST THEN, JUNGLE PRINCESS NOTICES A LOCAL NEWSSTAND...
LOOK— THE NEW COPY OF BIG CITY FASHION! IT GROANS, FAT WITH ADVERTISING!
BUT—WHAT IS THIS? ALL OF THE ADVERTISING IS FOR TRUSSES AND CEMETERY INSURANCE! AND DENTURE CREAM!

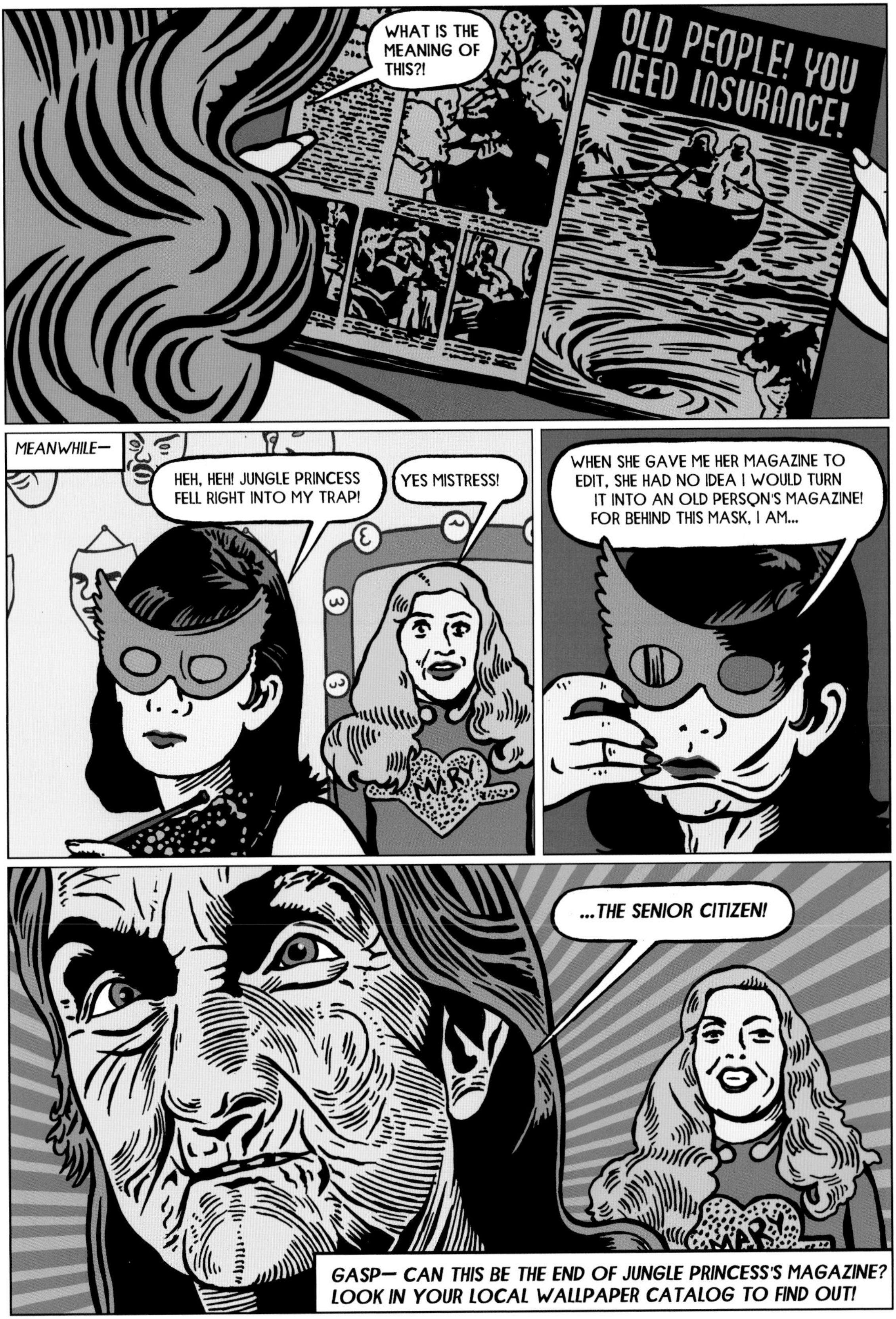
WHAT IS THE MEANING OF THIS?!
OLD PEOPLE! YOU NEED INSURANCE!
MEANWHILE—
HEH, HEH! JUNGLE PRINCESS FELL RIGHT INTO MY TRAP!
YES MISTRESS!
WHEN SHE GAVE ME HER MAGAZINE TO EDIT, SHE HAD NO IDEA I WOULD TURN IT INTO AN OLD PERSON'S MAGAZINE! FOR BEHIND THIS MASK, I AM...
...THE SENIOR CITIZEN!
GASP— CAN THIS BE THE END OF JUNGLE PRINCESS'S MAGAZINE? LOOK IN YOUR LOCAL WALLPAPER CATALOG TO FIND OUT!

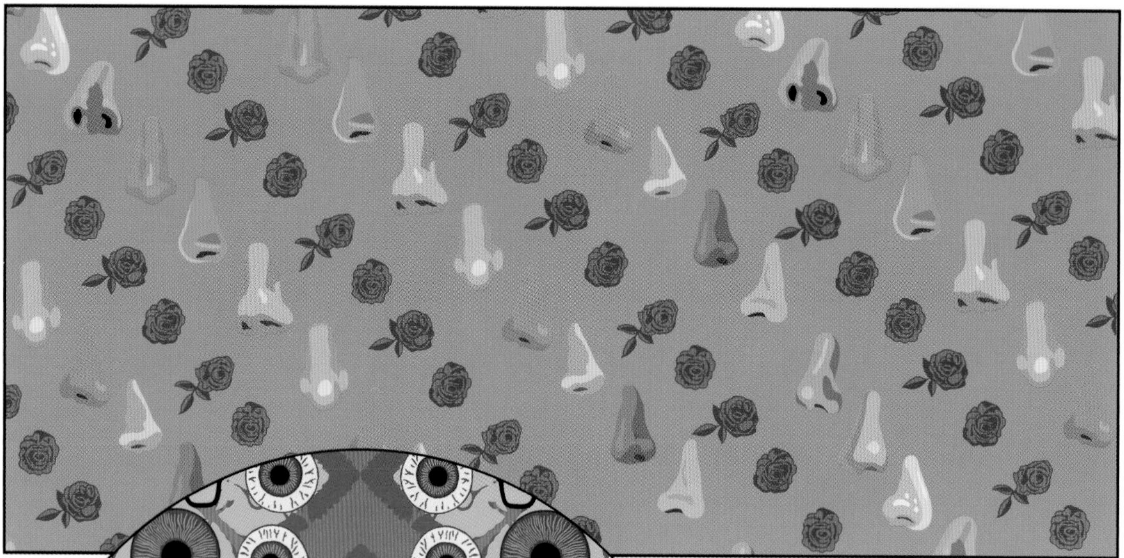

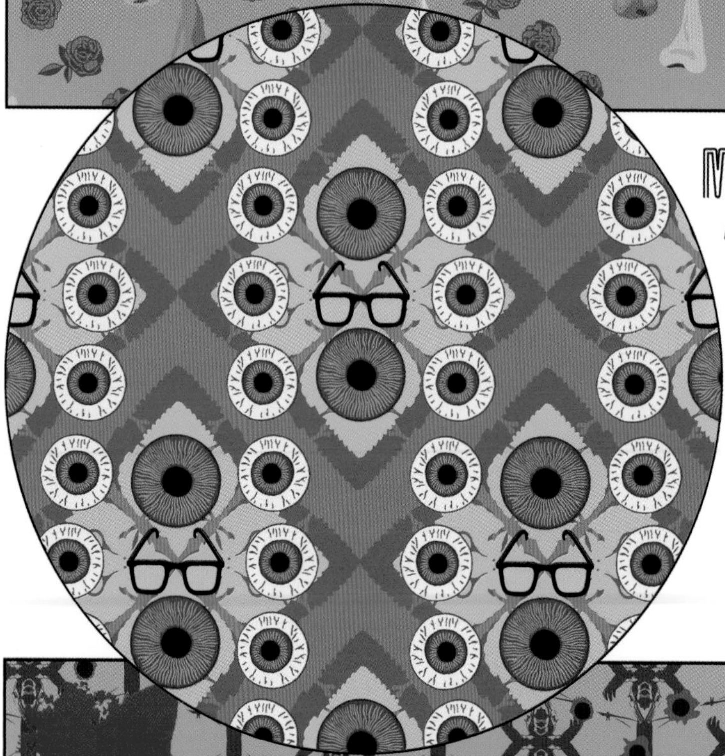

MODERN WALLPAPER

Bold Design Alternatives

57679 Noses And Roses

65488 Here's Looking At You, Kid

78993 A History Of Violence

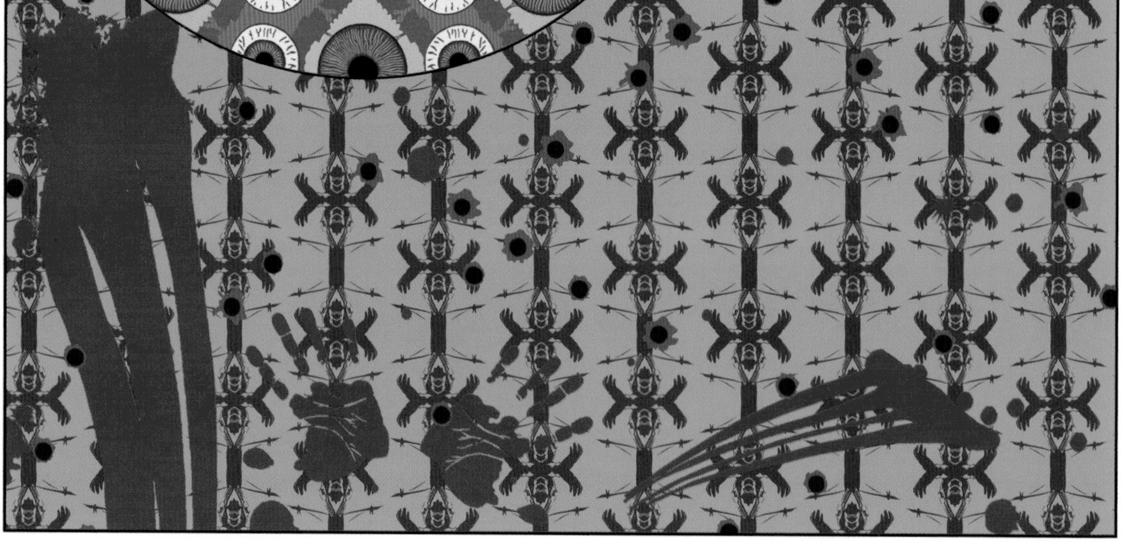

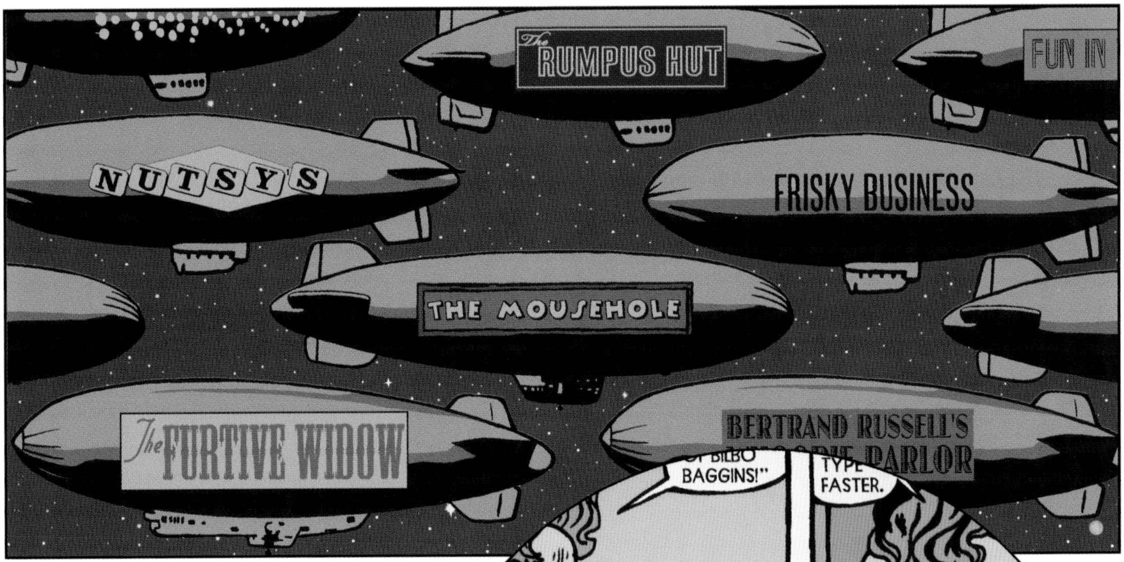
The RUMPUS HUT
FUN IN
NUTSYS
FRISKY BUSINESS
THE MOUSEHOLE
The FURTIVE WIDOW
BERTRAND RUSSELL'S

MODERN WALLPAPER

Popular Favorites

92114 Sex Blimps Ahoy

11345 The Continuing Adventures Of Jungle Princess

14987 Disco Veggies

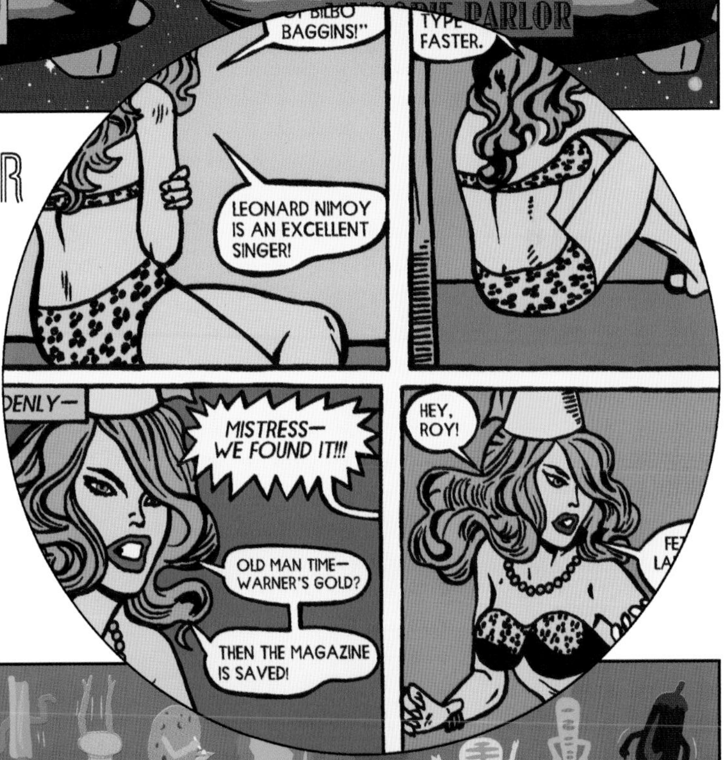
BAGGINS!"
LEONARD NIMOY IS AN EXCELLENT SINGER!
TYPE FASTER.
MISTRESS— WE FOUND IT!!!
OLD MAN TIME— WARNER'S GOLD?
THEN THE MAGAZINE IS SAVED!
HEY, ROY!

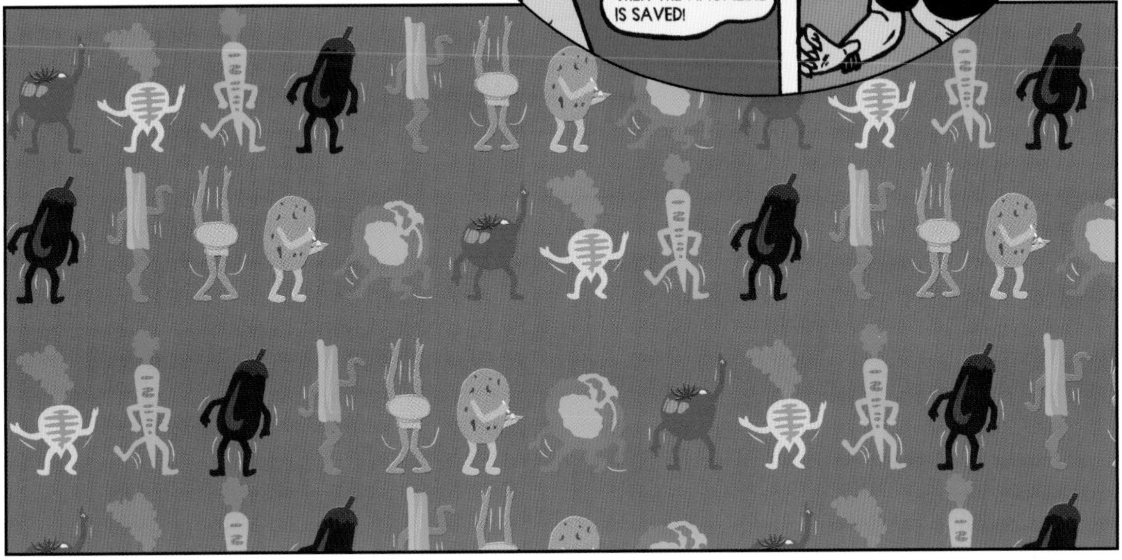

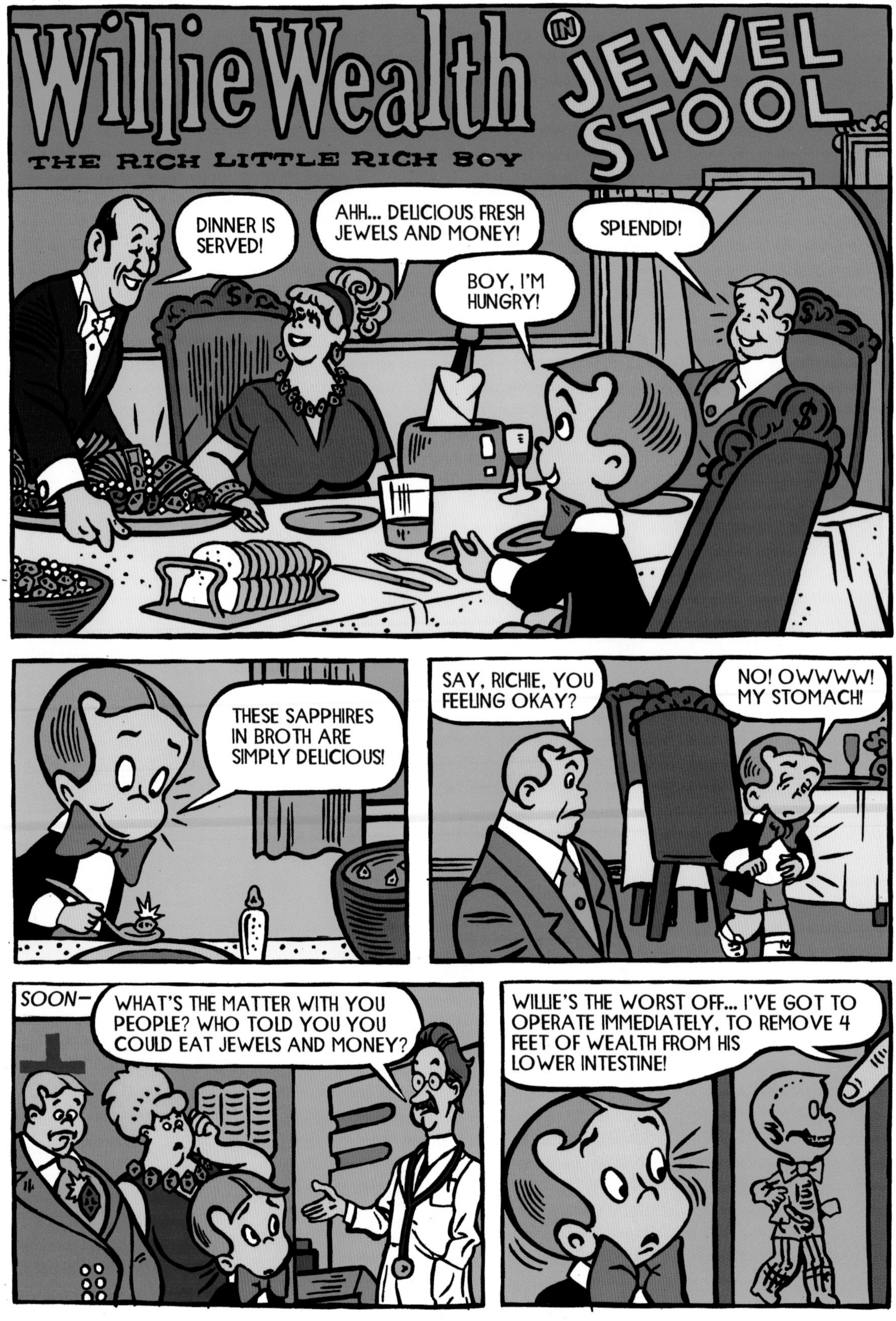
Willie Wealth
THE RICH LITTLE RICH BOY
IN
JEWEL STOOL
DINNER IS SERVED!
AHH... DELICIOUS FRESH JEWELS AND MONEY!
BOY, I'M HUNGRY!
SPLENDID!
THESE SAPPHIRES IN BROTH ARE SIMPLY DELICIOUS!
SAY, RICHIE, YOU FEELING OKAY?
NO! OWWWW! MY STOMACH!
SOON—
WHAT'S THE MATTER WITH YOU PEOPLE? WHO TOLD YOU YOU COULD EAT JEWELS AND MONEY?
WILLIE'S THE WORST OFF... I'VE GOT TO OPERATE IMMEDIATELY, TO REMOVE 4 FEET OF WEALTH FROM HIS LOWER INTESTINE!

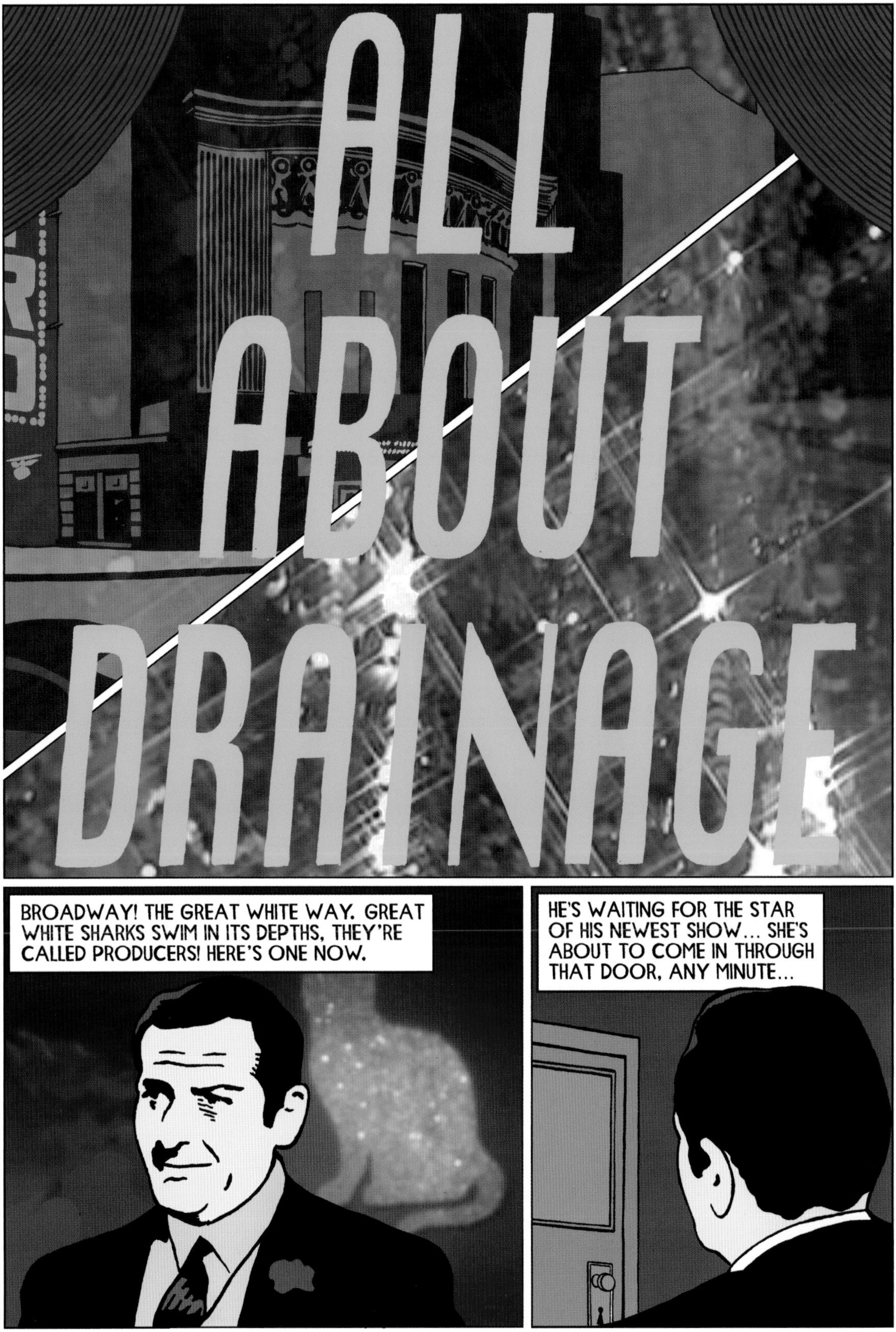
ALL ABOUT DRAINAGE
BROADWAY! THE GREAT WHITE WAY. GREAT WHITE SHARKS SWIM IN ITS DEPTHS, THEY'RE CALLED PRODUCERS! HERE'S ONE NOW.
HE'S WAITING FOR THE STAR OF HIS NEWEST SHOW... SHE'S ABOUT TO COME IN THROUGH THAT DOOR, ANY MINUTE...

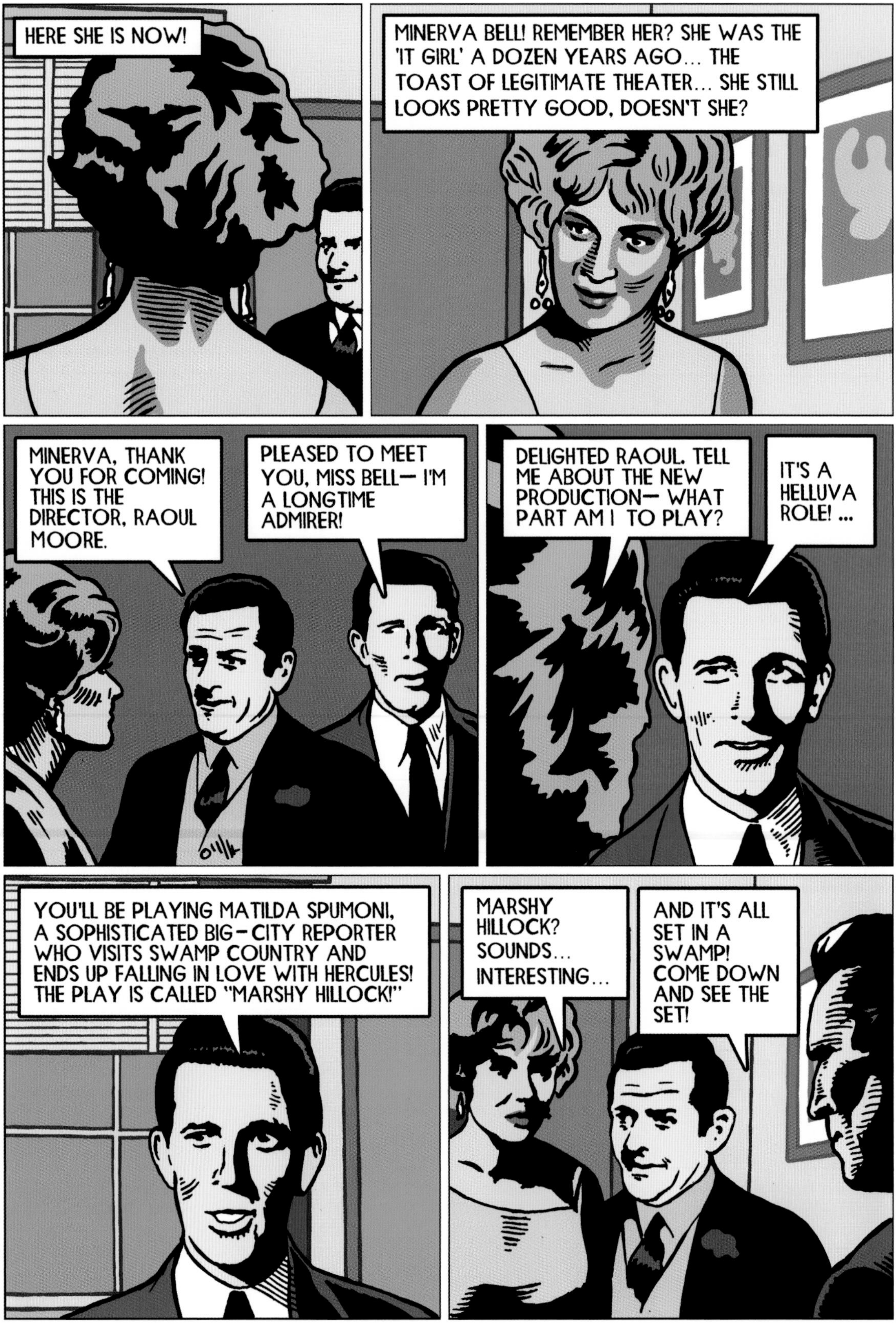
HERE SHE IS NOW!
MINERVA BELL! REMEMBER HER? SHE WAS THE 'IT GIRL' A DOZEN YEARS AGO... THE TOAST OF LEGITIMATE THEATER... SHE STILL LOOKS PRETTY GOOD, DOESN'T SHE?
MINERVA, THANK YOU FOR COMING! THIS IS THE DIRECTOR, RAOUL MOORE.
PLEASED TO MEET YOU, MISS BELL— I'M A LONGTIME ADMIRER!
DELIGHTED RAOUL. TELL ME ABOUT THE NEW PRODUCTION— WHAT PART AM I TO PLAY?
IT'S A HELLUVA ROLE! ...
YOU'LL BE PLAYING MATILDA SPUMONI, A SOPHISTICATED BIG-CITY REPORTER WHO VISITS SWAMP COUNTRY AND ENDS UP FALLING IN LOVE WITH HERCULES! THE PLAY IS CALLED "MARSHY HILLOCK!"
MARSHY HILLOCK? SOUNDS... INTERESTING...
AND IT'S ALL SET IN A SWAMP! COME DOWN AND SEE THE SET!

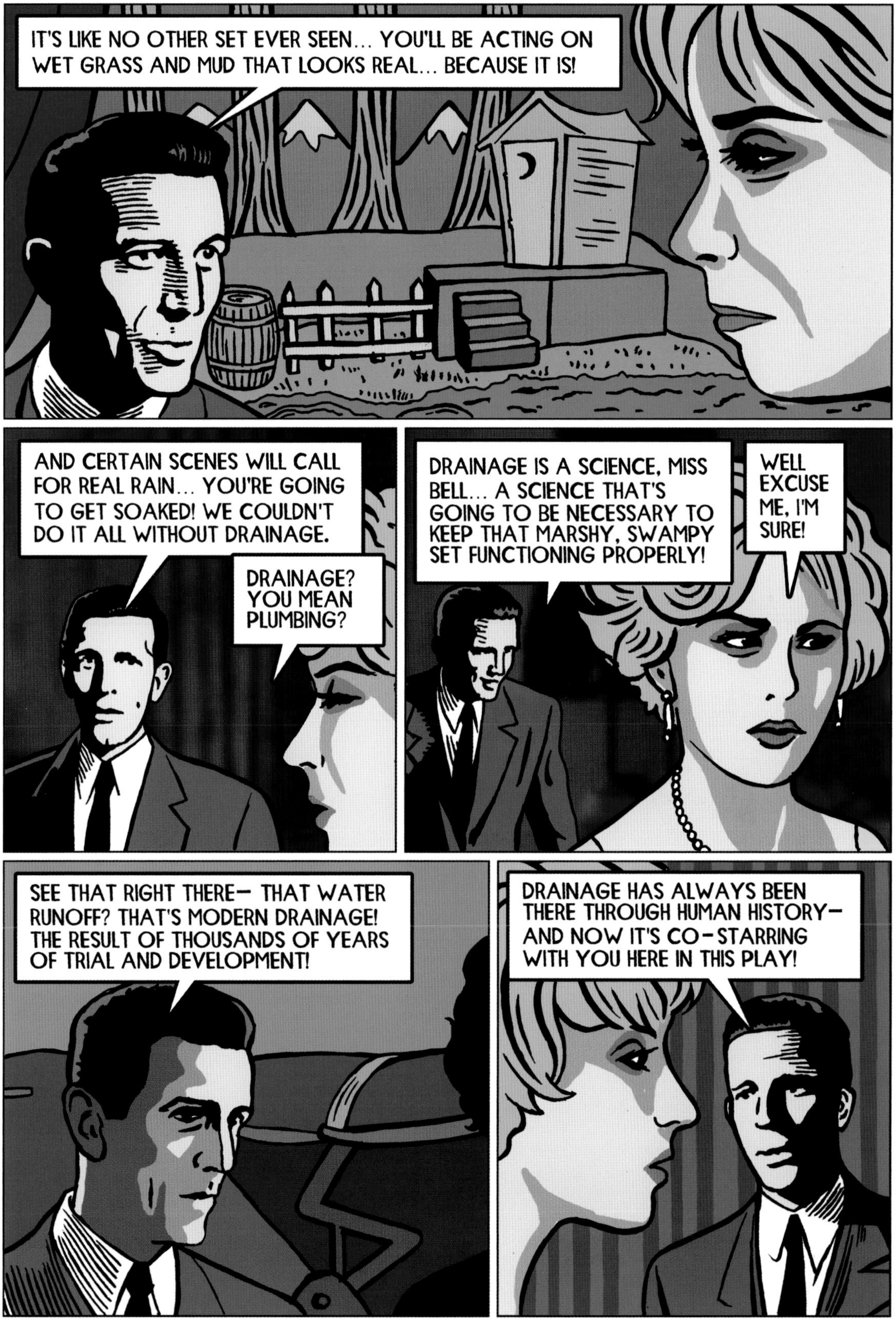
IT'S LIKE NO OTHER SET EVER SEEN... YOU'LL BE ACTING ON WET GRASS AND MUD THAT LOOKS REAL... BECAUSE IT IS!
AND CERTAIN SCENES WILL CALL FOR REAL RAIN... YOU'RE GOING TO GET SOAKED! WE COULDN'T DO IT ALL WITHOUT DRAINAGE.
DRAINAGE? YOU MEAN PLUMBING?
DRAINAGE IS A SCIENCE, MISS BELL... A SCIENCE THAT'S GOING TO BE NECESSARY TO KEEP THAT MARSHY, SWAMPY SET FUNCTIONING PROPERLY!
WELL EXCUSE ME, I'M SURE!
SEE THAT RIGHT THERE— THAT WATER RUNOFF? THAT'S MODERN DRAINAGE! THE RESULT OF THOUSANDS OF YEARS OF TRIAL AND DEVELOPMENT!
DRAINAGE HAS ALWAYS BEEN THERE THROUGH HUMAN HISTORY— AND NOW IT'S CO-STARRING WITH YOU HERE IN THIS PLAY!

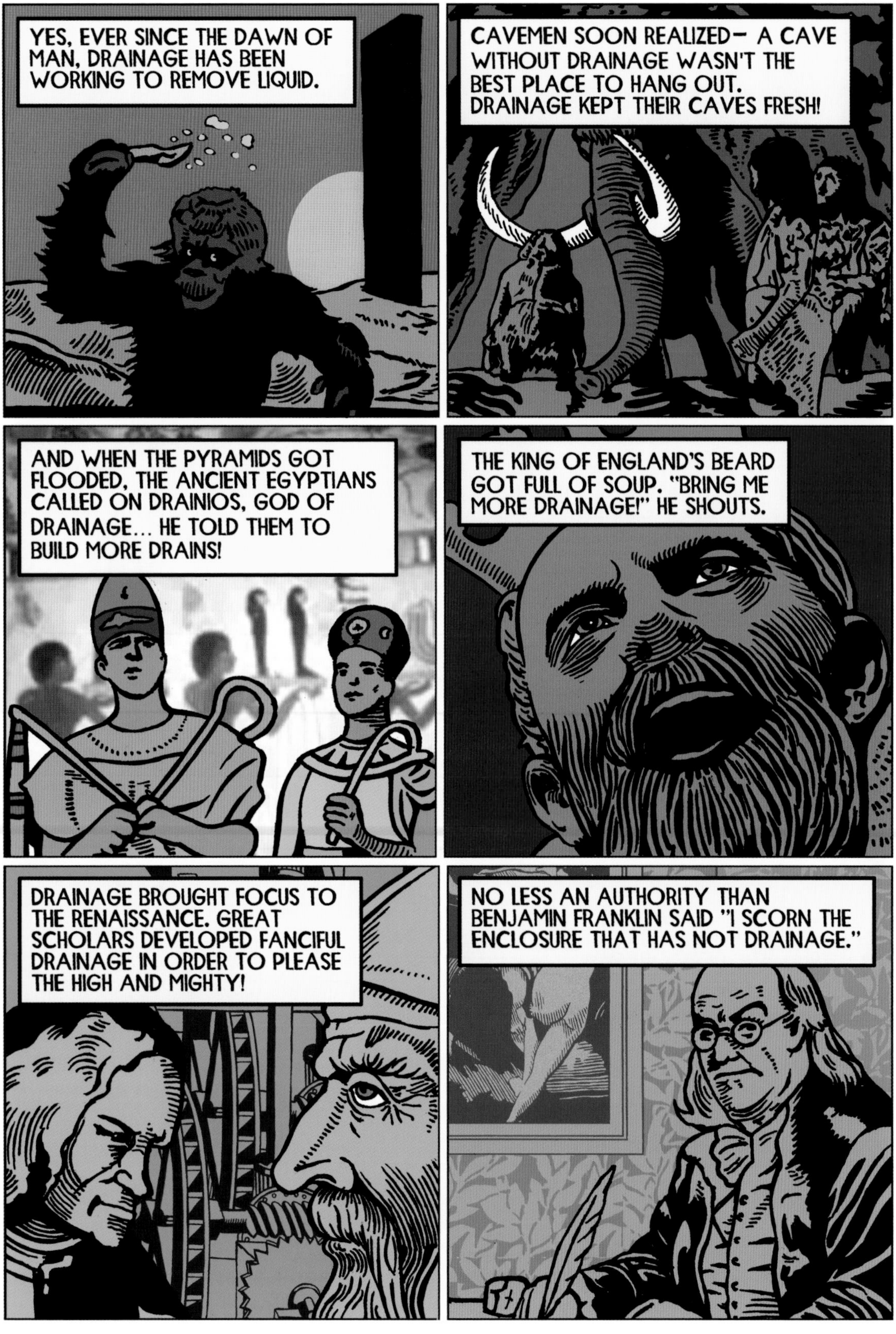
YES, EVER SINCE THE DAWN OF MAN, DRAINAGE HAS BEEN WORKING TO REMOVE LIQUID.
CAVEMEN SOON REALIZED— A CAVE WITHOUT DRAINAGE WASN'T THE BEST PLACE TO HANG OUT. DRAINAGE KEPT THEIR CAVES FRESH!
AND WHEN THE PYRAMIDS GOT FLOODED, THE ANCIENT EGYPTIANS CALLED ON DRAINIOS, GOD OF DRAINAGE… HE TOLD THEM TO BUILD MORE DRAINS!
THE KING OF ENGLAND'S BEARD GOT FULL OF SOUP. "BRING ME MORE DRAINAGE!" HE SHOUTS.
DRAINAGE BROUGHT FOCUS TO THE RENAISSANCE. GREAT SCHOLARS DEVELOPED FANCIFUL DRAINAGE IN ORDER TO PLEASE THE HIGH AND MIGHTY!
NO LESS AN AUTHORITY THAN BENJAMIN FRANKLIN SAID "I SCORN THE ENCLOSURE THAT HAS NOT DRAINAGE."

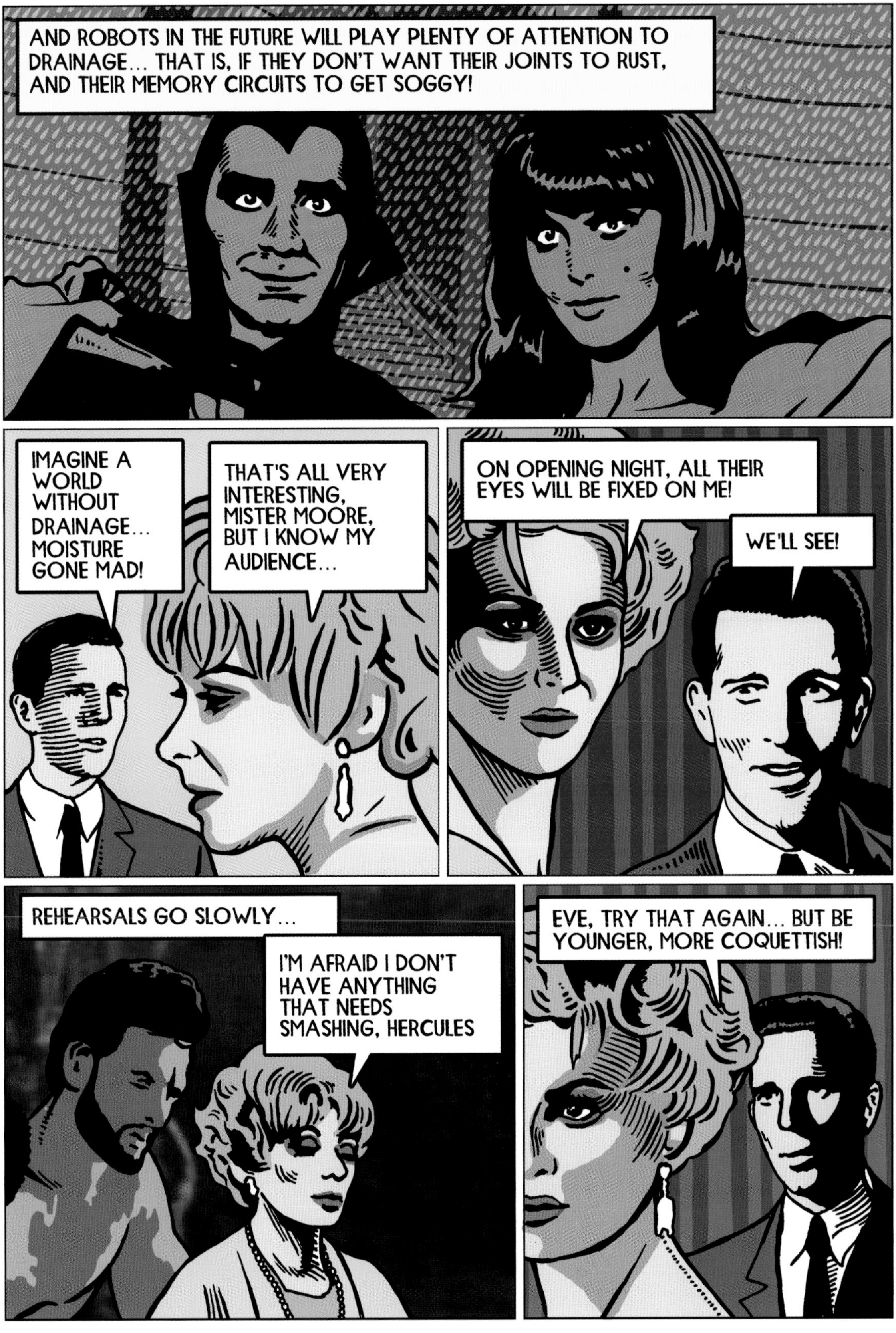
AND ROBOTS IN THE FUTURE WILL PLAY PLENTY OF ATTENTION TO DRAINAGE... THAT IS, IF THEY DON'T WANT THEIR JOINTS TO RUST, AND THEIR MEMORY CIRCUITS TO GET SOGGY!
IMAGINE A WORLD WITHOUT DRAINAGE... MOISTURE GONE MAD!
THAT'S ALL VERY INTERESTING, MISTER MOORE, BUT I KNOW MY AUDIENCE...
ON OPENING NIGHT, ALL THEIR EYES WILL BE FIXED ON ME!
WE'LL SEE!
REHEARSALS GO SLOWLY...
I'M AFRAID I DON'T HAVE ANYTHING THAT NEEDS SMASHING, HERCULES
EVE, TRY THAT AGAIN... BUT BE YOUNGER, MORE COQUETTISH!

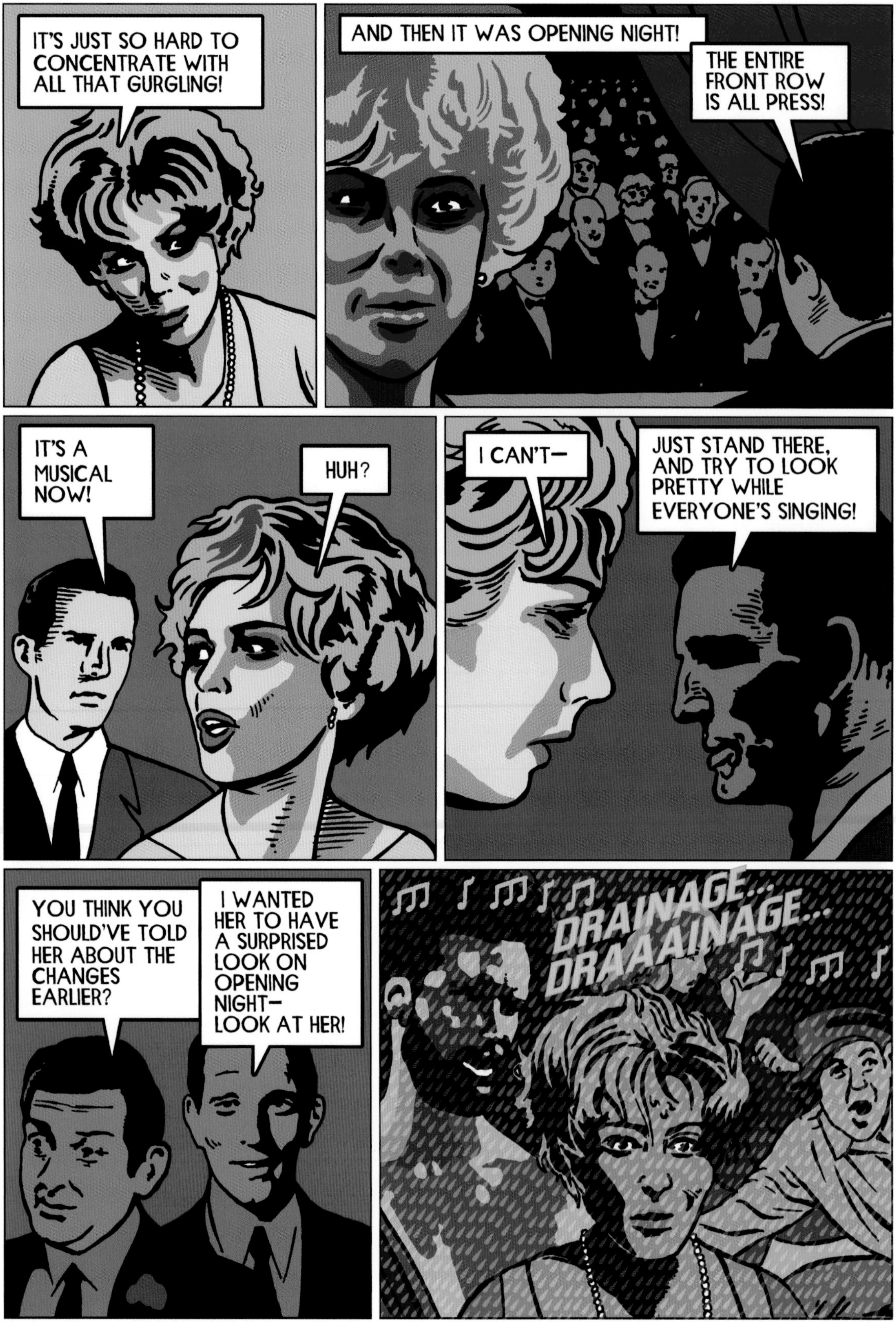
IT'S JUST SO HARD TO CONCENTRATE WITH ALL THAT GURGLING!
AND THEN IT WAS OPENING NIGHT!
THE ENTIRE FRONT ROW IS ALL PRESS!
IT'S A MUSICAL NOW!
HUH?
I CAN'T—
JUST STAND THERE, AND TRY TO LOOK PRETTY WHILE EVERYONE'S SINGING!
YOU THINK YOU SHOULD'VE TOLD HER ABOUT THE CHANGES EARLIER?
I WANTED HER TO HAVE A SURPRISED LOOK ON OPENING NIGHT— LOOK AT HER!
DRAINAGE... DRAAAINAGE...

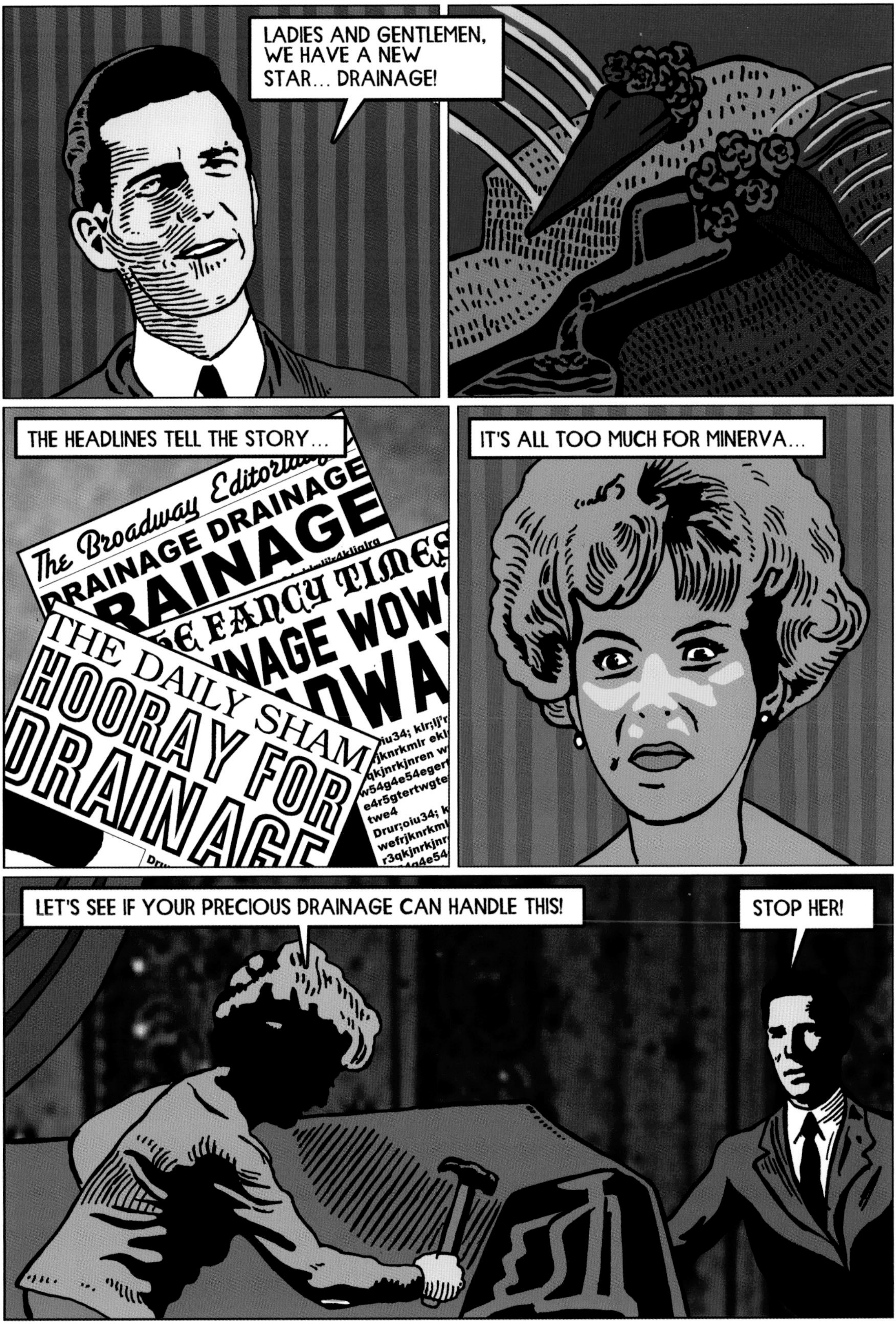
LADIES AND GENTLEMEN, WE HAVE A NEW STAR... DRAINAGE!
THE HEADLINES TELL THE STORY...
The Broadway
DRAINAGE DRAINAGE
THE DAILY SHAM
HOORAY FOR
IT'S ALL TOO MUCH FOR MINERVA...
LET'S SEE IF YOUR PRECIOUS DRAINAGE CAN HANDLE THIS!
STOP HER!

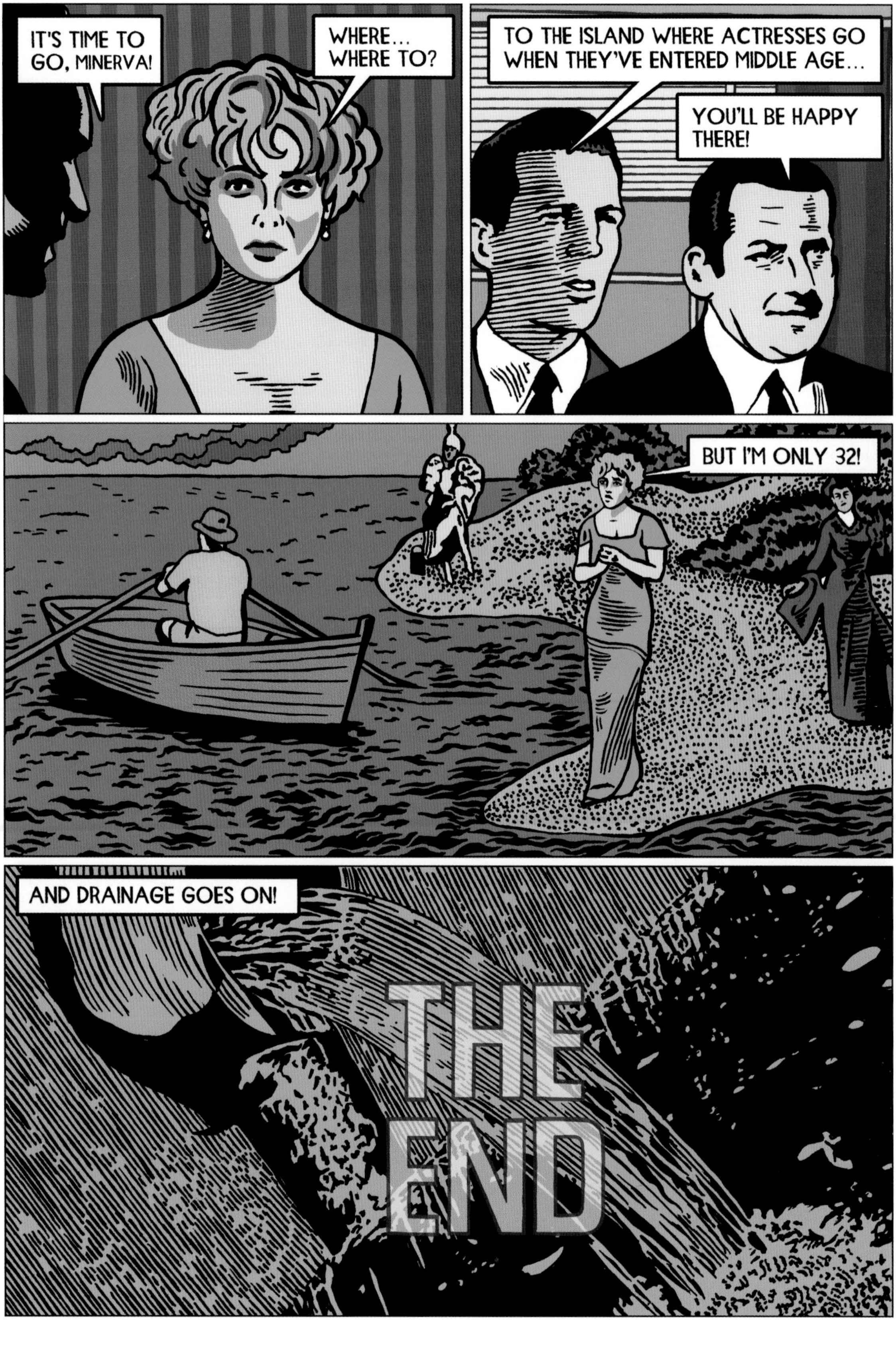
IT'S TIME TO GO, MINERVA!
WHERE... WHERE TO?
TO THE ISLAND WHERE ACTRESSES GO WHEN THEY'VE ENTERED MIDDLE AGE...
YOU'LL BE HAPPY THERE!
BUT I'M ONLY 32!
AND DRAINAGE GOES ON!
THE END

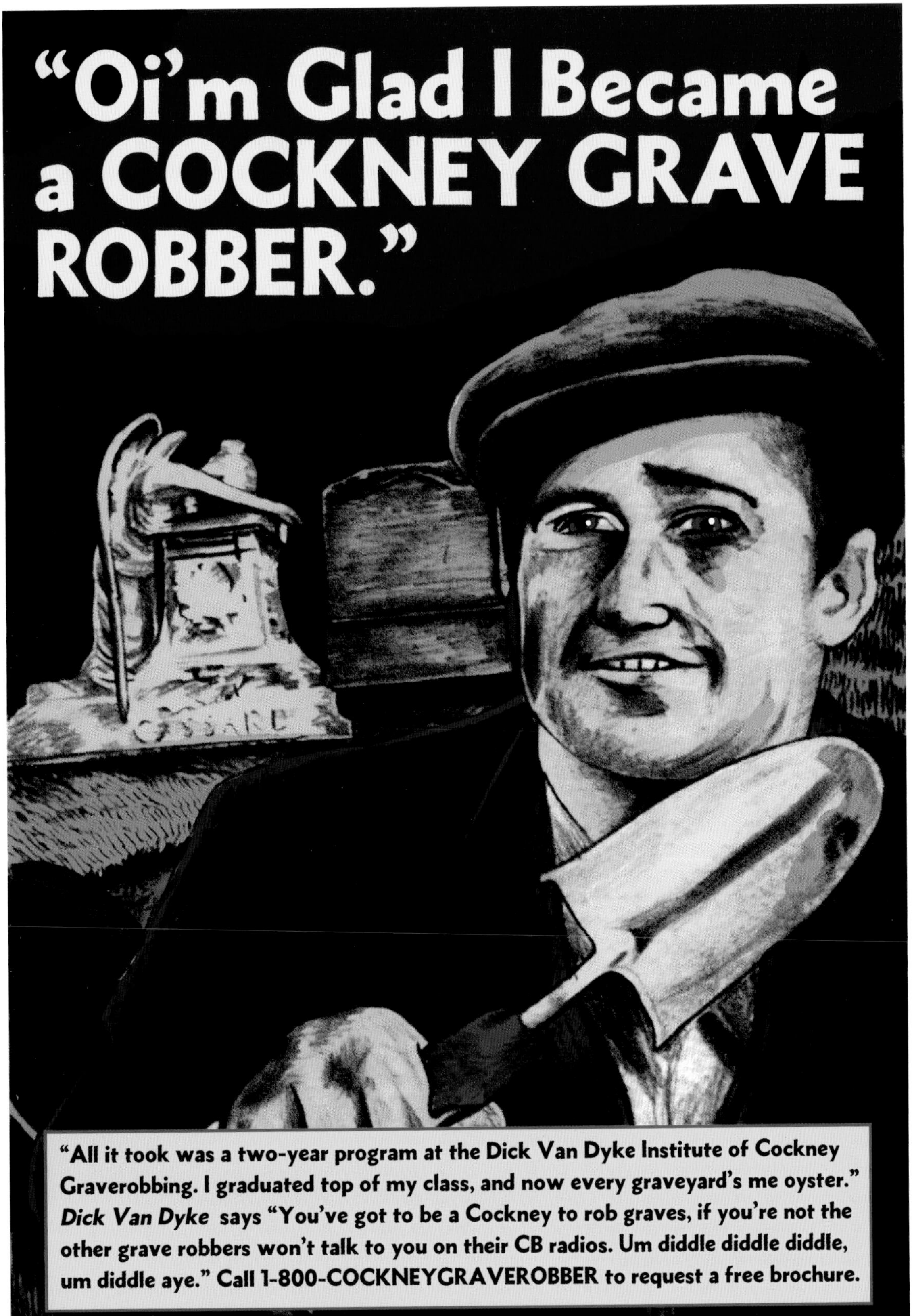
"Oi'm Glad I Became a COCKNEY GRAVE ROBBER."
"All it took was a two-year program at the Dick Van Dyke Institute of Cockney Graverobbing. I graduated top of my class, and now every graveyard's me oyster." *Dick Van Dyke* says "You've got to be a Cockney to rob graves, if you're not the other grave robbers won't talk to you on their CB radios. Um diddle diddle diddle, um diddle aye." Call 1-800-COCKNEYGRAVEROBBER to request a free brochure.

TWAIN & EINSTEIN *in* "CHASIN' THE DREAM"

Albert Einstein opened his mouth. "I–" he began, but Mark Twain cut him off. "Quit complaining, Al! I rented this steamboat so we could take a vacation together, we're both too stressed out from our jobs as lawmaking groundskeepers. You can finish your tests when we get back!"

"I just hope nothing goes giant-size," grouched Einstein, but Twain had a bite on his fishing line. "I just bought this fishing line!" he growled grimly around his cigar. "Whatever is biting it is getting a poke on the noggin." Quickly removing his jacket, he dived into the water and punching noises started coming out of it. Einstein took the opportunity to have a fantasy about an equation.

Twain climbed back out of the river. They were on the mighty Missisissippi and the paddlewheels made so much noise that they both had to shout. "That fish was a new breed of aggressive. I have to operate on the presumption that someone fed it drugs... it wasn't you, was it, Al?"

Einstein was horrified. "Of course not! I have only drugged fish in the pursuit of atomic immortality! But if some sinister figure has done this, then I hope it was not a fellow member of the Princeton Twelve, that shadowy organization that I have never mentioned I had been a part of." And he refused to say anything more.

Later they pulled into a riverside clam shack and had clam shakes. As they prepared to turn the keys in the steamboat's ignition Twain paused. "The driver of the boat ahead of us... he smelled like a criminal!" As his face hardened, the steamboat ahead suddenly shot off. "They saw my facial expression!" yelled Twain, and Einstein lost his balance as their boat lurched into high speed chase mode. "They're heading down the river!" pointed out the writer of such classics as "Tom Joad in Paris" and "The Prancing Pauper." "If we can go faster than them, we can possibly catch up. Paddle, wheels, paddle!"

"It's up to the boat now," observed Einstein, and he went to the lounge chairs to answer some fan mail. The first envelope he selected from the mailbag was decorated with smiley faces and hearts, as well as a carefully printed "LUV U." "This person or persons clearly like us a great deal," mused Einstein before opening it. Inside was a simple card: YOU STINK! "People are illogical creatures," chuckled Einstein as he prepared to write his reply.

"Hey, genius! How about some rockin' chase music?" snapped Twain. "Very well," grumbled Einstein, and, abandoning the mail for the time being, he shuffled over to the guitar locker. Taking out his favorite Stratocaster, he proceeded to play a blistering set of "chase rock" that included "Who's Chasin' Who?" "The Chase is the Game," and a dozen other hits. "Good thing I was wearing my silver lamé pantsuit and platform shoes," he smiled to himself while rocking out. Twain concentrated on the chase, and it continued fine until the river turned a corner and they found the other steamboat, abandoned.

"Look! They're getting into that submarine, over there!" shouted Einstein. "Who cares!" snarled Twain, who could really be quite moody and unpredictable sometimes. "Let it go– we got no jurisdiction!" He put on his sunglasses and

started to play sax as Einstein examined the sub through binoculars. "It has those Deluffenschrafft fan vents that were popular for a while... a wily old physicist could probably swim in through one of those, take over by impersonating the captain, and drive them all to the nearest police station" he mused to himself as he prepared to do just that. Later, as he counted his reward money, Einstein laughed while Twain shook his head. "You wanted us to have a vacation... but I am catching the, how you say, scum who give drugs to fish and getting paid well I am too in the bargain!"

"Sometimes you talk English as good as me, other times you sound like you just got off the boat," pointed out an exasperated Twain.

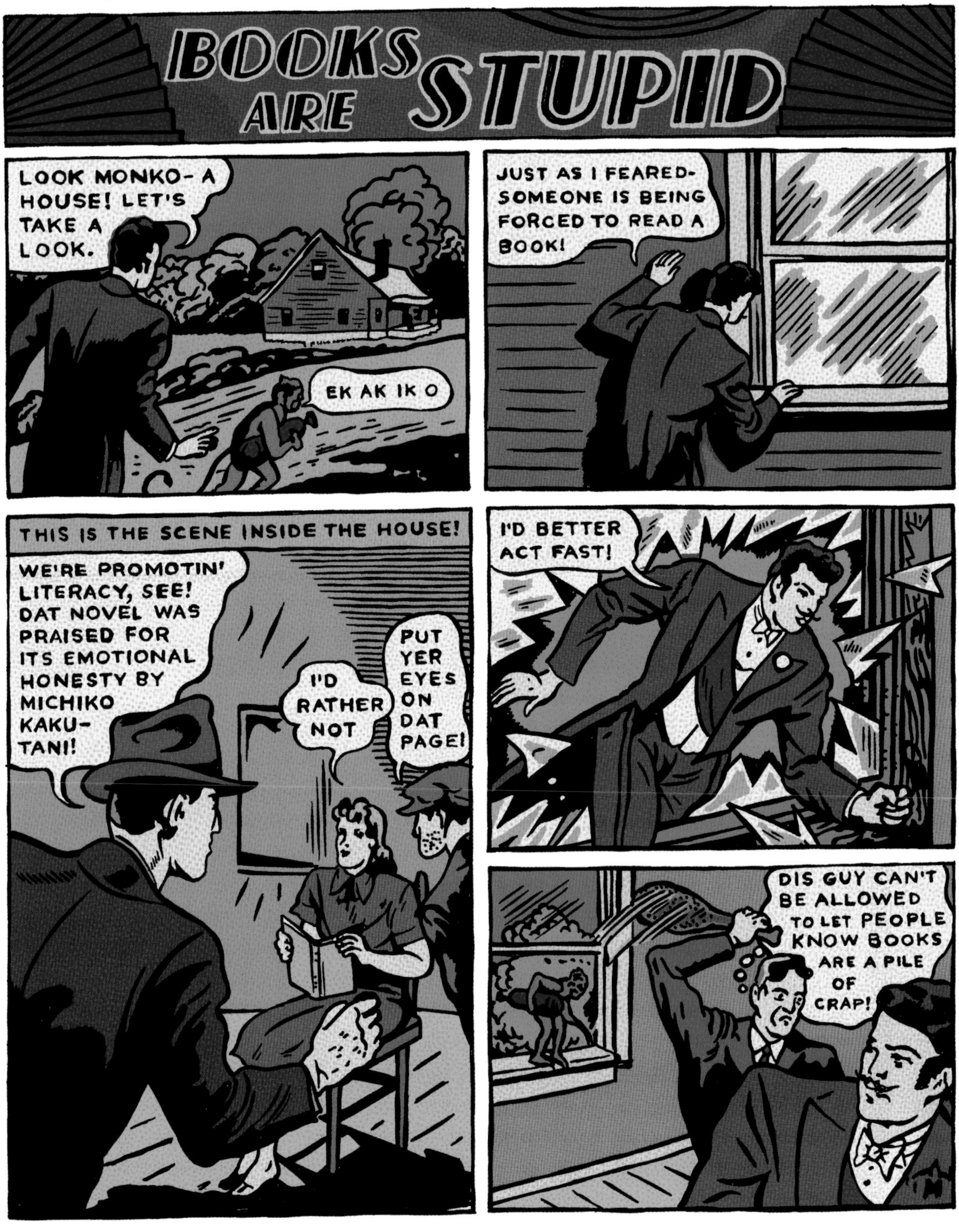
BOOKS ARE STUPID
LOOK MONKO- A HOUSE! LET'S TAKE A LOOK.
EK AK IK O
JUST AS I FEARED- SOMEONE IS BEING FORCED TO READ A BOOK!
THIS IS THE SCENE INSIDE THE HOUSE!
WE'RE PROMOTIN' LITERACY, SEE! DAT NOVEL WAS PRAISED FOR ITS EMOTIONAL HONESTY BY MICHIKO KAKU-TANI!
I'D RATHER NOT
PUT YER EYES ON DAT PAGE!
I'D BETTER ACT FAST!
DIS GUY CAN'T BE ALLOWED TO LET PEOPLE KNOW BOOKS ARE A PILE OF CRAP!

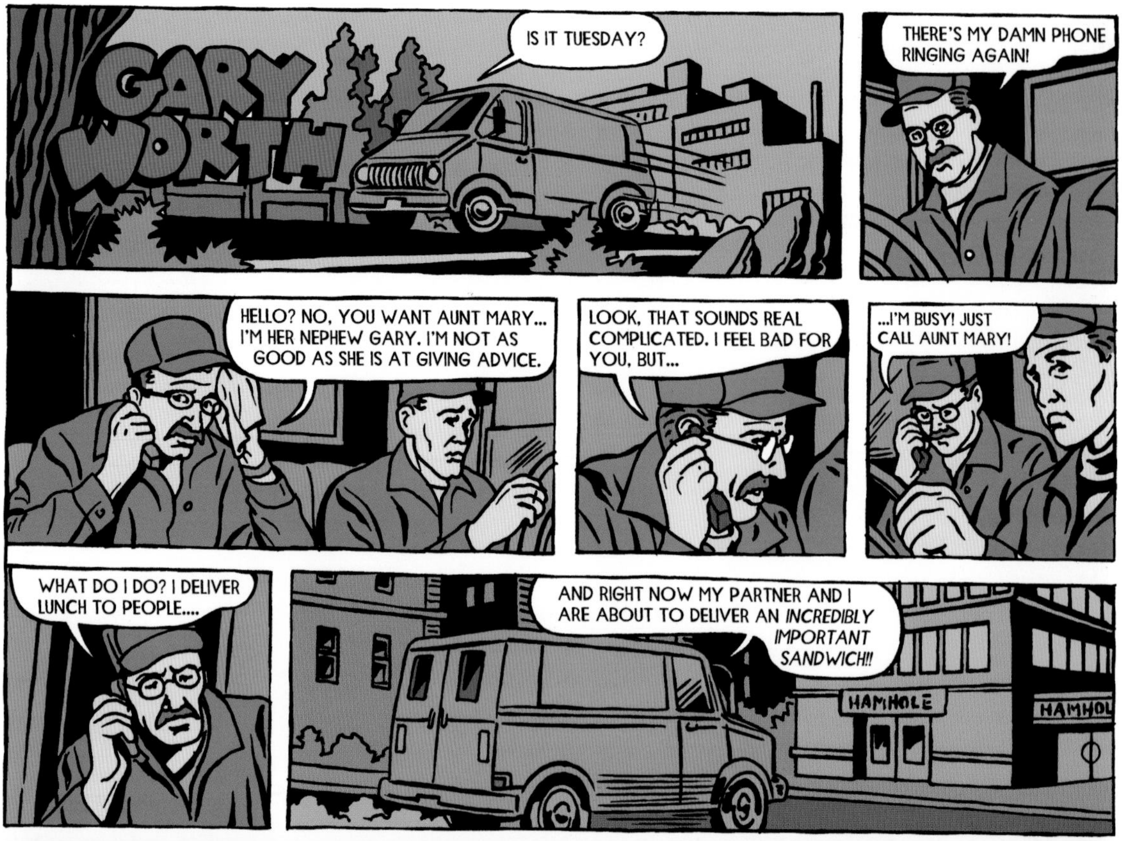
GARY WORTH
IS IT TUESDAY?
THERE'S MY DAMN PHONE RINGING AGAIN!
HELLO? NO, YOU WANT AUNT MARY... I'M HER NEPHEW GARY. I'M NOT AS GOOD AS SHE IS AT GIVING ADVICE.
LOOK, THAT SOUNDS REAL COMPLICATED. I FEEL BAD FOR YOU, BUT...
...I'M BUSY! JUST CALL AUNT MARY!
WHAT DO I DO? I DELIVER LUNCH TO PEOPLE....
AND RIGHT NOW MY PARTNER AND I ARE ABOUT TO DELIVER AN *INCREDIBLY IMPORTANT* SANDWICH!!
HAMHOLE
HAMHOL

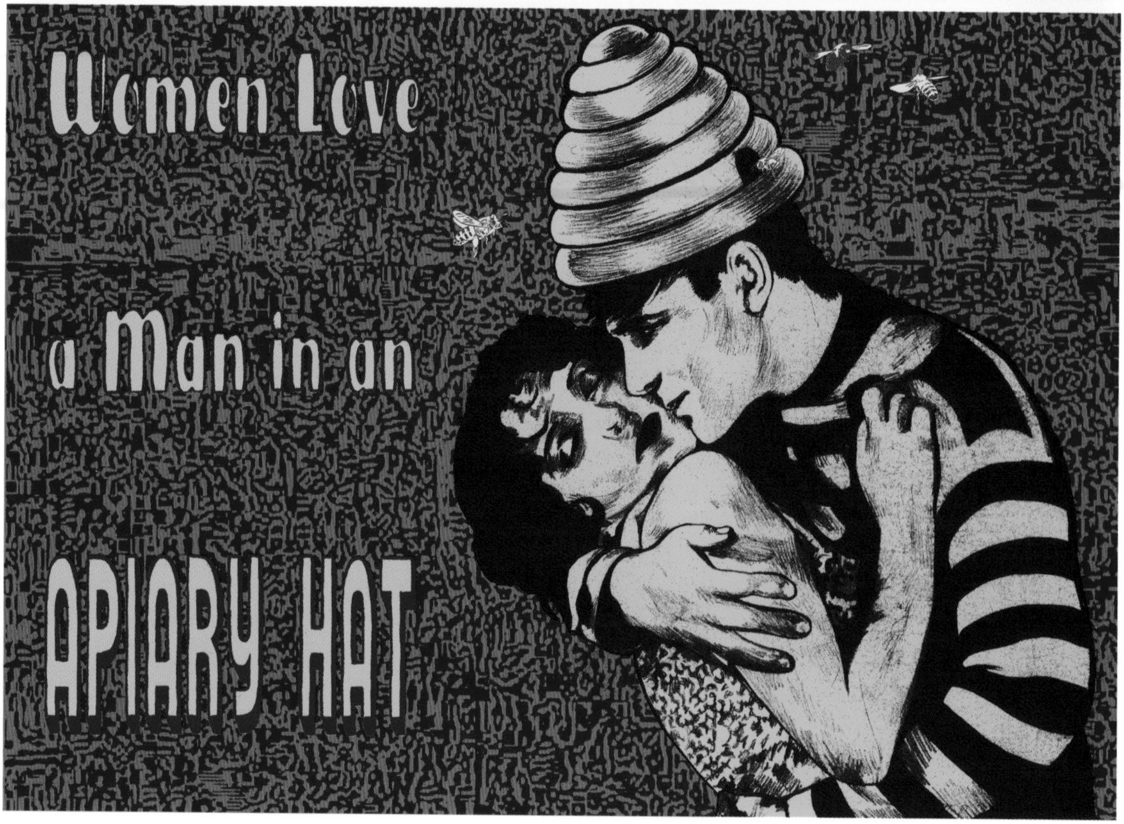
Women Love
a Man in an
APIARY HAT

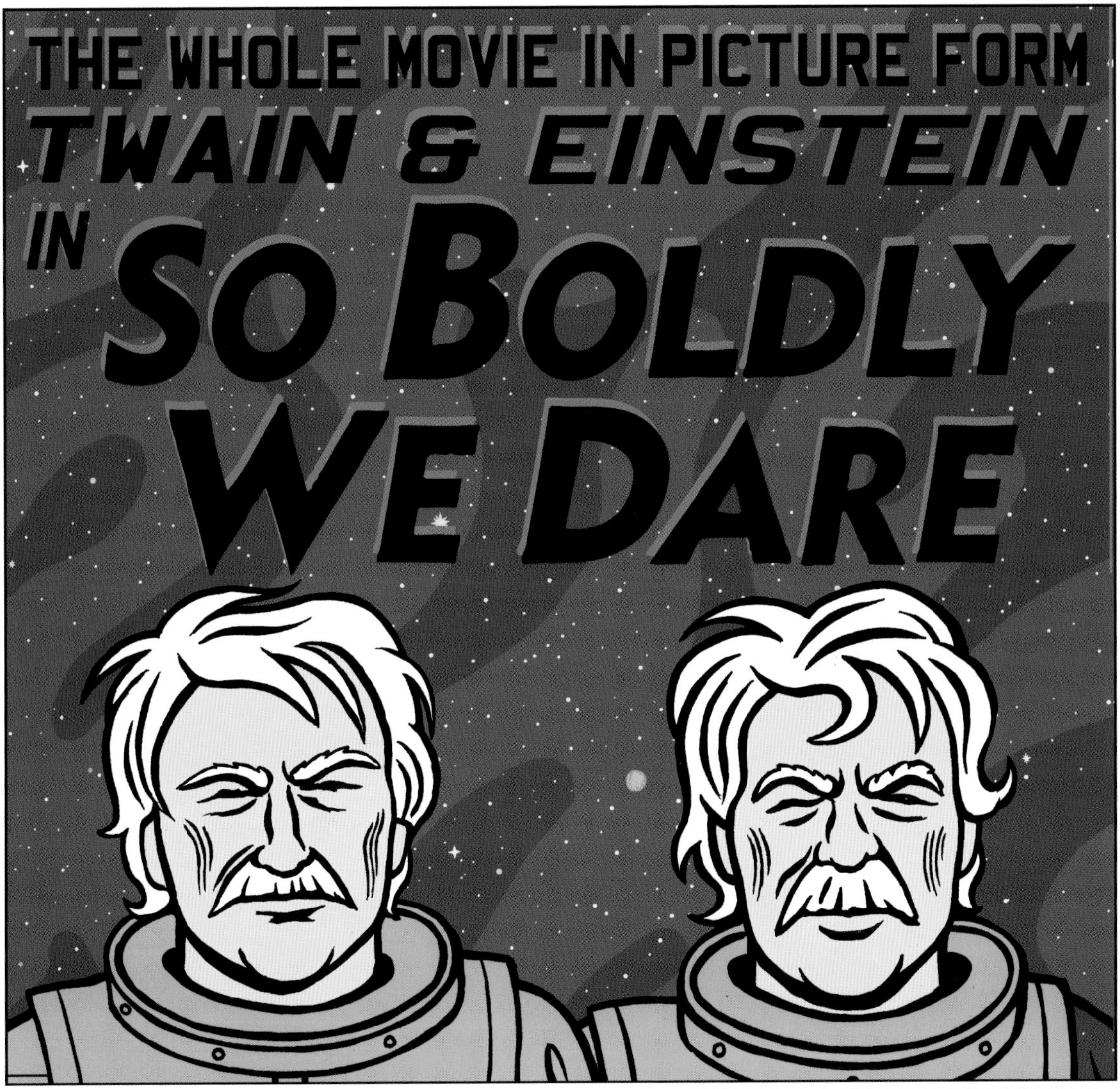
THE WHOLE MOVIE IN PICTURE FORM
TWAIN & EINSTEIN
IN SO BOLDLY WE DARE

1. Our story begins with the two heroes about to blast off in a rocket that will take them into space to destroy an asteroid that is menacing the Earth.

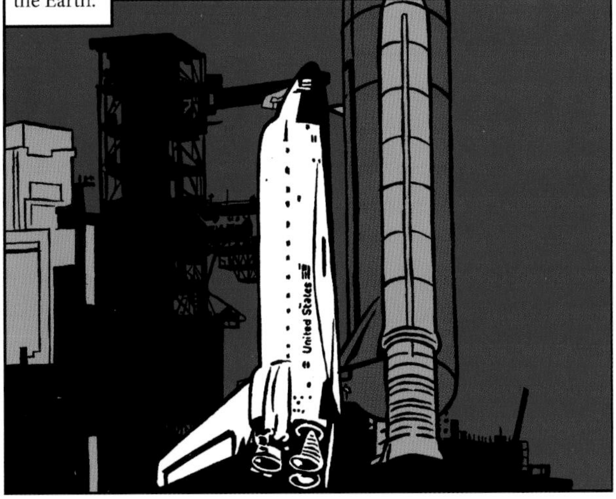
United States

2. "When you get a phone call from the President asking you to get rid of some aggressive debris, you say one thing: how high?" chuckles Twain.

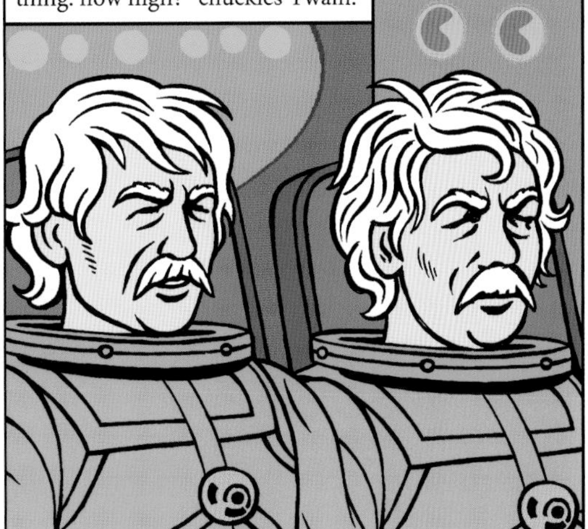

3. It's time for liftoff! "Prepare for blastoff!" shouts NASA. "10-9-8-7-6-5-4-3-2-1-0!"

4. And in a fireball of swirling gas, the rocket lifts!

5. The faces of the duo are mushed and smushed around by the terrific pressure of the G-forces.

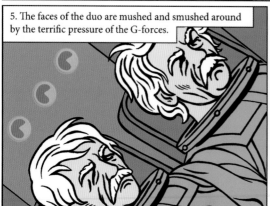

6. The ship hurtles through the atmosphere as exciting music plays.

7. Mercifully the two lose consciousness.

8. They awake to a meteorite storm. "Hard aft! Forward!" shouts Twain.

9. Einstein and Twain blast away at the meteorites with their laser cannons.

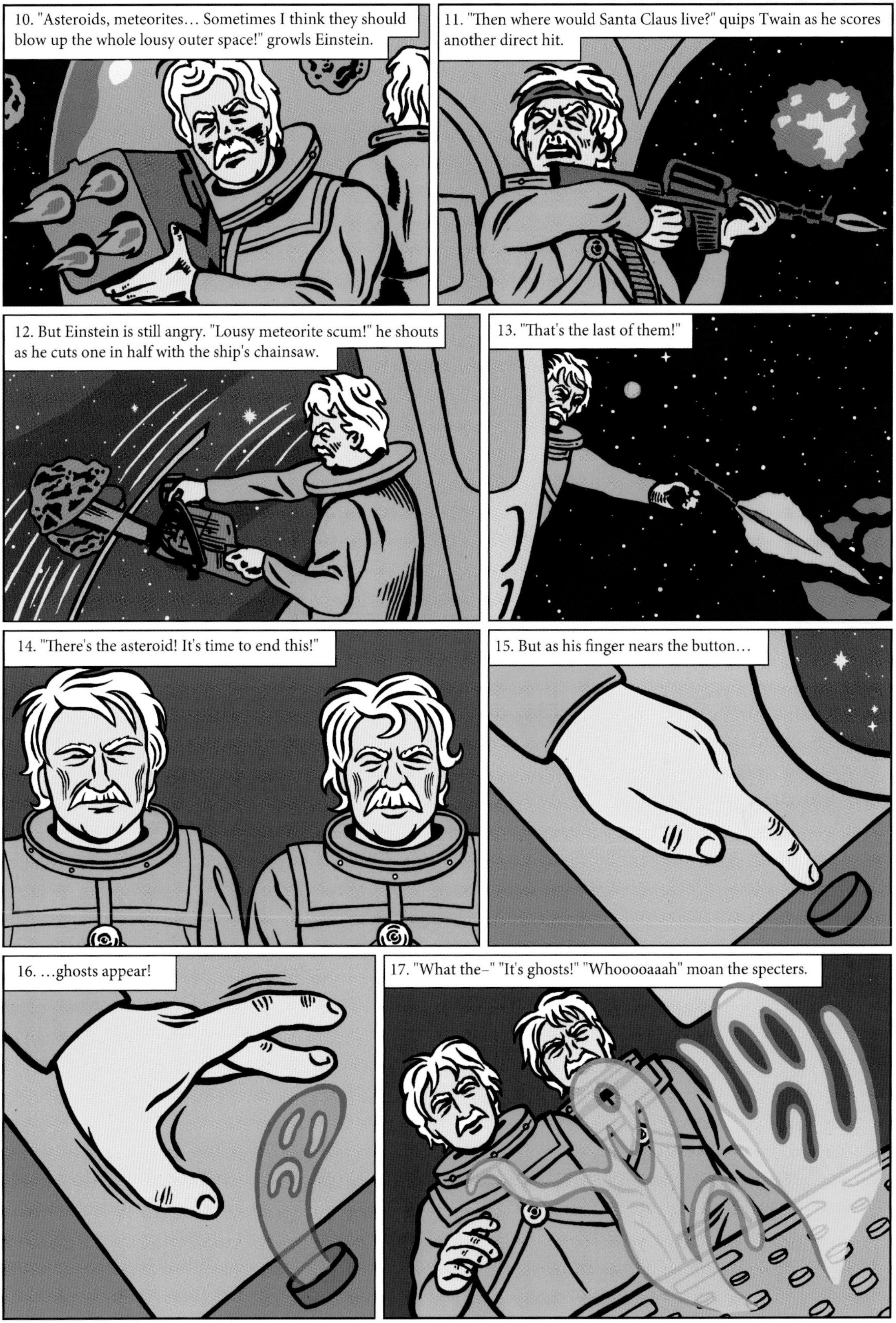
10. "Asteroids, meteorites… Sometimes I think they should blow up the whole lousy outer space!" growls Einstein.
11. "Then where would Santa Claus live?" quips Twain as he scores another direct hit.
12. But Einstein is still angry. "Lousy meteorite scum!" he shouts as he cuts one in half with the ship's chainsaw.
13. "That's the last of them!"
14. "There's the asteroid! It's time to end this!"
15. But as his finger nears the button…
16. …ghosts appear!
17. "What the–" "It's ghosts!" "Whoooooaaah" moan the specters.

18. "Hey, NASA, you gave us a haunted spaceship!" Twain barks into the communicator. "Over!"

19. "The top part is all new, but the basement is from the 19th century," admits the NASA man. "Over."

20. The literary/scientific duo prepare their weapons. "Time to broast some ghosts!" quips Twain. "Good thing I brought this harpoon," says Einstein.

BASEMENT

21. The pair descend to the basement. "Looks like nobody's cleaned here in years."

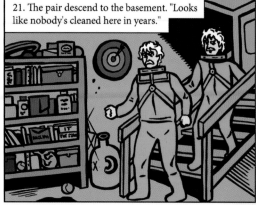

22. "Just a lotta junk," growls the scribe. "No—look!" shouts his partner.

23. "What about that skeleton chained to the wall?"

24. Writing on the wall in blood!

J. WALTER NASA KILLED ME

25. The two return grimly upstairs.

26. "Hey, are you J. Walter Nasa?"

27. "Yes, I…" "Take him away, boys!"

28. The ghosts leave, their thirst for justice satisfied. "Don't forget to write!" quips Einstein.

29. "Now, back to our original mission!"

30. "She's a beauty, but she's got to go!" "Time to take out the trash!"

31. Twain parks the rocket next to the asteroid. "Might as well get out and take a look around before we blow it up."

32. "Boy, what a dump."

33. Suddenly a floating alien head appears. "Attention, foolish humans!"

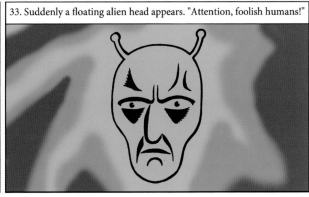

34. "Who's he calling foolish!" "Wait, let's hear what he has to say."

35. "Umm… ga ga… wa baah…"

36. "He sounds like a baby!" "That's because…"

37. "…he is a baby!"

38. "Aw, what a little cutie!" "Ickle tickle!"

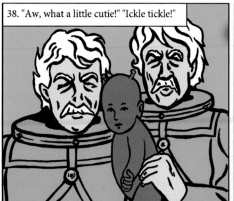

39. "Yes, Earthlings! Please take me home with you and change my zingnads!" "We call them diapers!" chuckles Twain.

40. Einstein sets the bomb timer. "Let's fly toward the viewer and yell 'Yahooo!' he suggests.

41. "Yaaahooo!"

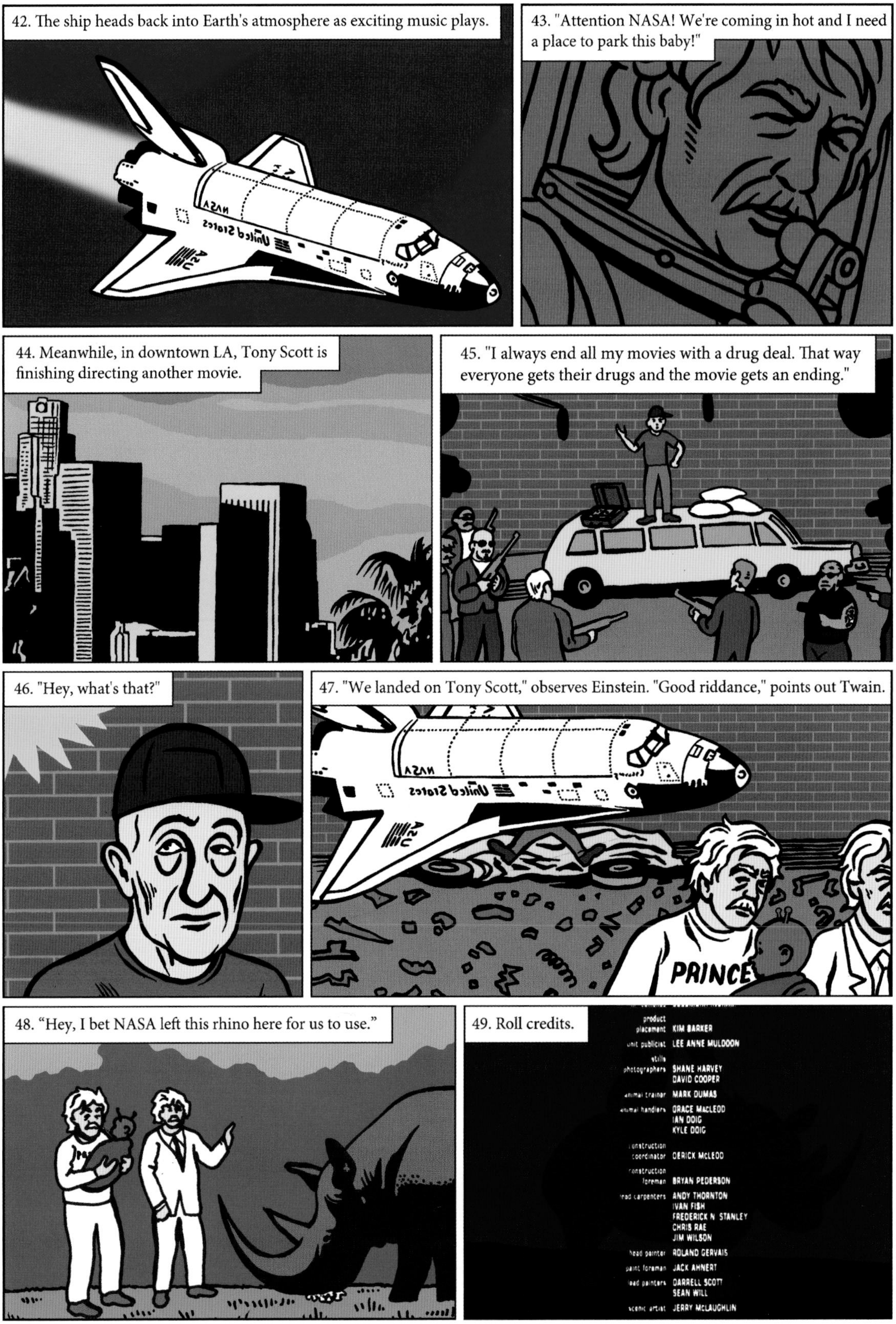
42. The ship heads back into Earth's atmosphere as exciting music plays.
NASA
United States
USA
43. "Attention NASA! We're coming in hot and I need a place to park this baby!"
44. Meanwhile, in downtown LA, Tony Scott is finishing directing another movie.
45. "I always end all my movies with a drug deal. That way everyone gets their drugs and the movie gets an ending."
46. "Hey, what's that?"
47. "We landed on Tony Scott," observes Einstein. "Good riddance," points out Twain.
NASA
United States
USA
PRINCE
48. "Hey, I bet NASA left this rhino here for us to use."
49. Roll credits.
product placement KIM BARKER
unit publicist LEE ANNE MULDOON
stills photographers SHANE HARVEY
DAVID COOPER
animal trainer MARK DUMAS
animal handlers GRACE MacLEOD
IAN DOIG
KYLE DOIG
construction coordinator DERICK McLEOD
construction foreman BRYAN PEDERSON
lead carpenters ANDY THORNTON
IVAN FISH
FREDERICK N. STANLEY
CHRIS RAE
JIM WILSON
head painter ROLAND GERVAIS
paint foreman JACK AHNERT
lead painters DARRELL SCOTT
SEAN WILL
scenic artist JERRY McLAUGHLIN

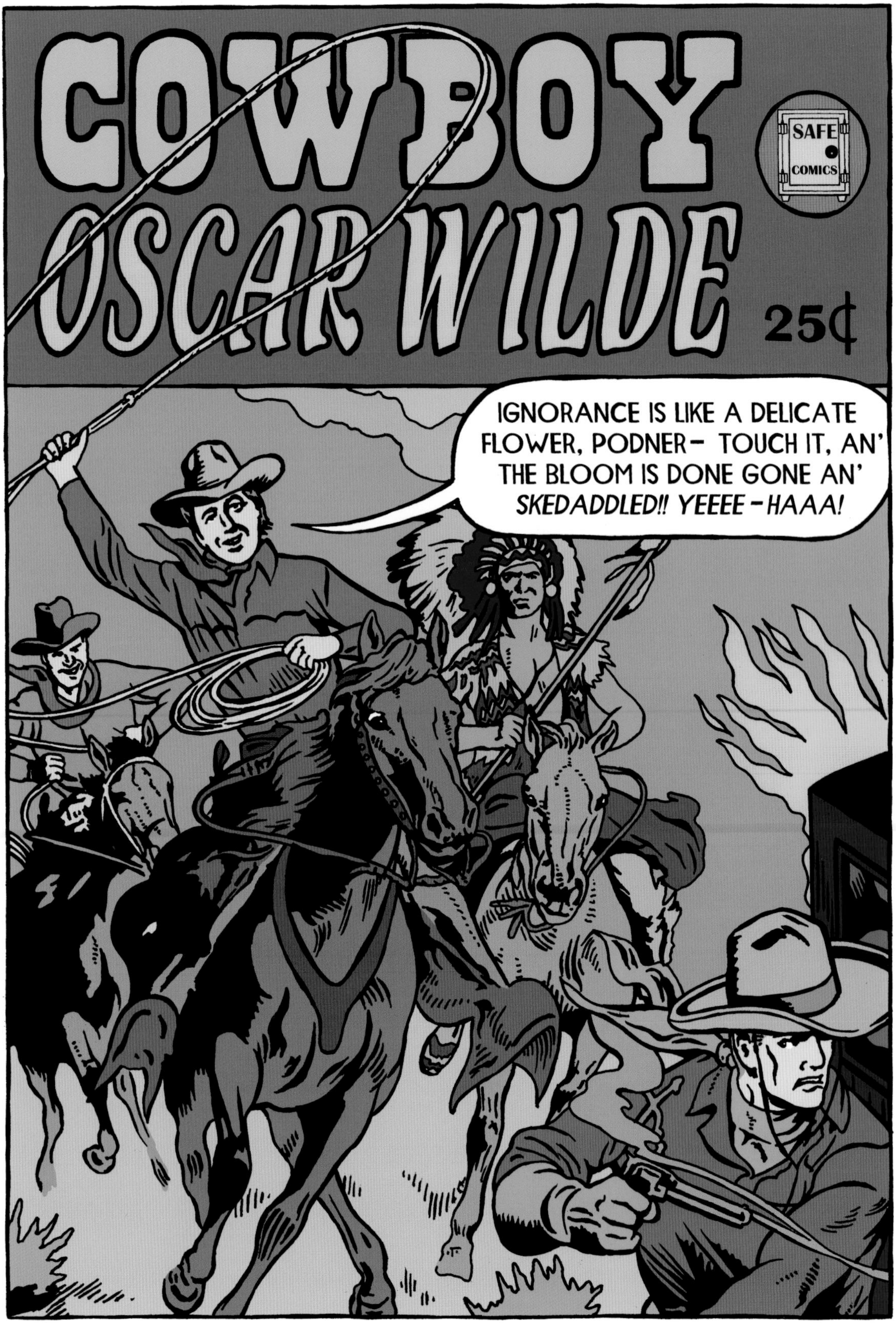
COWBOY OSCAR WILDE
SAFE COMICS
25¢
IGNORANCE IS LIKE A DELICATE FLOWER, PODNER— TOUCH IT, AN' THE BLOOM IS DONE GONE AN' SKEDADDLED!! YEEEE—HAAA!

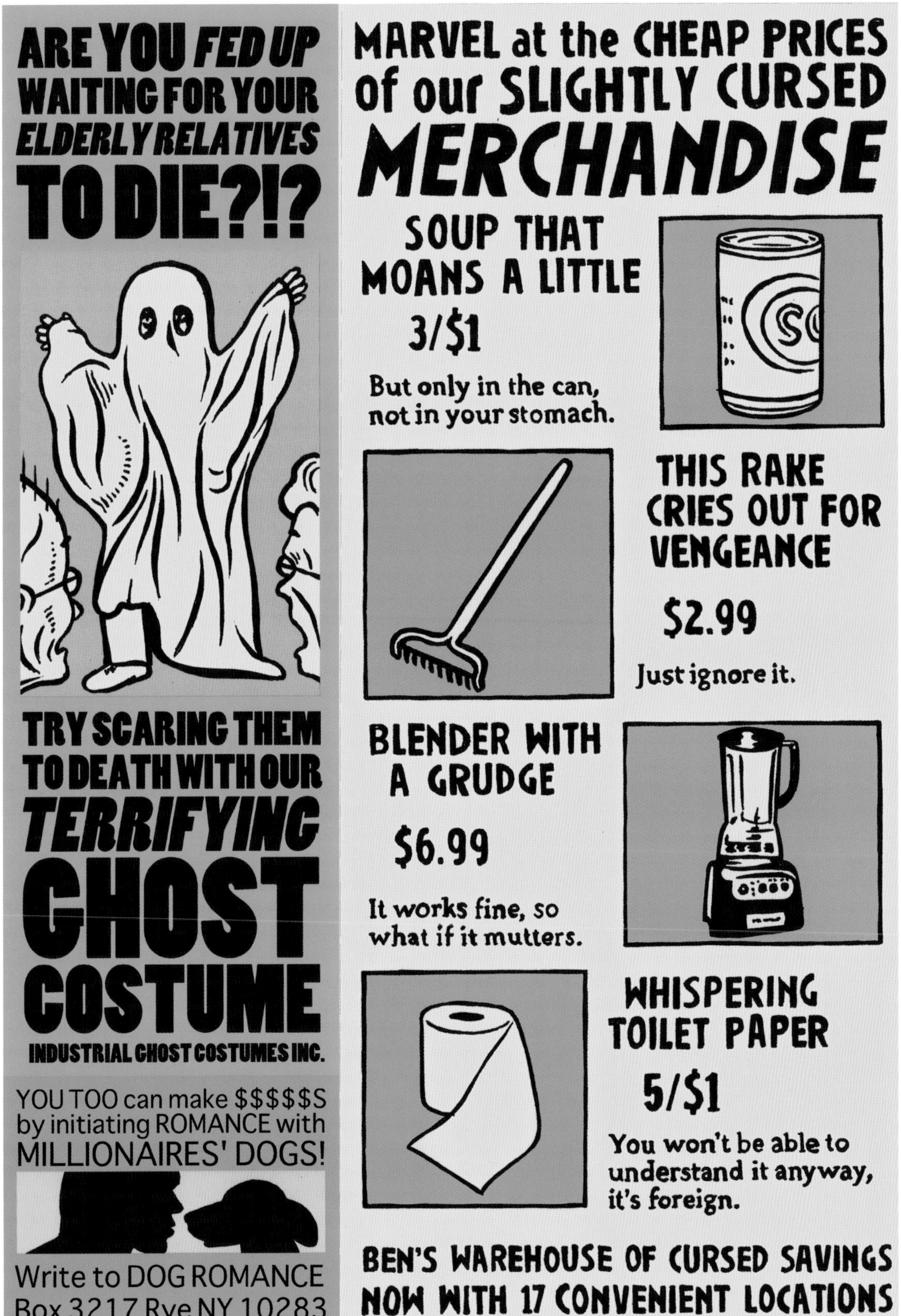
ARE YOU FED UP WAITING FOR YOUR ELDERLY RELATIVES TO DIE?!?
TRY SCARING THEM TO DEATH WITH OUR TERRIFYING GHOST COSTUME
INDUSTRIAL GHOST COSTUMES INC.
YOU TOO can make $$$$$S by initiating ROMANCE with MILLIONAIRES' DOGS!
Write to DOG ROMANCE Box 3217 Rye NY 10283
MARVEL at the CHEAP PRICES of our SLIGHTLY CURSED MERCHANDISE
SOUP THAT MOANS A LITTLE
3/$1
But only in the can, not in your stomach.
THIS RAKE CRIES OUT FOR VENGEANCE
$2.99
Just ignore it.
BLENDER WITH A GRUDGE
$6.99
It works fine, so what if it mutters.
WHISPERING TOILET PAPER
5/$1
You won't be able to understand it anyway, it's foreign.
BEN'S WAREHOUSE OF CURSED SAVINGS NOW WITH 17 CONVENIENT LOCATIONS

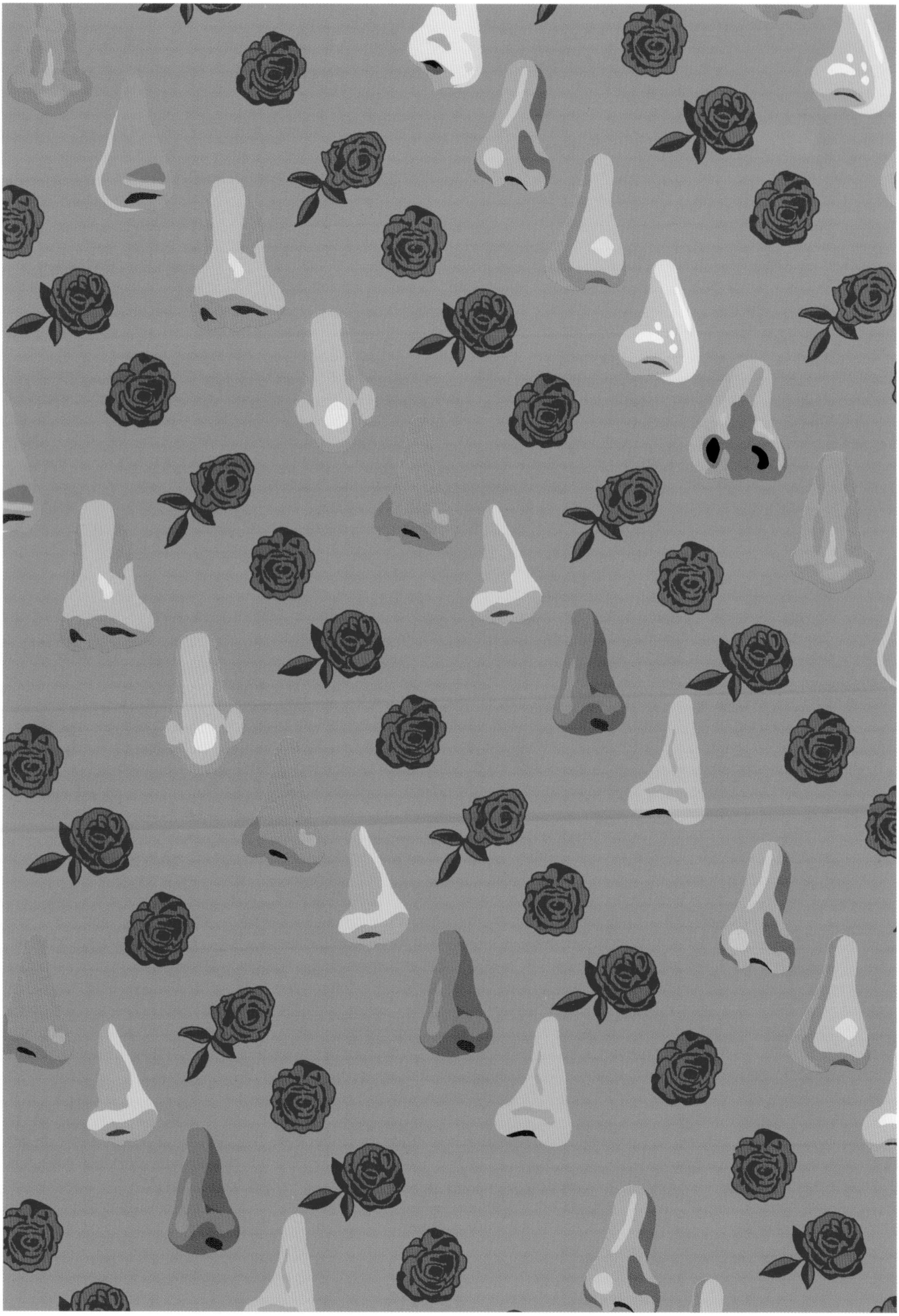

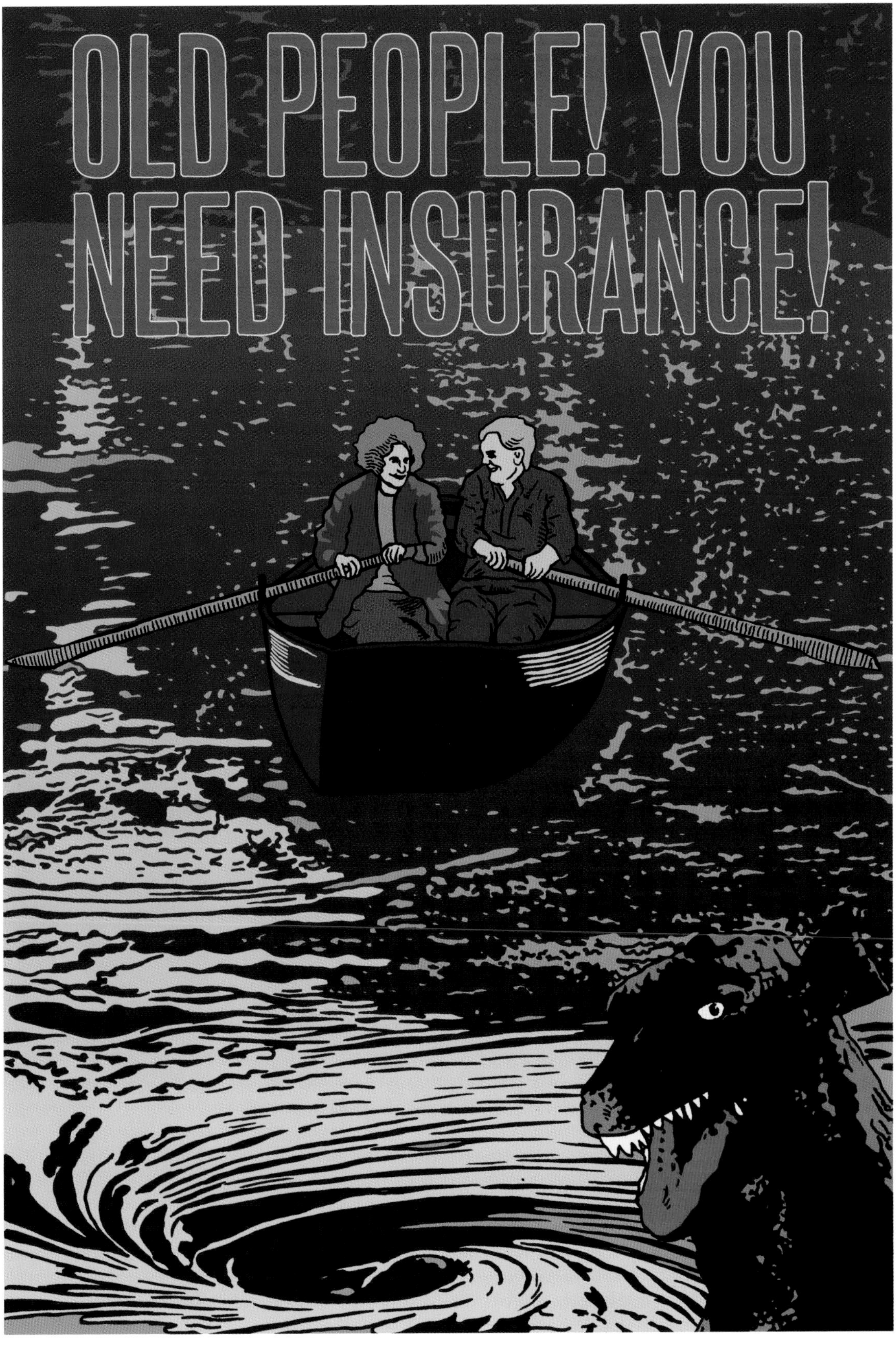
OLD PEOPLE! YOU NEED INSURANCE!

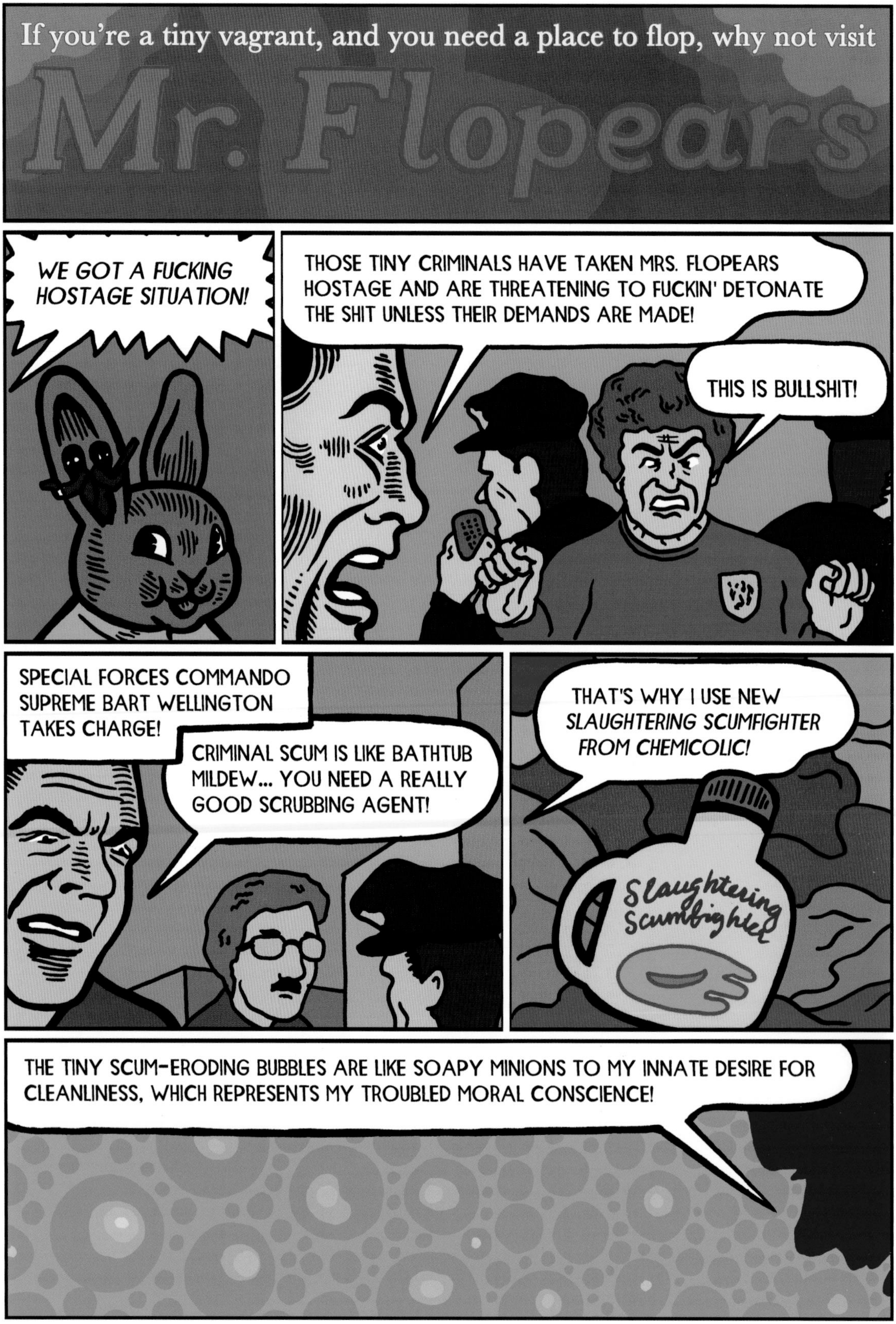
If you're a tiny vagrant, and you need a place to flop, why not visit
Mr. Flopears
WE GOT A FUCKING HOSTAGE SITUATION!
THOSE TINY CRIMINALS HAVE TAKEN MRS. FLOPEARS HOSTAGE AND ARE THREATENING TO FUCKIN' DETONATE THE SHIT UNLESS THEIR DEMANDS ARE MADE!
THIS IS BULLSHIT!
SPECIAL FORCES COMMANDO SUPREME BART WELLINGTON TAKES CHARGE!
CRIMINAL SCUM IS LIKE BATHTUB MILDEW... YOU NEED A REALLY GOOD SCRUBBING AGENT!
THAT'S WHY I USE NEW SLAUGHTERING SCUMFIGHTER FROM CHEMICOLIC!
Slaughtering Scumfighter
THE TINY SCUM-ERODING BUBBLES ARE LIKE SOAPY MINIONS TO MY INNATE DESIRE FOR CLEANLINESS, WHICH REPRESENTS MY TROUBLED MORAL CONSCIENCE!

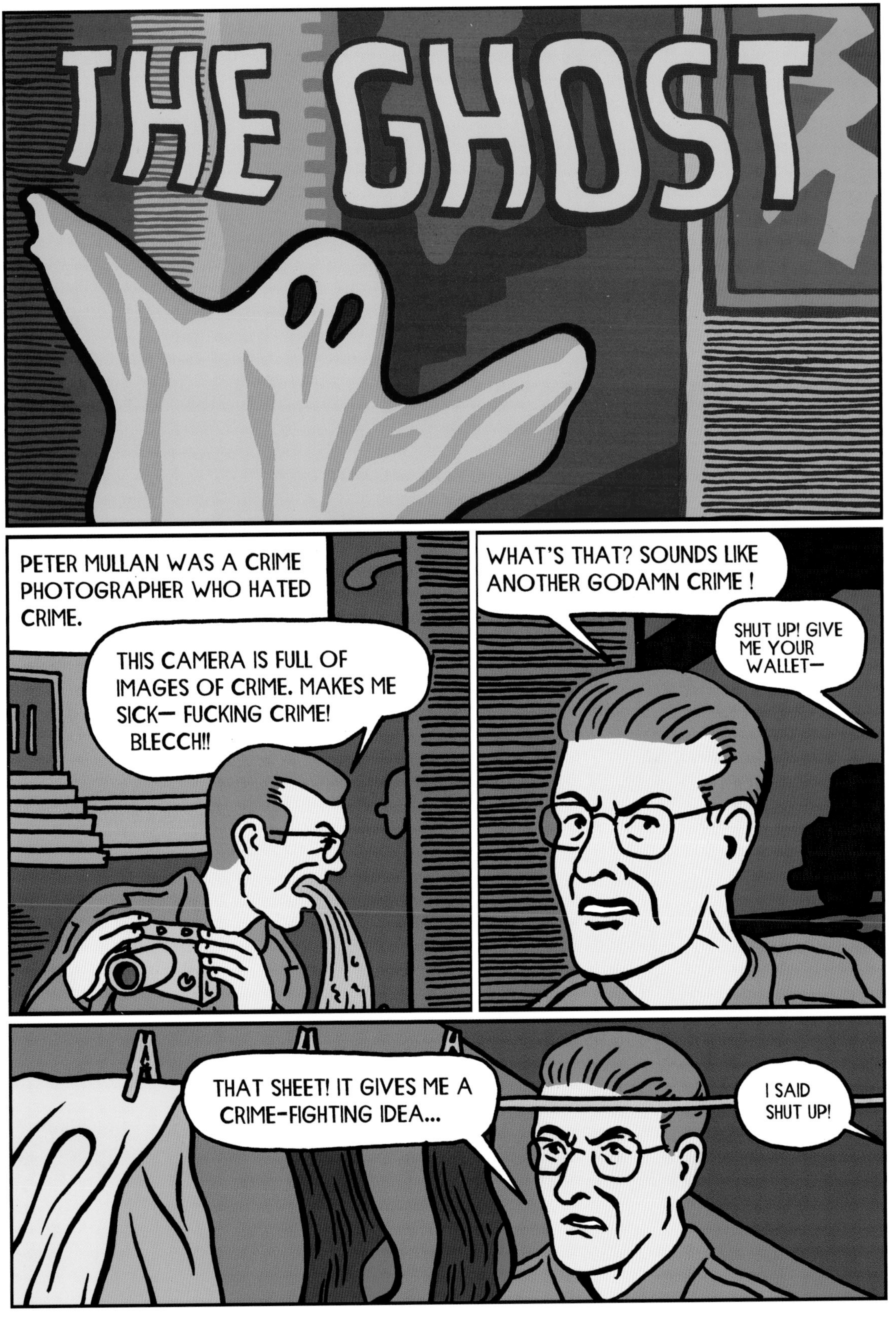
THE GHOST
PETER MULLAN WAS A CRIME PHOTOGRAPHER WHO HATED CRIME.
THIS CAMERA IS FULL OF IMAGES OF CRIME. MAKES ME SICK— FUCKING CRIME! BLECCH!!
WHAT'S THAT? SOUNDS LIKE ANOTHER GODAMN CRIME !
SHUT UP! GIVE ME YOUR WALLET—
THAT SHEET! IT GIVES ME A CRIME-FIGHTING IDEA...
I SAID SHUT UP!

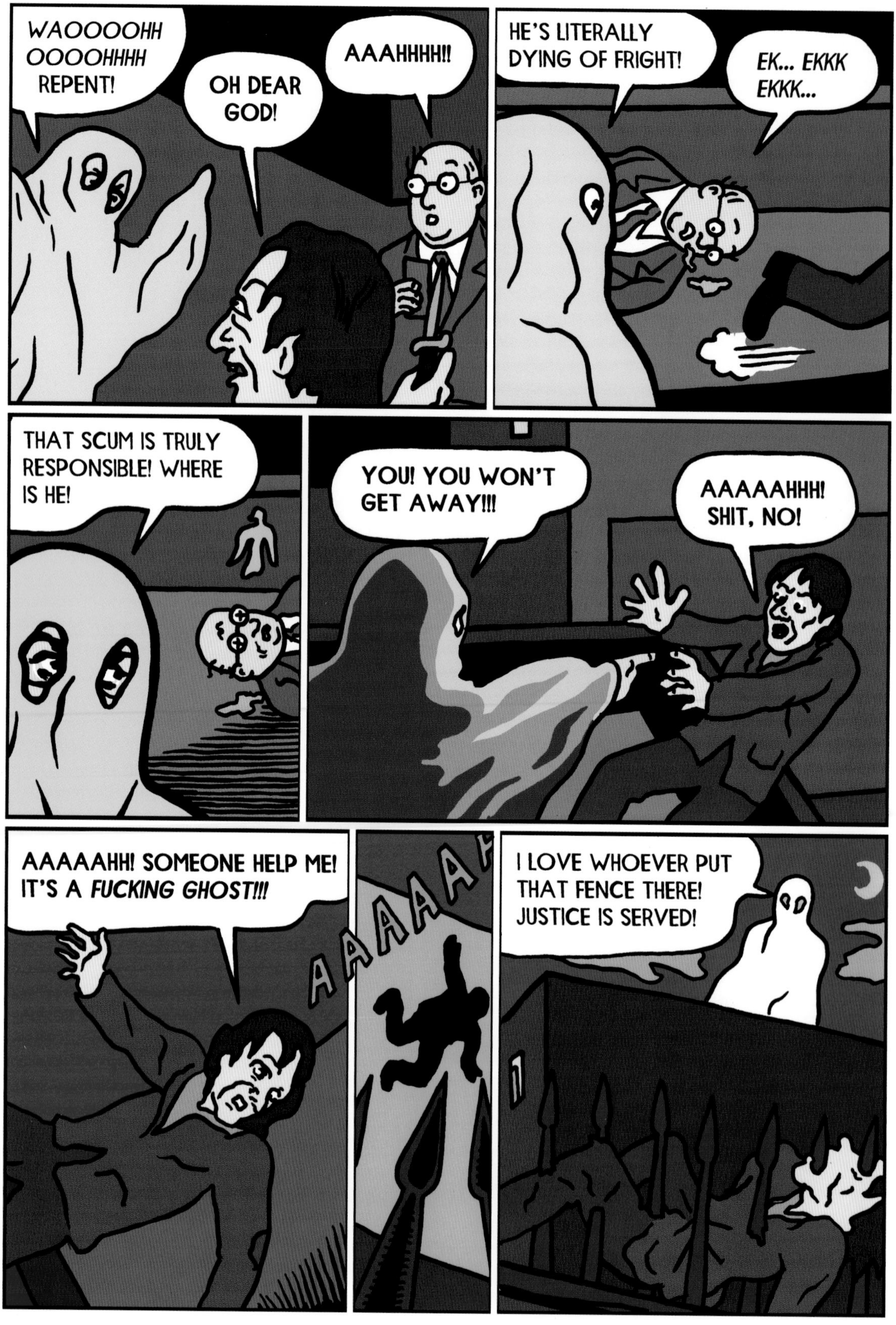
WAOOOOHH OOOOHHHH REPENT!
OH DEAR GOD!
AAAHHHH!!
HE'S LITERALLY DYING OF FRIGHT!
EK... EKKK EKKK...
THAT SCUM IS TRULY RESPONSIBLE! WHERE IS HE!
YOU! YOU WON'T GET AWAY!!!
AAAAAHHH! SHIT, NO!
AAAAAHH! SOMEONE HELP ME! IT'S A *FUCKING GHOST!!!*
AAAAAA
I LOVE WHOEVER PUT THAT FENCE THERE! JUSTICE IS SERVED!

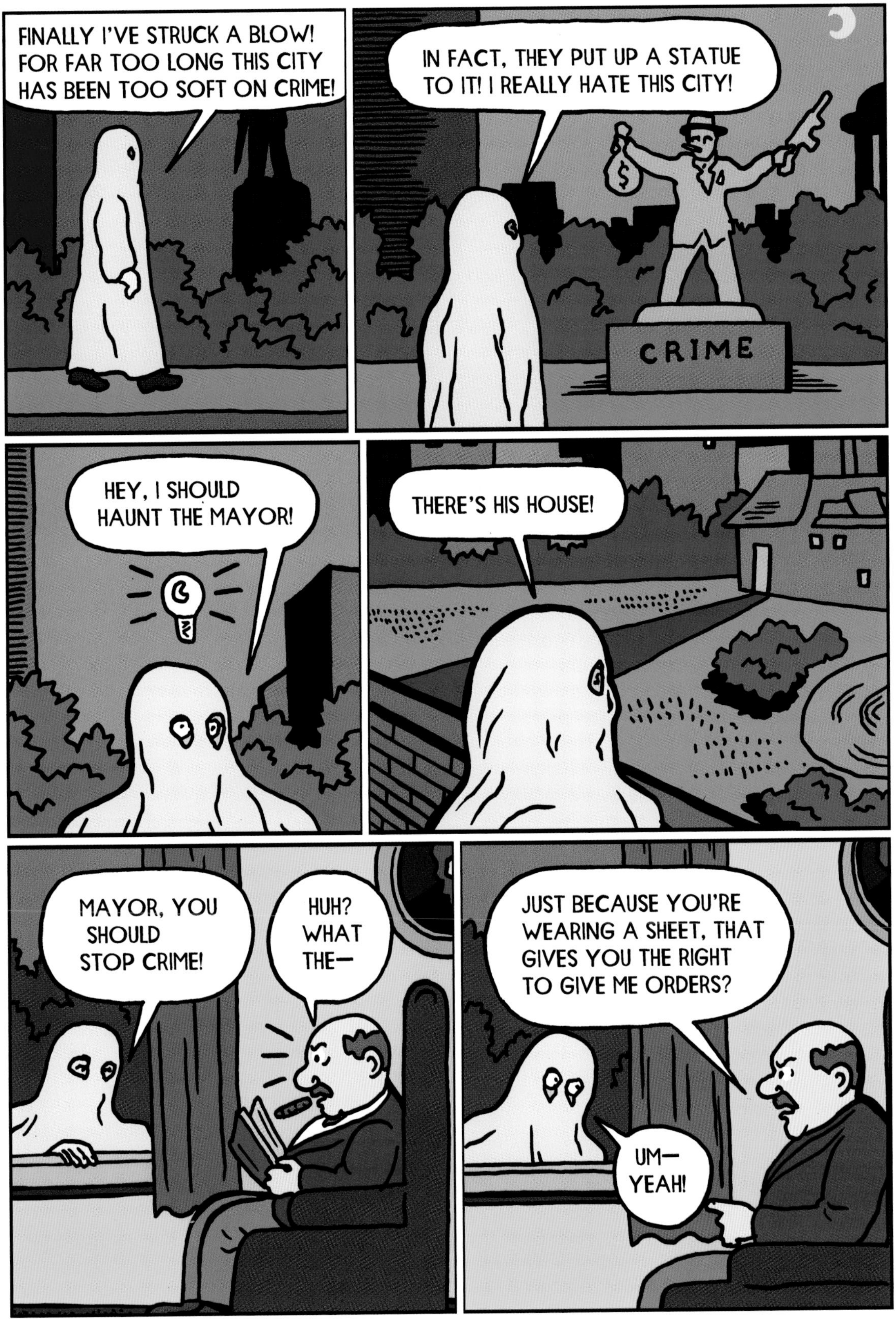
FINALLY I'VE STRUCK A BLOW! FOR FAR TOO LONG THIS CITY HAS BEEN TOO SOFT ON CRIME!
IN FACT, THEY PUT UP A STATUE TO IT! I REALLY HATE THIS CITY!
CRIME
HEY, I SHOULD HAUNT THE MAYOR!
THERE'S HIS HOUSE!
MAYOR, YOU SHOULD STOP CRIME!
HUH? WHAT THE—
JUST BECAUSE YOU'RE WEARING A SHEET, THAT GIVES YOU THE RIGHT TO GIVE ME ORDERS?
UM— YEAH!

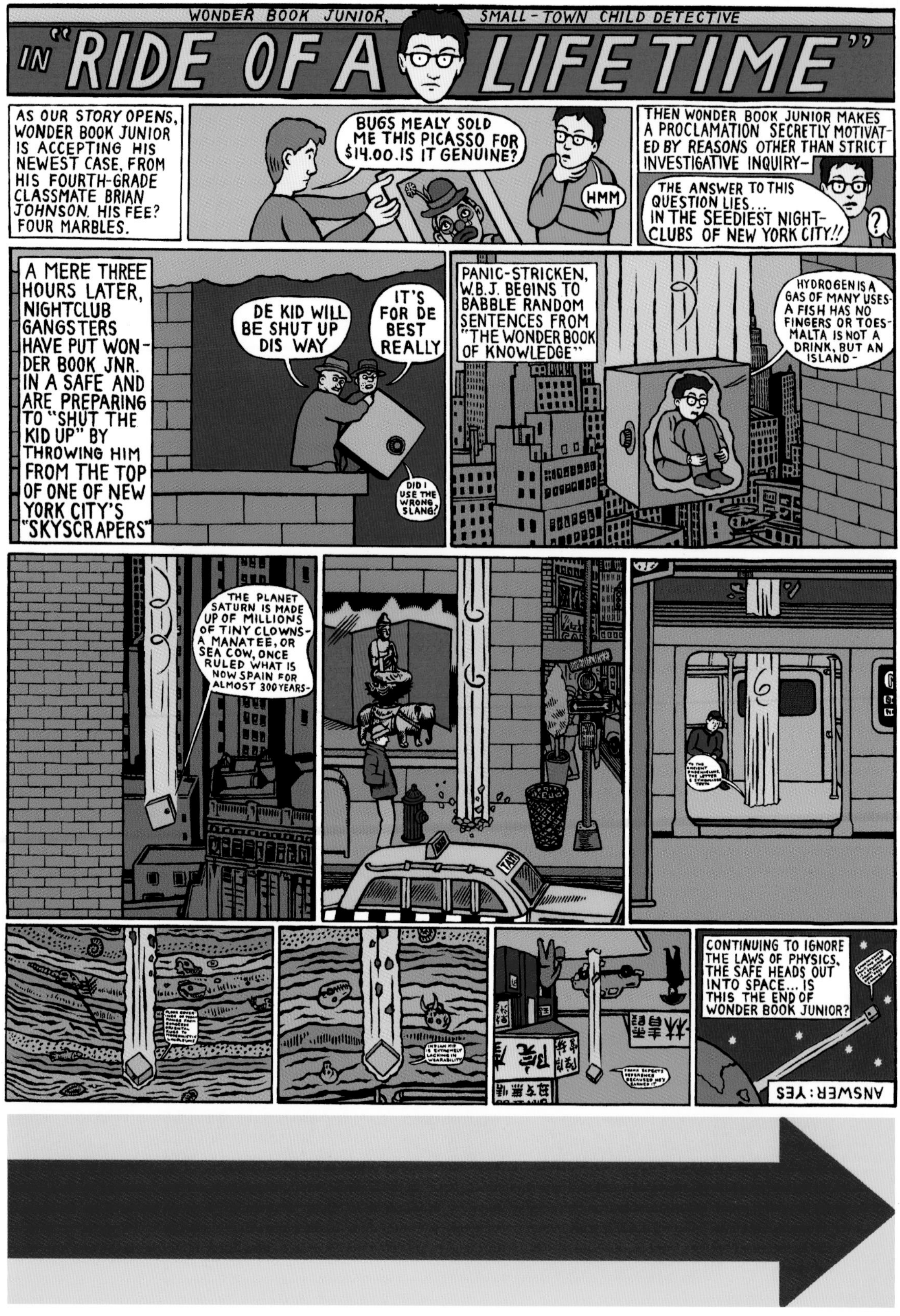
WONDER BOOK JUNIOR, SMALL-TOWN CHILD DETECTIVE
IN "RIDE OF A LIFETIME"
AS OUR STORY OPENS, WONDER BOOK JUNIOR IS ACCEPTING HIS NEWEST CASE, FROM HIS FOURTH-GRADE CLASSMATE BRIAN JOHNSON. HIS FEE? FOUR MARBLES.
BUGS MEALY SOLD ME THIS PICASSO FOR $14.00. IS IT GENUINE?
HMM
THEN WONDER BOOK JUNIOR MAKES A PROCLAMATION SECRETLY MOTIVATED BY REASONS OTHER THAN STRICT INVESTIGATIVE INQUIRY-
THE ANSWER TO THIS QUESTION LIES... IN THE SEEDIEST NIGHTCLUBS OF NEW YORK CITY!!
?
A MERE THREE HOURS LATER, NIGHTCLUB GANGSTERS HAVE PUT WONDER BOOK JNR. IN A SAFE AND ARE PREPARING TO "SHUT THE KID UP" BY THROWING HIM FROM THE TOP OF ONE OF NEW YORK CITY'S "SKYSCRAPERS"
DE KID WILL BE SHUT UP DIS WAY
IT'S FOR DE BEST REALLY
DID I USE THE WRONG SLANG?
PANIC-STRICKEN, W.B.J. BEGINS TO BABBLE RANDOM SENTENCES FROM "THE WONDER BOOK OF KNOWLEDGE"
HYDROGEN IS A GAS OF MANY USES- A FISH HAS NO FINGERS OR TOES- MALTA IS NOT A DRINK, BUT AN ISLAND-
THE PLANET SATURN IS MADE UP OF MILLIONS OF TINY CLOWNS- A MANATEE, OR SEA COW, ONCE RULED WHAT IS NOW SPAIN FOR ALMOST 300 YEARS-
TAXI
INDIAN KID IS EXTREMELY LACKING IN WEARABILITY
CONTINUING TO IGNORE THE LAWS OF PHYSICS, THE SAFE HEADS OUT INTO SPACE... IS THIS THE END OF WONDER BOOK JUNIOR?
ANSWER: YES

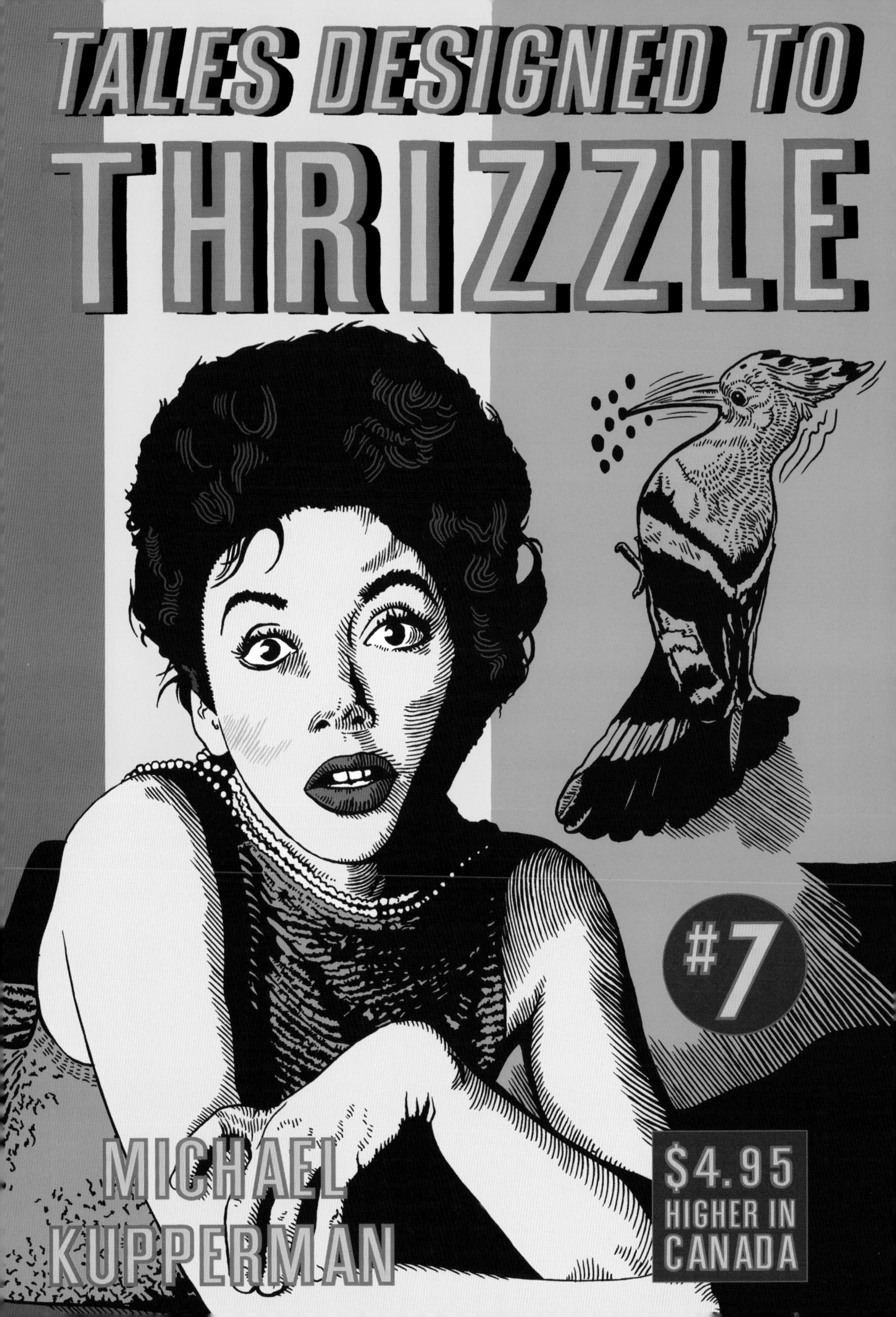
TALES DESIGNED TO
THRIZZLE
#7
MICHAEL
KUPPERMAN
$4.95
HIGHER IN
CANADA

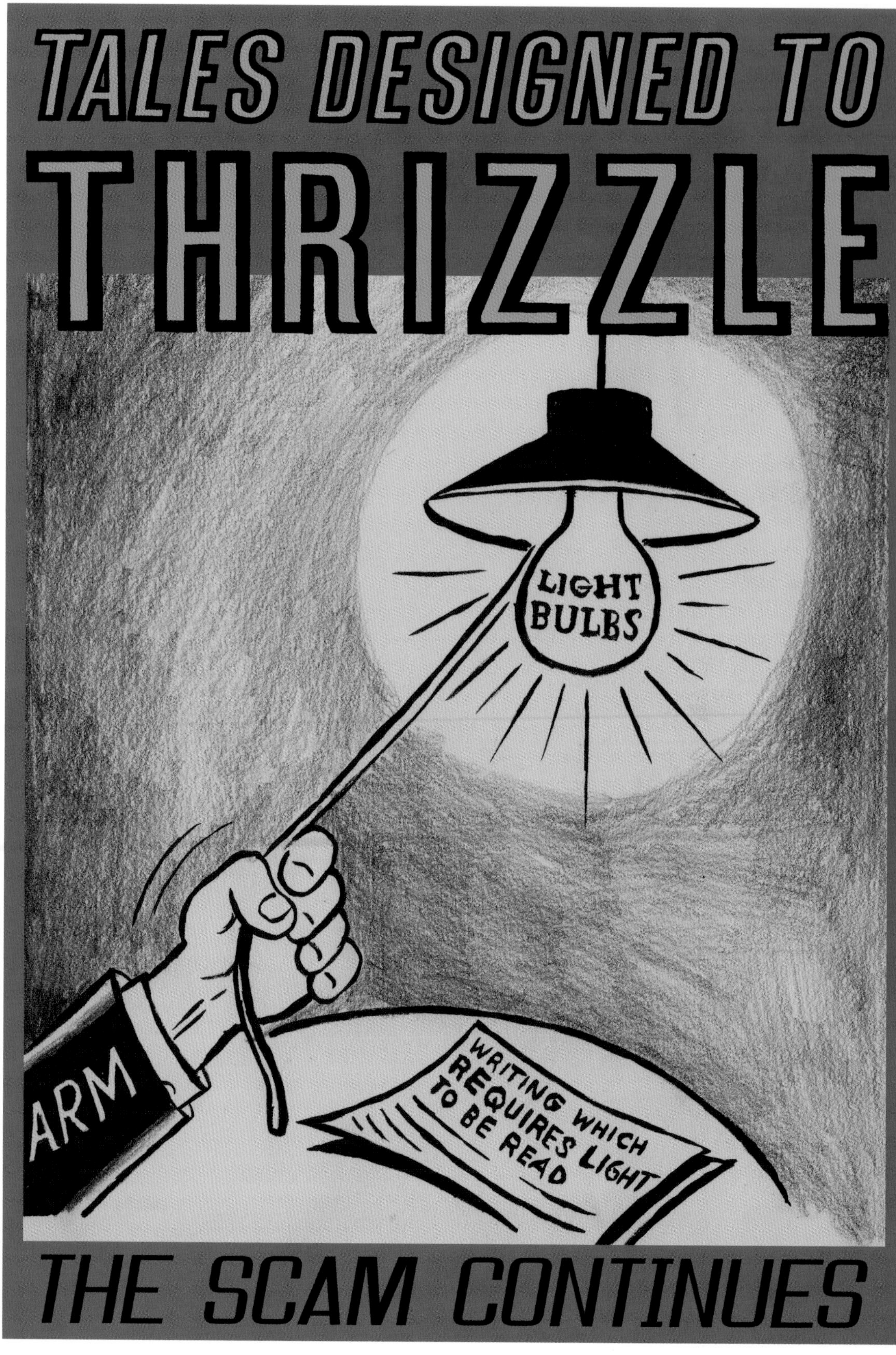
TALES DESIGNED TO
THRIZZLE
LIGHT BULBS
ARM
WRITING WHICH REQUIRES LIGHT TO BE READ
THE SCAM CONTINUES

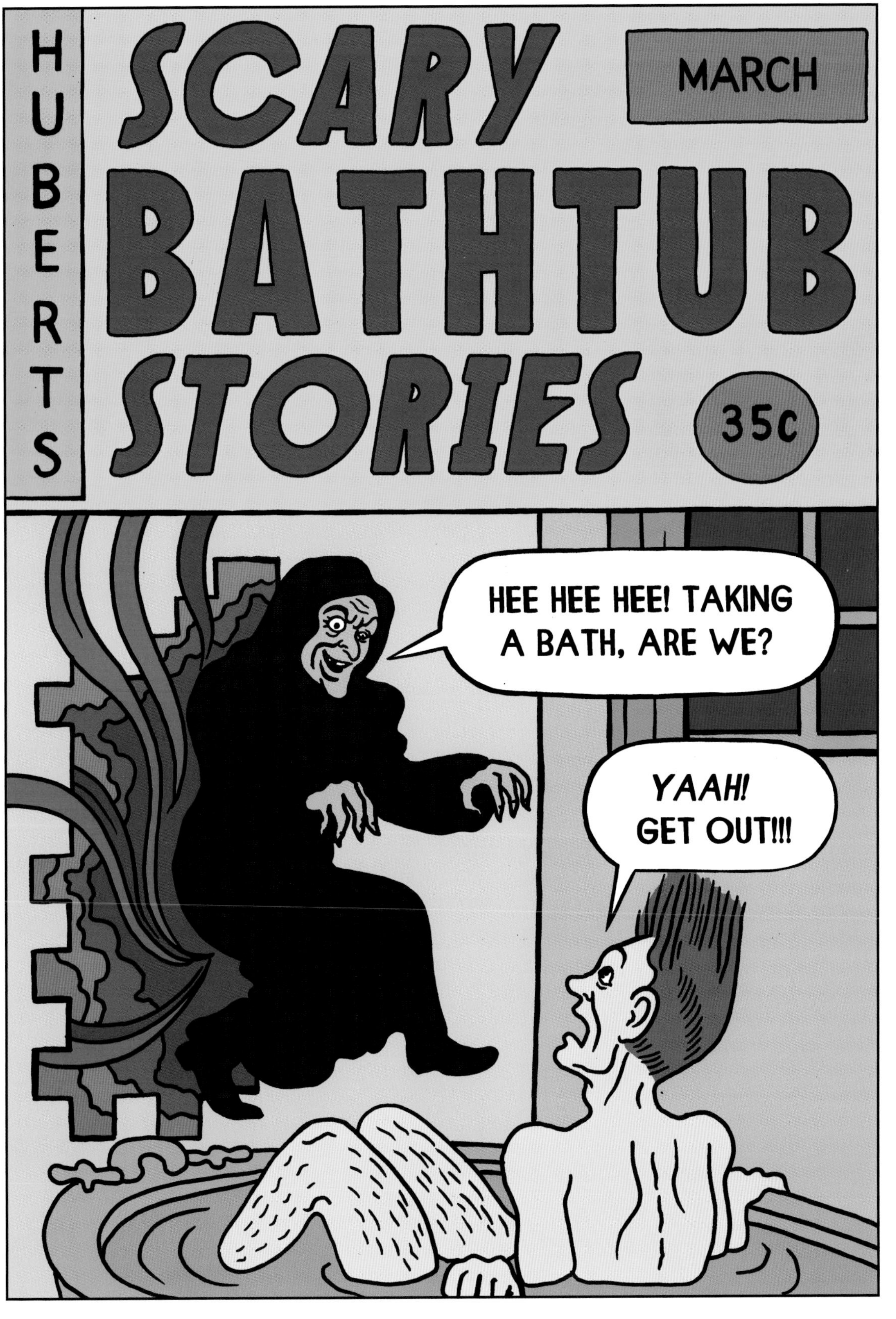
HUBERTS
SCARY BATHTUB STORIES
MARCH
35¢
HEE HEE HEE! TAKING A BATH, ARE WE?
YAAH! GET OUT!!!

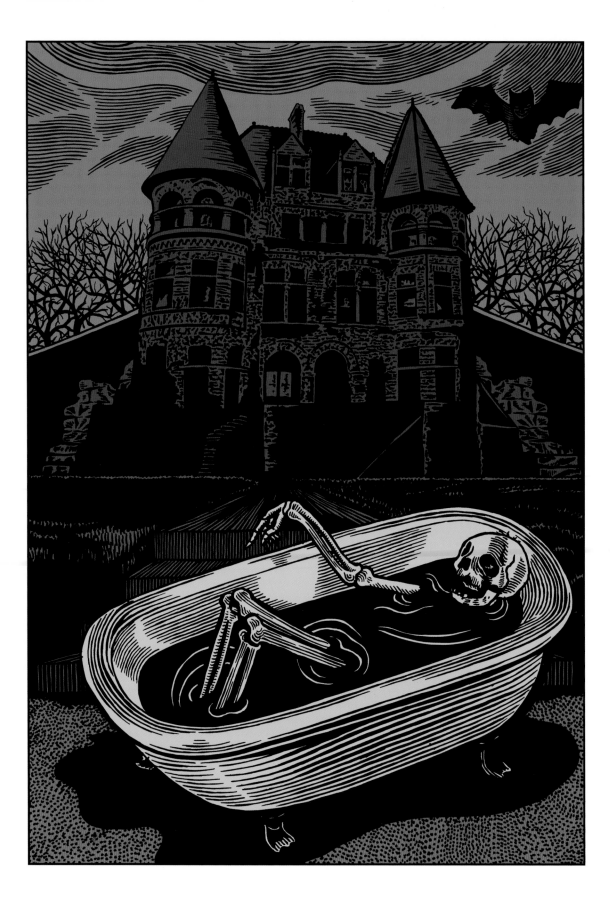

DID YOU KNOW MORE PEOPLE DIE IN BATHTUBS EVERY YEAR THAN IN ANY OTHER FORM OF BATHING TUB? NO WONDER TUBS HAVE A BAD REPUTATION— THEY'RE DEADLY!

EVERY YEAR, HUNDREDS OF PEOPLE ARE FOUND DEAD IN BATHTUBS, SOME OF THEM LOOKING LIKE THEY HAD SUFFERED UNSPEAKABLE HORROR BEFORE SHUFFLING OFF THIS MORTAL COIL.

SOME SAY THAT THE BATHTUB WAS INVENTED IN HELL, BY THE DEVIL HIMSELF!

OTHERS BELIEVE THAT IT REPRESENTS A SUBCONSCIOUS DESIRE OF MAN TO SUBMERGE HIMSELF IN HIS OWN EXCREMENT!

WHATEVER THE TRUE STORY, IT IS NOT UNREASONABLE TO FEEL SHEER NAKED TERROR WHEN CONTEMPLATING THIS UNHOLY VESSEL!

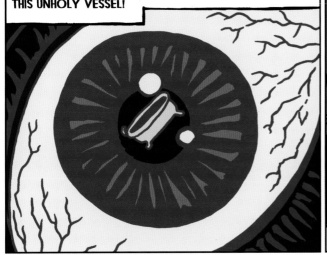

BATHTUBS... *BAH!*

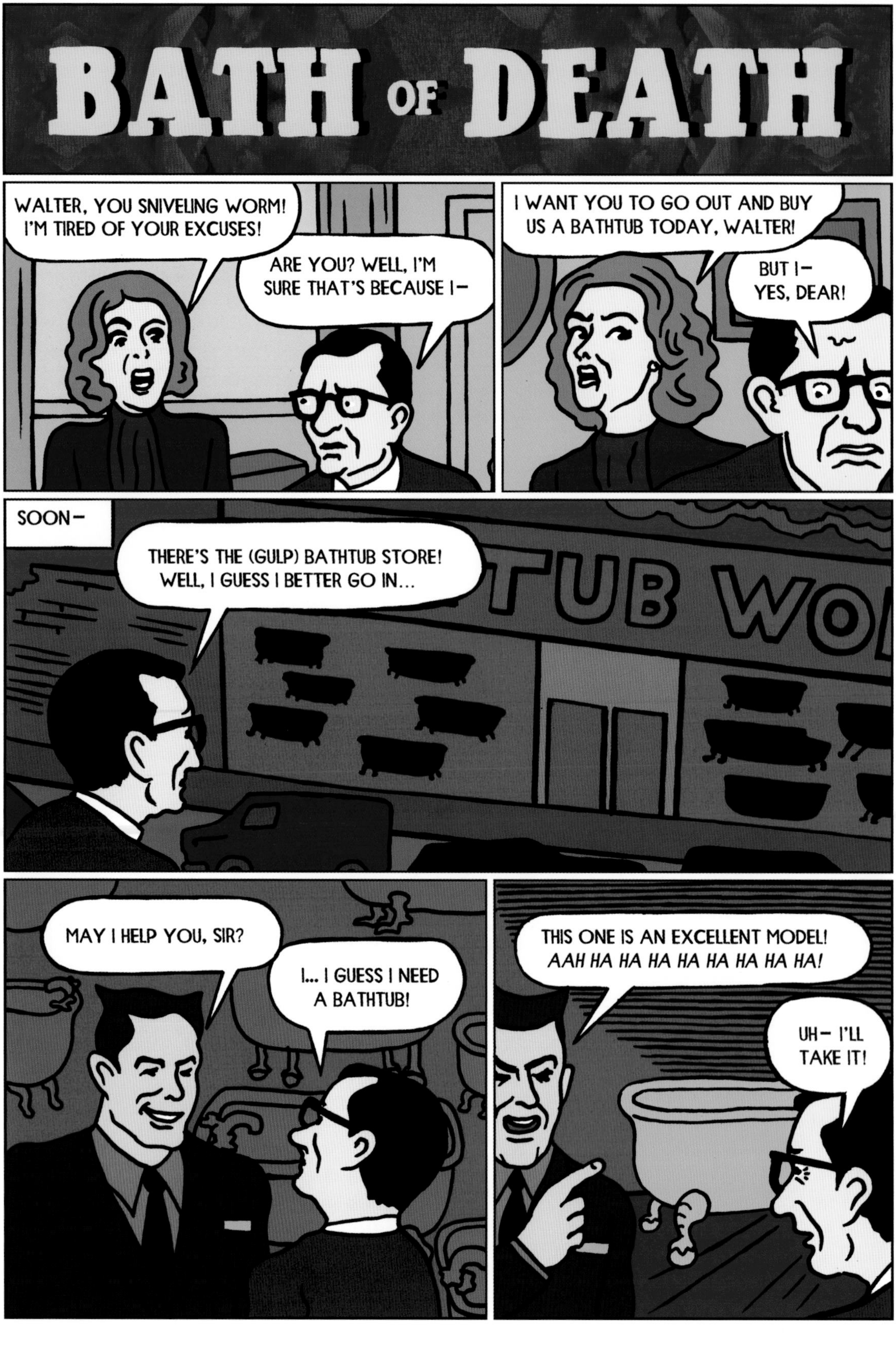
BATH OF DEATH
WALTER, YOU SNIVELING WORM! I'M TIRED OF YOUR EXCUSES!
ARE YOU? WELL, I'M SURE THAT'S BECAUSE I—
I WANT YOU TO GO OUT AND BUY US A BATHTUB TODAY, WALTER!
BUT I— YES, DEAR!
SOON—
THERE'S THE (GULP) BATHTUB STORE! WELL, I GUESS I BETTER GO IN...
TUB WO
MAY I HELP YOU, SIR?
I... I GUESS I NEED A BATHTUB!
THIS ONE IS AN EXCELLENT MODEL! AAH HA HA HA HA HA HA HA HA!
UH— I'LL TAKE IT!

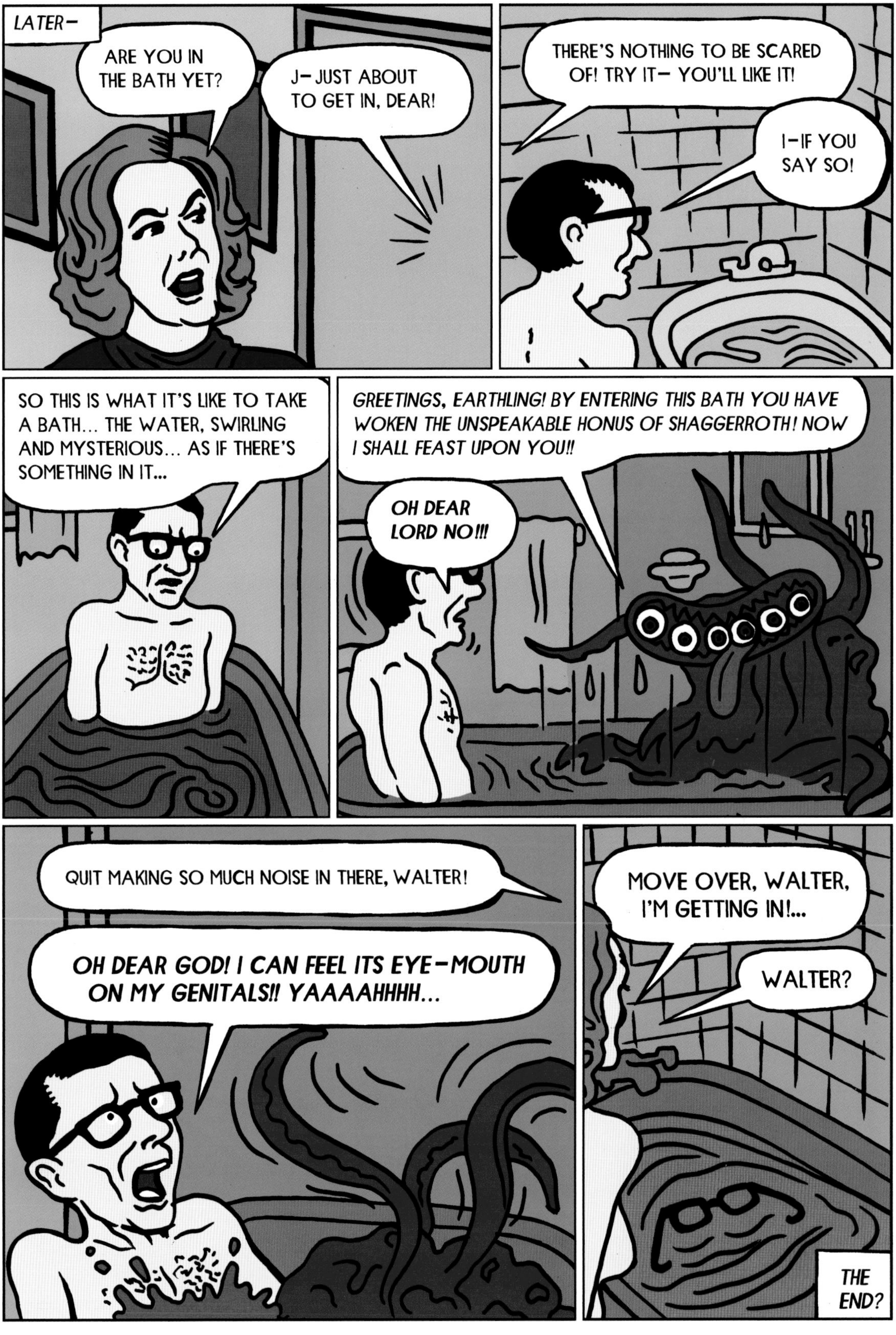
LATER—
ARE YOU IN THE BATH YET?
J— JUST ABOUT TO GET IN, DEAR!
THERE'S NOTHING TO BE SCARED OF! TRY IT— YOU'LL LIKE IT!
I—IF YOU SAY SO!
SO THIS IS WHAT IT'S LIKE TO TAKE A BATH... THE WATER, SWIRLING AND MYSTERIOUS... AS IF THERE'S SOMETHING IN IT...
GREETINGS, EARTHLING! BY ENTERING THIS BATH YOU HAVE WOKEN THE UNSPEAKABLE HONUS OF SHAGGERROTH! NOW I SHALL FEAST UPON YOU!!
OH DEAR LORD NO!!!
QUIT MAKING SO MUCH NOISE IN THERE, WALTER!
OH DEAR GOD! I CAN FEEL ITS EYE-MOUTH ON MY GENITALS!! YAAAAHHHH...
MOVE OVER, WALTER, I'M GETTING IN!...
WALTER?
THE END?

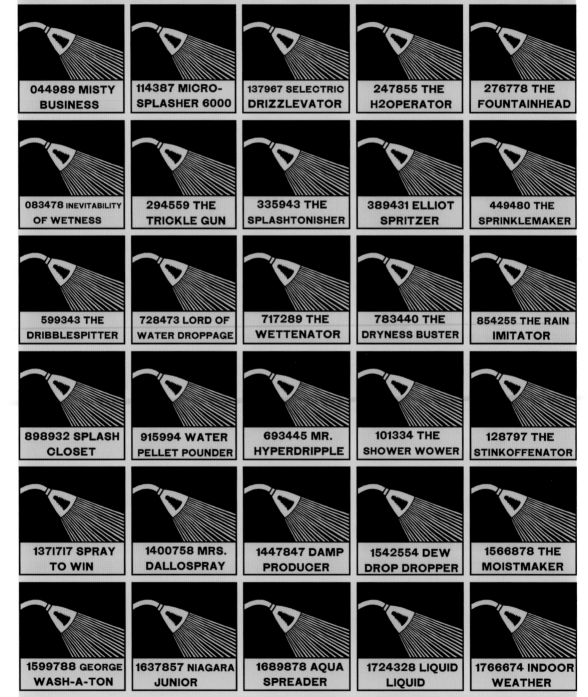

AVOID THE NIGHTMARE OF BATHS
VISIT HUBERT'S SHOWER WORLD AND
CHOOSE FROM ONE OF OUR THOUSANDS
OF SPECIALTY SHOWER HEADS

044989 MISTY BUSINESS

114387 MICRO-SPLASHER 6000

137967 SELECTRIC DRIZZLEVATOR

247855 THE H2OPERATOR

276778 THE FOUNTAINHEAD

083478 INEVITABILITY OF WETNESS

294559 THE TRICKLE GUN

335943 THE SPLASHTONISHER

389431 ELLIOT SPRITZER

449480 THE SPRINKLEMAKER

599343 THE DRIBBLESPITTER

728473 LORD OF WATER DROPPAGE

717289 THE WETTENATOR

783440 THE DRYNESS BUSTER

854255 THE RAIN IMITATOR

898932 SPLASH CLOSET

915994 WATER PELLET POUNDER

693445 MR. HYPERDRIPPLE

101334 THE SHOWER WOWER

128797 THE STINKOFFENATOR

1371717 SPRAY TO WIN

1400758 MRS. DALLOSPRAY

1447847 DAMP PRODUCER

1542554 DEW DROP DROPPER

1566878 THE MOISTMAKER

1599788 GEORGE WASH-A-TON

1637857 NIAGARA JUNIOR

1689878 AQUA SPREADER

1724328 LIQUID LIQUID

1766674 INDOOR WEATHER

HUBERT'S SHOWER WORLD - NOW WITH 17 CONVENIENT LOCATIONS

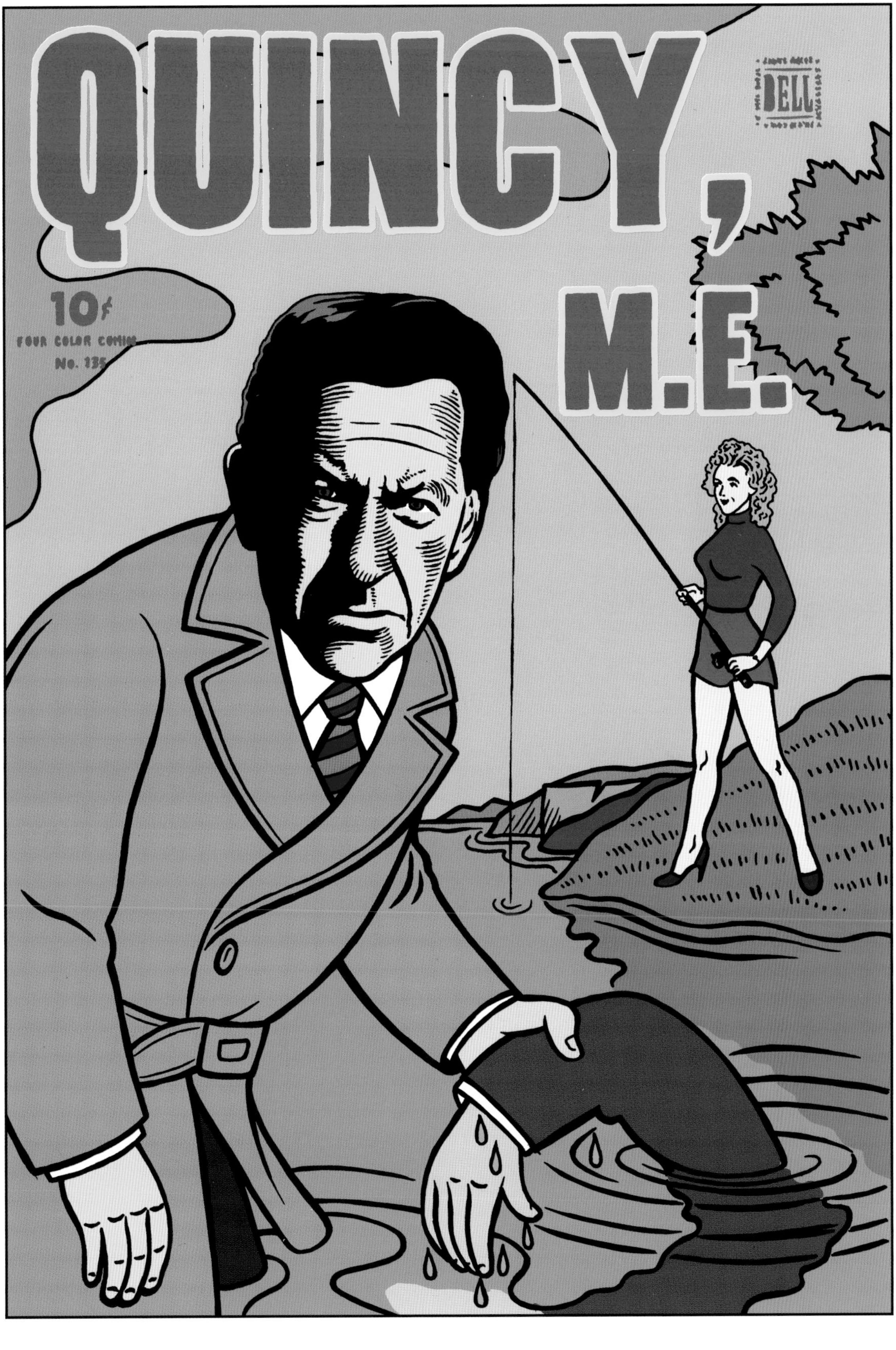
QUINCY,
M.E.
DELL
10¢
FOUR COLOR COMICS
No. 135

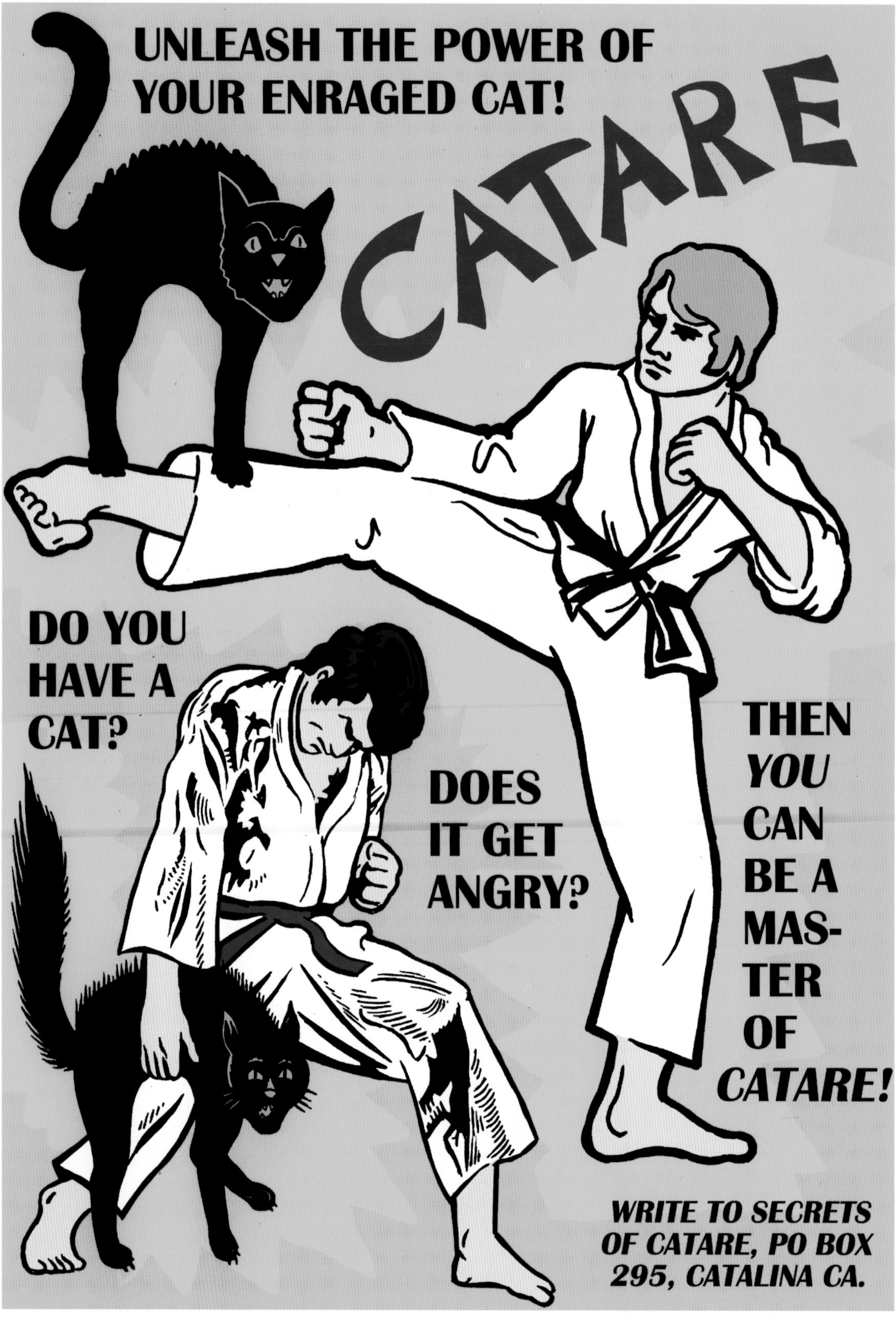
UNLEASH THE POWER OF YOUR ENRAGED CAT!
CATARE
DO YOU HAVE A CAT?
DOES IT GET ANGRY?
THEN *YOU* CAN BE A MAS-TER OF *CATARE!*
WRITE TO SECRETS OF CATARE, PO BOX 295, CATALINA CA.

QUINCY, M.E.

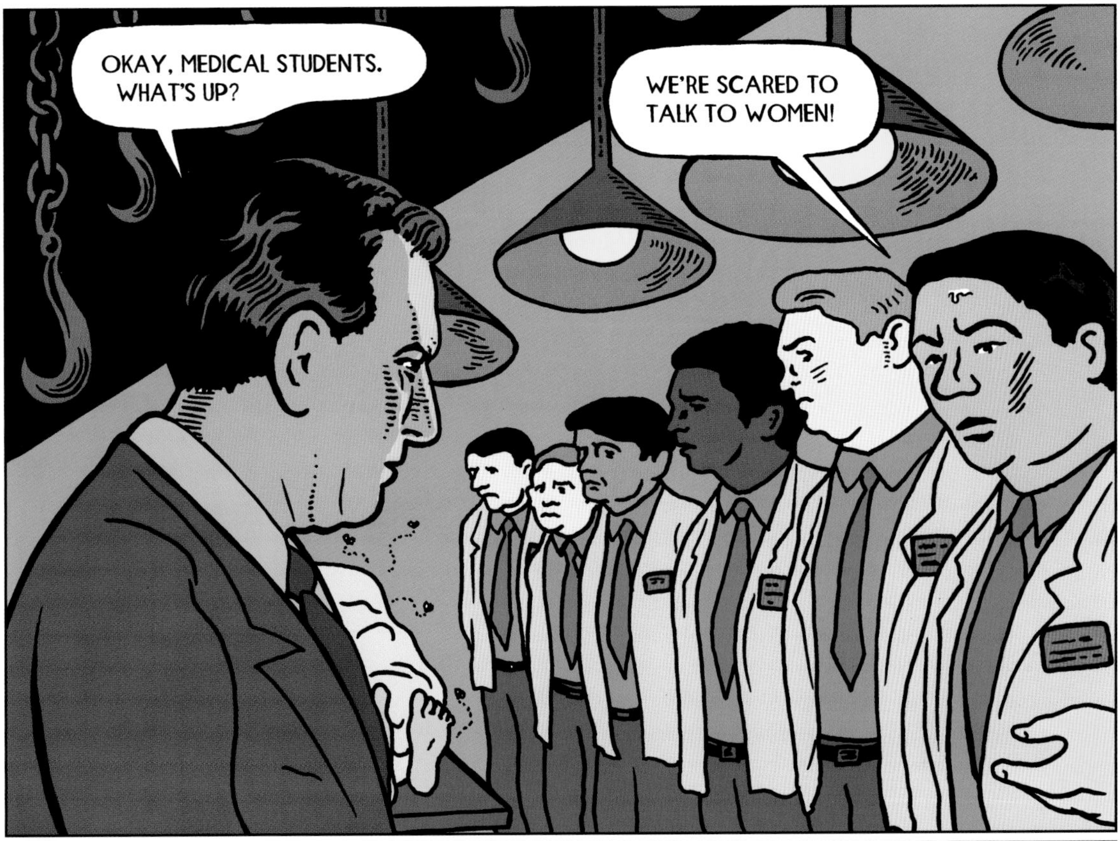
OKAY, MEDICAL STUDENTS. WHAT'S UP?
WE'RE SCARED TO TALK TO WOMEN!

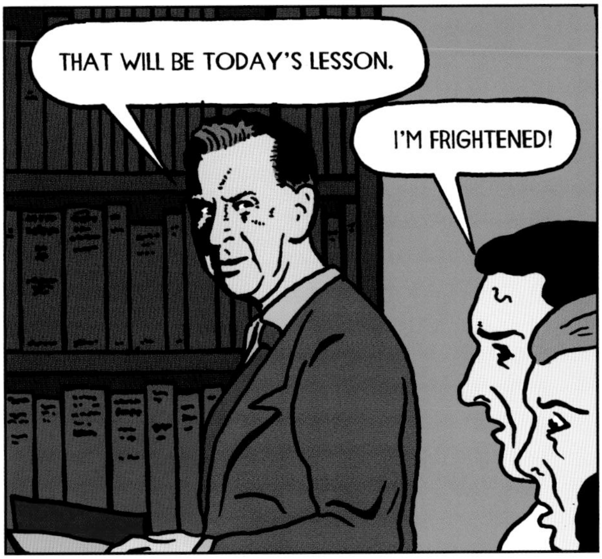
THAT WILL BE TODAY'S LESSON.
I'M FRIGHTENED!

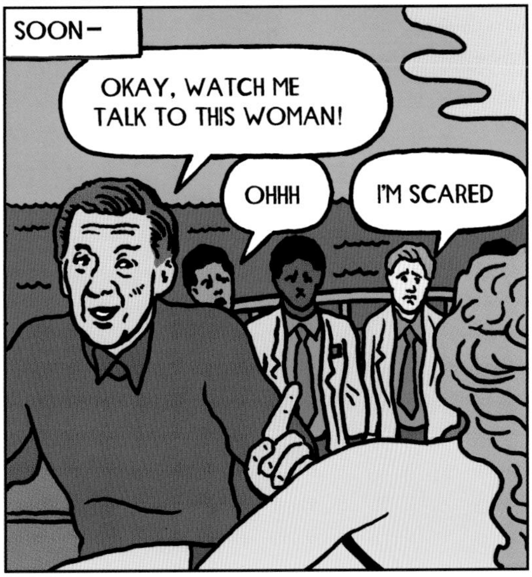
SOON—
OKAY, WATCH ME TALK TO THIS WOMAN!
OHHH
I'M SCARED

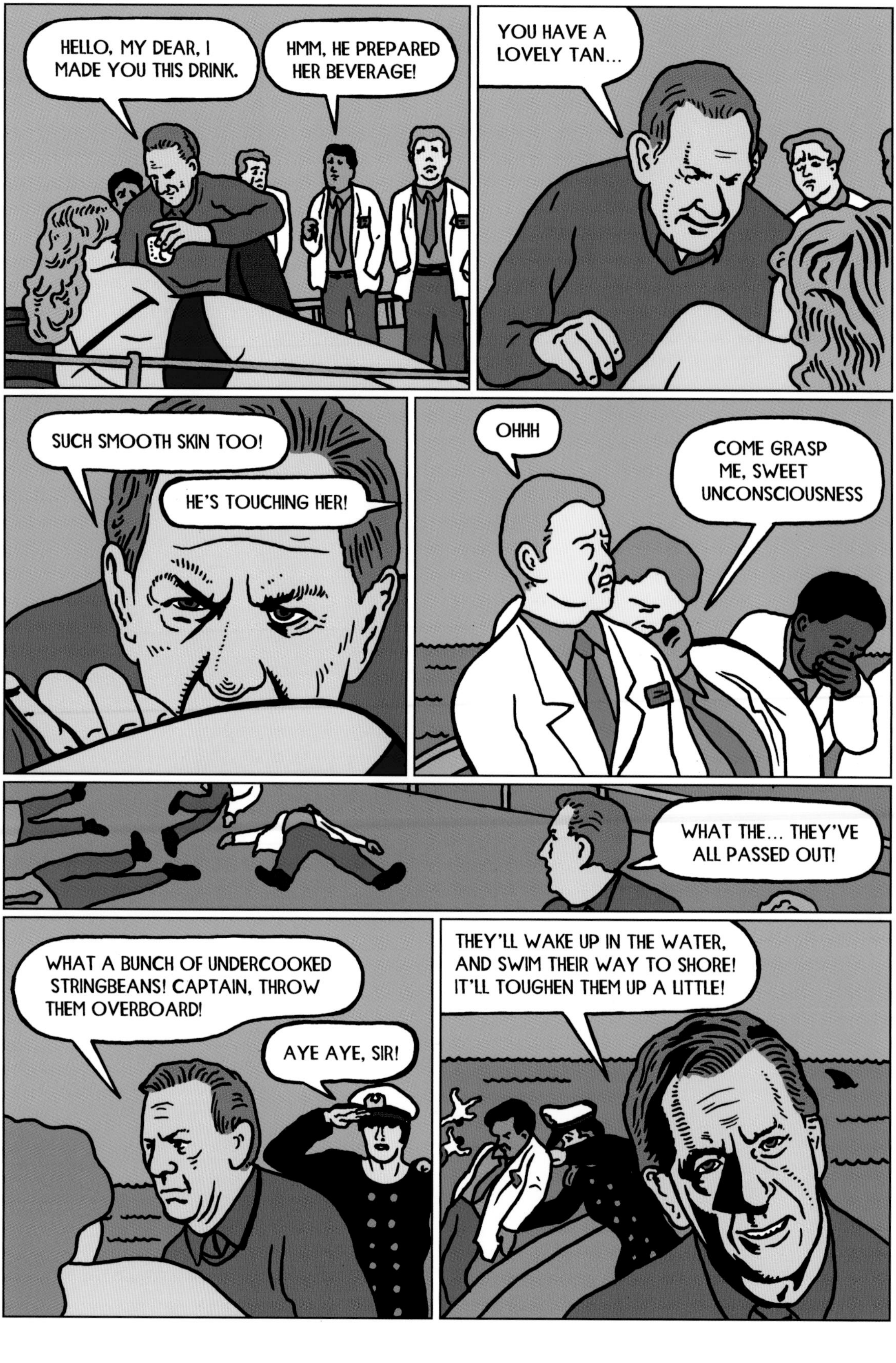
HELLO, MY DEAR, I MADE YOU THIS DRINK.
HMM, HE PREPARED HER BEVERAGE!
YOU HAVE A LOVELY TAN...
SUCH SMOOTH SKIN TOO!
HE'S TOUCHING HER!
OHHH
COME GRASP ME, SWEET UNCONSCIOUSNESS
WHAT THE... THEY'VE ALL PASSED OUT!
WHAT A BUNCH OF UNDERCOOKED STRINGBEANS! CAPTAIN, THROW THEM OVERBOARD!
AYE AYE, SIR!
THEY'LL WAKE UP IN THE WATER, AND SWIM THEIR WAY TO SHORE! IT'LL TOUGHEN THEM UP A LITTLE!

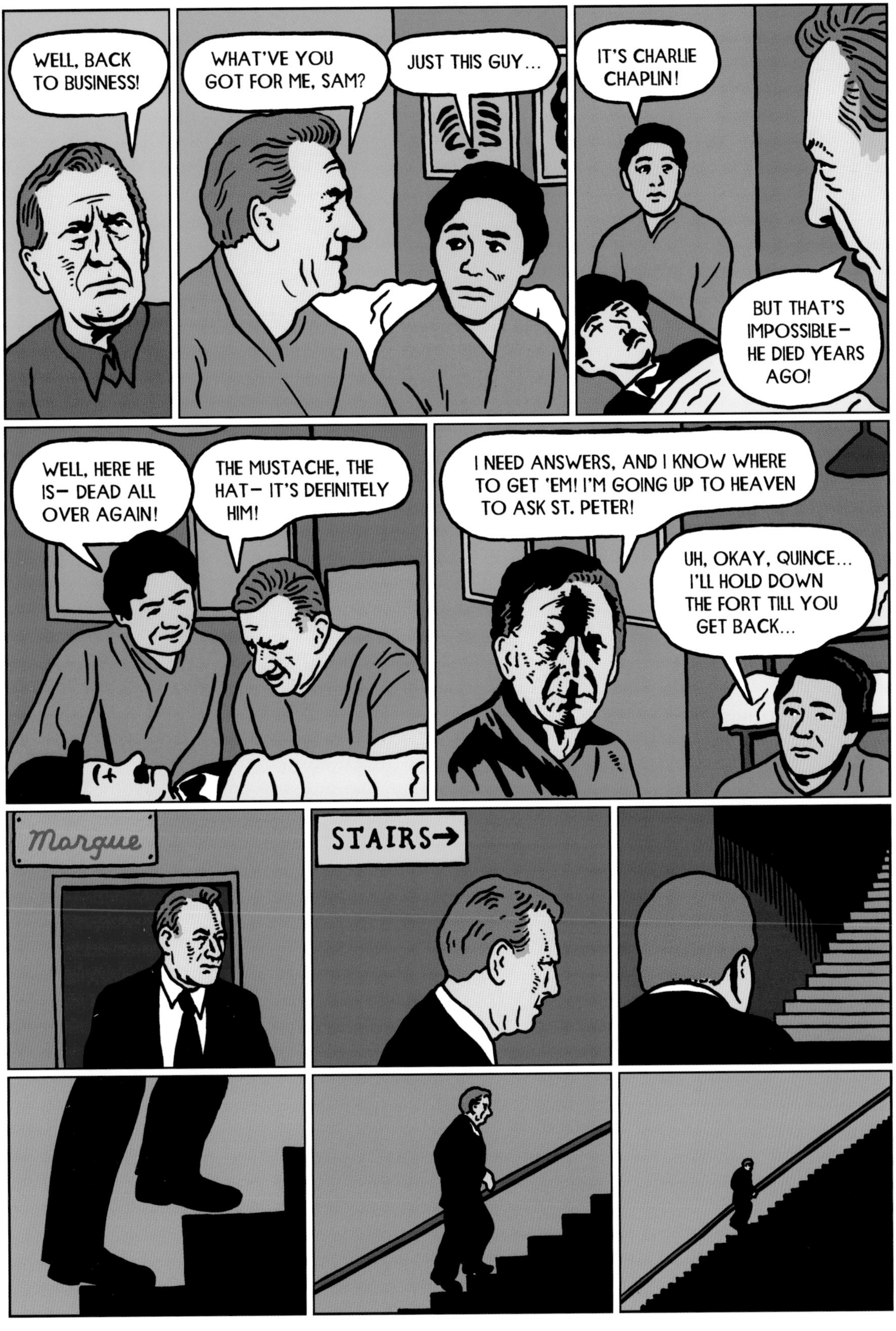
WELL, BACK TO BUSINESS!
WHAT'VE YOU GOT FOR ME, SAM?
JUST THIS GUY...
IT'S CHARLIE CHAPLIN!
BUT THAT'S IMPOSSIBLE— HE DIED YEARS AGO!
WELL, HERE HE IS— DEAD ALL OVER AGAIN!
THE MUSTACHE, THE HAT— IT'S DEFINITELY HIM!
I NEED ANSWERS, AND I KNOW WHERE TO GET 'EM! I'M GOING UP TO HEAVEN TO ASK ST. PETER!
UH, OKAY, QUINCE... I'LL HOLD DOWN THE FORT TILL YOU GET BACK...
Morgue
STAIRS→

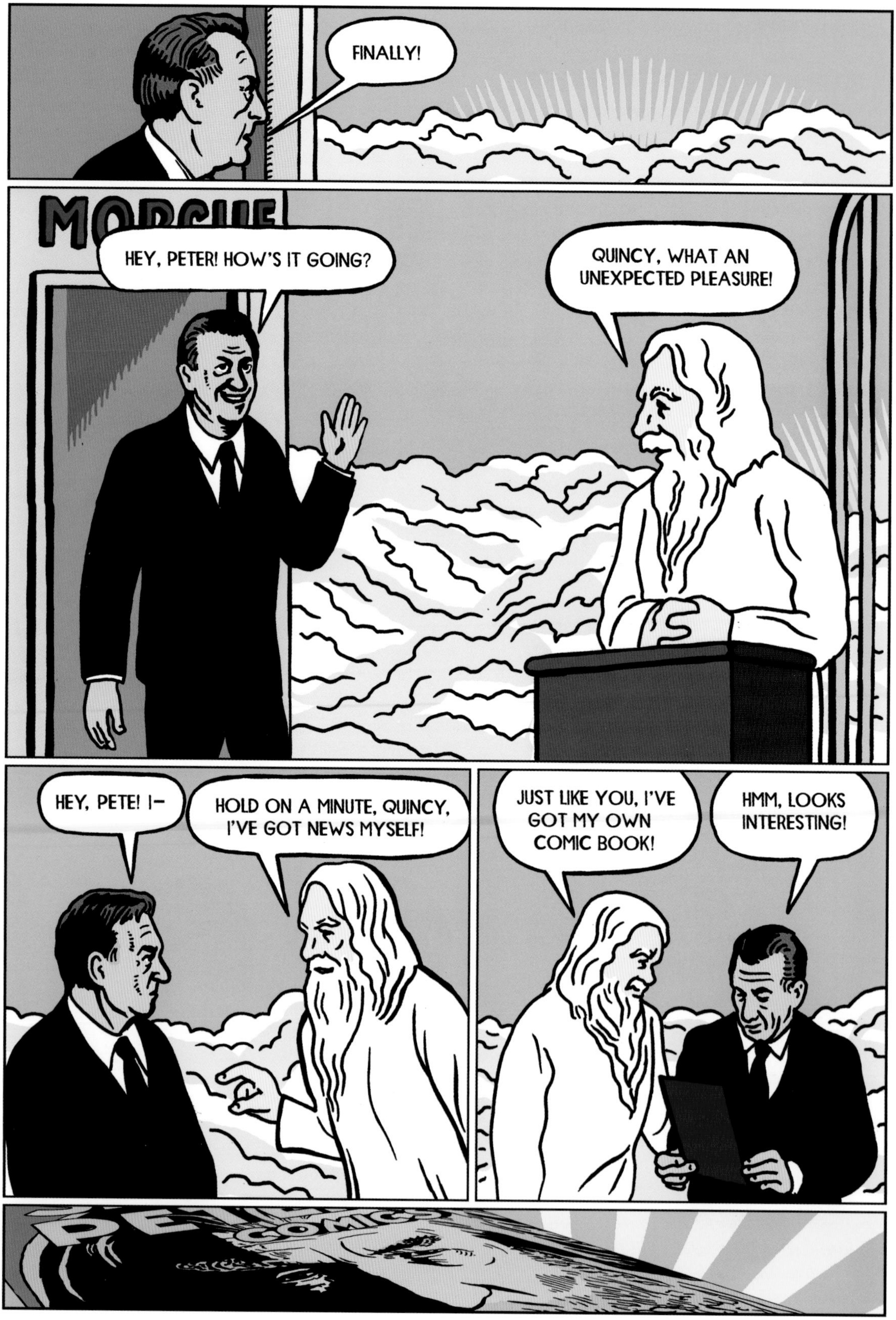
FINALLY!
MORGUE
HEY, PETER! HOW'S IT GOING?
QUINCY, WHAT AN UNEXPECTED PLEASURE!
HEY, PETE! I—
HOLD ON A MINUTE, QUINCY, I'VE GOT NEWS MYSELF!
JUST LIKE YOU, I'VE GOT MY OWN COMIC BOOK!
HMM, LOOKS INTERESTING!
COMICS

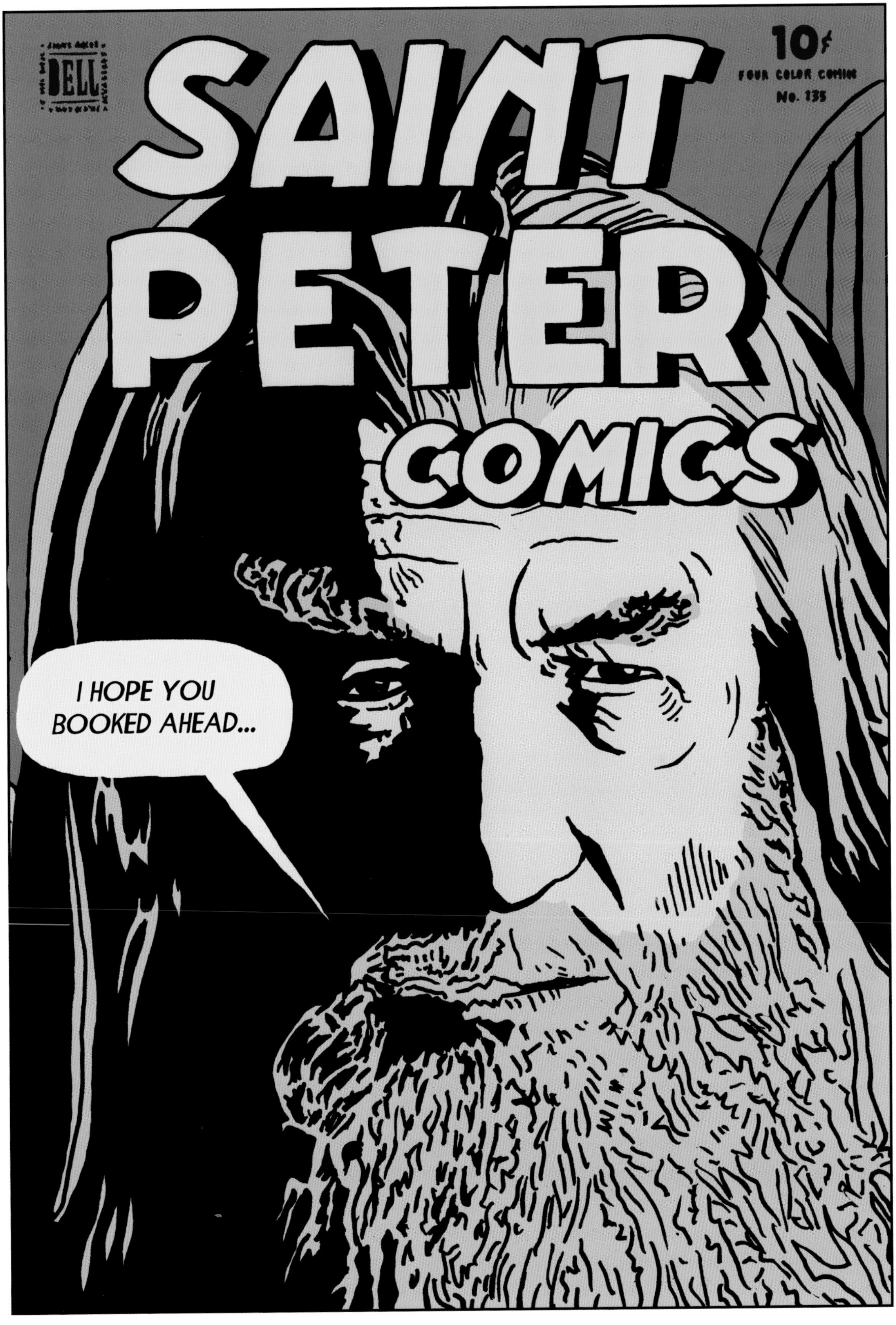
DELL
10¢
FOUR COLOR COMICS
No. 135
SAINT PETER COMICS
I HOPE YOU BOOKED AHEAD...

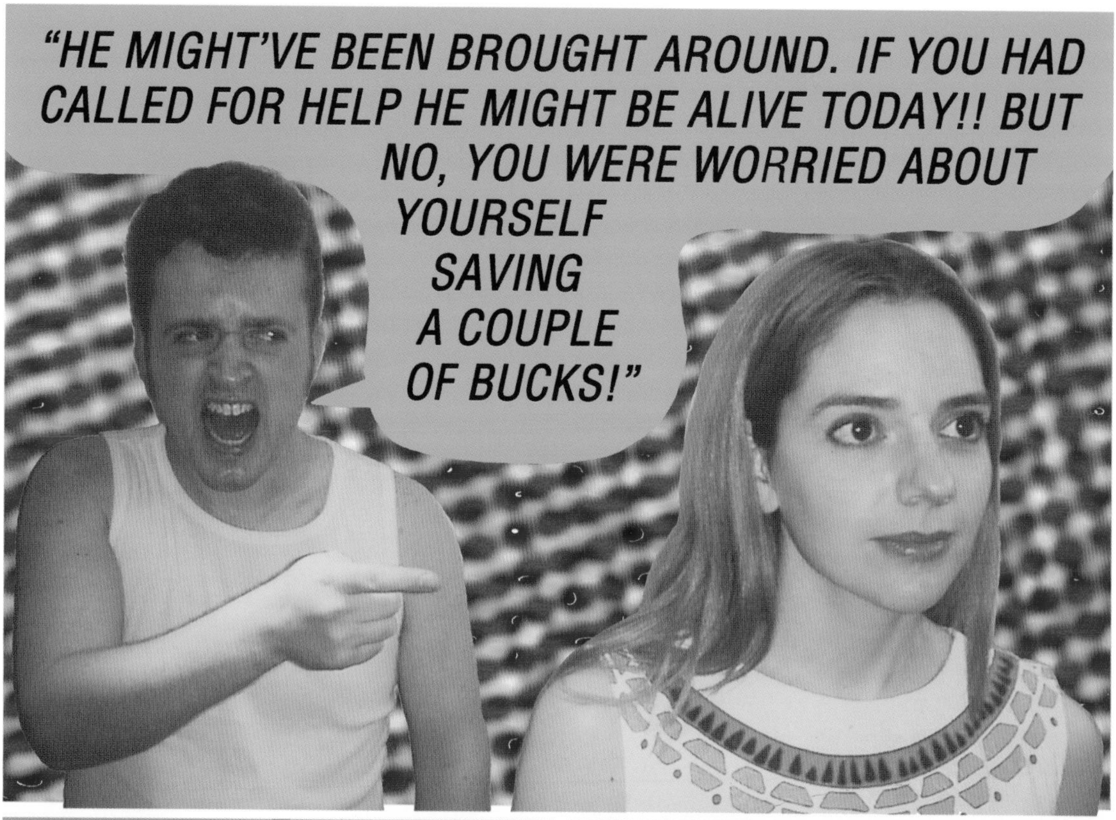
"HE MIGHT'VE BEEN BROUGHT AROUND. IF YOU HAD CALLED FOR HELP HE MIGHT BE ALIVE TODAY!! BUT NO, YOU WERE WORRIED ABOUT YOURSELF SAVING A COUPLE OF BUCKS!"

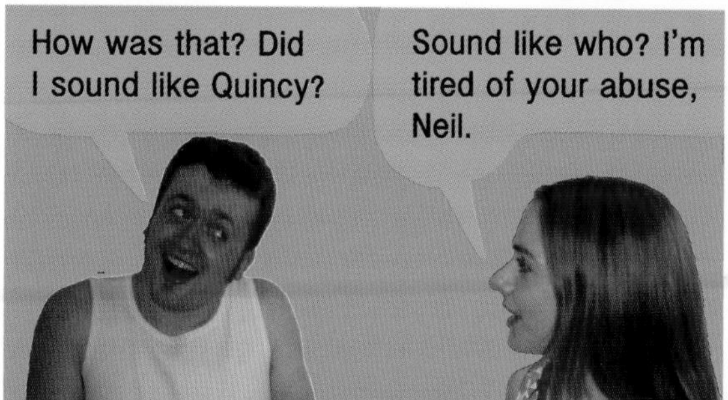
How was that? Did I sound like Quincy?
Sound like who? I'm tired of your abuse, Neil.

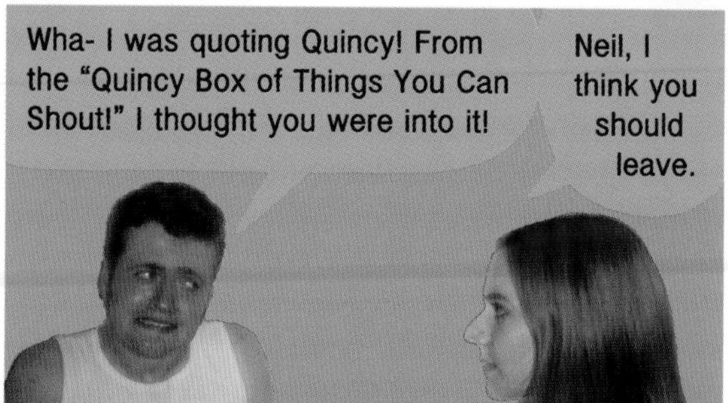
Wha- I was quoting Quincy! From the "Quincy Box of Things You Can Shout!" I thought you were into it!
Neil, I think you should leave.

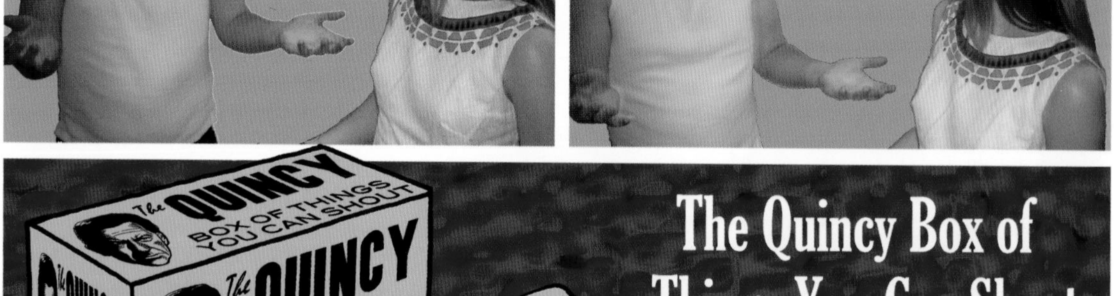
The QUINCY BOX OF THINGS YOU CAN SHOUT
"You sent those repairmen out to die, Senator- all cause you were worried about your dog getting the right to vote!"
AT BETTER STORES EVERYWHERE
The Quincy Box of Things You Can Shout. Just make sure your loved ones are into it.

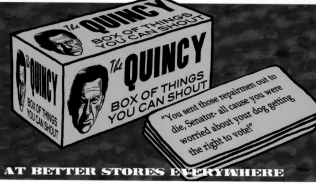

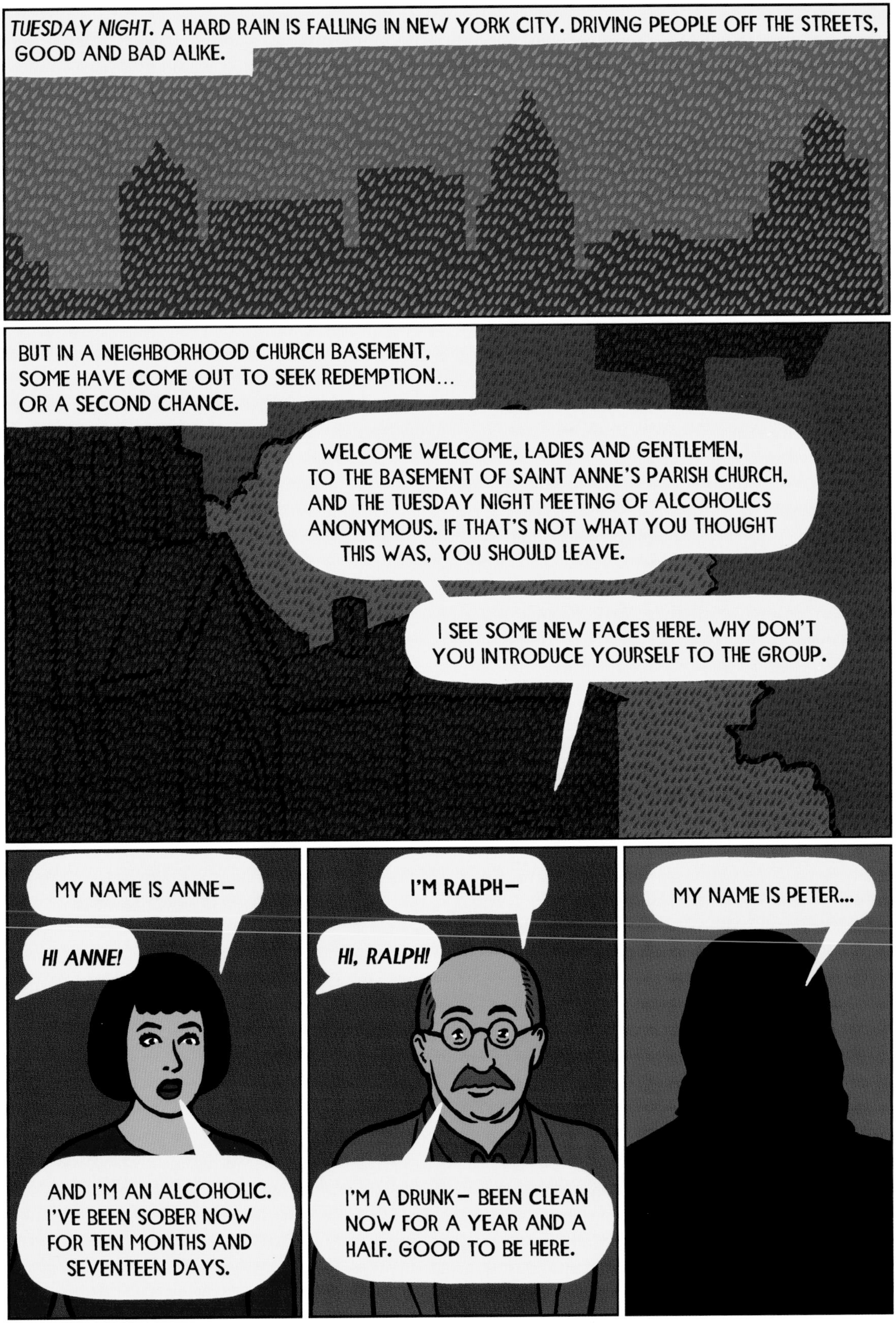
TUESDAY NIGHT. A HARD RAIN IS FALLING IN NEW YORK CITY. DRIVING PEOPLE OFF THE STREETS, GOOD AND BAD ALIKE.
BUT IN A NEIGHBORHOOD CHURCH BASEMENT, SOME HAVE COME OUT TO SEEK REDEMPTION... OR A SECOND CHANCE.
WELCOME WELCOME, LADIES AND GENTLEMEN, TO THE BASEMENT OF SAINT ANNE'S PARISH CHURCH, AND THE TUESDAY NIGHT MEETING OF ALCOHOLICS ANONYMOUS. IF THAT'S NOT WHAT YOU THOUGHT THIS WAS, YOU SHOULD LEAVE.
I SEE SOME NEW FACES HERE. WHY DON'T YOU INTRODUCE YOURSELF TO THE GROUP.
MY NAME IS ANNE–
HI ANNE!
AND I'M AN ALCOHOLIC. I'VE BEEN SOBER NOW FOR TEN MONTHS AND SEVENTEEN DAYS.
I'M RALPH–
HI, RALPH!
I'M A DRUNK– BEEN CLEAN NOW FOR A YEAR AND A HALF. GOOD TO BE HERE.
MY NAME IS PETER...

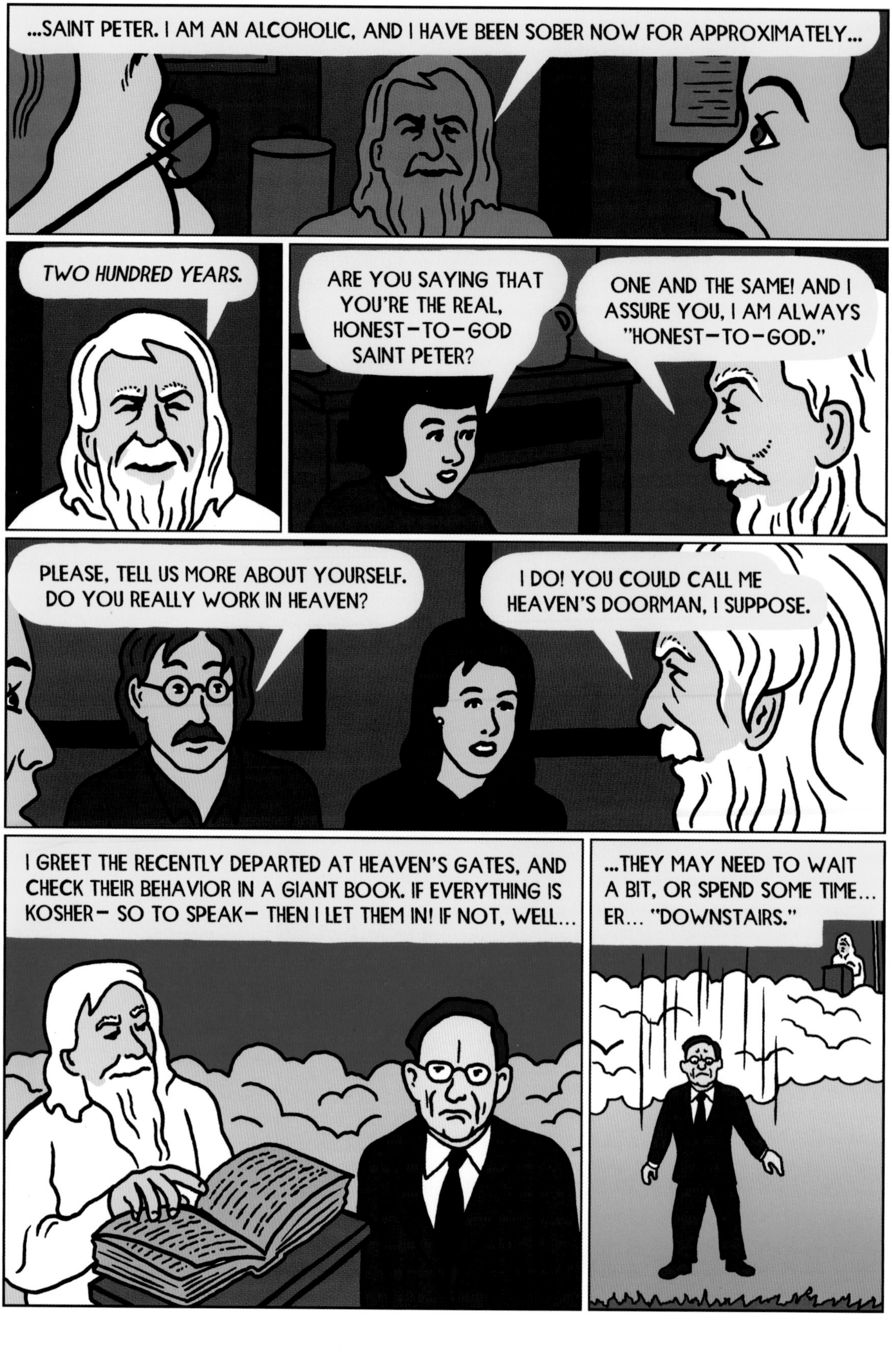
...SAINT PETER. I AM AN ALCOHOLIC, AND I HAVE BEEN SOBER NOW FOR APPROXIMATELY...
TWO HUNDRED YEARS.
ARE YOU SAYING THAT YOU'RE THE REAL, HONEST-TO-GOD SAINT PETER?
ONE AND THE SAME! AND I ASSURE YOU, I AM ALWAYS "HONEST-TO-GOD."
PLEASE, TELL US MORE ABOUT YOURSELF. DO YOU REALLY WORK IN HEAVEN?
I DO! YOU COULD CALL ME HEAVEN'S DOORMAN, I SUPPOSE.
I GREET THE RECENTLY DEPARTED AT HEAVEN'S GATES, AND CHECK THEIR BEHAVIOR IN A GIANT BOOK. IF EVERYTHING IS KOSHER– SO TO SPEAK– THEN I LET THEM IN! IF NOT, WELL...
...THEY MAY NEED TO WAIT A BIT, OR SPEND SOME TIME... ER... "DOWNSTAIRS."

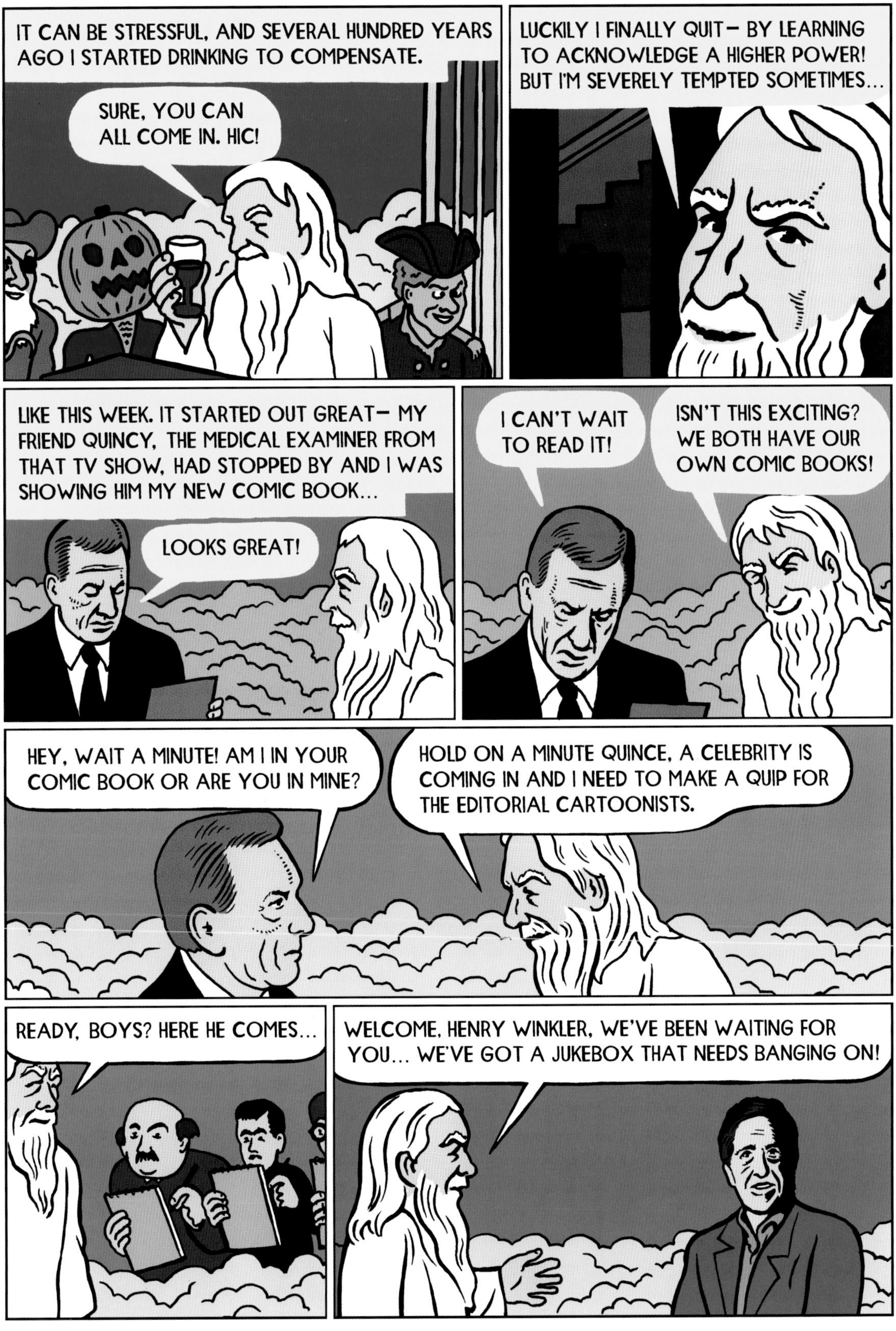
IT CAN BE STRESSFUL, AND SEVERAL HUNDRED YEARS AGO I STARTED DRINKING TO COMPENSATE.
SURE, YOU CAN ALL COME IN. HIC!
LUCKILY I FINALLY QUIT— BY LEARNING TO ACKNOWLEDGE A HIGHER POWER! BUT I'M SEVERELY TEMPTED SOMETIMES...
LIKE THIS WEEK. IT STARTED OUT GREAT— MY FRIEND QUINCY, THE MEDICAL EXAMINER FROM THAT TV SHOW, HAD STOPPED BY AND I WAS SHOWING HIM MY NEW COMIC BOOK...
LOOKS GREAT!
I CAN'T WAIT TO READ IT!
ISN'T THIS EXCITING? WE BOTH HAVE OUR OWN COMIC BOOKS!
HEY, WAIT A MINUTE! AM I IN YOUR COMIC BOOK OR ARE YOU IN MINE?
HOLD ON A MINUTE QUINCE, A CELEBRITY IS COMING IN AND I NEED TO MAKE A QUIP FOR THE EDITORIAL CARTOONISTS.
READY, BOYS? HERE HE COMES...
WELCOME, HENRY WINKLER, WE'VE BEEN WAITING FOR YOU... WE'VE GOT A JUKEBOX THAT NEEDS BANGING ON!

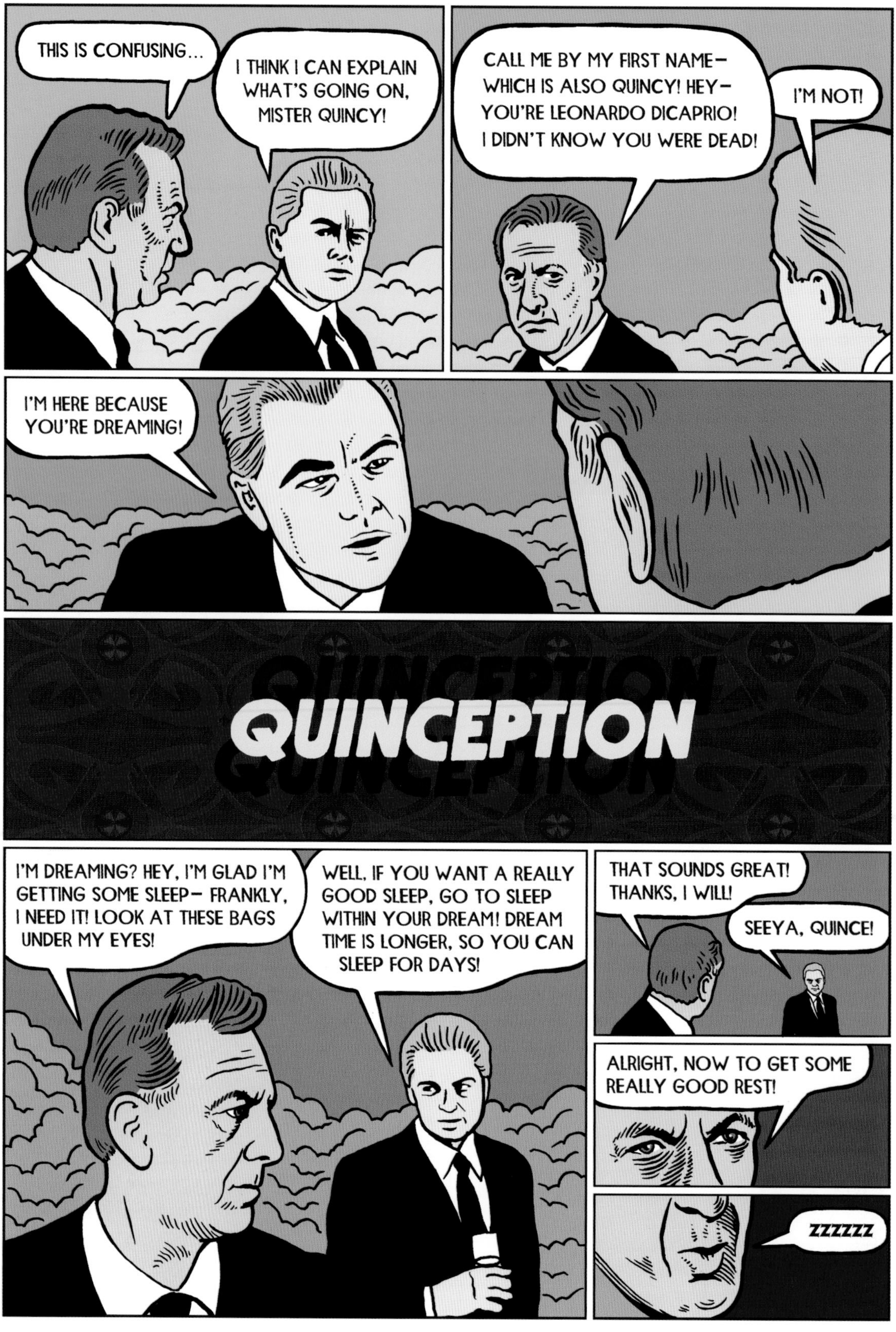
THIS IS CONFUSING...
I THINK I CAN EXPLAIN WHAT'S GOING ON, MISTER QUINCY!
CALL ME BY MY FIRST NAME— WHICH IS ALSO QUINCY! HEY— YOU'RE LEONARDO DICAPRIO! I DIDN'T KNOW YOU WERE DEAD!
I'M NOT!
I'M HERE BECAUSE YOU'RE DREAMING!
QUINCEPTION
I'M DREAMING? HEY, I'M GLAD I'M GETTING SOME SLEEP— FRANKLY, I NEED IT! LOOK AT THESE BAGS UNDER MY EYES!
WELL, IF YOU WANT A REALLY GOOD SLEEP, GO TO SLEEP WITHIN YOUR DREAM! DREAM TIME IS LONGER, SO YOU CAN SLEEP FOR DAYS!
THAT SOUNDS GREAT! THANKS, I WILL!
SEEYA, QUINCE!
ALRIGHT, NOW TO GET SOME REALLY GOOD REST!
ZZZZZZ

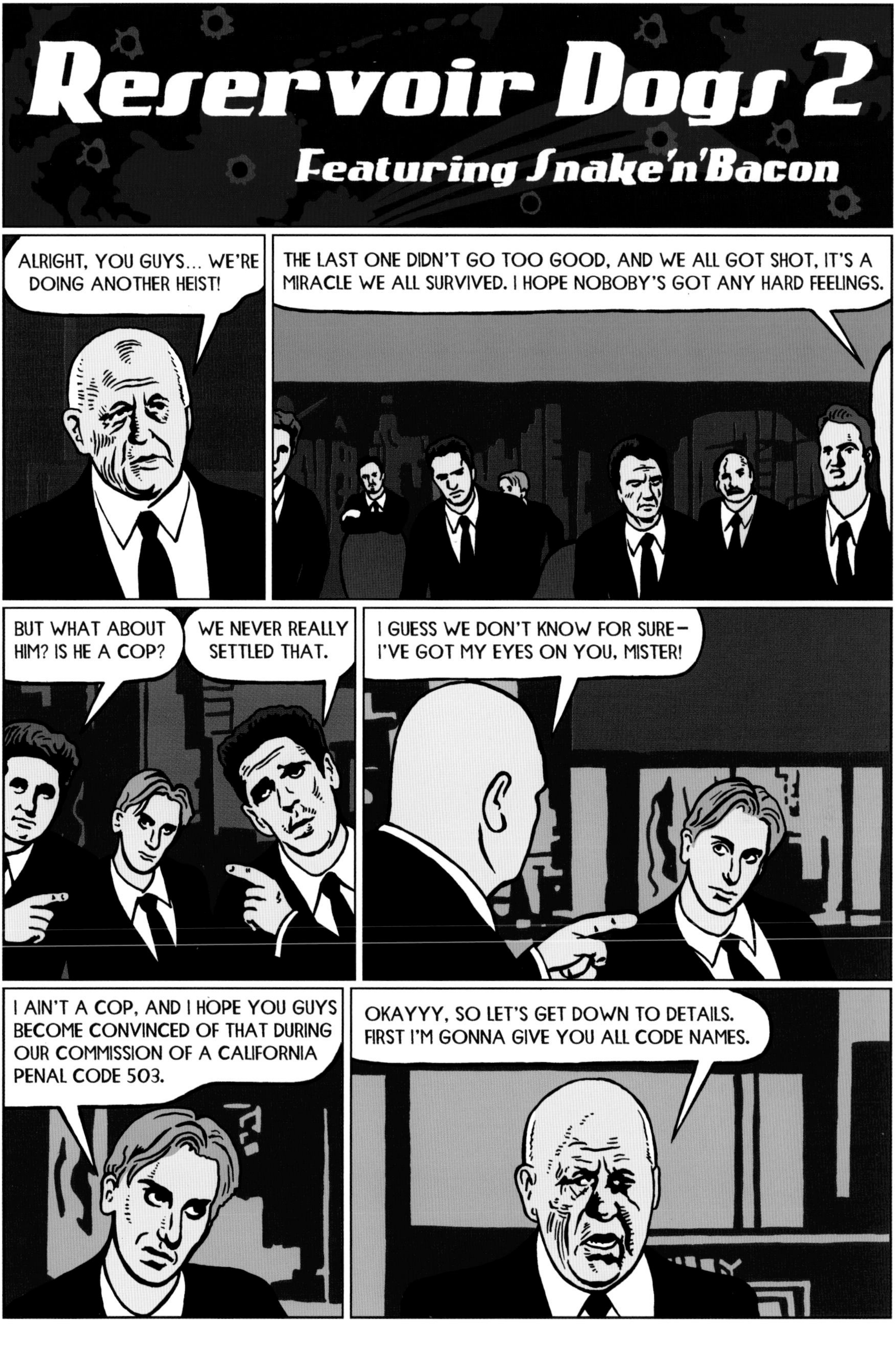
Reservoir Dogs 2
Featuring Snake'n'Bacon
ALRIGHT, YOU GUYS... WE'RE DOING ANOTHER HEIST!
THE LAST ONE DIDN'T GO TOO GOOD, AND WE ALL GOT SHOT, IT'S A MIRACLE WE ALL SURVIVED. I HOPE NOBOBY'S GOT ANY HARD FEELINGS.
BUT WHAT ABOUT HIM? IS HE A COP?
WE NEVER REALLY SETTLED THAT.
I GUESS WE DON'T KNOW FOR SURE— I'VE GOT MY EYES ON YOU, MISTER!
I AIN'T A COP, AND I HOPE YOU GUYS BECOME CONVINCED OF THAT DURING OUR COMMISSION OF A CALIFORNIA PENAL CODE 503.
OKAYYY, SO LET'S GET DOWN TO DETAILS. FIRST I'M GONNA GIVE YOU ALL CODE NAMES.

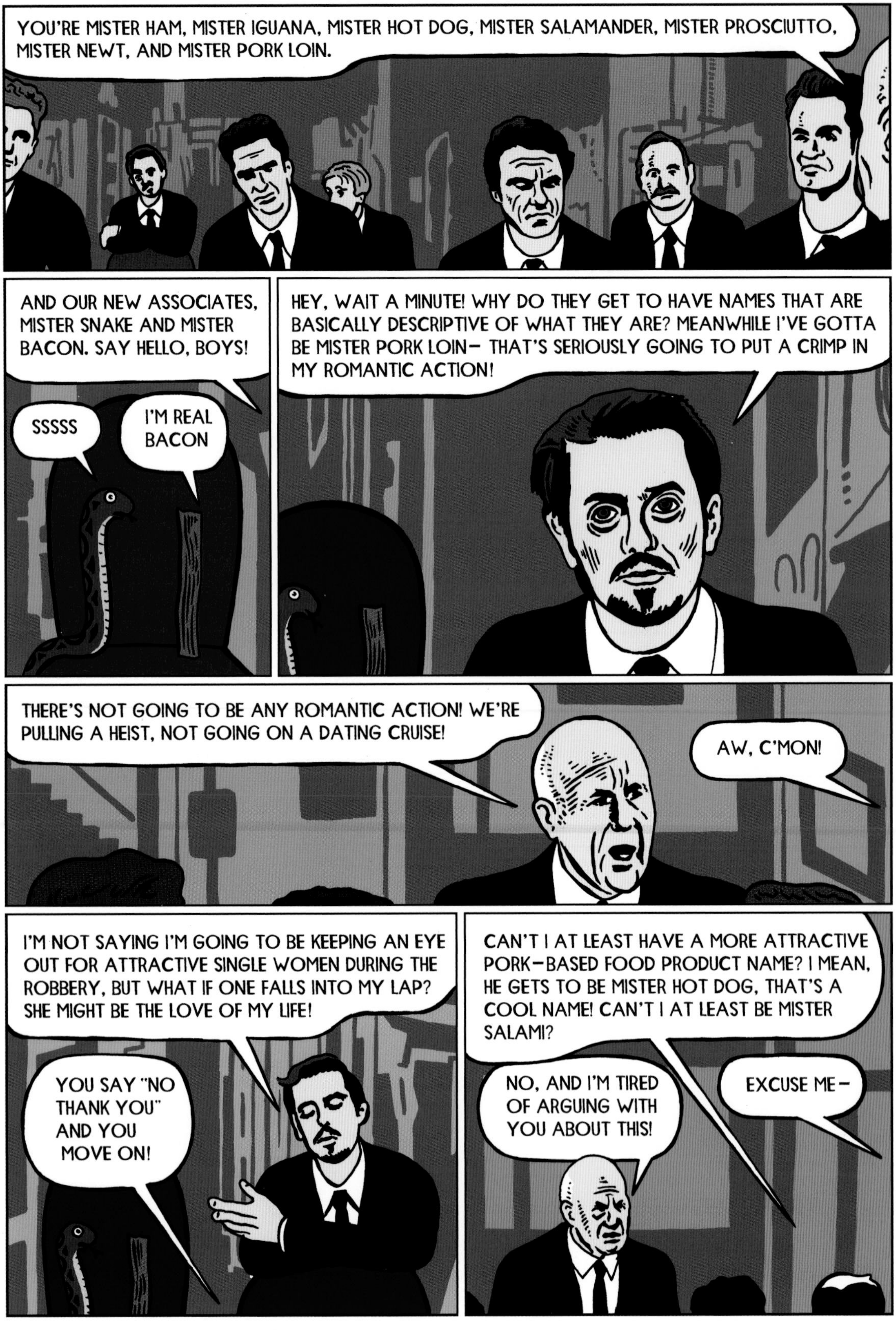
YOU'RE MISTER HAM, MISTER IGUANA, MISTER HOT DOG, MISTER SALAMANDER, MISTER PROSCIUTTO, MISTER NEWT, AND MISTER PORK LOIN.
AND OUR NEW ASSOCIATES, MISTER SNAKE AND MISTER BACON. SAY HELLO, BOYS!
SSSSS
I'M REAL BACON
HEY, WAIT A MINUTE! WHY DO THEY GET TO HAVE NAMES THAT ARE BASICALLY DESCRIPTIVE OF WHAT THEY ARE? MEANWHILE I'VE GOTTA BE MISTER PORK LOIN— THAT'S SERIOUSLY GOING TO PUT A CRIMP IN MY ROMANTIC ACTION!
THERE'S NOT GOING TO BE ANY ROMANTIC ACTION! WE'RE PULLING A HEIST, NOT GOING ON A DATING CRUISE!
AW, C'MON!
I'M NOT SAYING I'M GOING TO BE KEEPING AN EYE OUT FOR ATTRACTIVE SINGLE WOMEN DURING THE ROBBERY, BUT WHAT IF ONE FALLS INTO MY LAP? SHE MIGHT BE THE LOVE OF MY LIFE!
YOU SAY "NO THANK YOU" AND YOU MOVE ON!
CAN'T I AT LEAST HAVE A MORE ATTRACTIVE PORK—BASED FOOD PRODUCT NAME? I MEAN, HE GETS TO BE MISTER HOT DOG, THAT'S A COOL NAME! CAN'T I AT LEAST BE MISTER SALAMI?
NO, AND I'M TIRED OF ARGUING WITH YOU ABOUT THIS!
EXCUSE ME—

YES?

ARE WE GOING TO ELUDE PURSUERS IN BRIGHTLY-COLORED MINICARS WHILE COCKNEY MUSIC PLAYS?

NAH— WE'RE NOT GONNA DO THAT!

THEN I'M IN THE WRONG PLACE— EXCUSE ME.

WHAT THE HELL? THIS IS A HEIST MEETING. WE DON'T JUST LET CIVILIANS WALK IN OFF THE STREET!

THERE ARE CIVILIANS HERE? THAT'S REALLY UNPROFESSIONAL.

THERE'S ANOTHER ONE! HEY YOU! YEAH, I'M TALKING TO YOU!

WHO, ME?

YEAH, YOU! THIS AIN'T A BEACH CLUB. THIS AIN'T A SAUNA. YOU CAN SEE WE'RE ALL FULLY DRESSED!

SO WHY ARE YOU SITTING THERE IN YOUR UNDERWEAR. YOU HOPING TO START A TREND? WE'RE NOT INTERESTED!

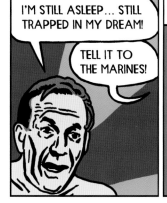

I'M STILL ASLEEP... STILL TRAPPED IN MY DREAM!

TELL IT TO THE MARINES!

THIS ISN'T RESTFUL! I'VE GOTTA FIND A PAIR OF PANTS!

YOU LEAVING? GOOD! WE'VE GOT A HEIST TO DISCUSS!

OKAY, NOW HE'S GONE I'VE GOT T-SHIRTS FOR EVERYBODY. HOPE I GOT YOUR SIZES RIGHT...

RESERVOIR DOGS

NICE, HUH? MY NEPHEW DID THE GRAPHICS.

WHOA, WHOA, WHOA WHOA. YELLOW? I WOULD MUCH PREFER A BLACK SHIRT.

IN HERE, QUINCE!

SAM? BOY, AM I GLAD TO SEE YOU!

COME STRAIGHT THROUGH QUINCE...

AND, ACCEPTING THE NOBEL PRIZE FOR FORENSIC MEDICINE... QUINCY MAURICE EDMUND QUINCY, M.E.!...

UH, THANKS... FOR THIS...

BOOOOOO!

GET SOME PANTS, YOU BUM!

NOBEL

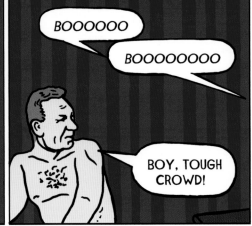

BOOOOOO

BOOOOOOOO

BOY, TOUGH CROWD!

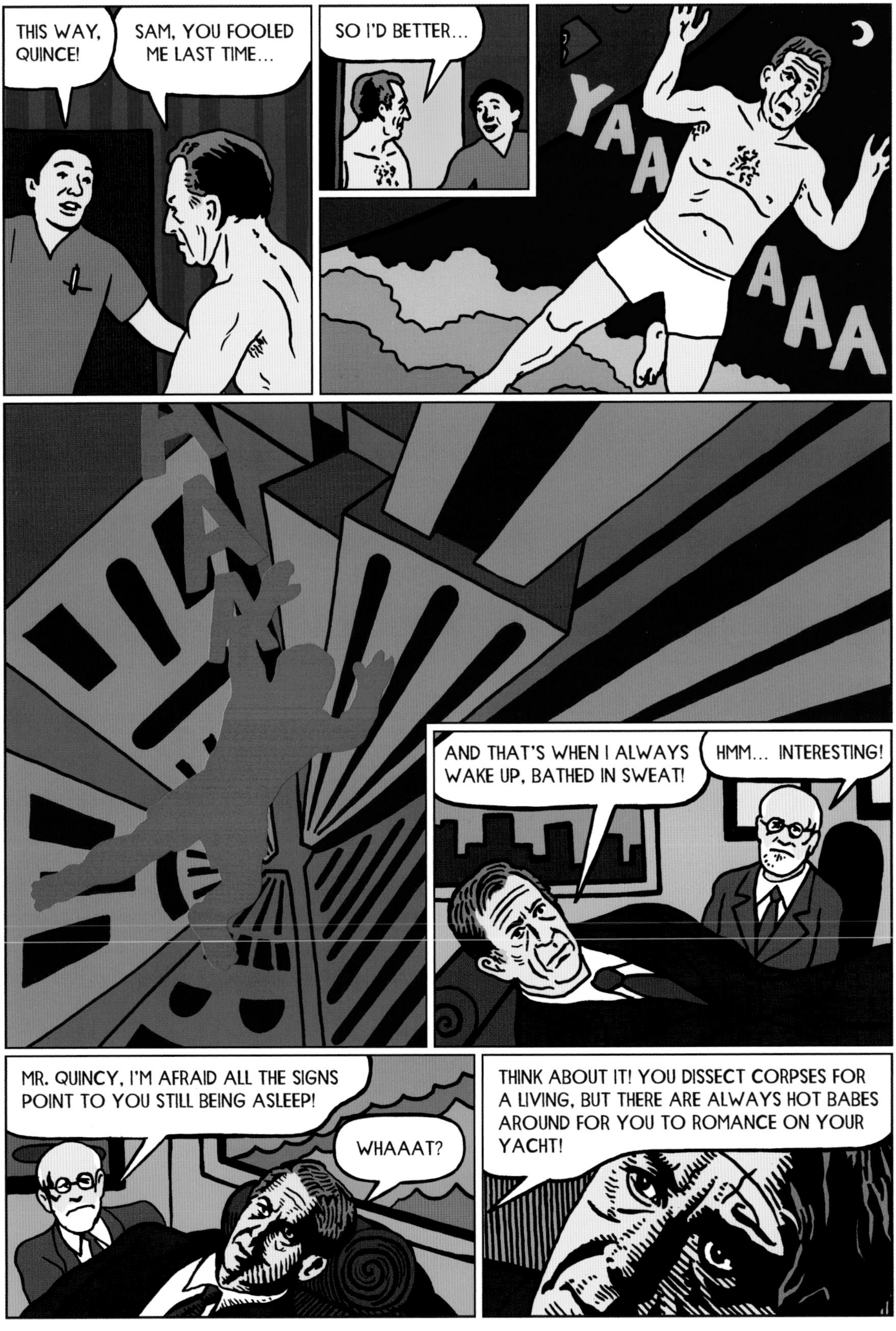
THIS WAY, QUINCE!
SAM, YOU FOOLED ME LAST TIME...
SO I'D BETTER...
YAAA AAAA
AND THAT'S WHEN I ALWAYS WAKE UP, BATHED IN SWEAT!
HMM... INTERESTING!
MR. QUINCY, I'M AFRAID ALL THE SIGNS POINT TO YOU STILL BEING ASLEEP!
WHAAAT?
THINK ABOUT IT! YOU DISSECT CORPSES FOR A LIVING, BUT THERE ARE ALWAYS HOT BABES AROUND FOR YOU TO ROMANCE ON YOUR YACHT!

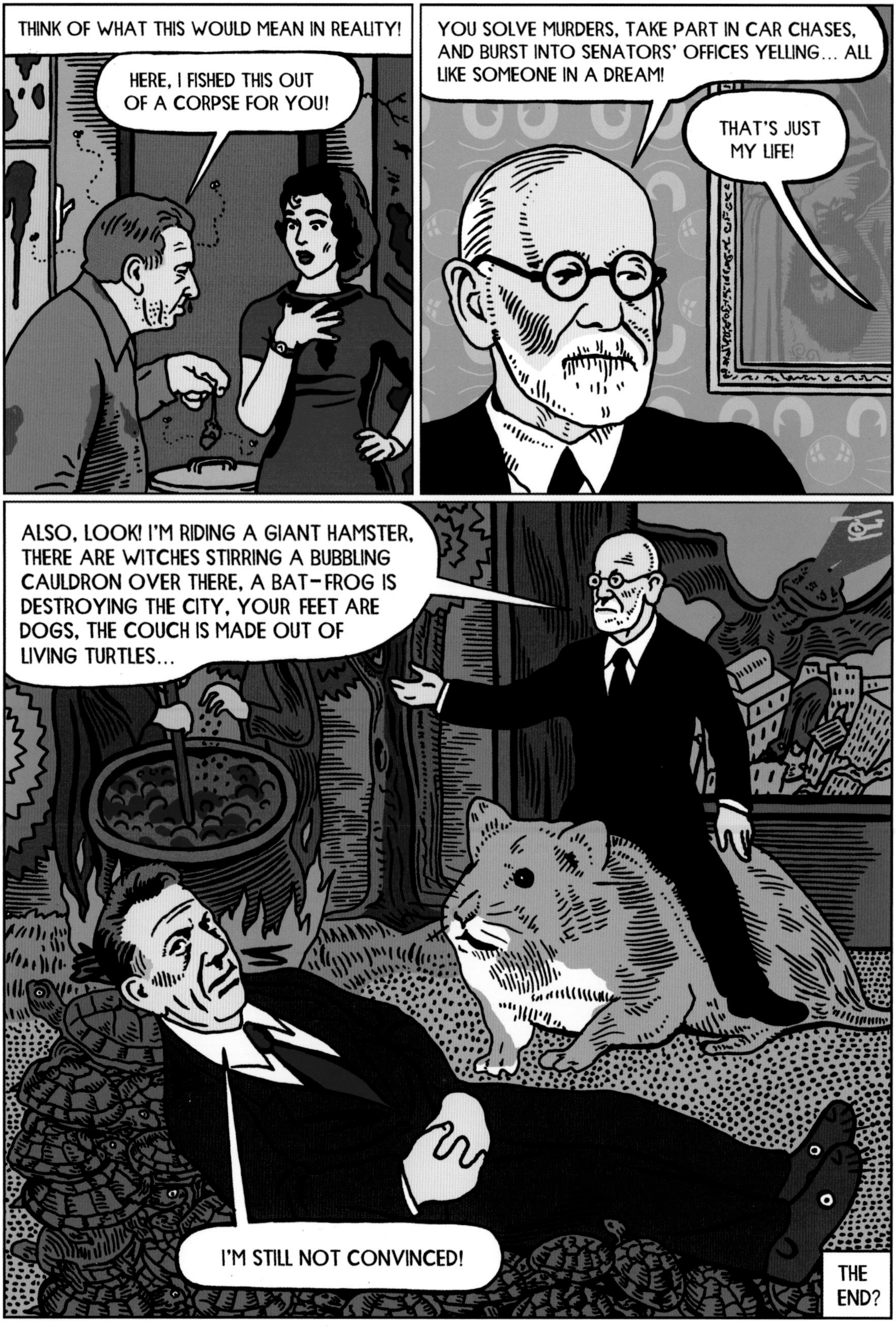
THINK OF WHAT THIS WOULD MEAN IN REALITY!
HERE, I FISHED THIS OUT OF A CORPSE FOR YOU!
YOU SOLVE MURDERS, TAKE PART IN CAR CHASES, AND BURST INTO SENATORS' OFFICES YELLING... ALL LIKE SOMEONE IN A DREAM!
THAT'S JUST MY LIFE!
ALSO, LOOK! I'M RIDING A GIANT HAMSTER, THERE ARE WITCHES STIRRING A BUBBLING CAULDRON OVER THERE, A BAT-FROG IS DESTROYING THE CITY, YOUR FEET ARE DOGS, THE COUCH IS MADE OUT OF LIVING TURTLES...
I'M STILL NOT CONVINCED!
THE END?

A Voyage to Narnia

I'm sorry I shouted like Quincy. I'm leaving now and going far away...

...to the fairytaleland of Narnia, an entrance to which lies in your closet. Farewell, my dear!

Later-

...and with those words he was gone, vanished into the magical recesses of my closet. I never knew he was so romantic!

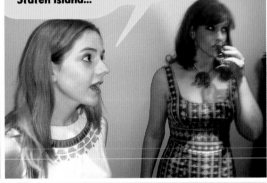

Maybe he'll return some day, laden with elf jewels, and we'll use them to put a down payment on a duplex in Staten Island...

Near where my mother lives...

Kate, you should've gone into that closet with him! He's going to be meeting all kinds of magical women in there! You blew it!

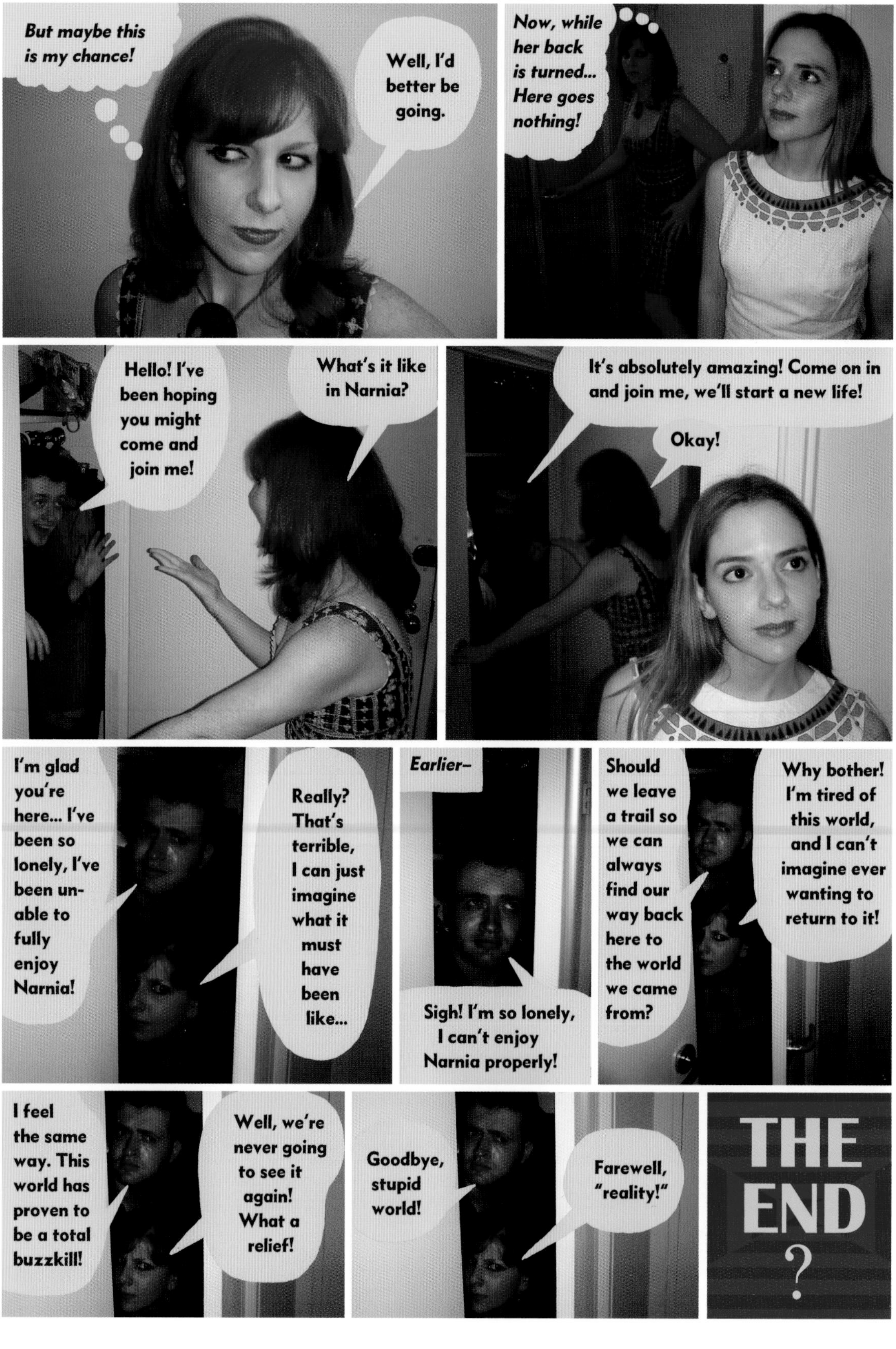
But maybe this is my chance!
Well, I'd better be going.
Now, while her back is turned... Here goes nothing!
Hello! I've been hoping you might come and join me!
What's it like in Narnia?
It's absolutely amazing! Come on in and join me, we'll start a new life!
Okay!
I'm glad you're here... I've been so lonely, I've been un-able to fully enjoy Narnia!
Really? That's terrible, I can just imagine what it must have been like...
Earlier–
Sigh! I'm so lonely, I can't enjoy Narnia properly!
Should we leave a trail so we can always find our way back here to the world we came from?
Why bother! I'm tired of this world, and I can't imagine ever wanting to return to it!
I feel the same way. This world has proven to be a total buzzkill!
Well, we're never going to see it again! What a relief!
Goodbye, stupid world!
Farewell, "reality!"
THE END ?

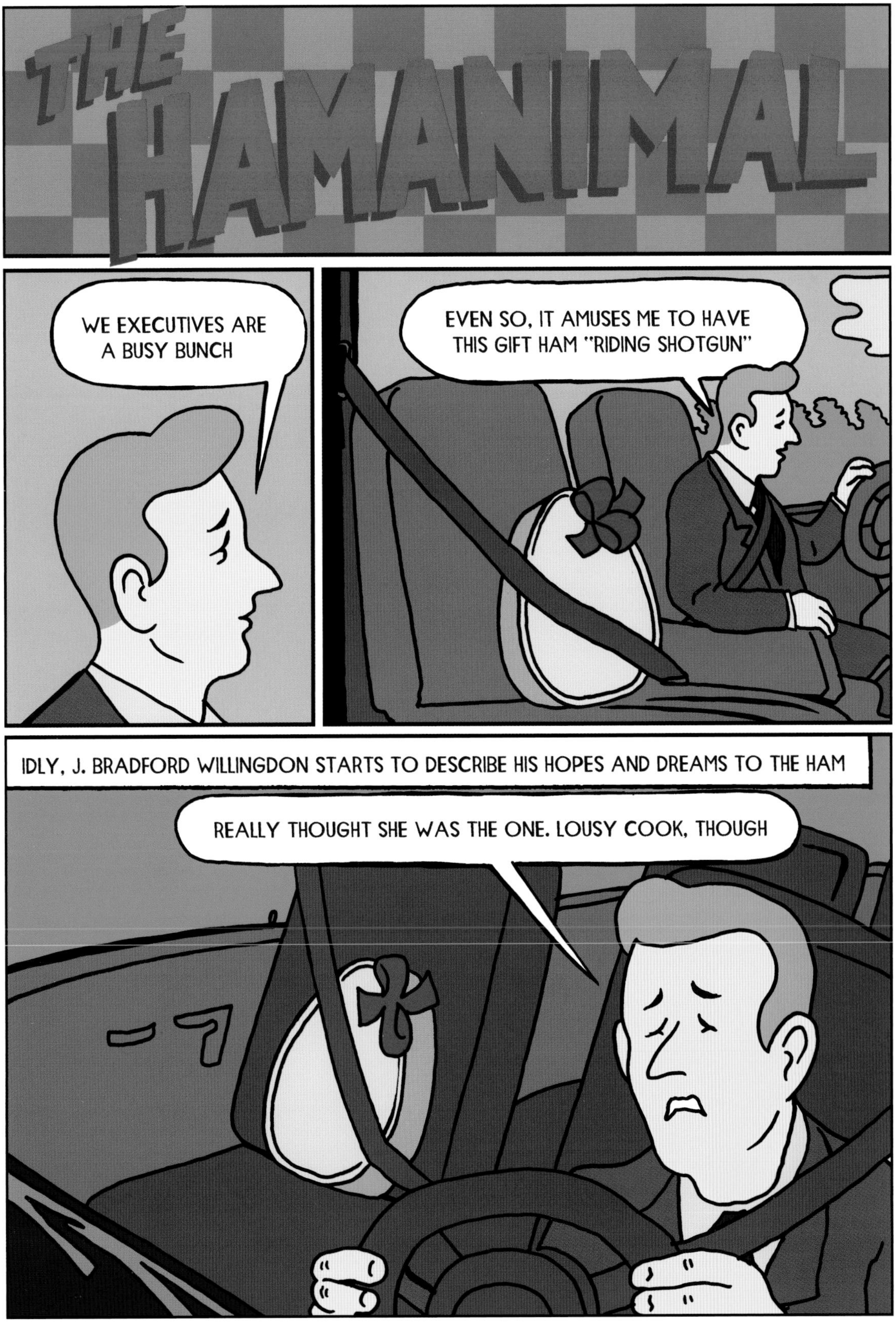
THE HAMANIMAL
WE EXECUTIVES ARE A BUSY BUNCH
EVEN SO, IT AMUSES ME TO HAVE THIS GIFT HAM "RIDING SHOTGUN"
IDLY, J. BRADFORD WILLINGDON STARTS TO DESCRIBE HIS HOPES AND DREAMS TO THE HAM
REALLY THOUGHT SHE WAS THE ONE. LOUSY COOK, THOUGH

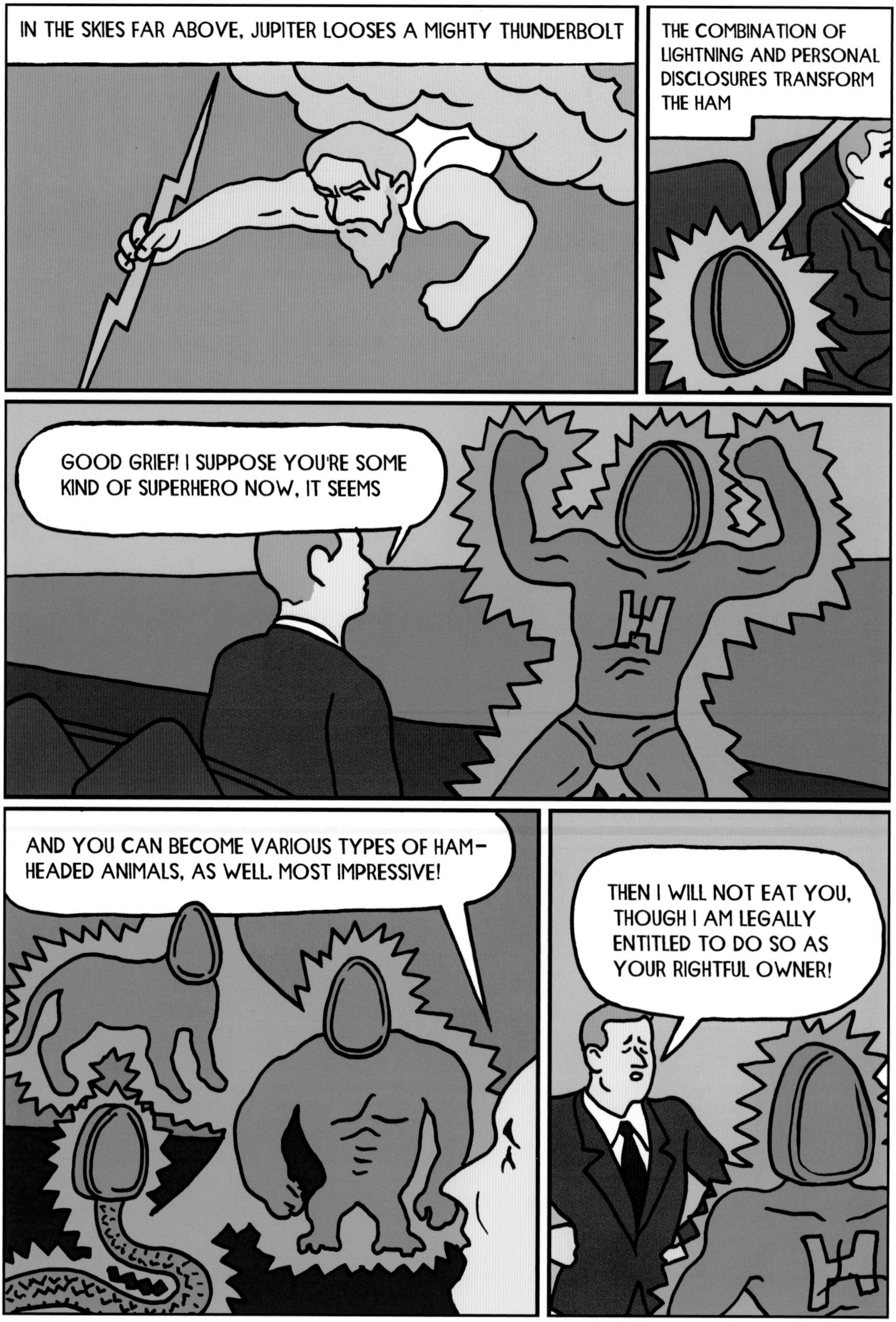
IN THE SKIES FAR ABOVE, JUPITER LOOSES A MIGHTY THUNDERBOLT
THE COMBINATION OF LIGHTNING AND PERSONAL DISCLOSURES TRANSFORM THE HAM
GOOD GRIEF! I SUPPOSE YOU'RE SOME KIND OF SUPERHERO NOW, IT SEEMS
AND YOU CAN BECOME VARIOUS TYPES OF HAM-HEADED ANIMALS, AS WELL. MOST IMPRESSIVE!
THEN I WILL NOT EAT YOU, THOUGH I AM LEGALLY ENTITLED TO DO SO AS YOUR RIGHTFUL OWNER!

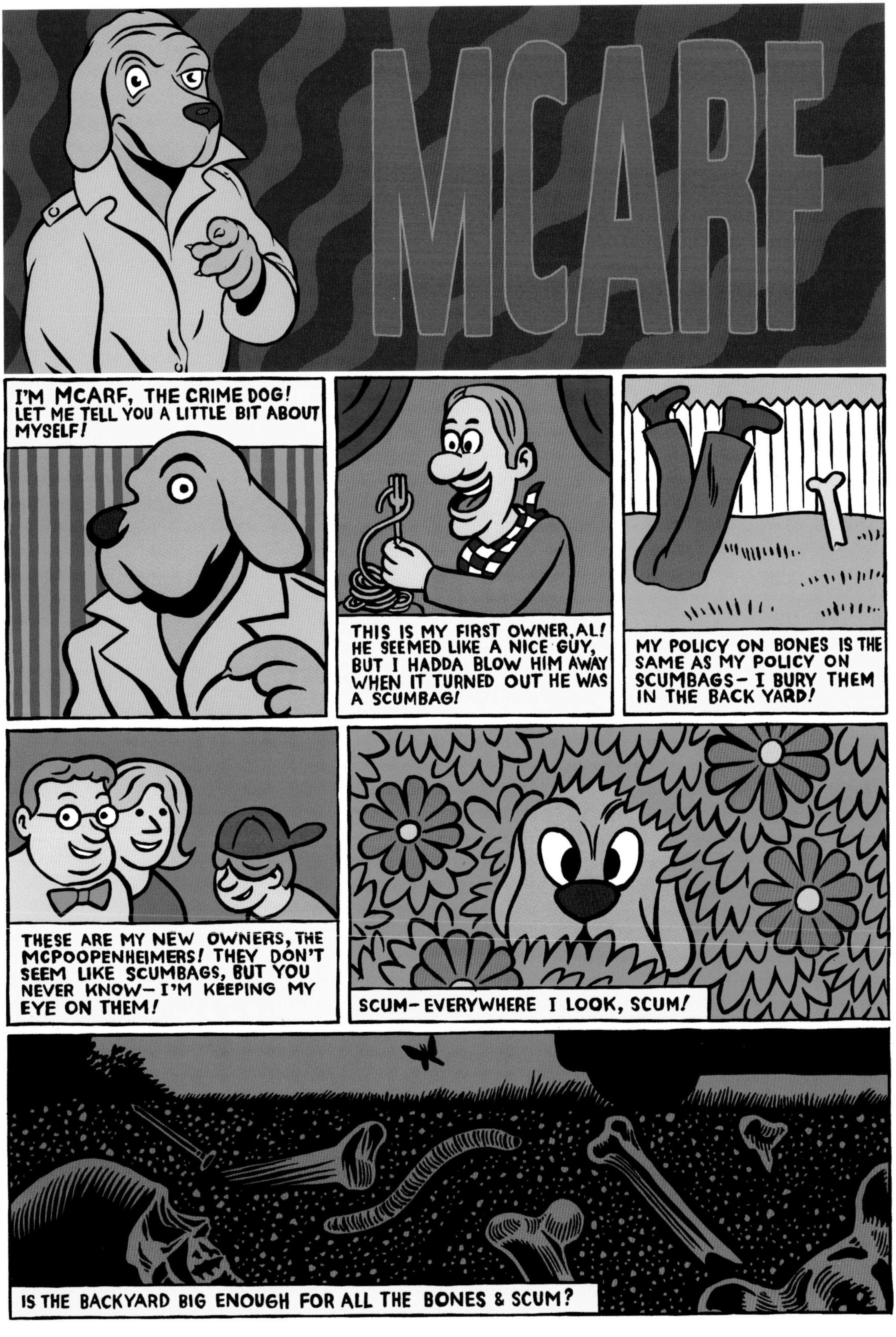
MCARF
I'M MCARF, THE CRIME DOG! LET ME TELL YOU A LITTLE BIT ABOUT MYSELF!
THIS IS MY FIRST OWNER, AL! HE SEEMED LIKE A NICE GUY, BUT I HADDA BLOW HIM AWAY WHEN IT TURNED OUT HE WAS A SCUMBAG!
MY POLICY ON BONES IS THE SAME AS MY POLICY ON SCUMBAGS– I BURY THEM IN THE BACK YARD!
THESE ARE MY NEW OWNERS, THE MCPOOPENHEIMERS! THEY DON'T SEEM LIKE SCUMBAGS, BUT YOU NEVER KNOW– I'M KEEPING MY EYE ON THEM!
SCUM– EVERYWHERE I LOOK, SCUM!
IS THE BACKYARD BIG ENOUGH FOR ALL THE BONES & SCUM?

I CAN'T REST WHILE THERE'S SCUM OUT THERE LIKE THE ALPHABET SOUP KILLER, WHO SPELLS OUT TAUNTING MESSAGES USING ALPHABET SOUP.

OR COUNTESS FLUFFY, MY ARCH-NEMESIS. I KNOW HER DEVIOUS MIND, INSIDE OUT, FOR WE WERE ONCE MARRIED. THE SEX WAS *DY-NO-MITE!*

LAST MONTH I FACED OFF AGAINST MOB BOSS TONY BALONEY... I BIT HIM ON THE CROTCH, REALLY GOOD!

THEN HIS OWN SOLDIERS FINISHED THE JOB — BLEW HIM AWAY WHILE HE WAS EATING A BIG, SPICY ITALIAN DINNER!

SCUM TURN MY STOMACH. YET I SPEND MOST OF MY LIFE AMONGST THEM...

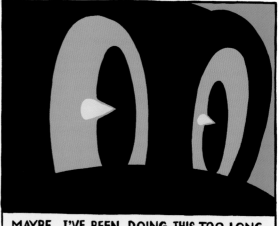

MAYBE I'VE BEEN DOING THIS TOO LONG. THE PILLS AREN'T HELPING...

TWAIN & EINSTEIN in "FAMILY AFFAIRS"

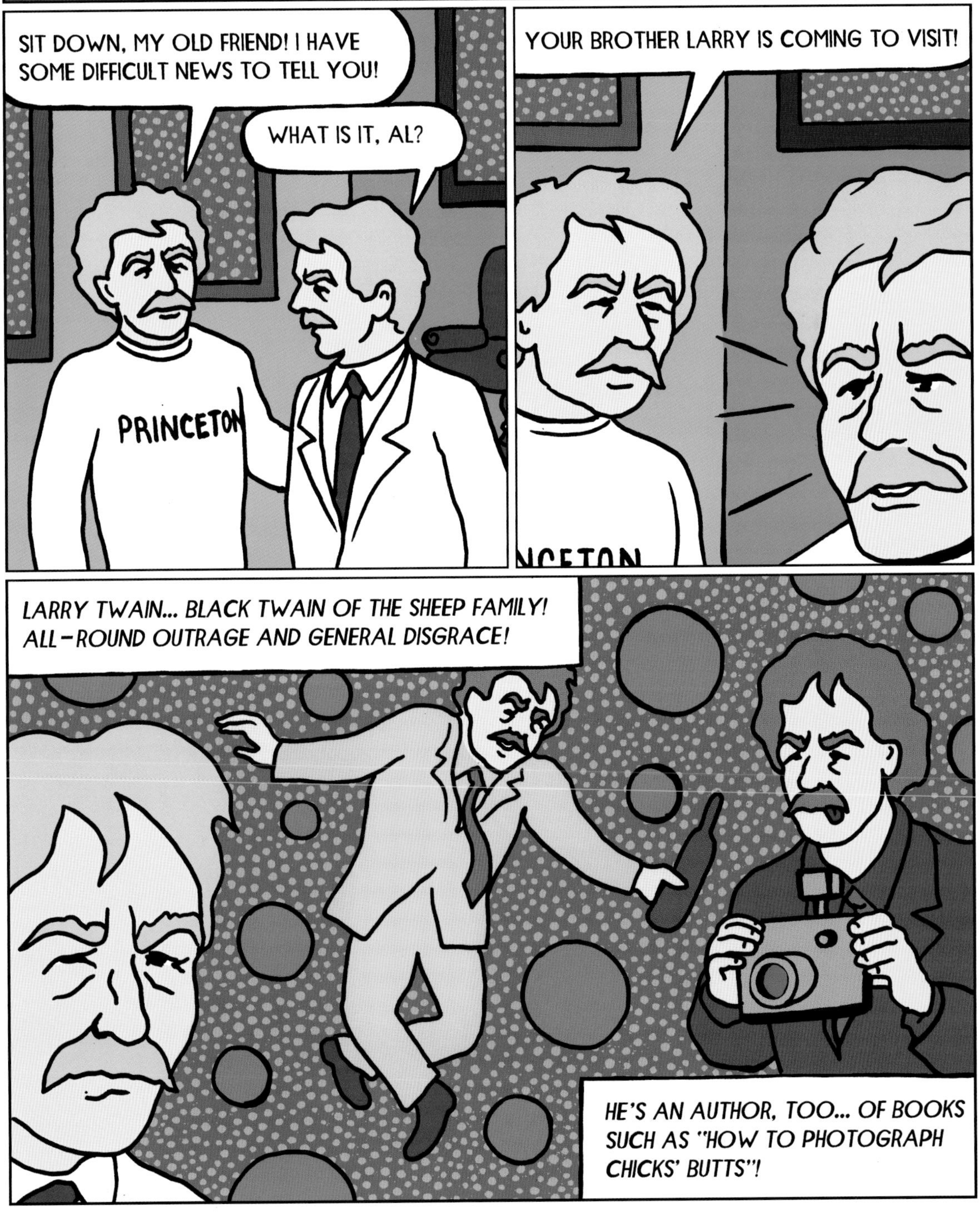
SIT DOWN, MY OLD FRIEND! I HAVE SOME DIFFICULT NEWS TO TELL YOU!
WHAT IS IT, AL?
PRINCETON
YOUR BROTHER LARRY IS COMING TO VISIT!
LARRY TWAIN... BLACK TWAIN OF THE SHEEP FAMILY! ALL-ROUND OUTRAGE AND GENERAL DISGRACE!
HE'S AN AUTHOR, TOO... OF BOOKS SUCH AS "HOW TO PHOTOGRAPH CHICKS' BUTTS"!

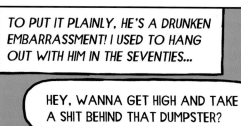

TO PUT IT PLAINLY, HE'S A DRUNKEN EMBARRASSMENT! I USED TO HANG OUT WITH HIM IN THE SEVENTIES...

HEY, WANNA GET HIGH AND TAKE A SHIT BEHIND THAT DUMPSTER?

WHY NOT? IT'S THE SEVENTIES!

WHEN NEXT I SAW HIM, IT WAS THE NINETIES...

THESE ARE DIFFERENT TIMES NOW, LARRY! I'D BETTER TAKE A RAIN CHECK!

AND I HAVEN'T SEEN HIM SINCE THEN!

SIT DOWN EVEN MORE, FRIEND TWAIN, THERE'S STILL MORE I MUST TELL YOU!

YOU SEE, LARRY TWAIN DOESN'T EXIST! YOUR MIND MADE HIM UP!

WHAT? BUT ALL THE PHOTOGRAPHS...

EXAMINE THEM AGAIN, SAM... THEY'RE ALL OF YOU WITH YOUR ARMS AROUND THIN AIR!

THE STRESS... THE CELEBRITY... YOUR MIND NEEDED A WAY TO ESCAPE! YOU "BECAME" LARRY TWAIN, BY DYING YOUR HAIR AND ASSUMING AN OBNOXIOUS ATTITUDE! NOW YOU MUST EXCUSE ME... I HAVE CORN ON THE STOVE!

THE END

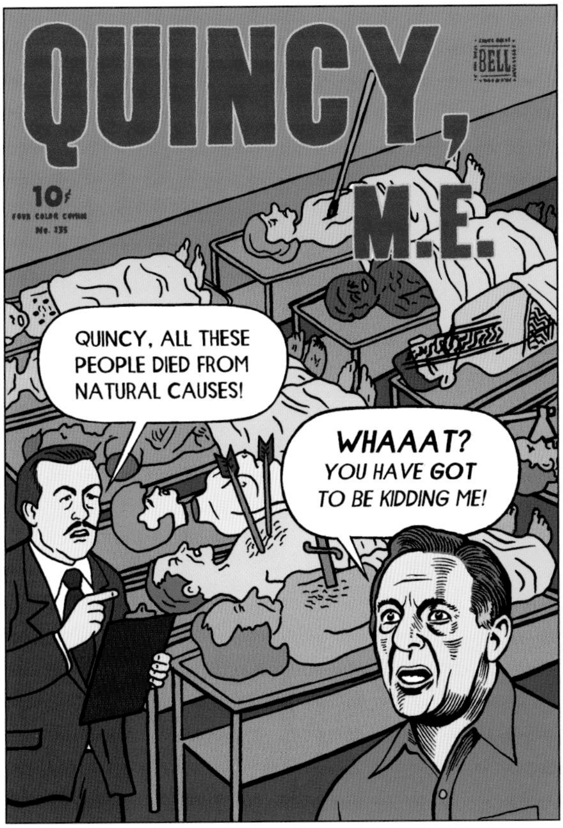
QUINCY, M.E.
BELL
10¢
FOUR COLOR COMICS
No. 135
QUINCY, ALL THESE PEOPLE DIED FROM NATURAL CAUSES!
WHAAAT? YOU HAVE GOT TO BE KIDDING ME!

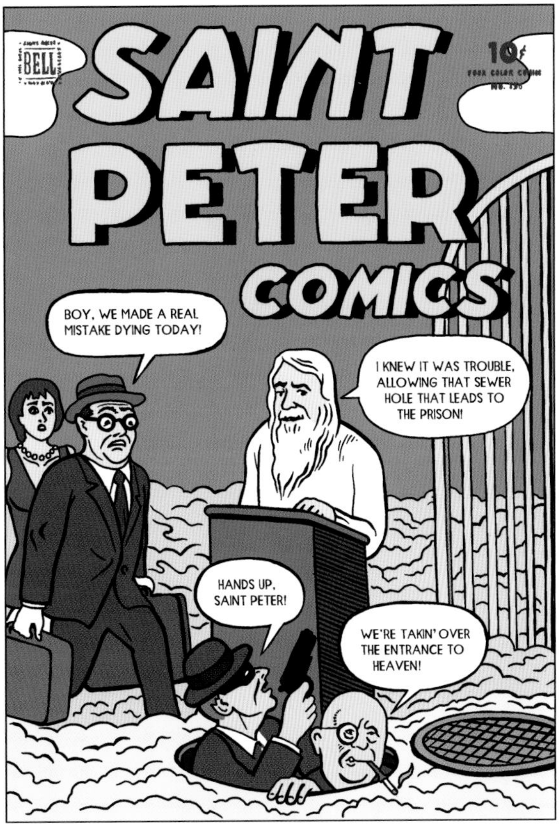
BELL
SAINT PETER COMICS
10¢
FOUR COLOR COMICS
BOY, WE MADE A REAL MISTAKE DYING TODAY!
I KNEW IT WAS TROUBLE, ALLOWING THAT SEWER HOLE THAT LEADS TO THE PRISON!
HANDS UP, SAINT PETER!
WE'RE TAKIN' OVER THE ENTRANCE TO HEAVEN!

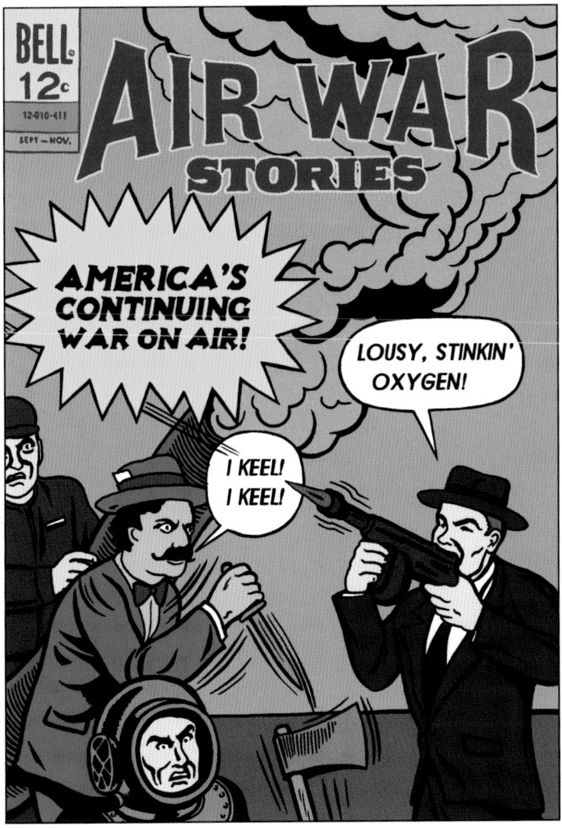
BELL
12¢
12-010-411
SEPT.—NOV.
AIR WAR STORIES
AMERICA'S CONTINUING WAR ON AIR!
LOUSY, STINKIN' OXYGEN!
I KEEL! I KEEL!

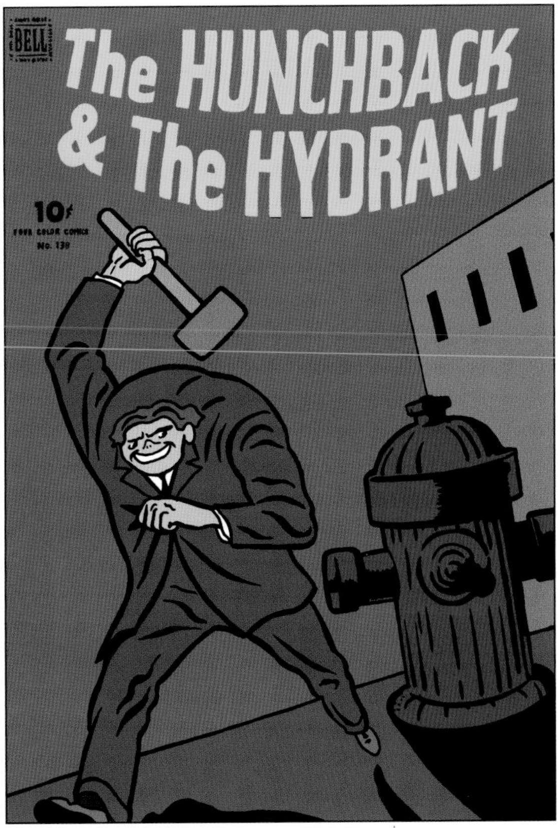
BELL
The HUNCHBACK & The HYDRANT
10¢
FOUR COLOR COMICS
No. 138

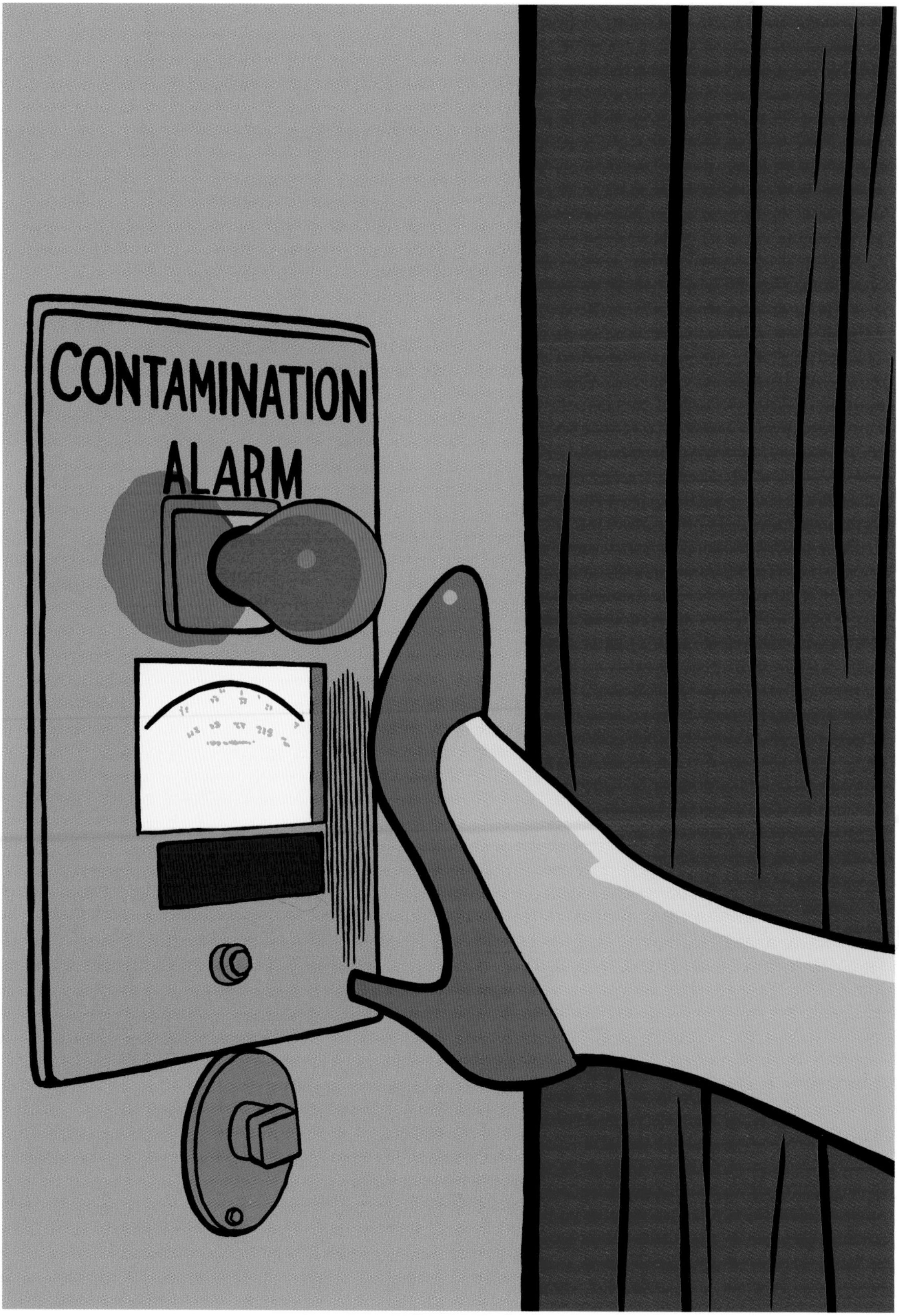
CONTAMINATION
ALARM

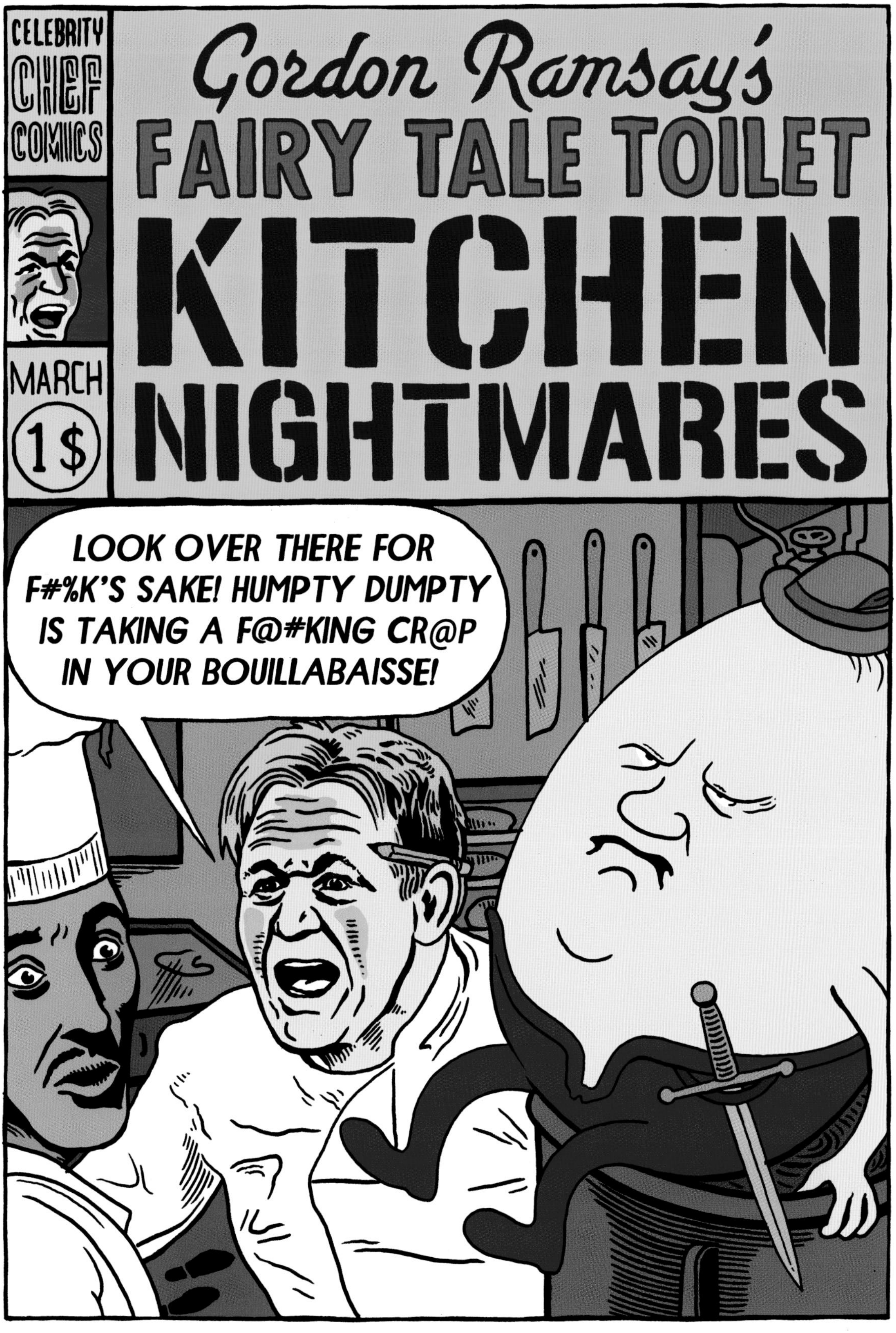
CELEBRITY CHEF COMICS
Gordon Ramsay's
FAIRY TALE TOILET
KITCHEN NIGHTMARES
MARCH
1$
LOOK OVER THERE FOR F#%K'S SAKE! HUMPTY DUMPTY IS TAKING A F@#KING CR@P IN YOUR BOUILLABAISSE!

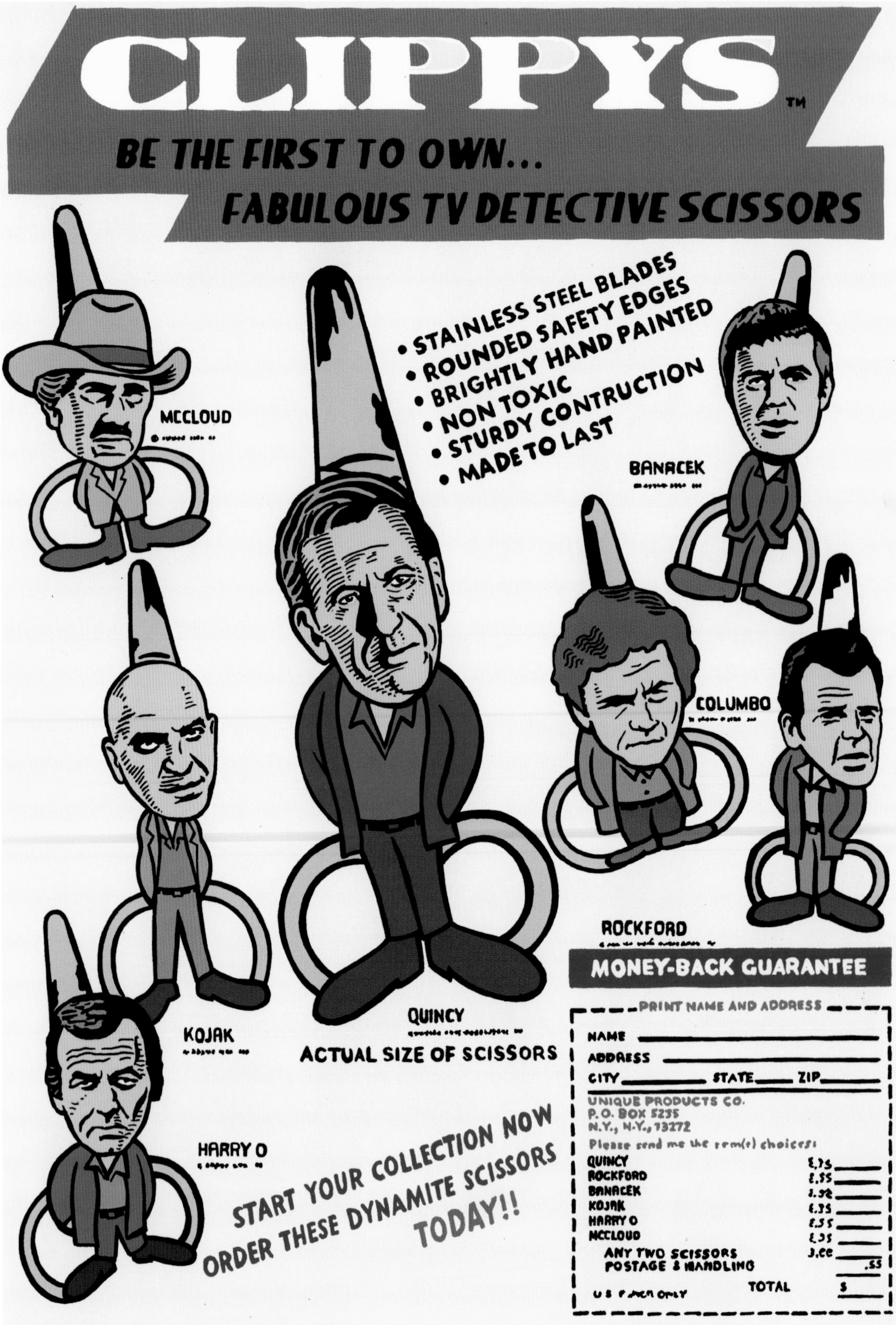

CLIPPYS
TM
BE THE FIRST TO OWN...
FABULOUS TV DETECTIVE SCISSORS
• STAINLESS STEEL BLADES
• ROUNDED SAFETY EDGES
• BRIGHTLY HAND PAINTED
• NON TOXIC
• STURDY CONTRUCTION
• MADE TO LAST
MCCLOUD
BANACEK
COLUMBO
KOJAK
QUINCY
ROCKFORD
HARRY O
ACTUAL SIZE OF SCISSORS
START YOUR COLLECTION NOW
ORDER THESE DYNAMITE SCISSORS
TODAY!!
MONEY-BACK GUARANTEE
PRINT NAME AND ADDRESS
NAME
ADDRESS
CITY
STATE
ZIP
UNIQUE PRODUCTS CO.
P.O. BOX 5235
N.Y., N.Y., 73272
QUINCY
ROCKFORD
BANACEK
KOJAK
HARRY O
MCCLOUD
ANY TWO SCISSORS
POSTAGE & HANDLING
.55
TOTAL
$

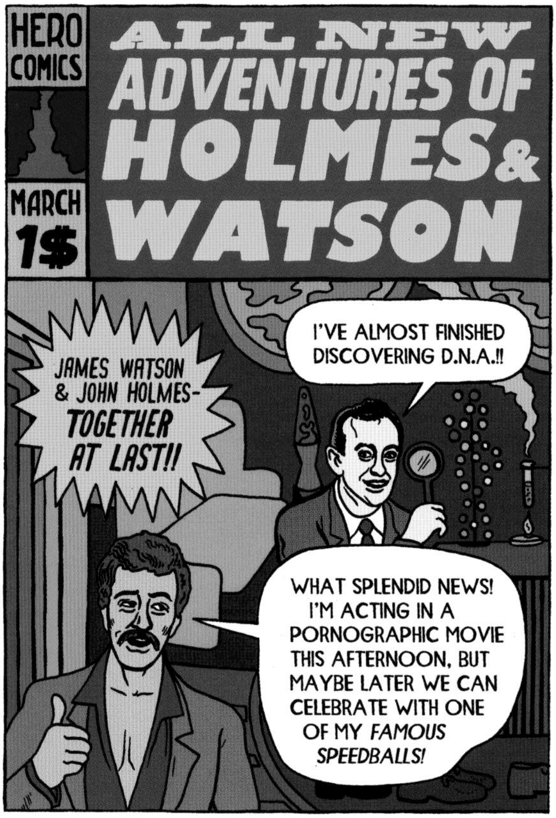
HERO COMICS
ALL NEW ADVENTURES OF HOLMES & WATSON
MARCH 1$
JAMES WATSON & JOHN HOLMES- TOGETHER AT LAST!!
I'VE ALMOST FINISHED DISCOVERING D.N.A.!!
WHAT SPLENDID NEWS! I'M ACTING IN A PORNOGRAPHIC MOVIE THIS AFTERNOON, BUT MAYBE LATER WE CAN CELEBRATE WITH ONE OF MY FAMOUS SPEEDBALLS!
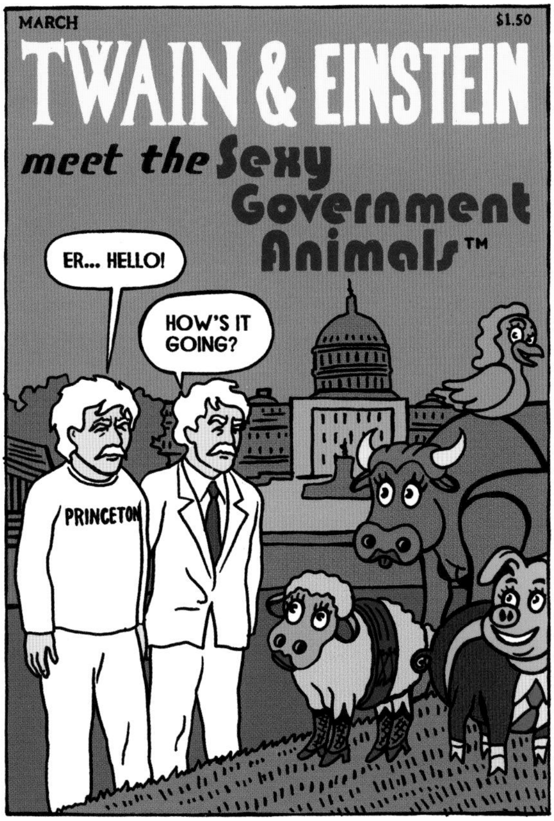
MARCH
$1.50
TWAIN & EINSTEIN
meet the Sexy Government Animals™
ER... HELLO!
HOW'S IT GOING?
PRINCETON
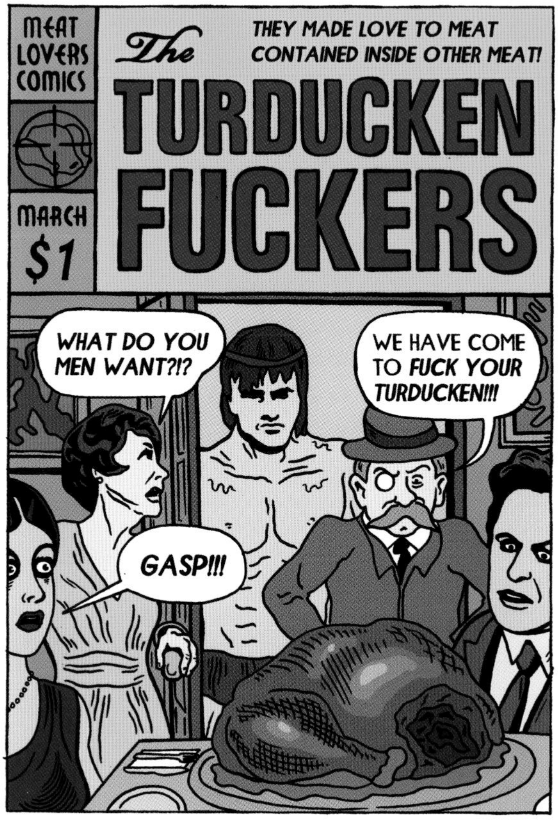
MEAT LOVERS COMICS
The
THEY MADE LOVE TO MEAT CONTAINED INSIDE OTHER MEAT!
TURDUCKEN FUCKERS
MARCH $1
WHAT DO YOU MEN WANT?!?
WE HAVE COME TO FUCK YOUR TURDUCKEN!!!
GASP!!!
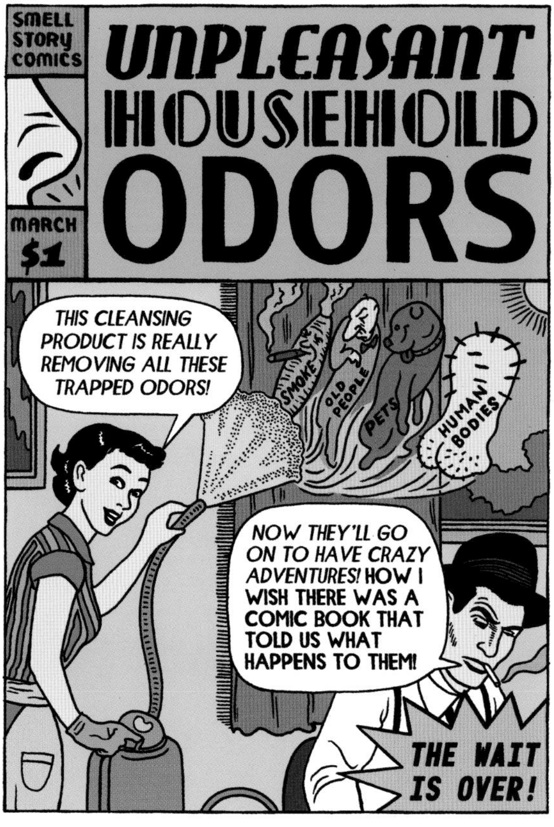
SMELL STORY COMICS
UNPLEASANT HOUSEHOLD ODORS
MARCH $1
THIS CLEANSING PRODUCT IS REALLY REMOVING ALL THESE TRAPPED ODORS!
SMOKE
OLD PEOPLE
PETS
HUMAN BODIES
NOW THEY'LL GO ON TO HAVE CRAZY ADVENTURES! HOW I WISH THERE WAS A COMIC BOOK THAT TOLD US WHAT HAPPENS TO THEM!
THE WAIT IS OVER!

BUDDY BAKER in the 25TH CENTURY

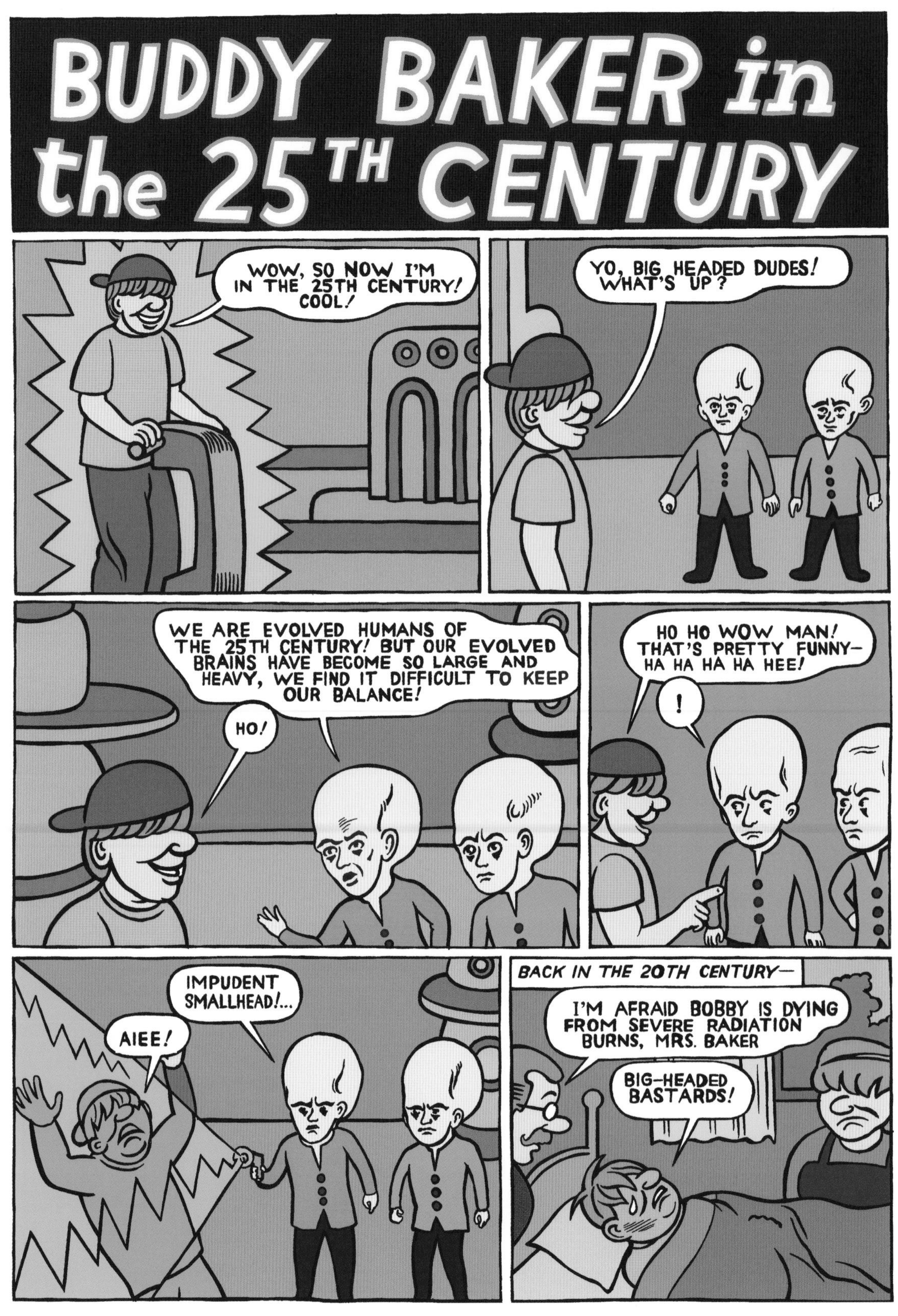

WOW, SO NOW I'M IN THE 25TH CENTURY! COOL!
YO, BIG HEADED DUDES! WHAT'S UP?
WE ARE EVOLVED HUMANS OF THE 25TH CENTURY! BUT OUR EVOLVED BRAINS HAVE BECOME SO LARGE AND HEAVY, WE FIND IT DIFFICULT TO KEEP OUR BALANCE!
HO!
HO HO WOW MAN! THAT'S PRETTY FUNNY— HA HA HA HA HEE!
!
IMPUDENT SMALLHEAD!...
AIEE!
BACK IN THE 20TH CENTURY—
I'M AFRAID BOBBY IS DYING FROM SEVERE RADIATION BURNS, MRS. BAKER
BIG-HEADED BASTARDS!

BILLY & THE GIANT GANGSTER

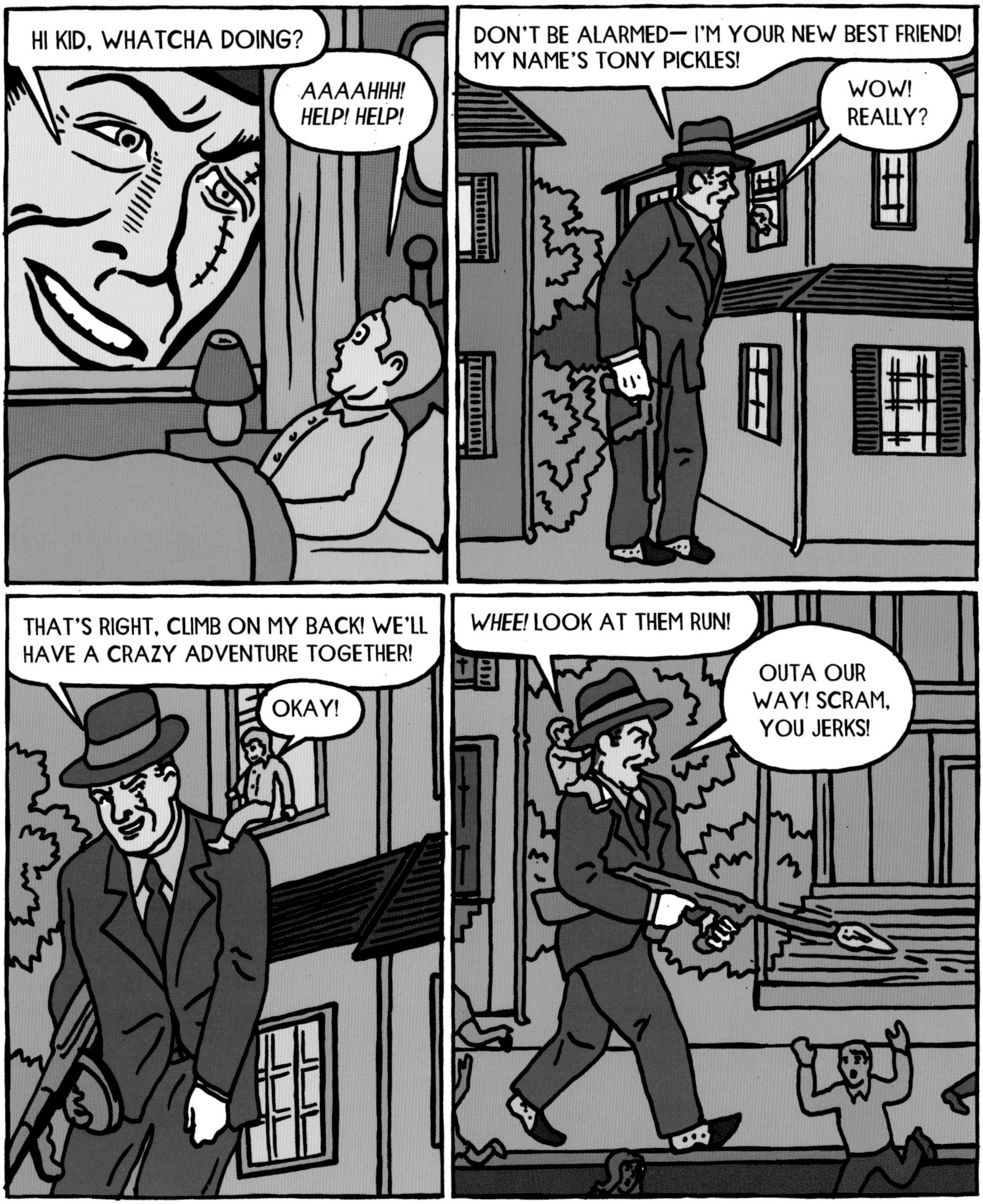
HI KID, WHATCHA DOING?
AAAAHHH! HELP! HELP!
DON'T BE ALARMED— I'M YOUR NEW BEST FRIEND! MY NAME'S TONY PICKLES!
WOW! REALLY?
THAT'S RIGHT, CLIMB ON MY BACK! WE'LL HAVE A CRAZY ADVENTURE TOGETHER!
OKAY!
WHEE! LOOK AT THEM RUN!
OUTA OUR WAY! SCRAM, YOU JERKS!

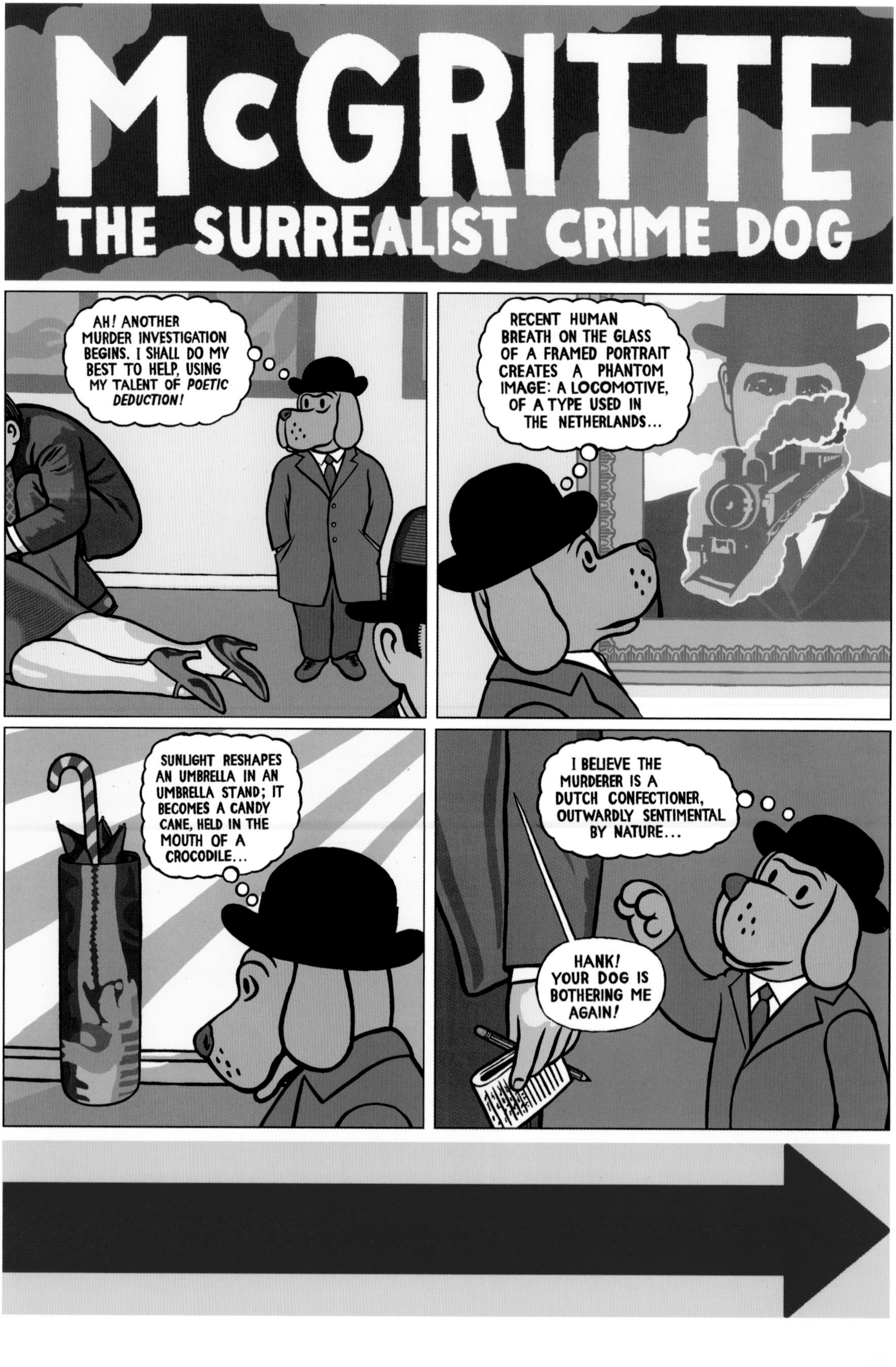
McGRITTE
THE SURREALIST CRIME DOG
AH! ANOTHER MURDER INVESTIGATION BEGINS. I SHALL DO MY BEST TO HELP, USING MY TALENT OF *POETIC DEDUCTION!*
RECENT HUMAN BREATH ON THE GLASS OF A FRAMED PORTRAIT CREATES A PHANTOM IMAGE: A LOCOMOTIVE, OF A TYPE USED IN THE NETHERLANDS...
SUNLIGHT RESHAPES AN UMBRELLA IN AN UMBRELLA STAND; IT BECOMES A CANDY CANE, HELD IN THE MOUTH OF A CROCODILE...
I BELIEVE THE MURDERER IS A DUTCH CONFECTIONER, OUTWARDLY SENTIMENTAL BY NATURE...
HANK! YOUR DOG IS BOTHERING ME AGAIN!

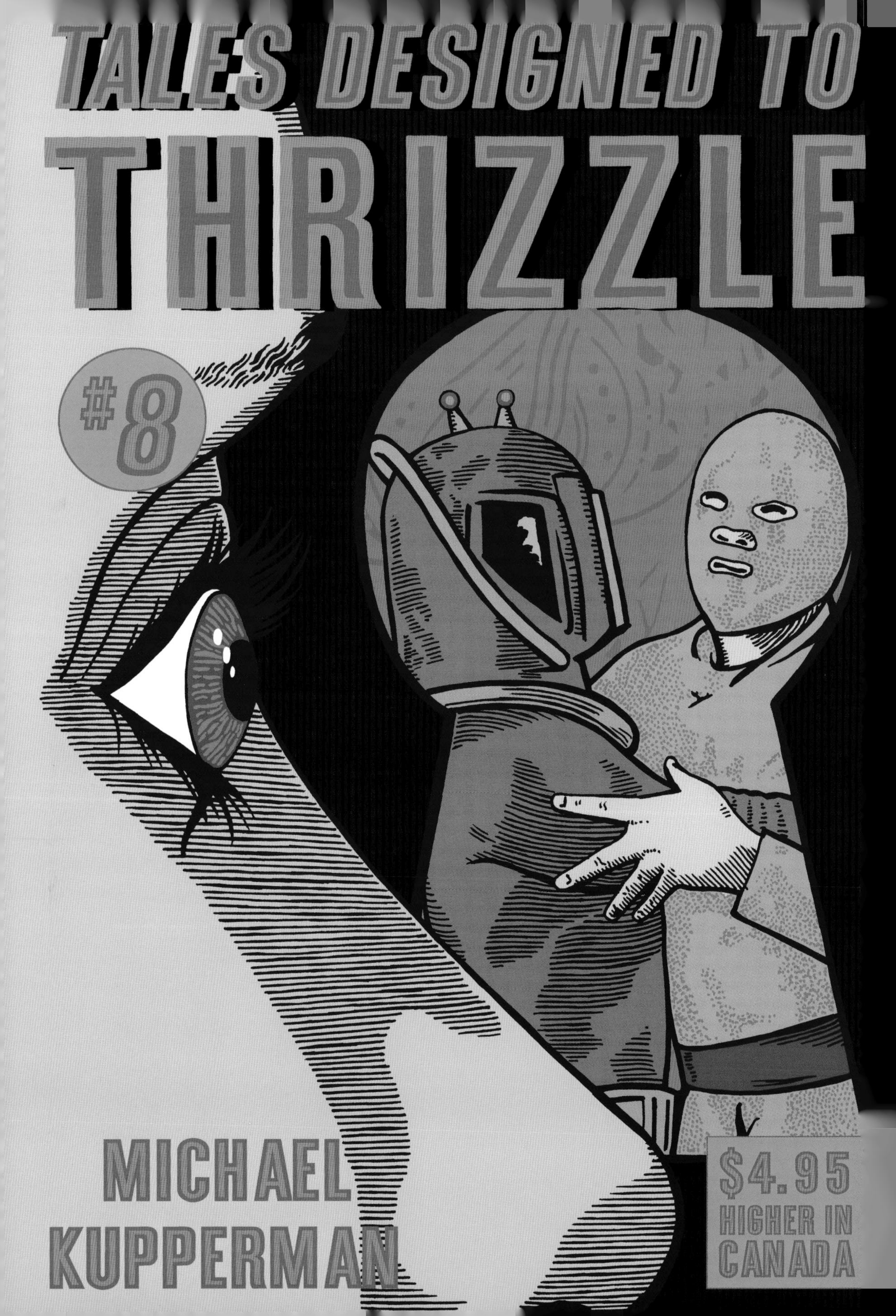
TALES DESIGNED TO
THRIZZLE
#8
MICHAEL
KUPPERMAN
$4.95
HIGHER IN
CANADA

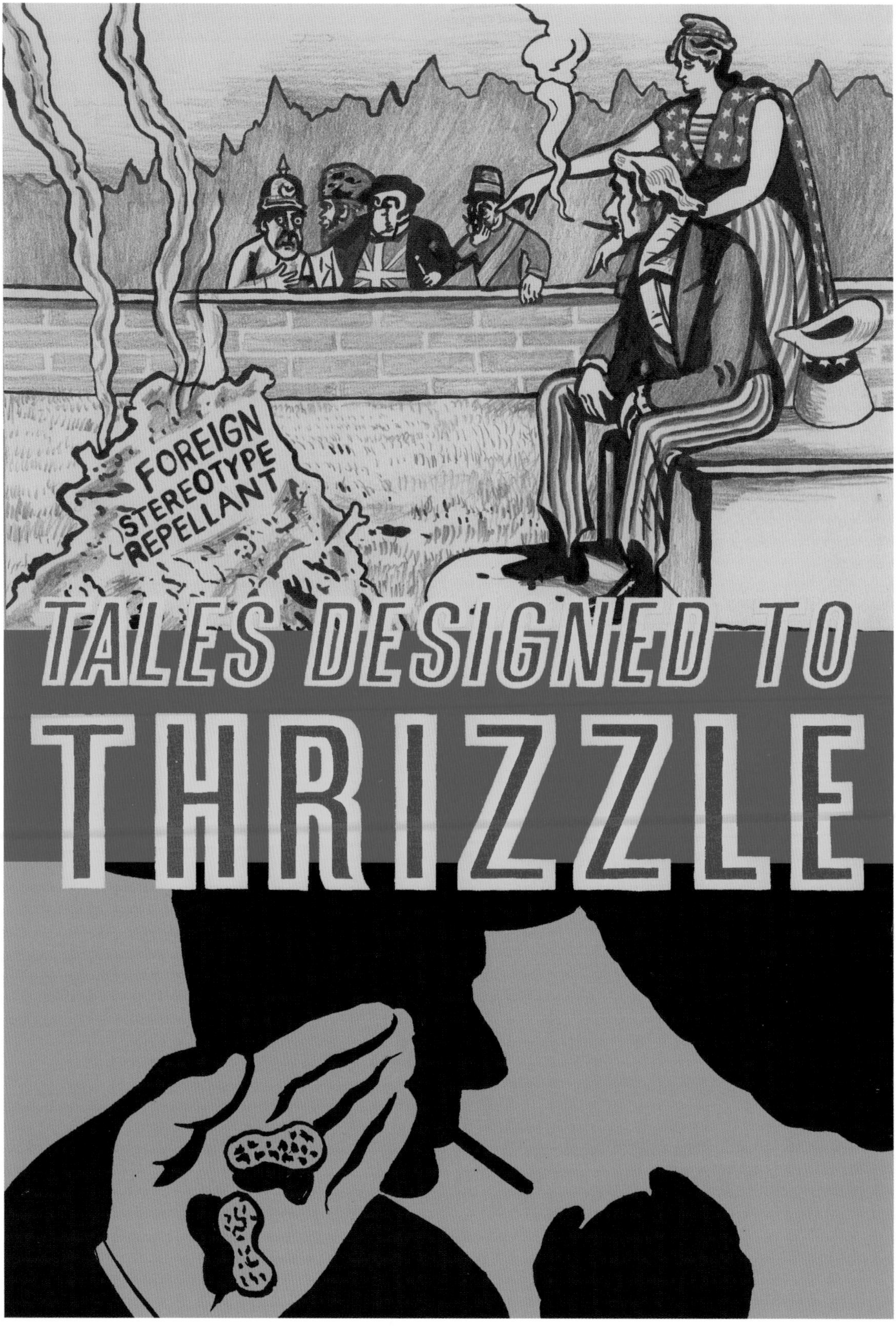
FOREIGN
STEREOTYPE
REPELLANT
TALES DESIGNED TO
THRIZZLE

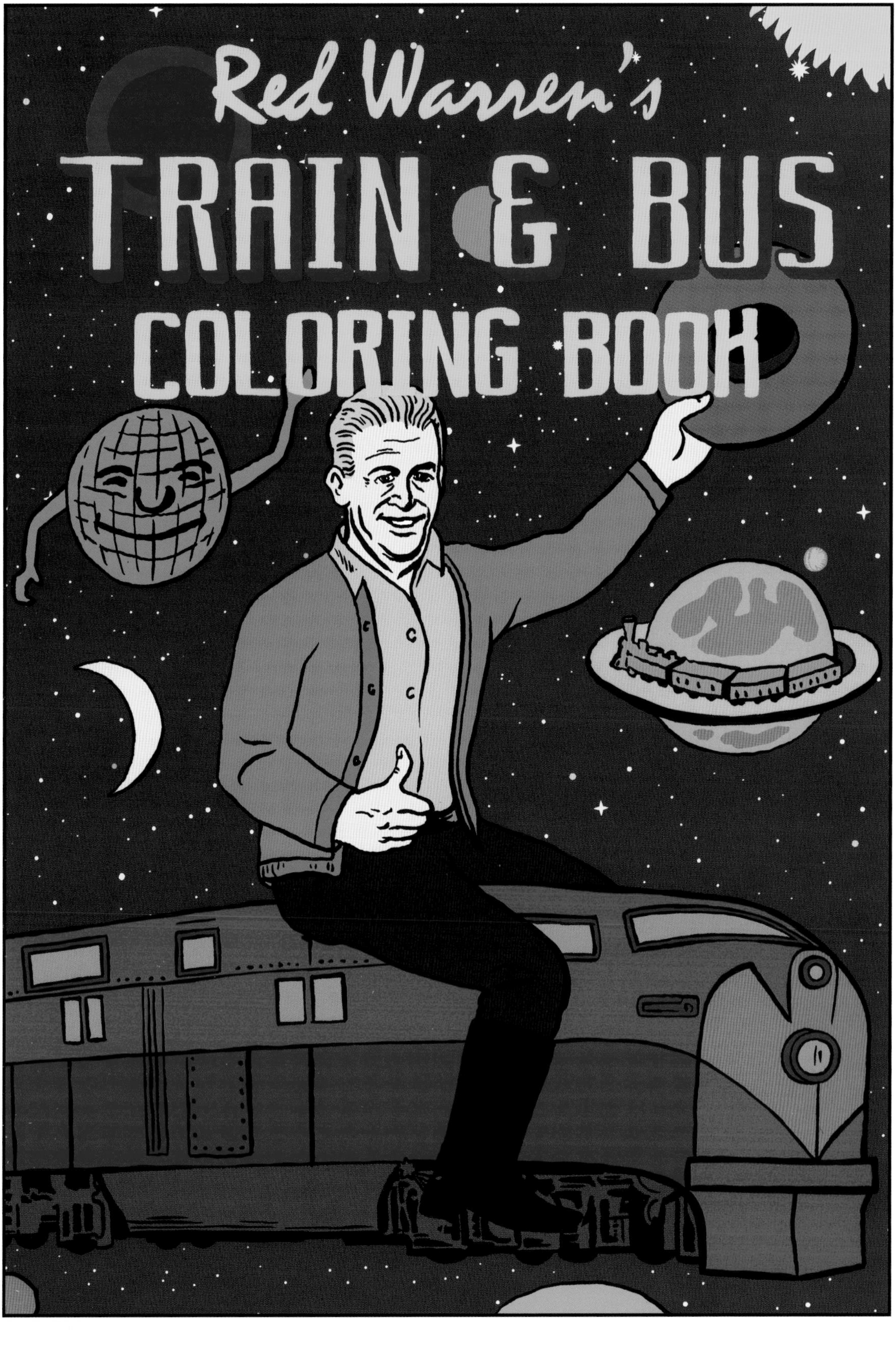
Red Warren's
TRAIN & BUS
COLORING BOOK

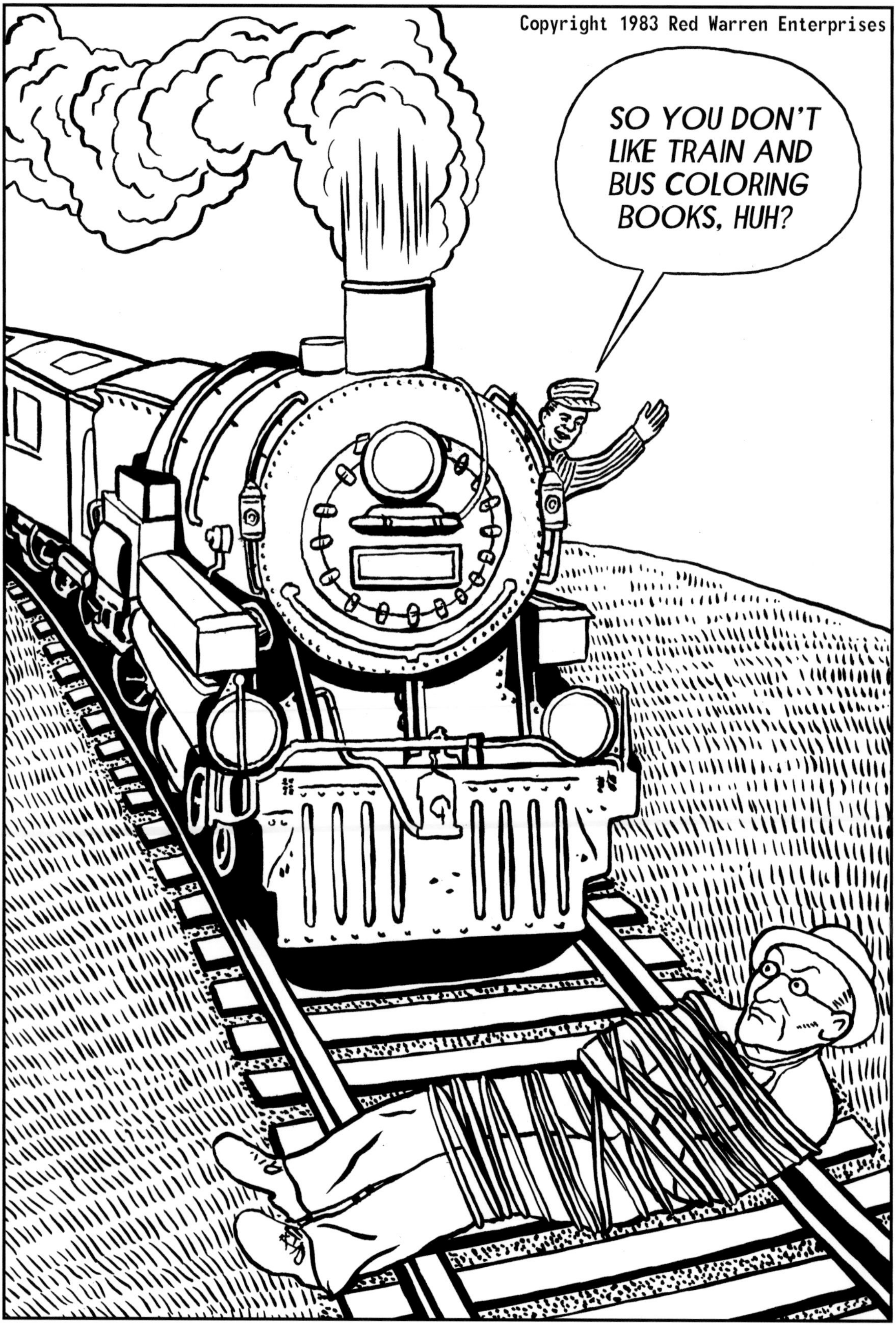
Copyright 1983 Red Warren Enterprises
SO YOU DON'T LIKE TRAIN AND BUS COLORING BOOKS, HUH?

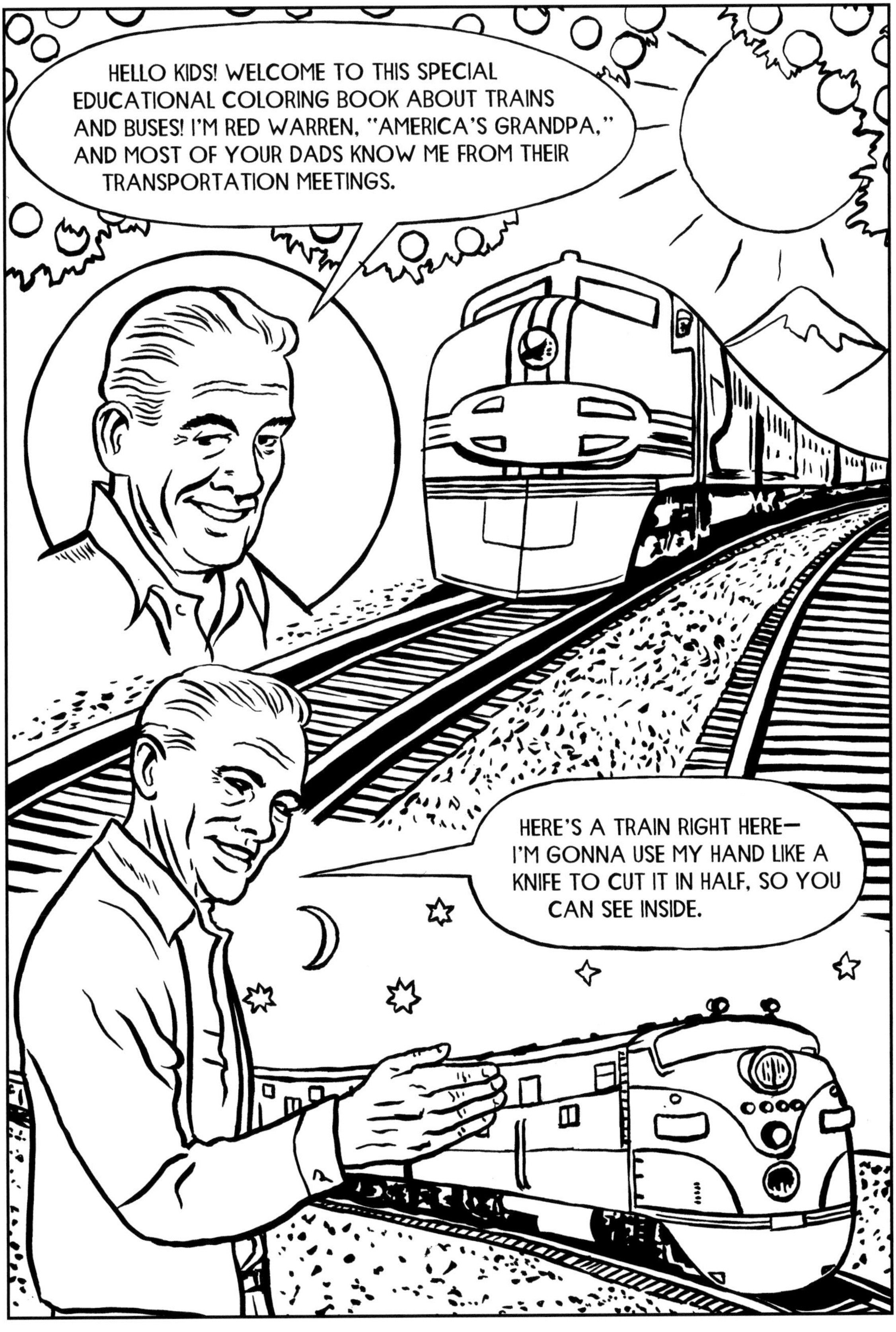
HELLO KIDS! WELCOME TO THIS SPECIAL EDUCATIONAL COLORING BOOK ABOUT TRAINS AND BUSES! I'M RED WARREN, "AMERICA'S GRANDPA," AND MOST OF YOUR DADS KNOW ME FROM THEIR TRANSPORTATION MEETINGS.
HERE'S A TRAIN RIGHT HERE— I'M GONNA USE MY HAND LIKE A KNIFE TO CUT IT IN HALF, SO YOU CAN SEE INSIDE.

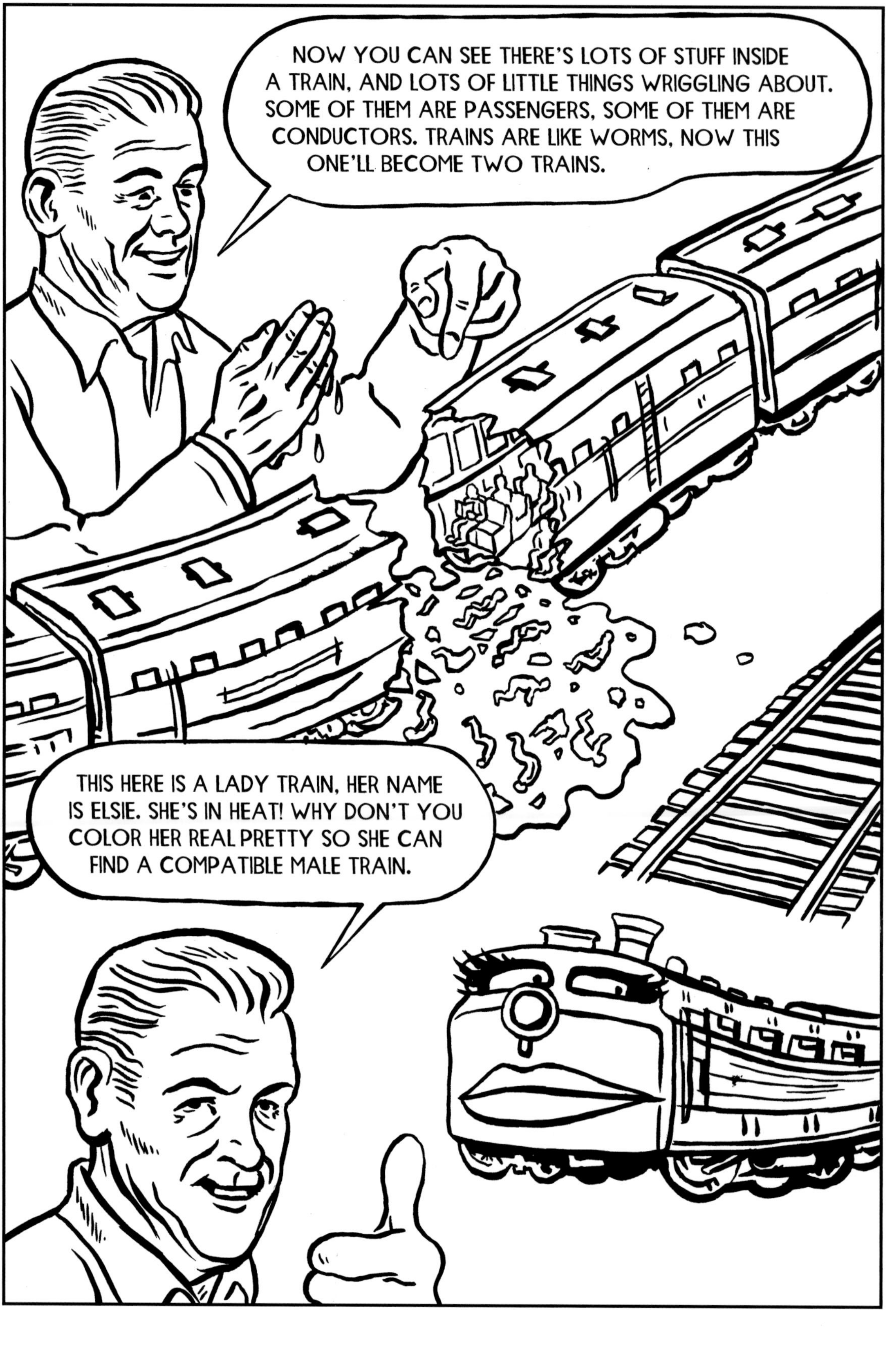
NOW YOU CAN SEE THERE'S LOTS OF STUFF INSIDE A TRAIN, AND LOTS OF LITTLE THINGS WRIGGLING ABOUT. SOME OF THEM ARE PASSENGERS, SOME OF THEM ARE CONDUCTORS. TRAINS ARE LIKE WORMS, NOW THIS ONE'LL BECOME TWO TRAINS.
THIS HERE IS A LADY TRAIN, HER NAME IS ELSIE. SHE'S IN HEAT! WHY DON'T YOU COLOR HER REAL PRETTY SO SHE CAN FIND A COMPATIBLE MALE TRAIN.

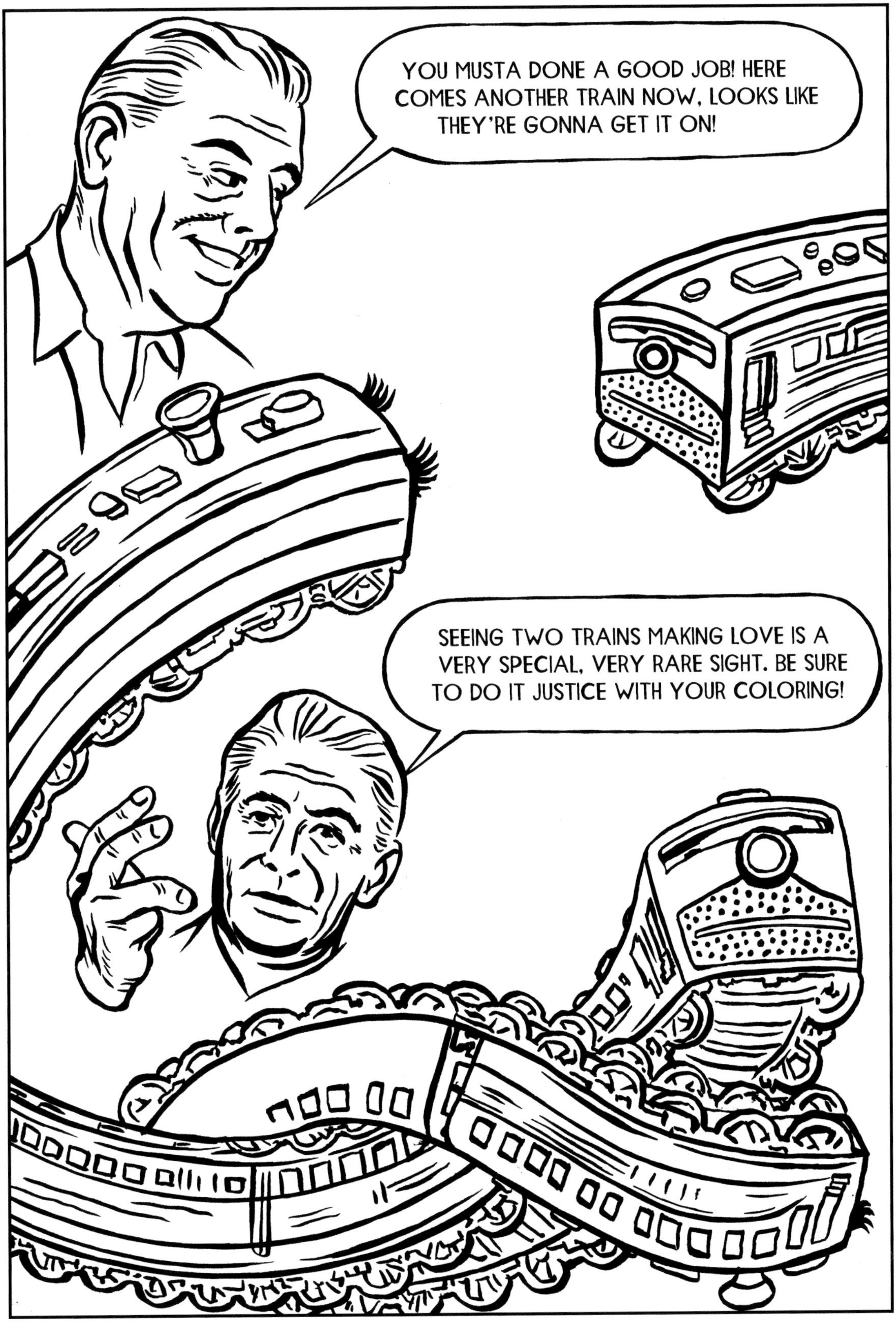
YOU MUSTA DONE A GOOD JOB! HERE COMES ANOTHER TRAIN NOW, LOOKS LIKE THEY'RE GONNA GET IT ON!
SEEING TWO TRAINS MAKING LOVE IS A VERY SPECIAL, VERY RARE SIGHT. BE SURE TO DO IT JUSTICE WITH YOUR COLORING!

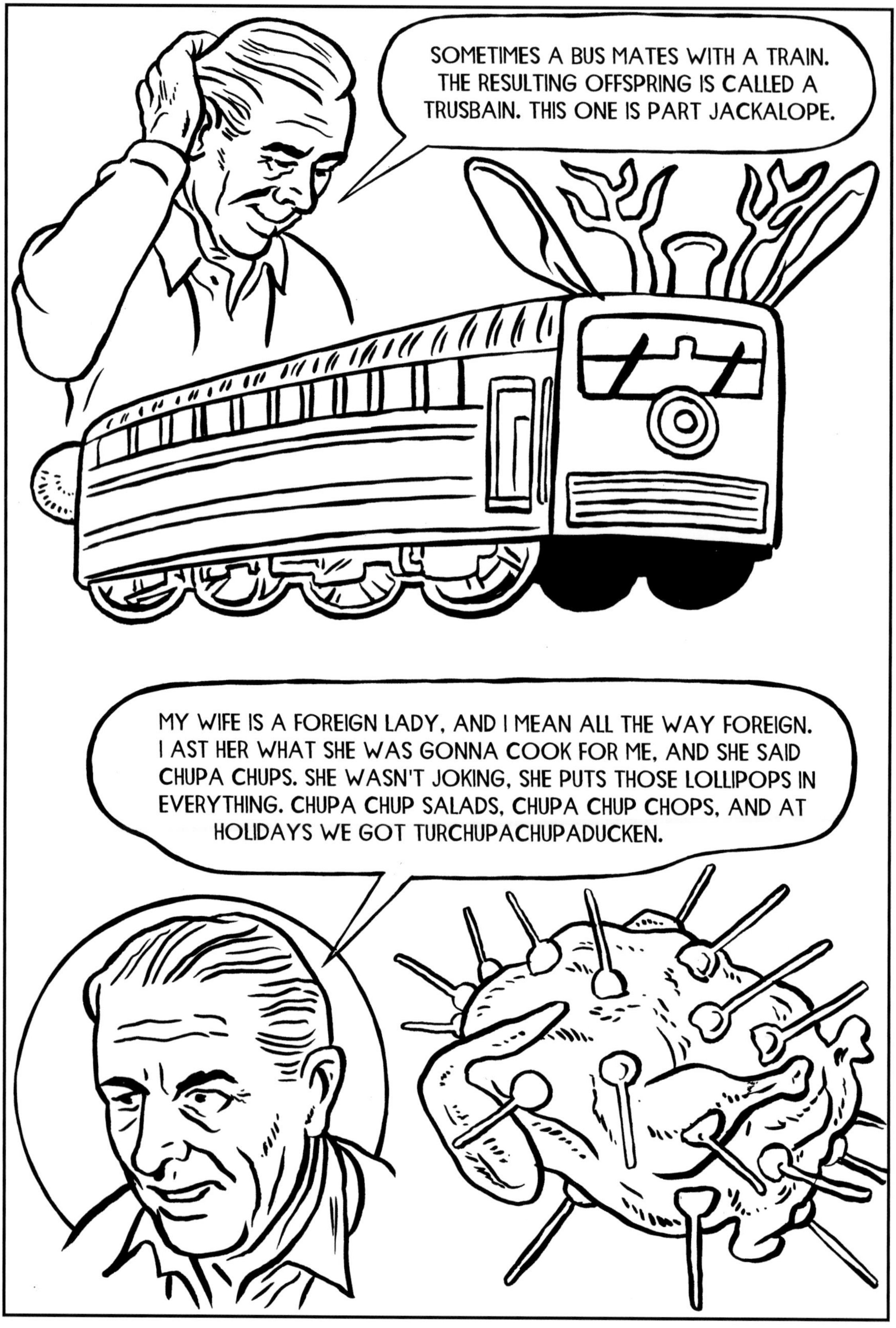
SOMETIMES A BUS MATES WITH A TRAIN. THE RESULTING OFFSPRING IS CALLED A TRUSBAIN. THIS ONE IS PART JACKALOPE.
MY WIFE IS A FOREIGN LADY, AND I MEAN ALL THE WAY FOREIGN. I AST HER WHAT SHE WAS GONNA COOK FOR ME, AND SHE SAID CHUPA CHUPS. SHE WASN'T JOKING, SHE PUTS THOSE LOLLIPOPS IN EVERYTHING. CHUPA CHUP SALADS, CHUPA CHUP CHOPS, AND AT HOLIDAYS WE GOT TURCHUPACHUPADUCKEN.

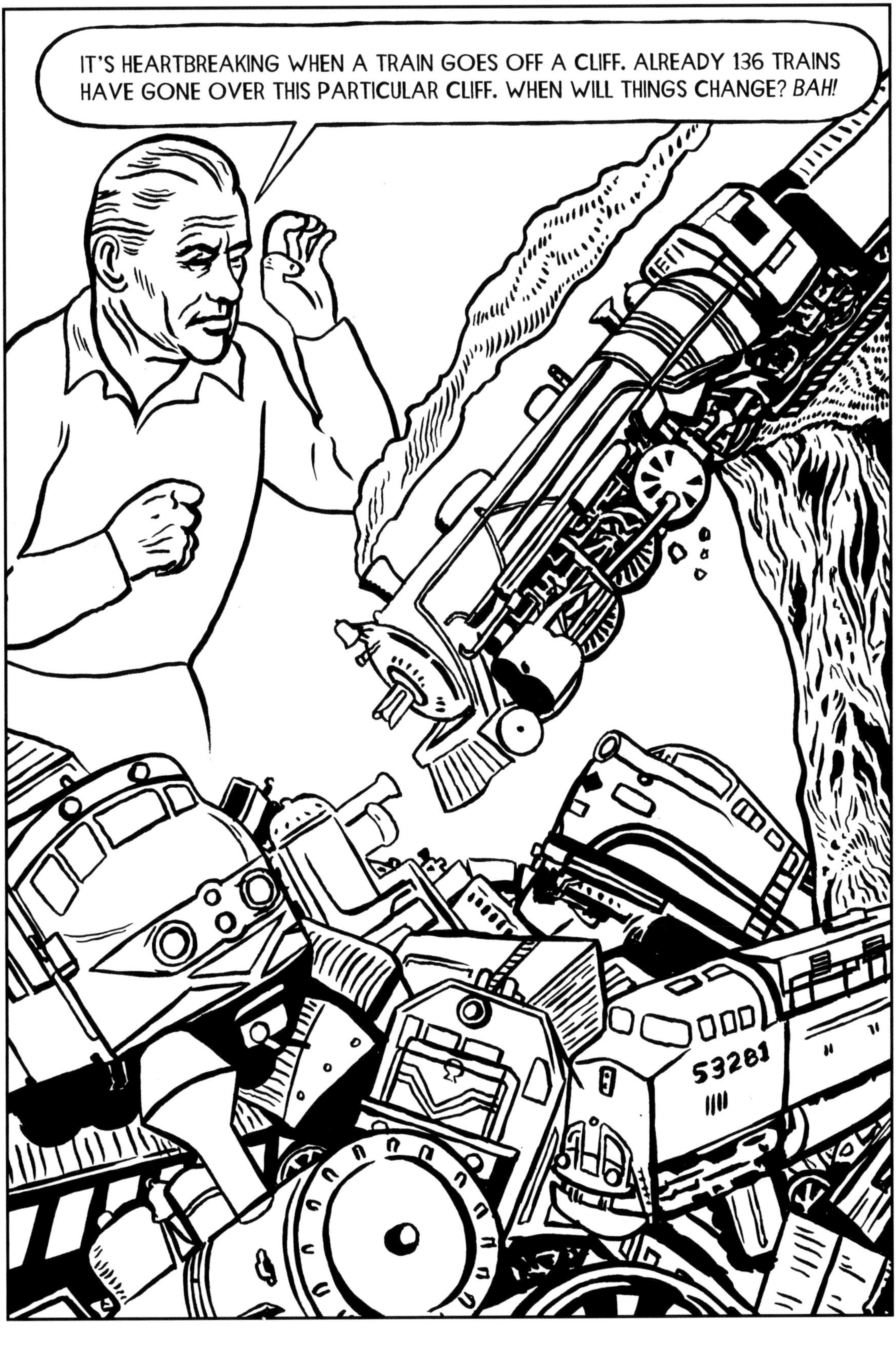
IT'S HEARTBREAKING WHEN A TRAIN GOES OFF A CLIFF. ALREADY 136 TRAINS HAVE GONE OVER THIS PARTICULAR CLIFF. WHEN WILL THINGS CHANGE? *BAH!*
53281

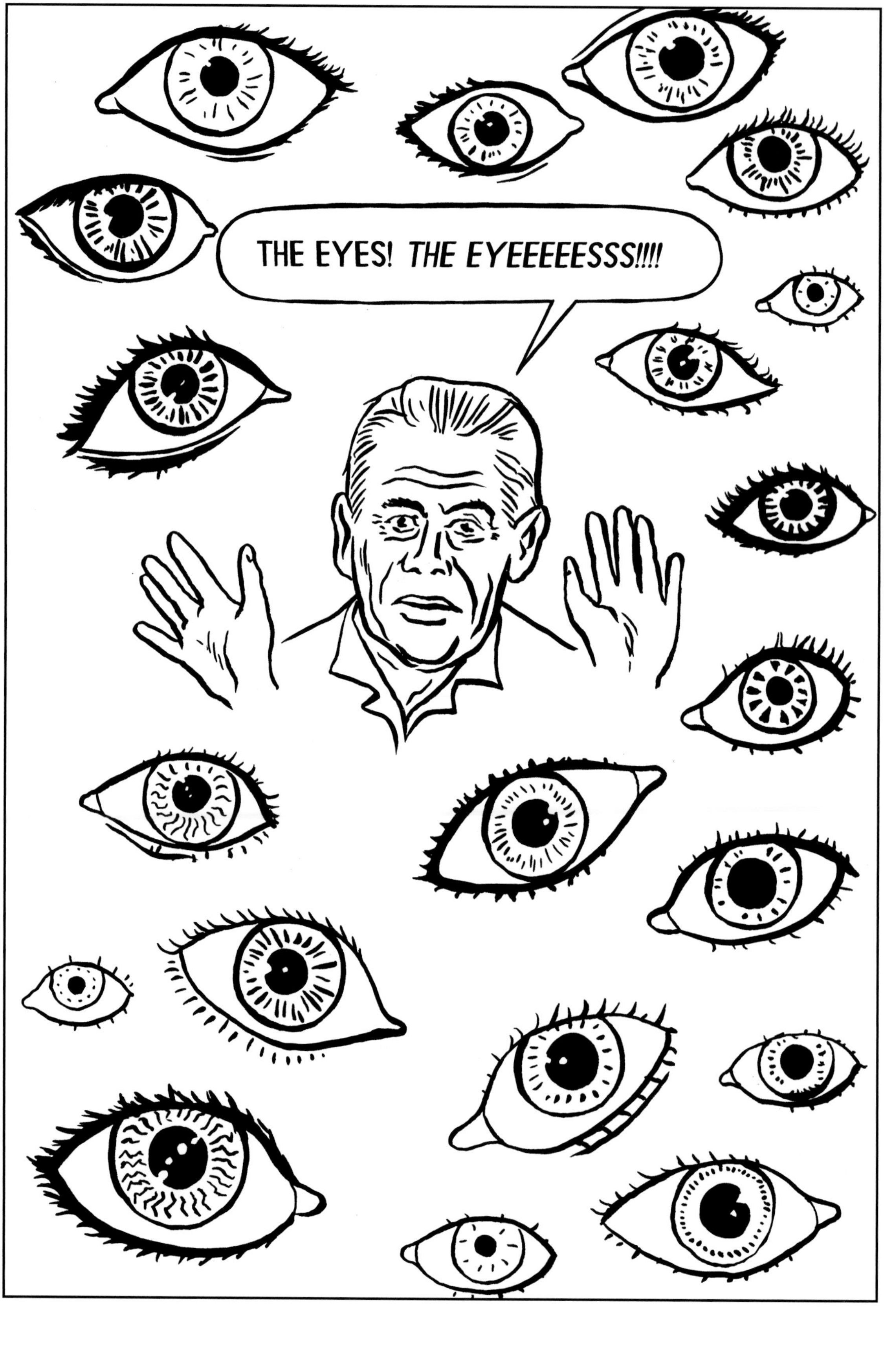
THE EYES! THE EYEEEEESSS!!!!

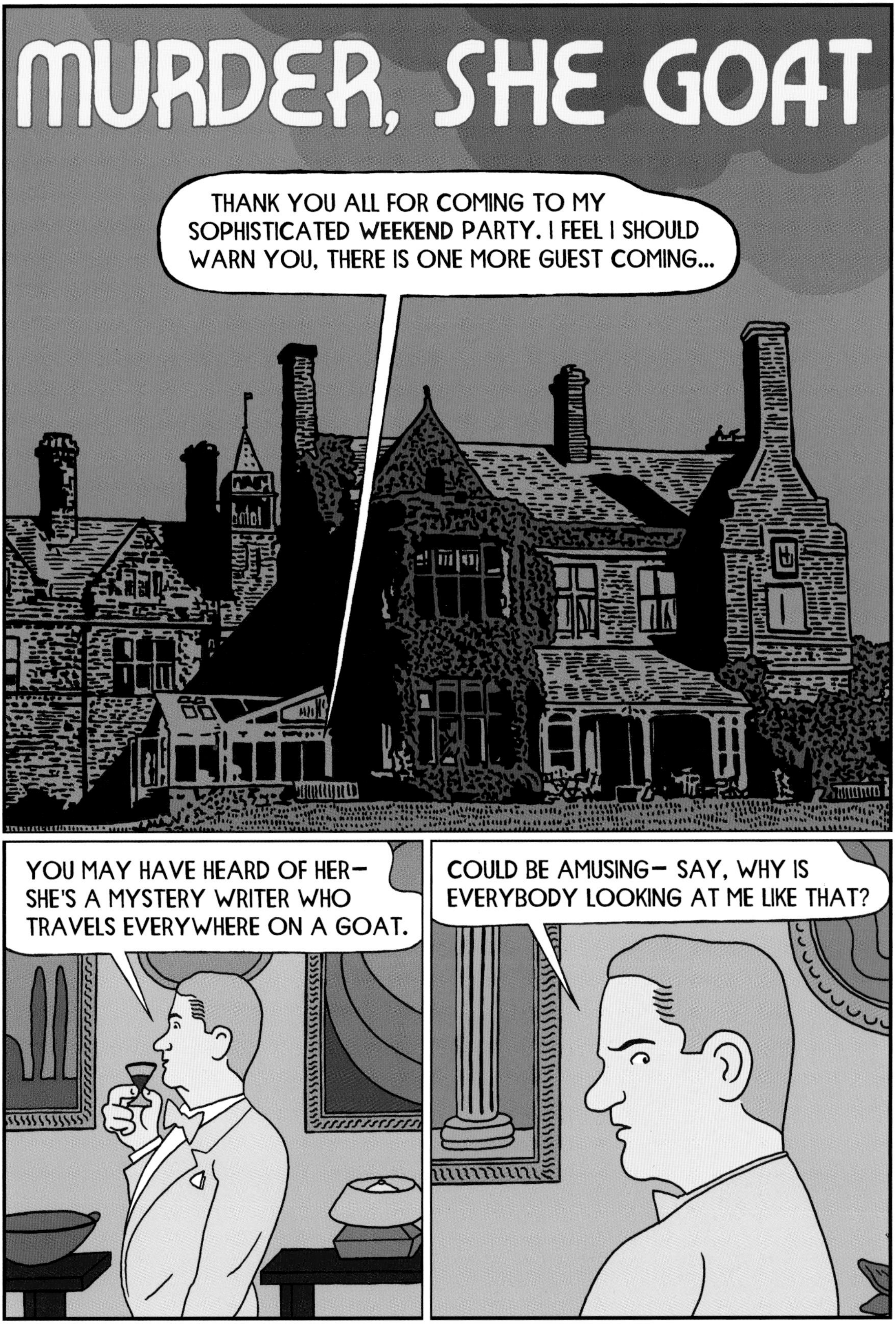
MURDER, SHE GOAT
THANK YOU ALL FOR COMING TO MY SOPHISTICATED WEEKEND PARTY. I FEEL I SHOULD WARN YOU, THERE IS ONE MORE GUEST COMING...
YOU MAY HAVE HEARD OF HER— SHE'S A MYSTERY WRITER WHO TRAVELS EVERYWHERE ON A GOAT.
COULD BE AMUSING— SAY, WHY IS EVERYBODY LOOKING AT ME LIKE THAT?

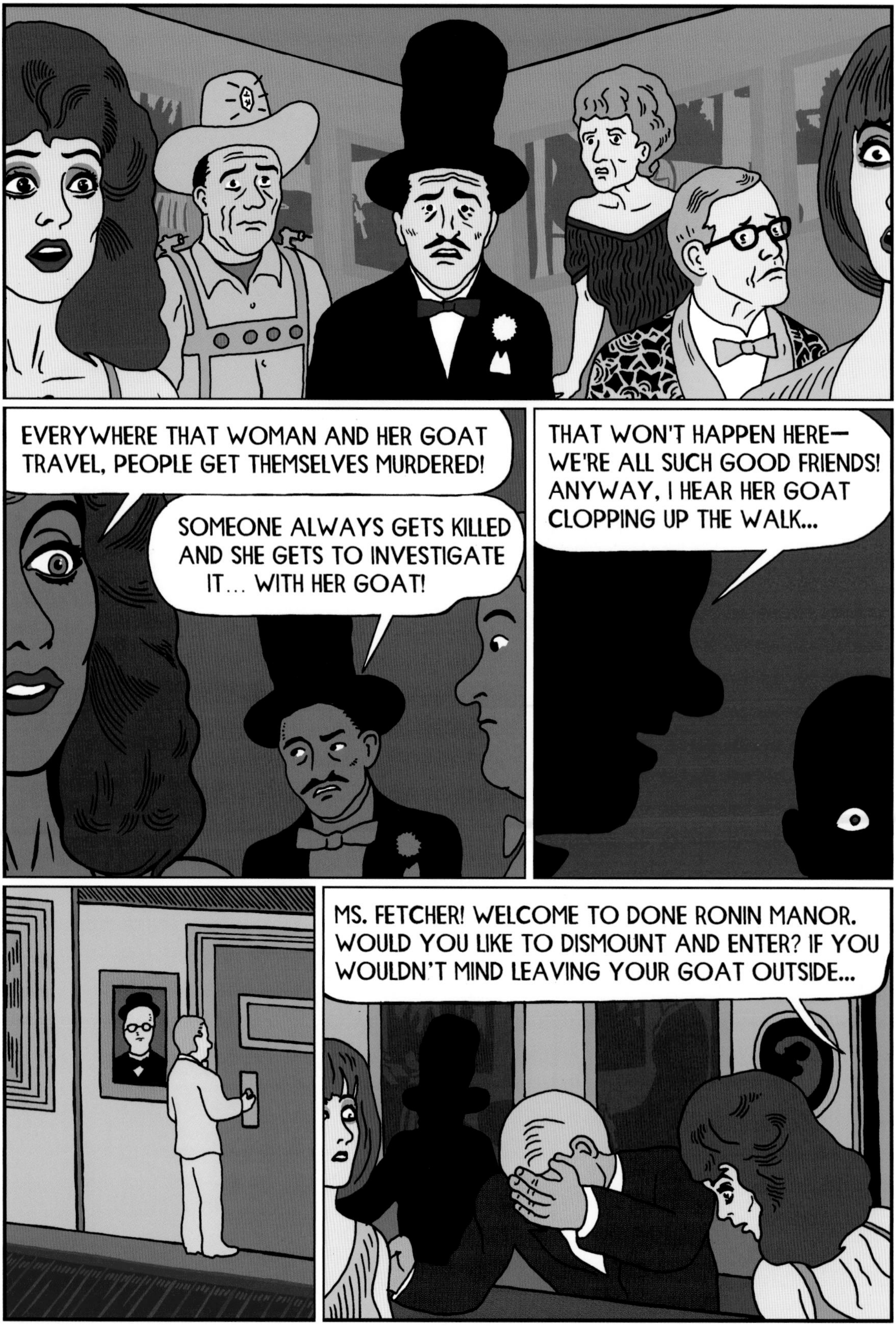
EVERYWHERE THAT WOMAN AND HER GOAT TRAVEL, PEOPLE GET THEMSELVES MURDERED!
SOMEONE ALWAYS GETS KILLED AND SHE GETS TO INVESTIGATE IT... WITH HER GOAT!
THAT WON'T HAPPEN HERE— WE'RE ALL SUCH GOOD FRIENDS! ANYWAY, I HEAR HER GOAT CLOPPING UP THE WALK...
MS. FETCHER! WELCOME TO DONE RONIN MANOR. WOULD YOU LIKE TO DISMOUNT AND ENTER? IF YOU WOULDN'T MIND LEAVING YOUR GOAT OUTSIDE...

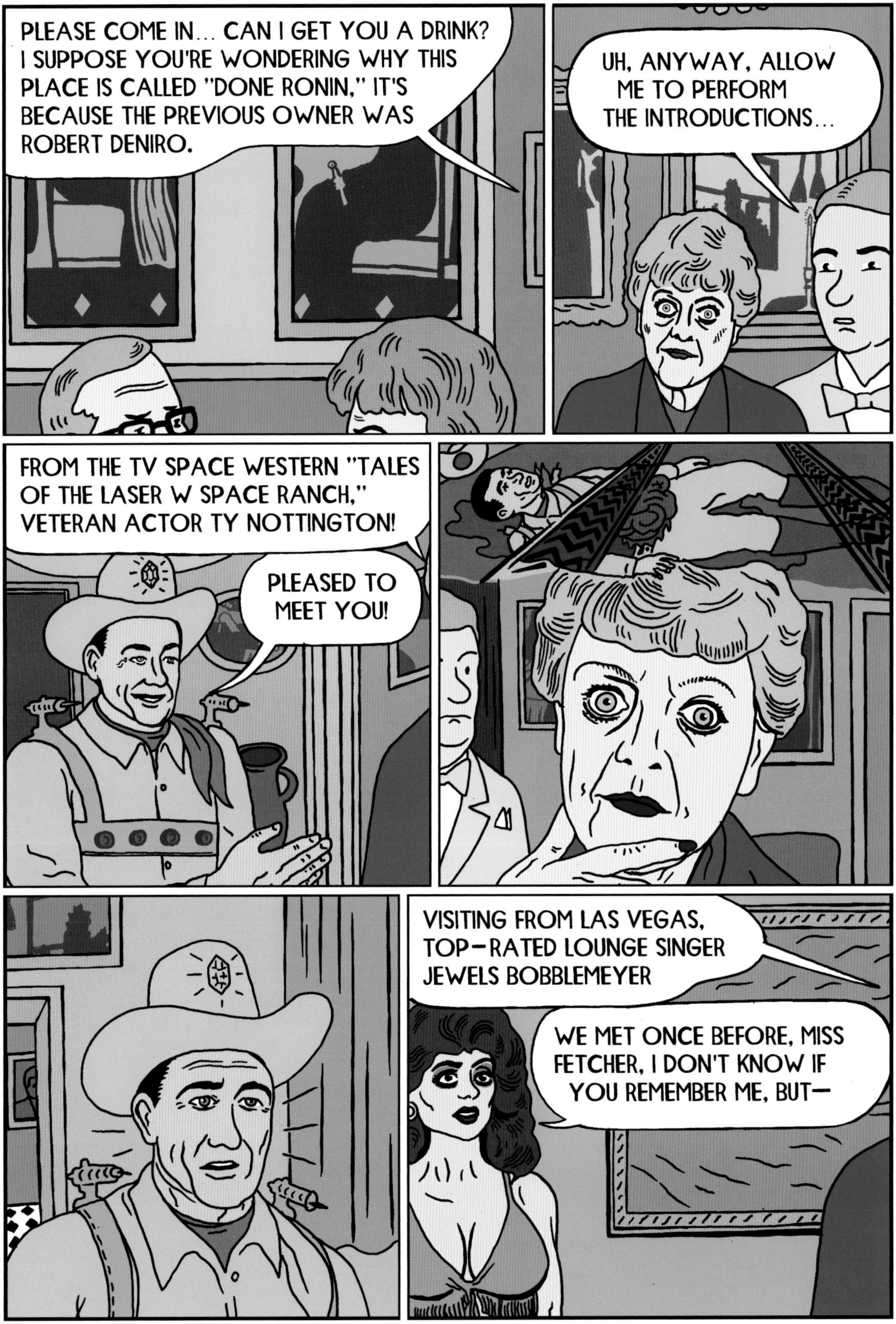
PLEASE COME IN... CAN I GET YOU A DRINK? I SUPPOSE YOU'RE WONDERING WHY THIS PLACE IS CALLED "DONE RONIN," IT'S BECAUSE THE PREVIOUS OWNER WAS ROBERT DENIRO.
UH, ANYWAY, ALLOW ME TO PERFORM THE INTRODUCTIONS...
FROM THE TV SPACE WESTERN "TALES OF THE LASER W SPACE RANCH," VETERAN ACTOR TY NOTTINGTON!
PLEASED TO MEET YOU!
VISITING FROM LAS VEGAS, TOP-RATED LOUNGE SINGER JEWELS BOBBLEMEYER
WE MET ONCE BEFORE, MISS FETCHER, I DON'T KNOW IF YOU REMEMBER ME, BUT—

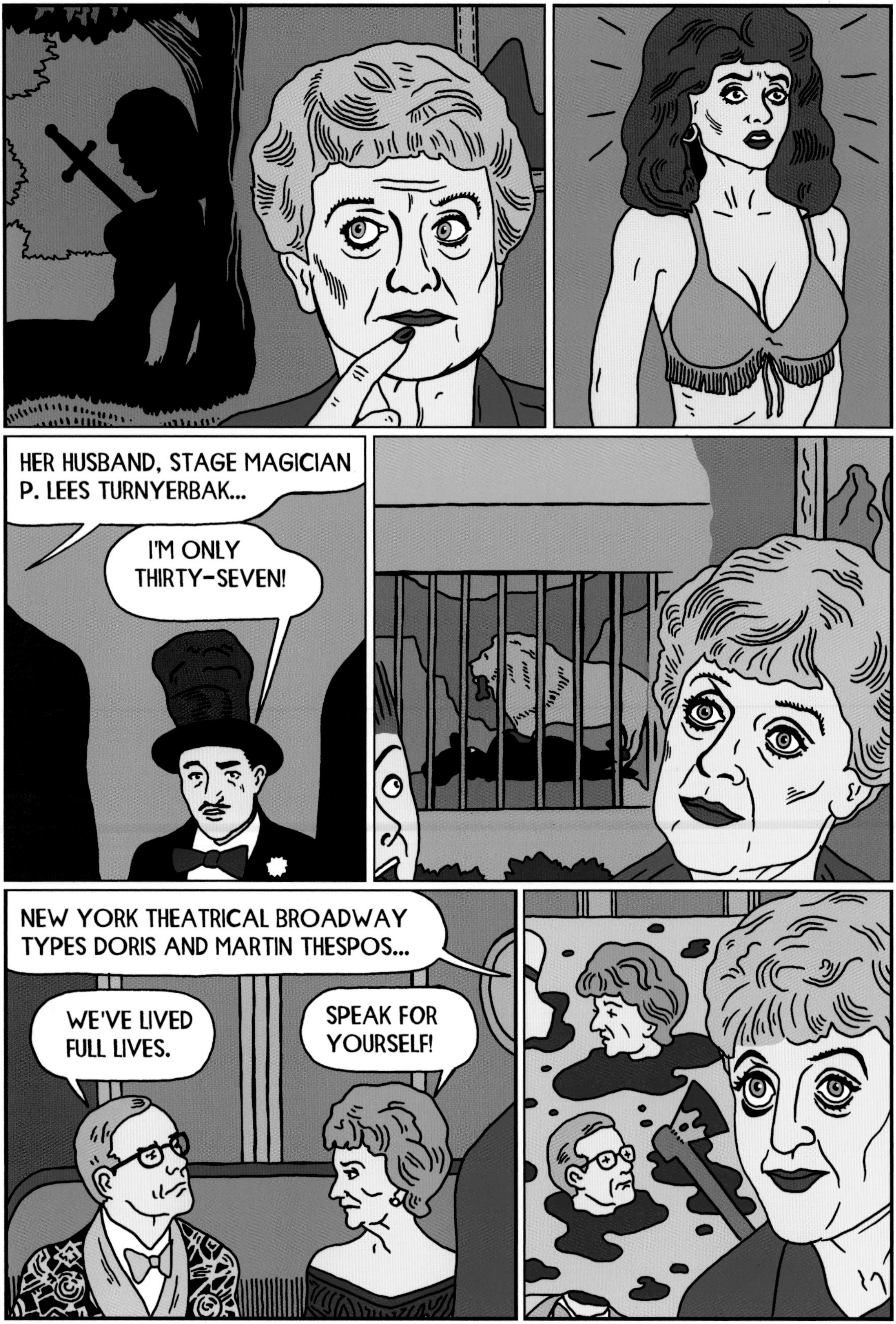
HER HUSBAND, STAGE MAGICIAN P. LEES TURNYERBAK...
I'M ONLY THIRTY-SEVEN!
NEW YORK THEATRICAL BROADWAY TYPES DORIS AND MARTIN THESPOS...
WE'VE LIVED FULL LIVES.
SPEAK FOR YOURSELF!

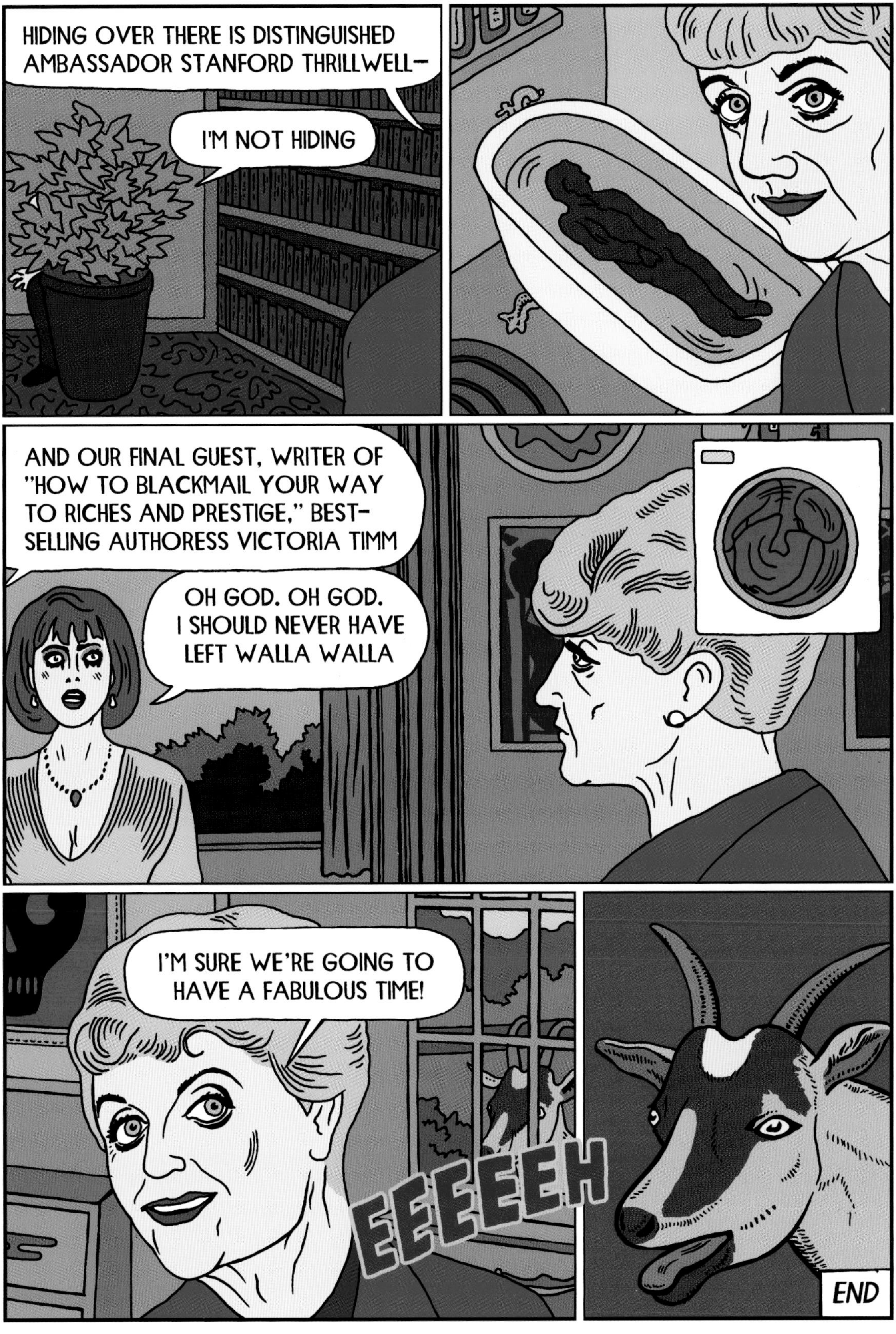
HIDING OVER THERE IS DISTINGUISHED AMBASSADOR STANFORD THRILLWELL—
I'M NOT HIDING
AND OUR FINAL GUEST, WRITER OF "HOW TO BLACKMAIL YOUR WAY TO RICHES AND PRESTIGE," BEST-SELLING AUTHORESS VICTORIA TIMM
OH GOD. OH GOD. I SHOULD NEVER HAVE LEFT WALLA WALLA
I'M SURE WE'RE GOING TO HAVE A FABULOUS TIME!
EEEEEH
END

DO YOU HAVE
THIN, WISPY PUBIC HAIR? IS IT CAUSING YOU TO MAKE FACIAL EXPRESSIONS LIKE THIS ONE?

Today's fashions involve elaborately stenciled pubic hair for both men and women. It's embarrassing when you don't have enough hair down there to form Che's face.

It's time to join the Pubic Association.

Your commitment to healthier, more luxurious pubic hair will be announced by the Pubic Association's Town Crier, who will come to your place of business to ring his bell and read your name off his parchment. You'll be presented with the gold medal that indicates pubic beginner status, and every month you'll receive Pubic Club pamphlets with ghost stories about haunted bushes of pubic hair. It really works. Scared pubic hair grows faster. Your co-workers will beam when we call to inform them of your attempts.

Listen to these testimonials from real members.

"I can't believe the results. My pubic hair has never been more terrified or more luxurious. It was worth the public humiliation."

"Before, I could hardly manage a smiley face– now my pubic hair is thick enough for a reproduction of Bronzino's Venus and Mars. I miss my job, though!"

"It's a miracle. I felt like a failure with my scraggly groin, but now I'm a success with my extravagant dong marquee! It makes being homeless that much more bearable."

"HEAR YE HEAR YE"

Send 2$ for our catalogue to:
PUBIC GROWTH, PO BOX 69,
LOVEWELL NY.

WHEN THE MOON HITS YOUR EYE LIKE A BIG PIZZA PIE- THAT'S ASSAULT!

–WHEN an asteroid hits your ear like a dessert liqueur

–WHEN Mars hits your knee like a fine aged brie

–WHEN a star hits your nose like a veal clemenceau

CALL 1-888-SUE-THE-SKY

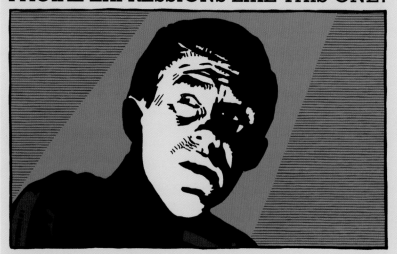

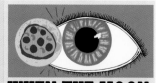

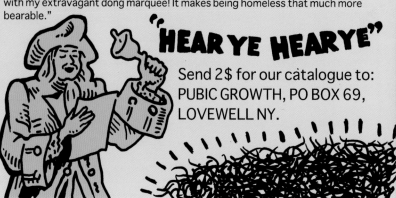

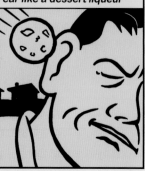

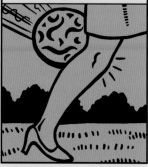

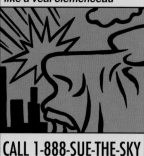

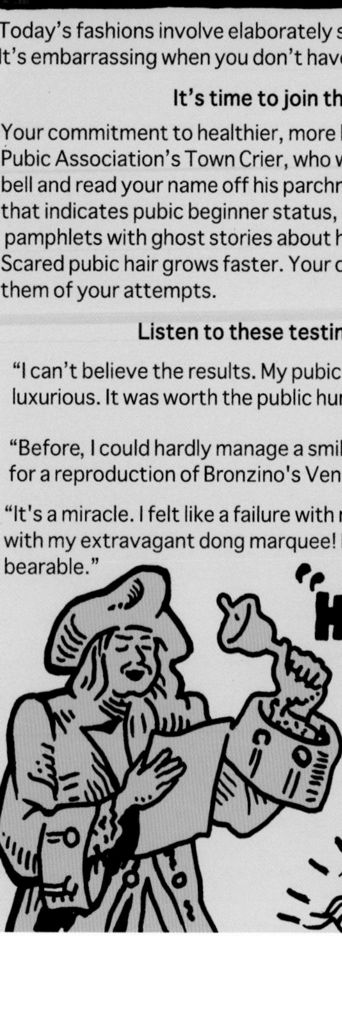

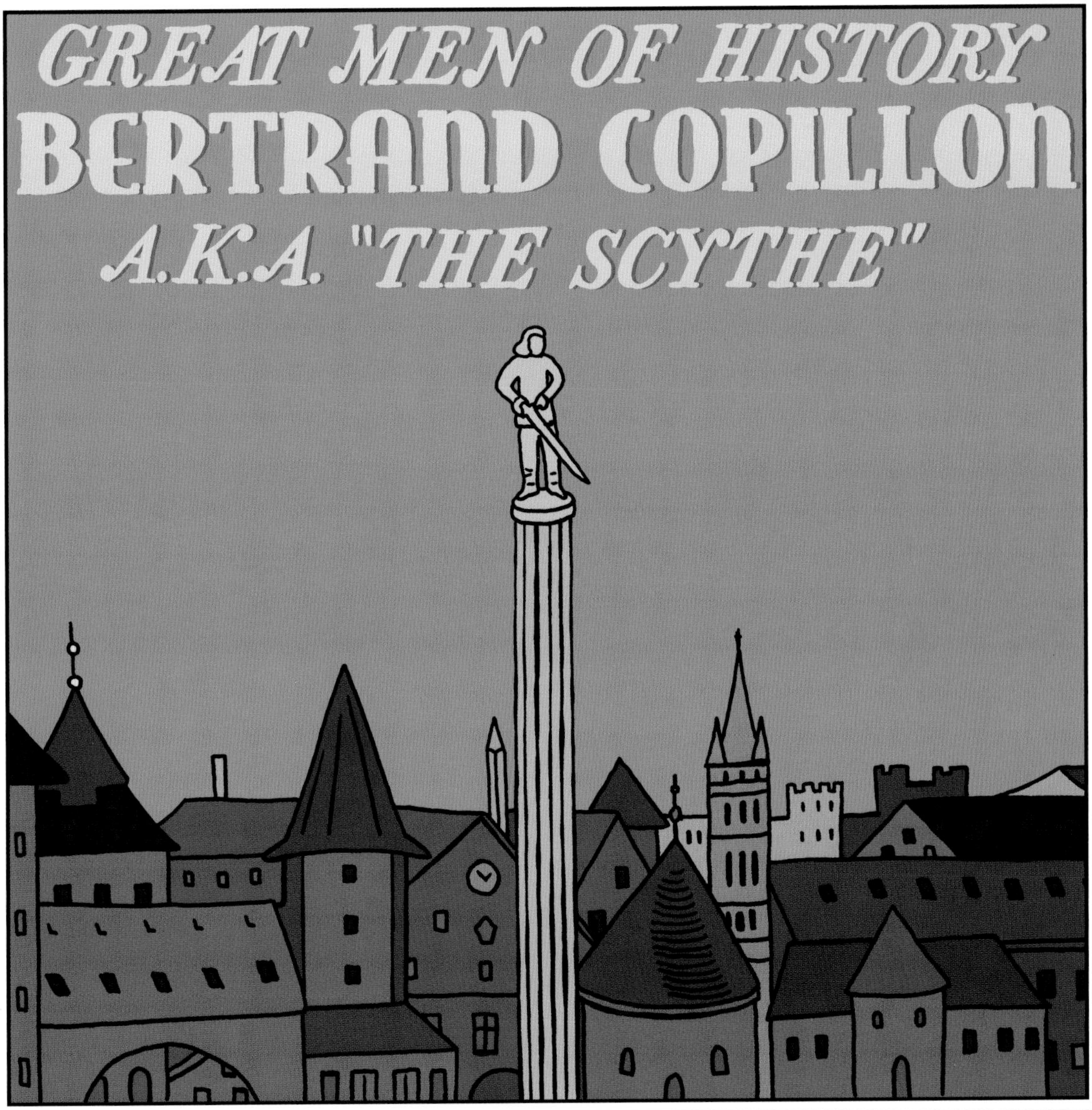
GREAT MEN OF HISTORY
BERTRAND COPILLON
A.K.A. "THE SCYTHE"

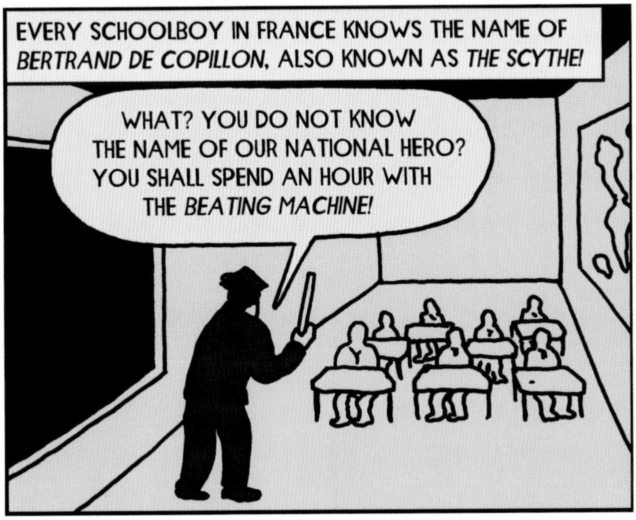
EVERY SCHOOLBOY IN FRANCE KNOWS THE NAME OF *BERTRAND DE COPILLON*, ALSO KNOWN AS *THE SCYTHE!*
WHAT? YOU DO NOT KNOW THE NAME OF OUR NATIONAL HERO? YOU SHALL SPEND AN HOUR WITH THE *BEATING MACHINE!*

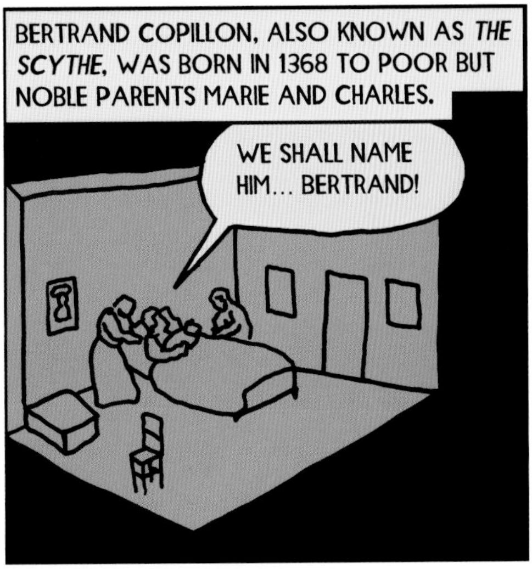
BERTRAND COPILLON, ALSO KNOWN AS *THE SCYTHE*, WAS BORN IN 1368 TO POOR BUT NOBLE PARENTS MARIE AND CHARLES.
WE SHALL NAME HIM... BERTRAND!

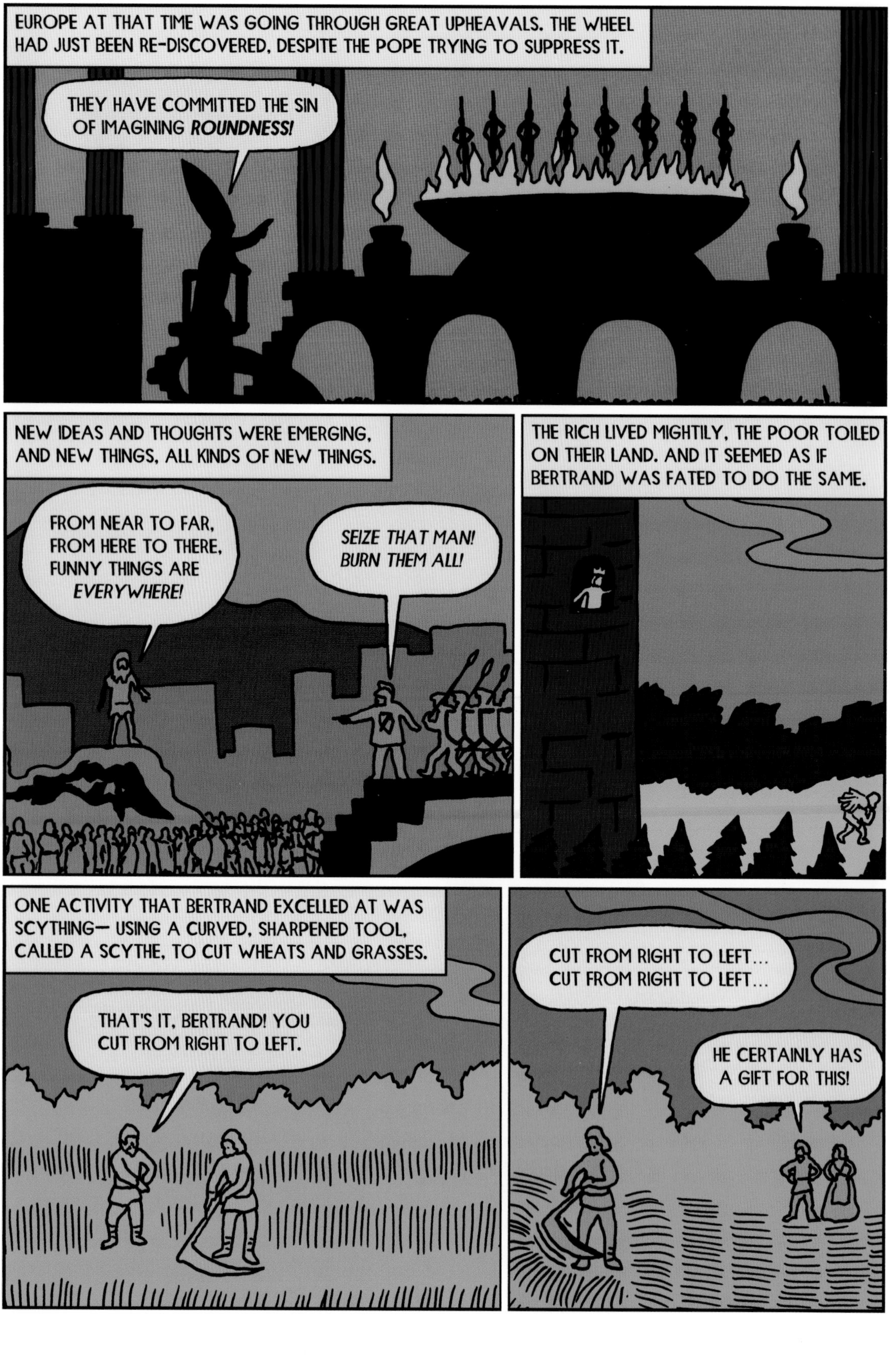
EUROPE AT THAT TIME WAS GOING THROUGH GREAT UPHEAVALS. THE WHEEL HAD JUST BEEN RE-DISCOVERED, DESPITE THE POPE TRYING TO SUPPRESS IT.
THEY HAVE COMMITTED THE SIN OF IMAGINING *ROUNDNESS!*
NEW IDEAS AND THOUGHTS WERE EMERGING, AND NEW THINGS, ALL KINDS OF NEW THINGS.
FROM NEAR TO FAR, FROM HERE TO THERE, FUNNY THINGS ARE *EVERYWHERE!*
SEIZE THAT MAN! BURN THEM ALL!
THE RICH LIVED MIGHTILY, THE POOR TOILED ON THEIR LAND. AND IT SEEMED AS IF BERTRAND WAS FATED TO DO THE SAME.
ONE ACTIVITY THAT BERTRAND EXCELLED AT WAS SCYTHING— USING A CURVED, SHARPENED TOOL, CALLED A SCYTHE, TO CUT WHEATS AND GRASSES.
THAT'S IT, BERTRAND! YOU CUT FROM RIGHT TO LEFT.
CUT FROM RIGHT TO LEFT... CUT FROM RIGHT TO LEFT...
HE CERTAINLY HAS A GIFT FOR THIS!

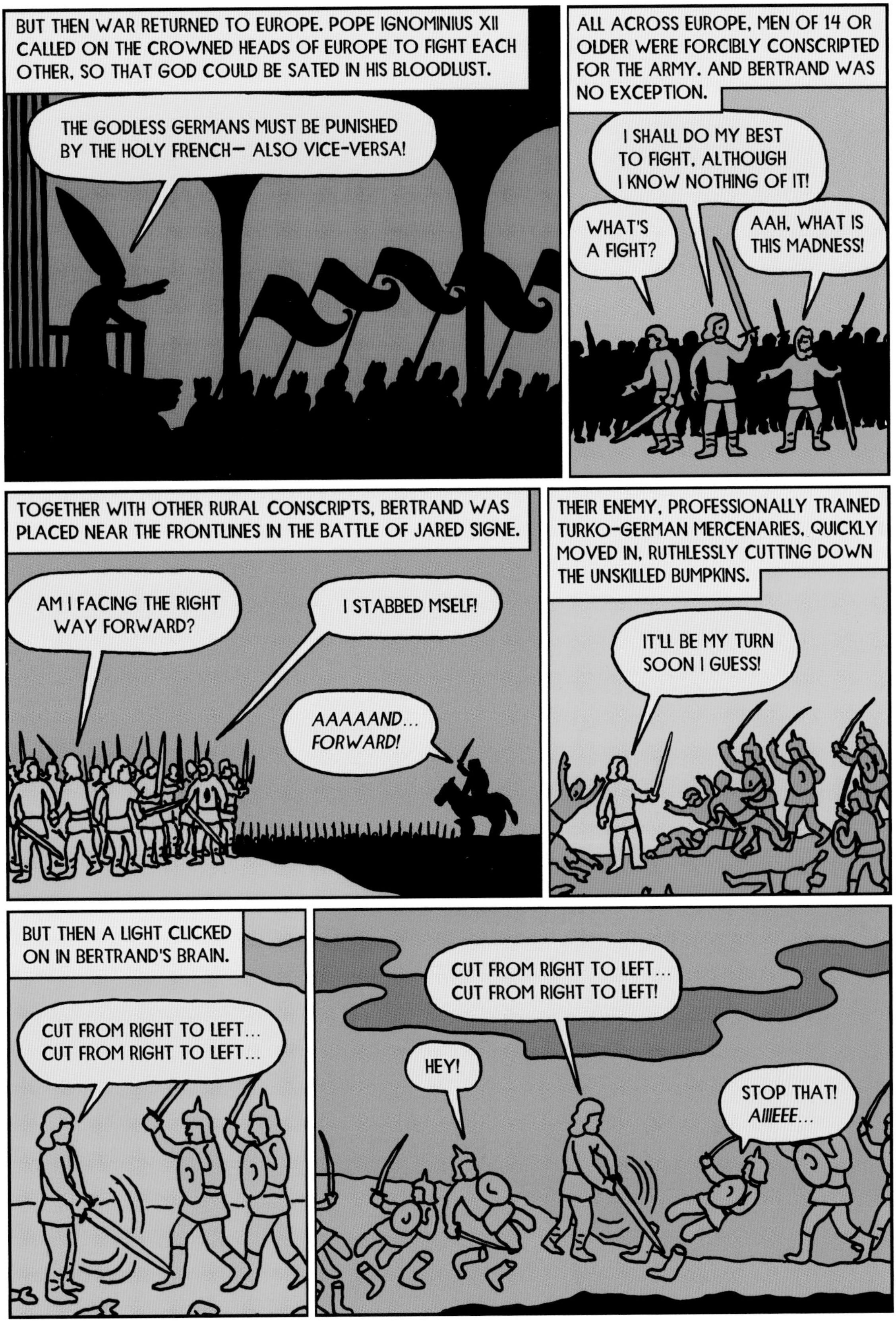
BUT THEN WAR RETURNED TO EUROPE. POPE IGNOMINIUS XII CALLED ON THE CROWNED HEADS OF EUROPE TO FIGHT EACH OTHER, SO THAT GOD COULD BE SATED IN HIS BLOODLUST.
THE GODLESS GERMANS MUST BE PUNISHED BY THE HOLY FRENCH— ALSO VICE-VERSA!
ALL ACROSS EUROPE, MEN OF 14 OR OLDER WERE FORCIBLY CONSCRIPTED FOR THE ARMY. AND BERTRAND WAS NO EXCEPTION.
I SHALL DO MY BEST TO FIGHT, ALTHOUGH I KNOW NOTHING OF IT!
WHAT'S A FIGHT?
AAH, WHAT IS THIS MADNESS!
TOGETHER WITH OTHER RURAL CONSCRIPTS, BERTRAND WAS PLACED NEAR THE FRONTLINES IN THE BATTLE OF JARED SIGNE.
AM I FACING THE RIGHT WAY FORWARD?
I STABBED MSELF!
AAAAAND... FORWARD!
THEIR ENEMY, PROFESSIONALLY TRAINED TURKO-GERMAN MERCENARIES, QUICKLY MOVED IN, RUTHLESSLY CUTTING DOWN THE UNSKILLED BUMPKINS.
IT'LL BE MY TURN SOON I GUESS!
BUT THEN A LIGHT CLICKED ON IN BERTRAND'S BRAIN.
CUT FROM RIGHT TO LEFT... CUT FROM RIGHT TO LEFT...
CUT FROM RIGHT TO LEFT... CUT FROM RIGHT TO LEFT!
HEY!
STOP THAT! AIIIEEE...

WHEN BERTRAND FINALLY PAUSED, 287 MEN LAY BEHIND HIM, LEGLESS.

WELL DONE, PRIVATE!

BERTRAND WAS GIVEN SPECIAL ATTENTION FOR HIS MAIMING SKILLS.

SO... A HUMAN SCYTHE, EH? WE SHALL SEE IF YOUR SKILLS CONTINUE TO DELIVER!

EXTRA PORRIDGE FOR THIS MAN!

BERTRAND'S NEXT BATTLE WAS AT POOTERS, ON JULY 29TH.

YOU, MY BOY, SHALL ADVANCE IN FRONT!

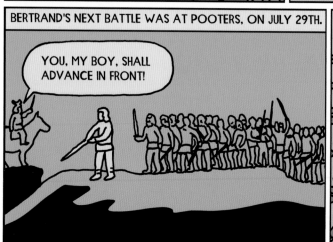

CUT FROM RIGHT TO LEFT... CUT FROM RIGHT TO LEFT...

THE BATTLE WAS A GREAT SUCCESS. AND BERTRAND WAS PROMOTED TO CAPTAIN.

CONGRATULATIONS, MY BOY!

BERTRAND CONTINUED TO WIN GREAT VICTORIES FOR HIS NATION, AND HIS FORTUNES ROSE. HE HACKED AND SLASHED HIS WAY ACROSS EUROPE.

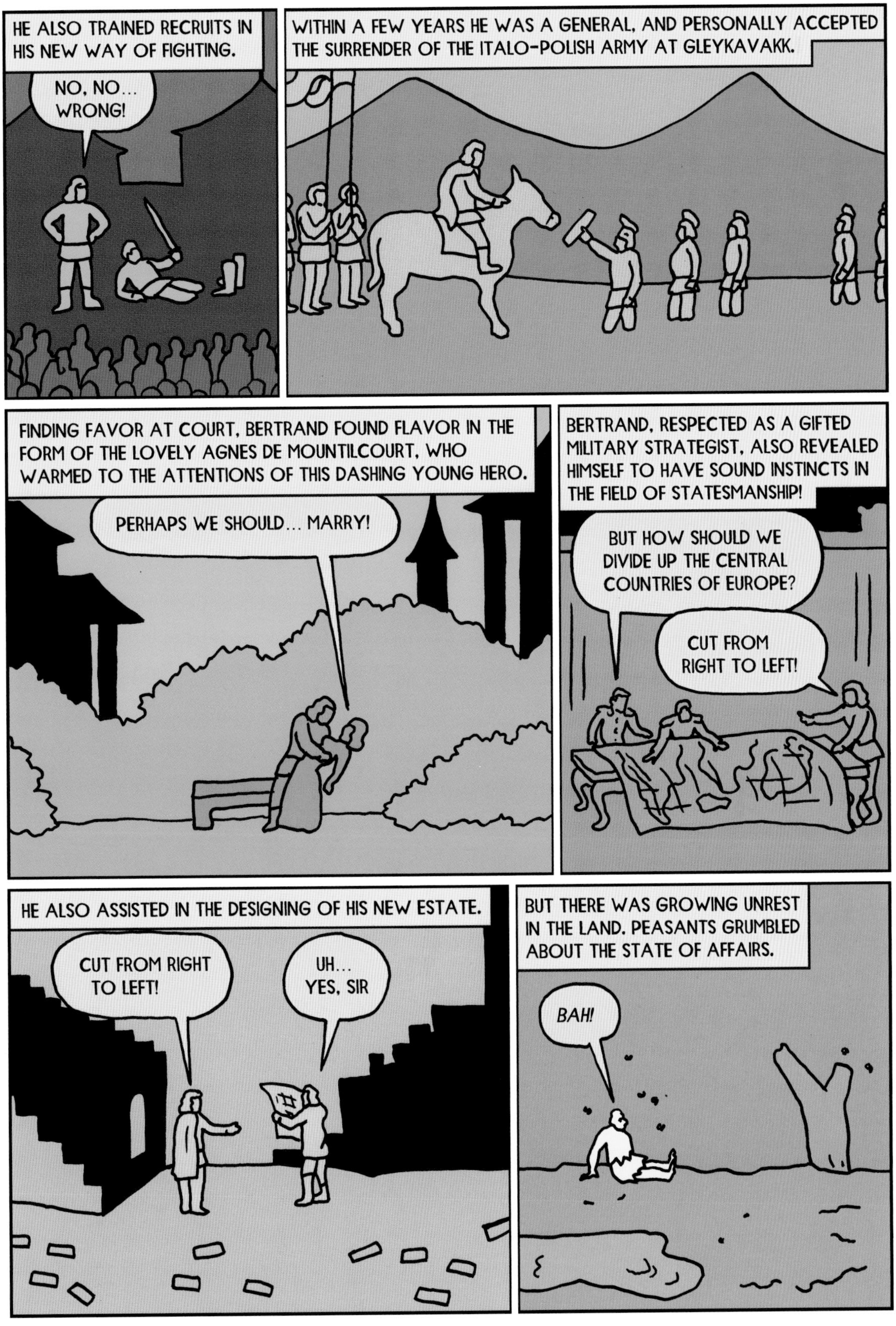
HE ALSO TRAINED RECRUITS IN HIS NEW WAY OF FIGHTING.
NO, NO... WRONG!
WITHIN A FEW YEARS HE WAS A GENERAL, AND PERSONALLY ACCEPTED THE SURRENDER OF THE ITALO-POLISH ARMY AT GLEYKAVAKK.
FINDING FAVOR AT COURT, BERTRAND FOUND FLAVOR IN THE FORM OF THE LOVELY AGNES DE MOUNTILCOURT, WHO WARMED TO THE ATTENTIONS OF THIS DASHING YOUNG HERO.
PERHAPS WE SHOULD... MARRY!
BERTRAND, RESPECTED AS A GIFTED MILITARY STRATEGIST, ALSO REVEALED HIMSELF TO HAVE SOUND INSTINCTS IN THE FIELD OF STATESMANSHIP!
BUT HOW SHOULD WE DIVIDE UP THE CENTRAL COUNTRIES OF EUROPE?
CUT FROM RIGHT TO LEFT!
HE ALSO ASSISTED IN THE DESIGNING OF HIS NEW ESTATE.
CUT FROM RIGHT TO LEFT!
UH... YES, SIR
BUT THERE WAS GROWING UNREST IN THE LAND. PEASANTS GRUMBLED ABOUT THE STATE OF AFFAIRS.
BAH!

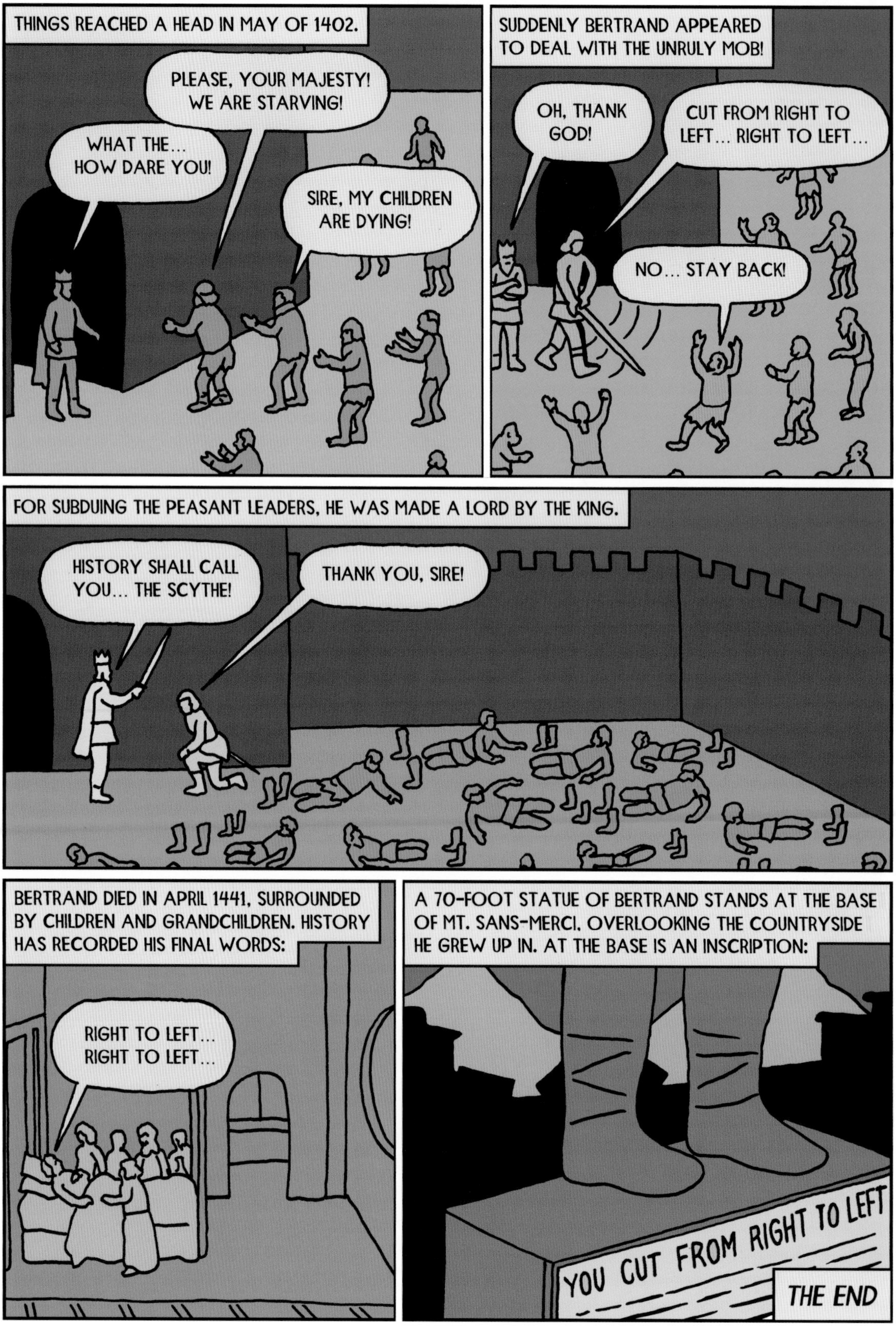
THINGS REACHED A HEAD IN MAY OF 1402.
PLEASE, YOUR MAJESTY! WE ARE STARVING!
WHAT THE... HOW DARE YOU!
SIRE, MY CHILDREN ARE DYING!
SUDDENLY BERTRAND APPEARED TO DEAL WITH THE UNRULY MOB!
OH, THANK GOD!
CUT FROM RIGHT TO LEFT... RIGHT TO LEFT...
NO... STAY BACK!
FOR SUBDUING THE PEASANT LEADERS, HE WAS MADE A LORD BY THE KING.
HISTORY SHALL CALL YOU... THE SCYTHE!
THANK YOU, SIRE!
BERTRAND DIED IN APRIL 1441, SURROUNDED BY CHILDREN AND GRANDCHILDREN. HISTORY HAS RECORDED HIS FINAL WORDS:
RIGHT TO LEFT... RIGHT TO LEFT...
A 70-FOOT STATUE OF BERTRAND STANDS AT THE BASE OF MT. SANS-MERCI, OVERLOOKING THE COUNTRYSIDE HE GREW UP IN. AT THE BASE IS AN INSCRIPTION:
YOU CUT FROM RIGHT TO LEFT
THE END

MOON 69
THE TRUE STORY
OF THE
1969 MOON LAUNCH

IN 1969 RICHARD NIXON IS COURTING THE HIPPY VOTE.

69ING AND ACID ARE GROOVY! LET'S GO TO THE MOON!

NASA KNOWS THAT IF THEY DON'T BUILD AND LAUNCH A WORKING MOON ROCKET IMMEDIATELY, NIXON WILL HAVE THEM ALL MURDERED.

YOU HAVE THIRTY DAYS. DO YOU HEAR ME? THIRTY DAYS.

BUT WE DON'T HAVE A ROCKET CAPABLE—

DESPERATE, NASA HOLDS A NEWSPAPER CONTEST.

DESIGN THE MOON ROCKET AND WIN TWO FREE TICKETS TO THE MGM MOVIE "THE BRAVE AND THE OLD."

THEIR LUCK CHANGES WHEN A WORKING ROCKET IS DONATED BY A MYSTERIOUS "MR. GORSKY."

IT IS MAGNIFICENT— AND COMES WITH ITS OWN LOADING GANTRY, LAUNCH PAD, ETC.

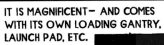

NASA HAS A ROCKET— NOW THEY NEED ASTRONAUTS TO FLY IN IT.

CONDEMNED PRISONERS— THAT'S WHO'LL FLY OUR SPACESHIP!

TWELVE DESPERATE MEN ARE GIVEN A REPRIEVE FROM DEATH ROW AND TRAINED IN RHYME.

ARMSTRONG STEPS OUT, THEN A SPEECH HE DOES SHOUT. ALDRIN COMES NEXT, JUGGLING SOME EGGS.

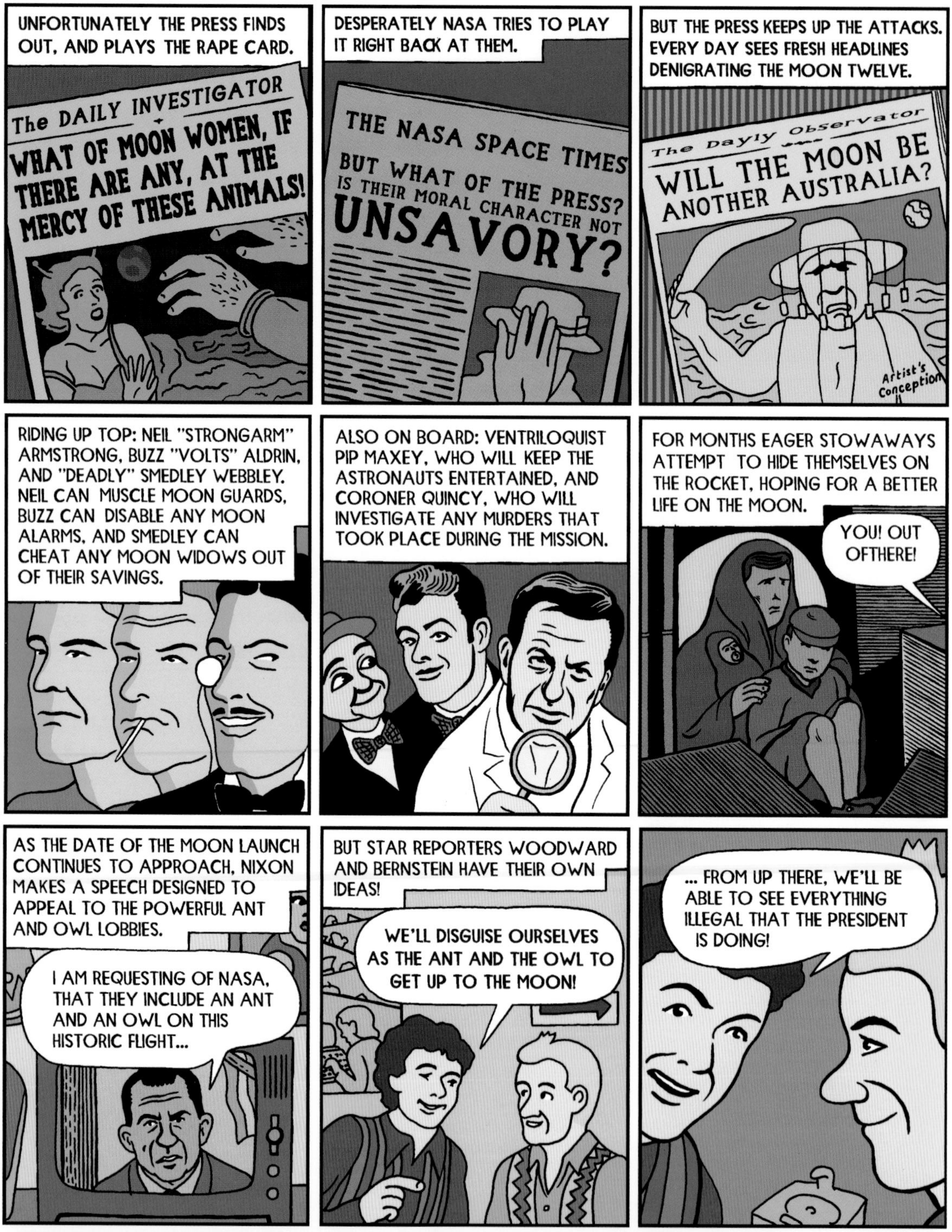
UNFORTUNATELY THE PRESS FINDS OUT, AND PLAYS THE RAPE CARD.
The DAILY INVESTIGATOR
WHAT OF MOON WOMEN, IF THERE ARE ANY, AT THE MERCY OF THESE ANIMALS!
DESPERATELY NASA TRIES TO PLAY IT RIGHT BACK AT THEM.
THE NASA SPACE TIMES
BUT WHAT OF THE PRESS? IS THEIR MORAL CHARACTER NOT UNSAVORY?
BUT THE PRESS KEEPS UP THE ATTACKS. EVERY DAY SEES FRESH HEADLINES DENIGRATING THE MOON TWELVE.
The Dayly Observator
WILL THE MOON BE ANOTHER AUSTRALIA?
Artist's Conception
RIDING UP TOP: NEIL "STRONGARM" ARMSTRONG, BUZZ "VOLTS" ALDRIN, AND "DEADLY" SMEDLEY WEBBLEY. NEIL CAN MUSCLE MOON GUARDS, BUZZ CAN DISABLE ANY MOON ALARMS, AND SMEDLEY CAN CHEAT ANY MOON WIDOWS OUT OF THEIR SAVINGS.
ALSO ON BOARD: VENTRILOQUIST PIP MAXEY, WHO WILL KEEP THE ASTRONAUTS ENTERTAINED, AND CORONER QUINCY, WHO WILL INVESTIGATE ANY MURDERS THAT TOOK PLACE DURING THE MISSION.
FOR MONTHS EAGER STOWAWAYS ATTEMPT TO HIDE THEMSELVES ON THE ROCKET, HOPING FOR A BETTER LIFE ON THE MOON.
YOU! OUT OFTHERE!
AS THE DATE OF THE MOON LAUNCH CONTINUES TO APPROACH, NIXON MAKES A SPEECH DESIGNED TO APPEAL TO THE POWERFUL ANT AND OWL LOBBIES.
I AM REQUESTING OF NASA, THAT THEY INCLUDE AN ANT AND AN OWL ON THIS HISTORIC FLIGHT...
BUT STAR REPORTERS WOODWARD AND BERNSTEIN HAVE THEIR OWN IDEAS!
WE'LL DISGUISE OURSELVES AS THE ANT AND THE OWL TO GET UP TO THE MOON!
... FROM UP THERE, WE'LL BE ABLE TO SEE EVERYTHING ILLEGAL THAT THE PRESIDENT IS DOING!

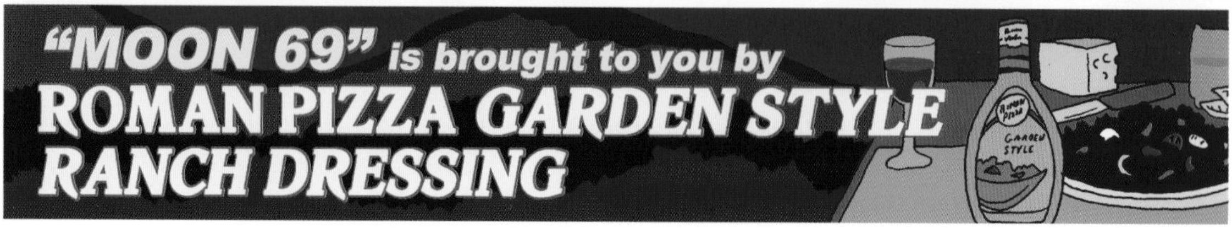
"MOON 69" is brought to you by
ROMAN PIZZA GARDEN STYLE RANCH DRESSING
GARDEN STYLE

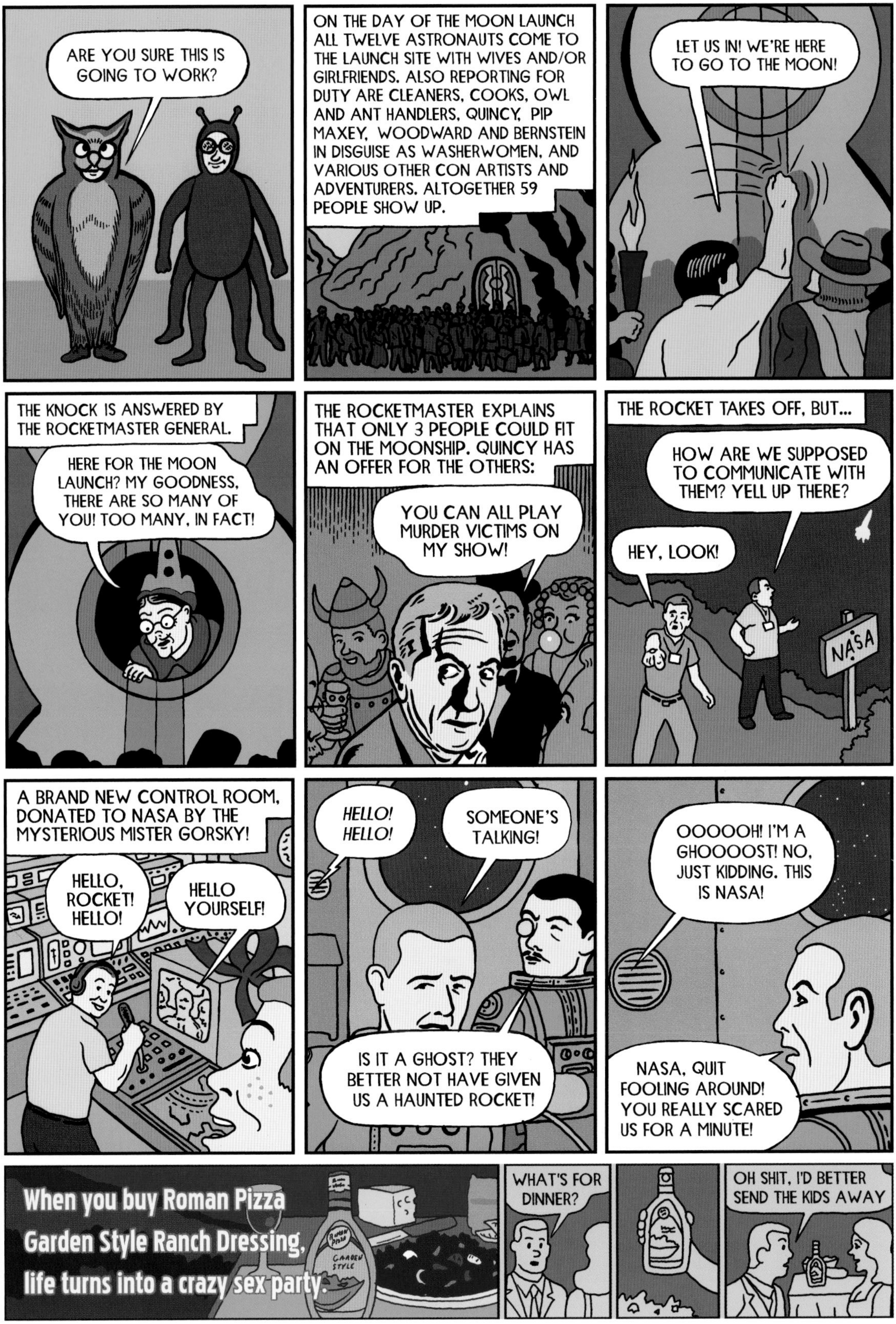
ARE YOU SURE THIS IS GOING TO WORK?
ON THE DAY OF THE MOON LAUNCH ALL TWELVE ASTRONAUTS COME TO THE LAUNCH SITE WITH WIVES AND/OR GIRLFRIENDS. ALSO REPORTING FOR DUTY ARE CLEANERS, COOKS, OWL AND ANT HANDLERS, QUINCY, PIP MAXEY, WOODWARD AND BERNSTEIN IN DISGUISE AS WASHERWOMEN, AND VARIOUS OTHER CON ARTISTS AND ADVENTURERS. ALTOGETHER 59 PEOPLE SHOW UP.
LET US IN! WE'RE HERE TO GO TO THE MOON!
THE KNOCK IS ANSWERED BY THE ROCKETMASTER GENERAL.
HERE FOR THE MOON LAUNCH? MY GOODNESS, THERE ARE SO MANY OF YOU! TOO MANY, IN FACT!
THE ROCKETMASTER EXPLAINS THAT ONLY 3 PEOPLE COULD FIT ON THE MOONSHIP. QUINCY HAS AN OFFER FOR THE OTHERS:
YOU CAN ALL PLAY MURDER VICTIMS ON MY SHOW!
THE ROCKET TAKES OFF, BUT...
HOW ARE WE SUPPOSED TO COMMUNICATE WITH THEM? YELL UP THERE?
HEY, LOOK!
NASA
A BRAND NEW CONTROL ROOM, DONATED TO NASA BY THE MYSTERIOUS MISTER GORSKY!
HELLO, ROCKET! HELLO!
HELLO YOURSELF!
HELLO! HELLO!
SOMEONE'S TALKING!
IS IT A GHOST? THEY BETTER NOT HAVE GIVEN US A HAUNTED ROCKET!
OOOOOH! I'M A GHOOOOST! NO, JUST KIDDING. THIS IS NASA!
NASA, QUIT FOOLING AROUND! YOU REALLY SCARED US FOR A MINUTE!
When you buy Roman Pizza Garden Style Ranch Dressing, life turns into a crazy sex party.
WHAT'S FOR DINNER?
OH SHIT, I'D BETTER SEND THE KIDS AWAY

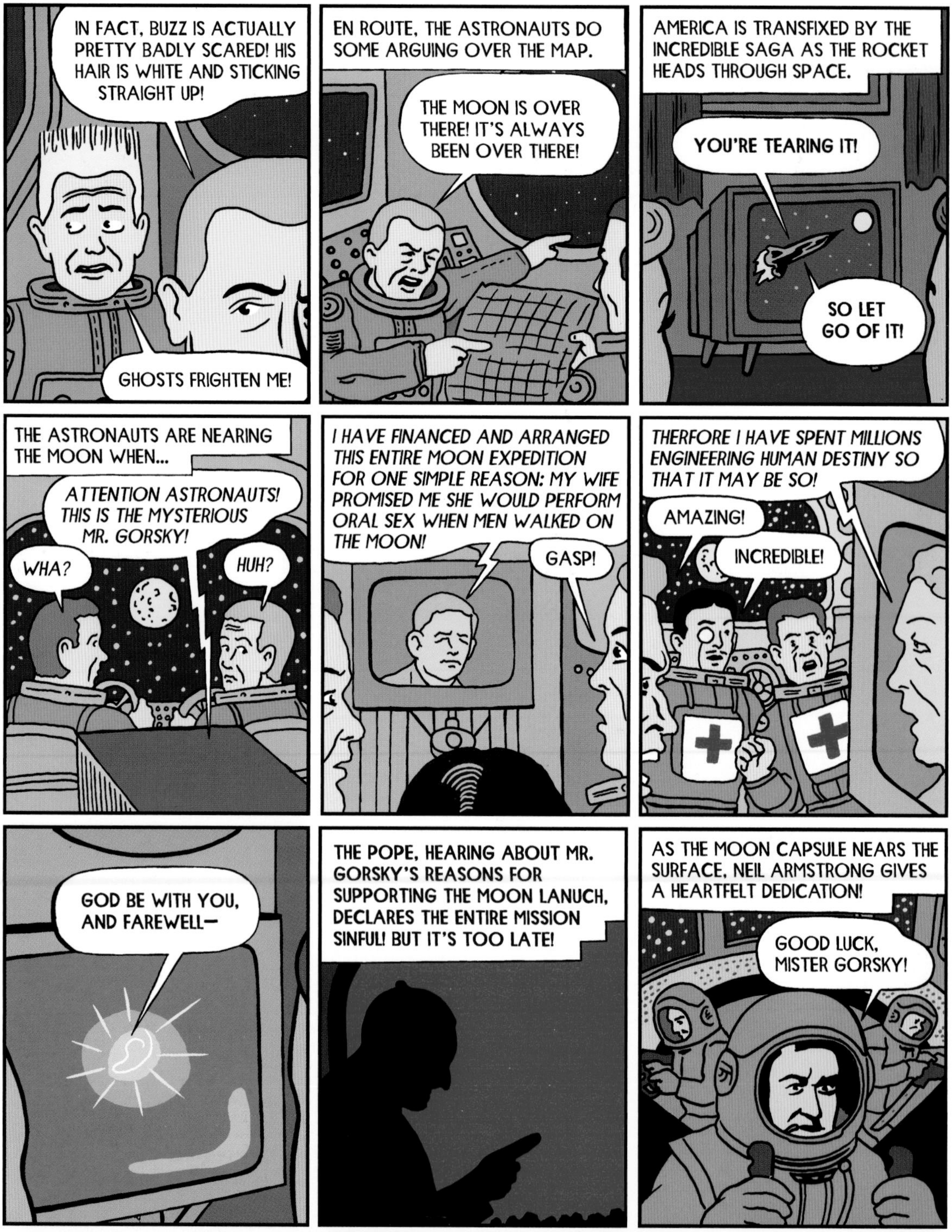
IN FACT, BUZZ IS ACTUALLY PRETTY BADLY SCARED! HIS HAIR IS WHITE AND STICKING STRAIGHT UP!
GHOSTS FRIGHTEN ME!
EN ROUTE, THE ASTRONAUTS DO SOME ARGUING OVER THE MAP.
THE MOON IS OVER THERE! IT'S ALWAYS BEEN OVER THERE!
AMERICA IS TRANSFIXED BY THE INCREDIBLE SAGA AS THE ROCKET HEADS THROUGH SPACE.
YOU'RE TEARING IT!
SO LET GO OF IT!
THE ASTRONAUTS ARE NEARING THE MOON WHEN...
ATTENTION ASTRONAUTS! THIS IS THE MYSTERIOUS MR. GORSKY!
WHA?
HUH?
I HAVE FINANCED AND ARRANGED THIS ENTIRE MOON EXPEDITION FOR ONE SIMPLE REASON: MY WIFE PROMISED ME SHE WOULD PERFORM ORAL SEX WHEN MEN WALKED ON THE MOON!
GASP!
THERFORE I HAVE SPENT MILLIONS ENGINEERING HUMAN DESTINY SO THAT IT MAY BE SO!
AMAZING!
INCREDIBLE!
GOD BE WITH YOU, AND FAREWELL—
THE POPE, HEARING ABOUT MR. GORSKY'S REASONS FOR SUPPORTING THE MOON LANUCH, DECLARES THE ENTIRE MISSION SINFUL! BUT IT'S TOO LATE!
AS THE MOON CAPSULE NEARS THE SURFACE, NEIL ARMSTRONG GIVES A HEARTFELT DEDICATION!
GOOD LUCK, MISTER GORSKY!

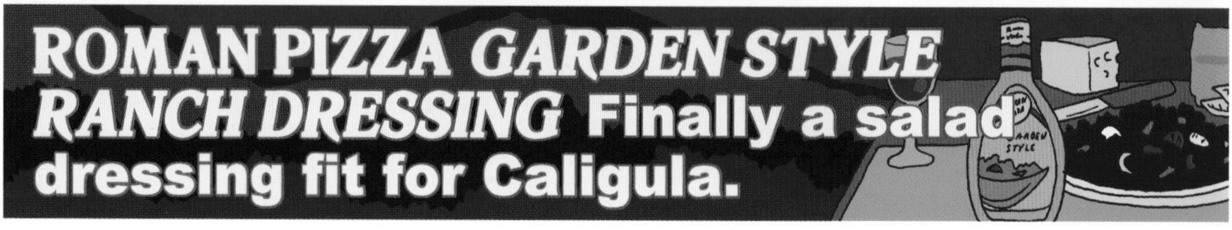
ROMAN PIZZA GARDEN STYLE RANCH DRESSING Finally a salad dressing fit for Caligula.

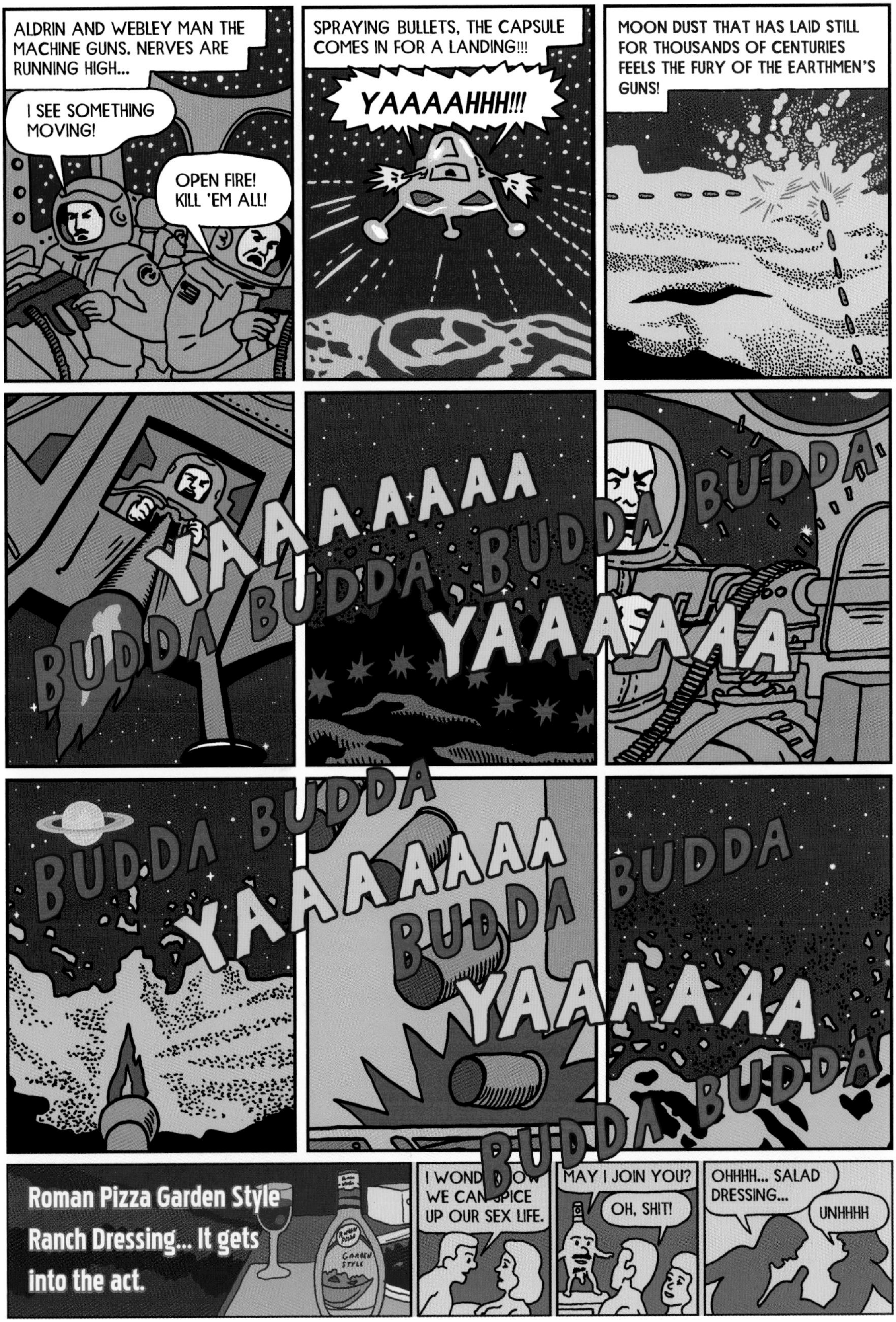
ALDRIN AND WEBLEY MAN THE MACHINE GUNS. NERVES ARE RUNNING HIGH...
I SEE SOMETHING MOVING!
OPEN FIRE! KILL 'EM ALL!
SPRAYING BULLETS, THE CAPSULE COMES IN FOR A LANDING!!!
YAAAAHHH!!!
MOON DUST THAT HAS LAID STILL FOR THOUSANDS OF CENTURIES FEELS THE FURY OF THE EARTHMEN'S GUNS!
YAAAAAAAA
BUDDA BUDDA BUDDA BUDDA
YAAAAAAA
BUDDA BUDDA
YAAAAAAAA
BUDDA
BUDDA
YAAAAAAA
BUDDA BUDDA
Roman Pizza Garden Style Ranch Dressing... It gets into the act.
GARDEN STYLE
I WOND OW WE CAN SPICE UP OUR SEX LIFE.
MAY I JOIN YOU?
OH, SHIT!
OHHHH... SALAD DRESSING...
UNHHHH

ALRIGHT— I THINK THAT'S ENOUGH.

WHATEVER'S DOWN THERE KNOWS THE TYPE OF PUNISHMENT WE CAN PROVIDE— HOPEFULLY THEY'LL THINK TWICE ABOUT MAKING A MOVE.

ALSO, I DON'T THINK THERE IS ANYONE DOWN THERE. TIME TO MAKE HISTORY, BOYS!

FOR THE FIRST TIME WE KNOW OF, HUMAN BOOTS STEP ONTO THE MOON'S SURFACE.

AND NEIL ARMSTRONG SAYS SOME FAMOUS WORDS!

ONE SMALL STEP FOR THIS MAN, AND I'M STANDING ON THE MOON!!!

ME, WHO THEY SAID WOULD NEVER AMOUNT TO ANYTHING! ALL MY LIFE, THE MAN ON MY BACK, KEEPING ME DOWN...

ARMSTRONG LETS A LIFETIME OF ANGER LOOSE, RANTING FOR OVER FIFTEEN MINUTES!

BY THE END HE IS WEEPING.

BUT I SHOWED 'EM.... I SHOWED 'EM ALL...

HE IS FOLLOWED BY BUZZ ALDRIN, JUGGLING SOME EGGS!

THE REST OF THE MOON LANDING GOES SMOOTHLY. THE ANT AND THE OWL DO THEIR BIT WHILE THE ASTRONAUTS COLLECT MOON ROCKS.

WHEN THE WORK IS DONE THE ASTRONAUTS PLAY A FEW ROUNDS OF VOLLEYBALL...

...AND THEN IT'S TIME TO LEAVE.

GOODNIGHT, MOON!

AS THE ASTRONAUTS PREPARE TO HEAD HOME, THEY PAUSE TO ENJOY THEIR VICTORY SANDWICHES.

EVERYTHING TASTES BETTER IN SPACE!

BUT, UNBEKNOWNST TO THEM, NIXON HAD PACKED THE SANDWICHES WITH EXPLOSIVES!

EXPLODE THEM!

NIXON WANTS ALL THE ASTRONAUTS DEAD FOR SOME REASON!

BLOW THEM UP!

BUT SUDDENLY —

THE *NEW THREE MUSKETEERS!*

HALT THEE, MONSIEUR PRESIDENT!

WE SHALL REPLACE THEE WITH THE *NIXON IN THE IRON MASK!* AND YOU SHALL TAKE HIS PLACE IN THE WHITE HOUSE DUNGEON!

AW, DARNIT!

THE WORLD HASN'T SEEN THE LAST OF ME!

WHATEVER HAPPENED TO ED BEDD? I HAVEN'T SEEN HIM IN A LONG TIME.

HAVEN'T YOU HEARD? HIM AND HIS WIFE STARTED HAVING SEX WITH THEIR SALAD DRESSING, THEN THEY BOTH LITERALLY WENT INSANE!

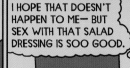

I HOPE THAT DOESN'T HAPPEN TO ME— BUT SEX WITH THAT SALAD DRESSING IS SOO GOOD.

HEY, WHAT ARE YOU THINKING ABOUT?

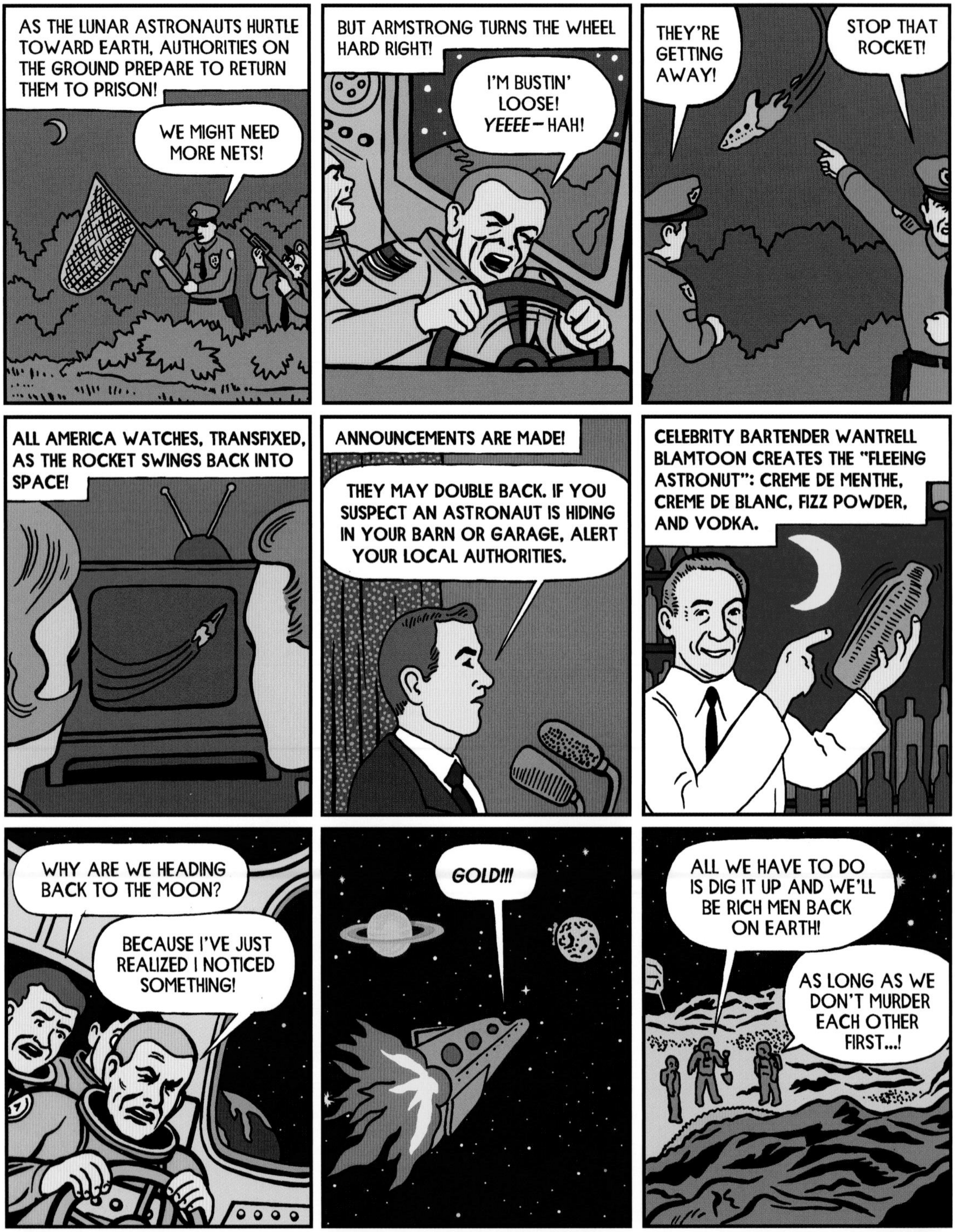
AS THE LUNAR ASTRONAUTS HURTLE TOWARD EARTH, AUTHORITIES ON THE GROUND PREPARE TO RETURN THEM TO PRISON!
WE MIGHT NEED MORE NETS!
BUT ARMSTRONG TURNS THE WHEEL HARD RIGHT!
I'M BUSTIN' LOOSE! *YEEEE*—HAH!
THEY'RE GETTING AWAY!
STOP THAT ROCKET!
ALL AMERICA WATCHES, TRANSFIXED, AS THE ROCKET SWINGS BACK INTO SPACE!
ANNOUNCEMENTS ARE MADE!
THEY MAY DOUBLE BACK. IF YOU SUSPECT AN ASTRONAUT IS HIDING IN YOUR BARN OR GARAGE, ALERT YOUR LOCAL AUTHORITIES.
CELEBRITY BARTENDER WANTRELL BLAMTOON CREATES THE "FLEEING ASTRONUT": CREME DE MENTHE, CREME DE BLANC, FIZZ POWDER, AND VODKA.
WHY ARE WE HEADING BACK TO THE MOON?
BECAUSE I'VE JUST REALIZED I NOTICED SOMETHING!
GOLD!!!
ALL WE HAVE TO DO IS DIG IT UP AND WE'LL BE RICH MEN BACK ON EARTH!
AS LONG AS WE DON'T MURDER EACH OTHER FIRST...!

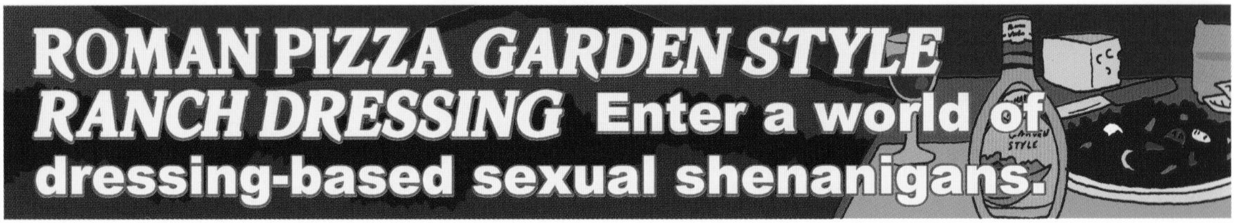
ROMAN PIZZA *GARDEN STYLE RANCH DRESSING*
Enter a world of dressing-based sexual shenanigans.

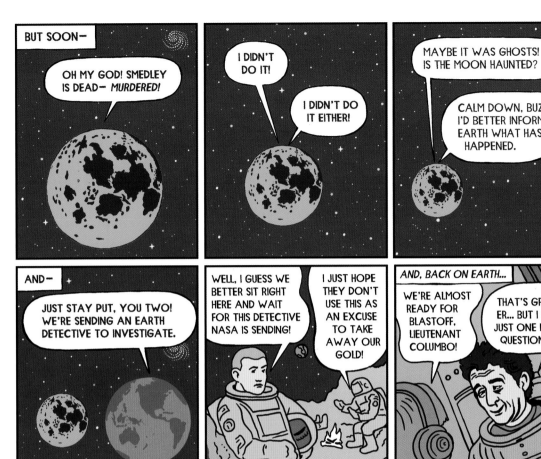

BUT SOON—

OH MY GOD! SMEDLEY IS DEAD— *MURDERED!*

I DIDN'T DO IT!

I DIDN'T DO IT EITHER!

MAYBE IT WAS GHOSTS! IS THE MOON HAUNTED?

CALM DOWN, BUZZ. I'D BETTER INFORM EARTH WHAT HAS HAPPENED.

AND—

JUST STAY PUT, YOU TWO! WE'RE SENDING AN EARTH DETECTIVE TO INVESTIGATE.

WELL, I GUESS WE BETTER SIT RIGHT HERE AND WAIT FOR THIS DETECTIVE NASA IS SENDING!

I JUST HOPE THEY DON'T USE THIS AS AN EXCUSE TO TAKE AWAY OUR GOLD!

AND, BACK ON EARTH...

WE'RE ALMOST READY FOR BLASTOFF, LIEUTENANT COLUMBO!

THAT'S GREAT! ER... BUT I HAVE JUST ONE MORE QUESTION...

WHEN YOU GET CLOSE TO THE MOON, IS IT FULL ALL THE TIME? THAT IS TO SAY, ER...

WORRIED ABOUT THAT GUY WHO BIT ME LAST NIGHT... THINK HE WAS A WEREWOLF!

WITH THE ASTRONAUTS BACK ON THE MOON, ONE OF THEM HAS BEEN MURDERED, AND NASA ARE SENDING THE RENOWNED DETECTIVE LT. COLUMBO TO INVESTIGATE...

THIS WILL BE A REAL CHALLENGE, SOLVING A CRIME IN SPACE! BUT I'M WORRIED I'LL TURN INTO A WEREWOLF!

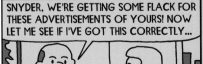

SNYDER, WE'RE GETTING SOME FLACK FOR THESE ADVERTISEMENTS OF YOURS! NOW LET ME SEE IF I'VE GOT THIS CORRECTLY...

KROFT FOODS HIRED US TO PRODUCE FAMILY TV ADS FOR THEIR NEW ROMAN PIZZA GARDEN STYLE RANCH DRESSING! WE LET YOU HANDLE IT, NOW YOU'VE GOT ADS WITH BIZARRE EROTIC CONCEPTS, WOMEN AND MEN HAVING SEX WITH TALKING SALAD DRESSING, IS THAT RIGHT?

YEP.

WELL DONE!

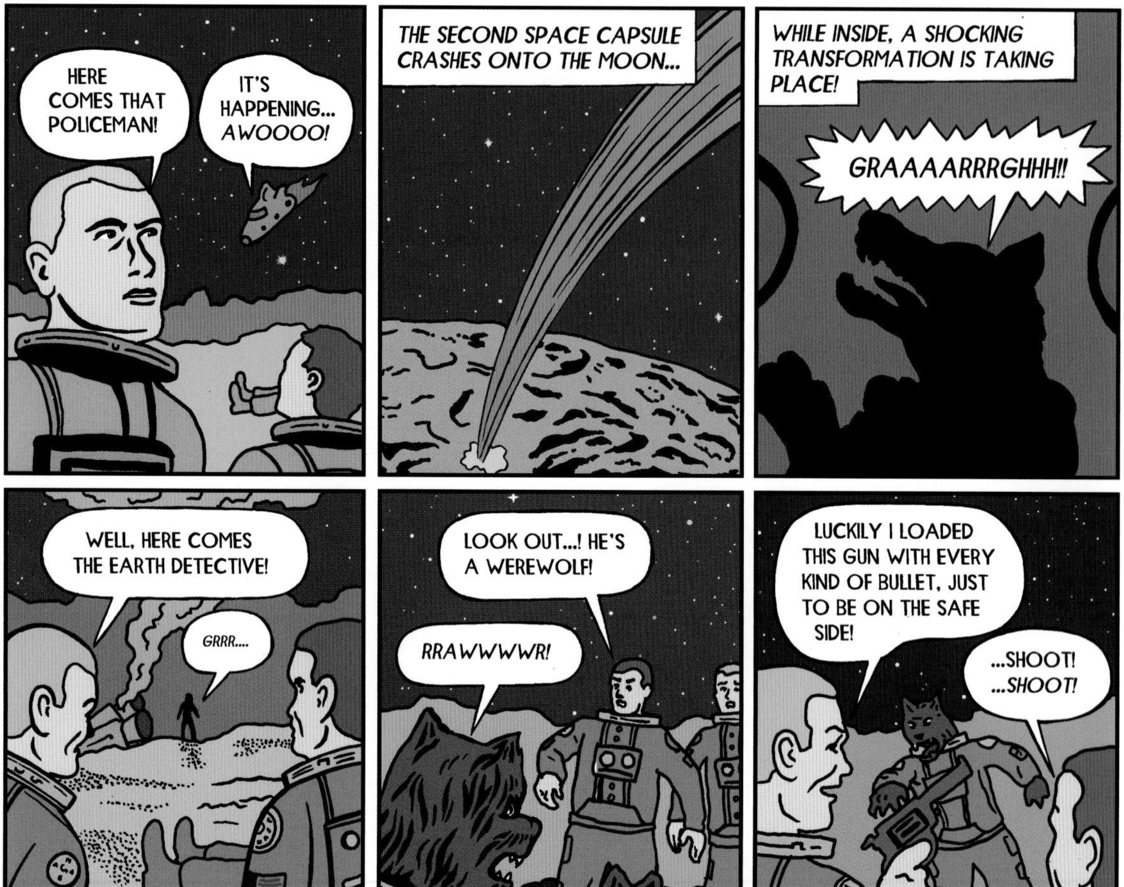
HERE COMES THAT POLICEMAN!
IT'S HAPPENING... AWOOOO!
THE SECOND SPACE CAPSULE CRASHES ONTO THE MOON...
WHILE INSIDE, A SHOCKING TRANSFORMATION IS TAKING PLACE!
GRAAAARRRGHHH!!
WELL, HERE COMES THE EARTH DETECTIVE!
GRRR....
LOOK OUT...! HE'S A WEREWOLF!
RRAWWWWR!
LUCKILY I LOADED THIS GUN WITH EVERY KIND OF BULLET, JUST TO BE ON THE SAFE SIDE!
...SHOOT! ...SHOOT!
I'VE GOT SIX DIFFERENT KINDS OF BULLET IN THIS GUN! CHOCOLATE, CHALK, CHEESE, GOLD, SILVER AND SPICY ITALIAN SAUSAGE!
HIS FINGER TIGHTENS ON THE TRIGGER...
BUT—
WAARROHHH.....
HE'S CHANGING BACK TO HUMAN!

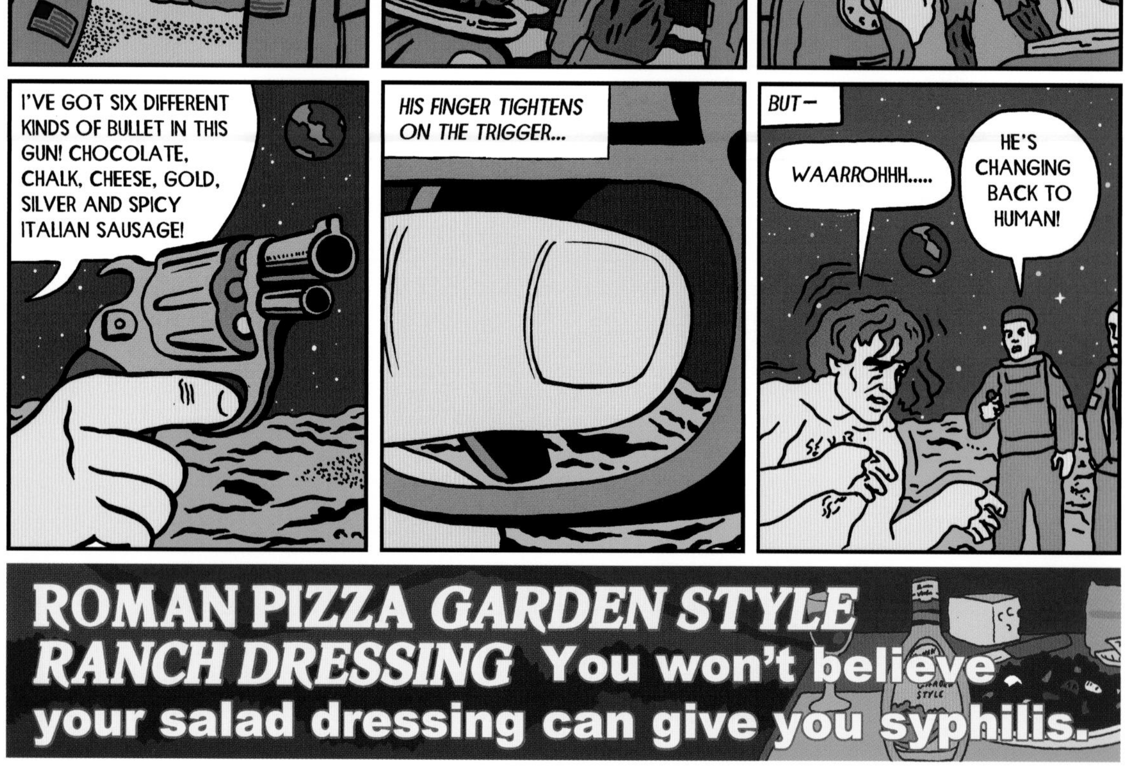
ROMAN PIZZA GARDEN STYLE RANCH DRESSING You won't believe your salad dressing can give you syphilis.

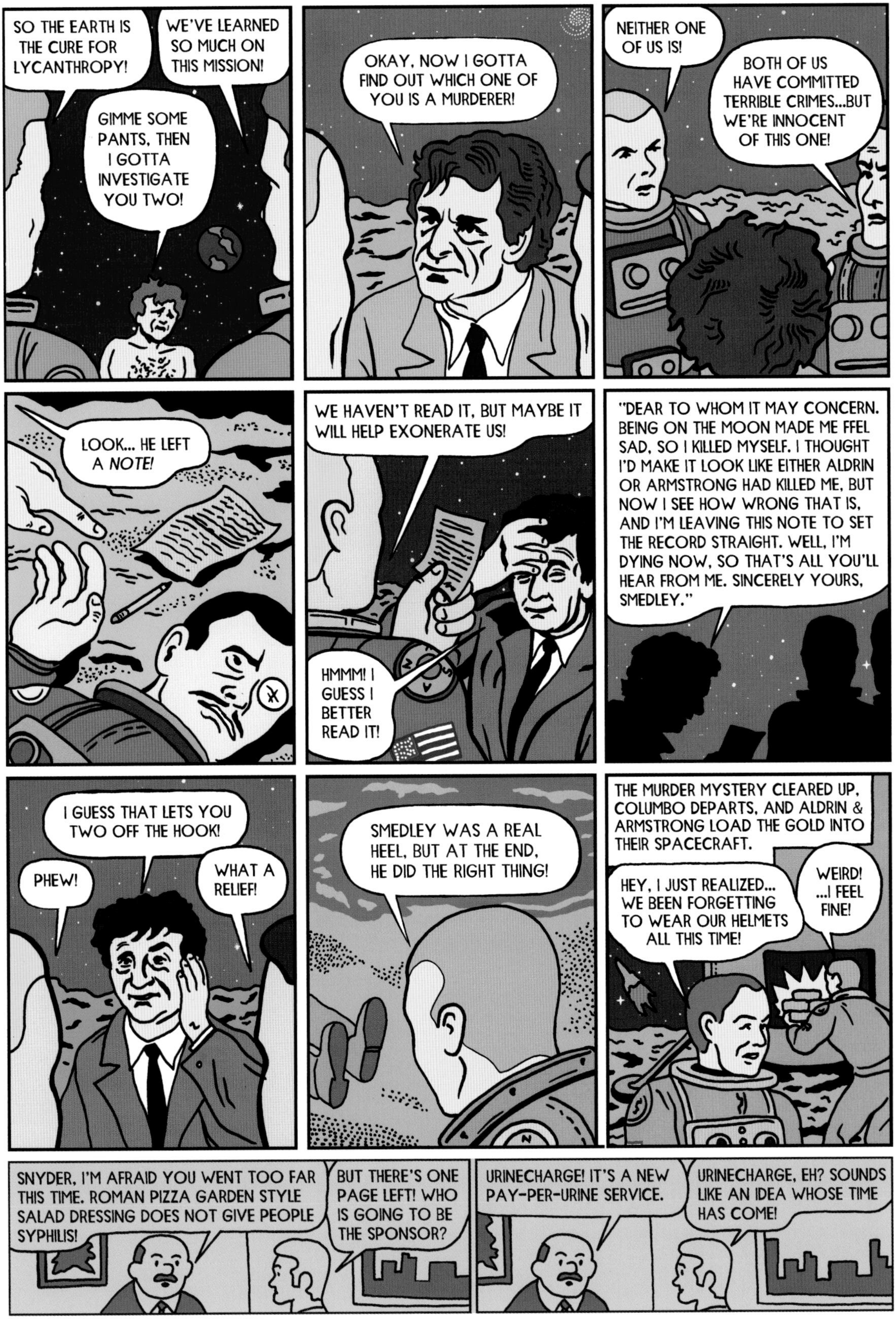
SO THE EARTH IS THE CURE FOR LYCANTHROPY!
WE'VE LEARNED SO MUCH ON THIS MISSION!
GIMME SOME PANTS, THEN I GOTTA INVESTIGATE YOU TWO!
OKAY, NOW I GOTTA FIND OUT WHICH ONE OF YOU IS A MURDERER!
NEITHER ONE OF US IS!
BOTH OF US HAVE COMMITTED TERRIBLE CRIMES...BUT WE'RE INNOCENT OF THIS ONE!
LOOK... HE LEFT A NOTE!
WE HAVEN'T READ IT, BUT MAYBE IT WILL HELP EXONERATE US!
HMMM! I GUESS I BETTER READ IT!
"DEAR TO WHOM IT MAY CONCERN. BEING ON THE MOON MADE ME FFEL SAD, SO I KILLED MYSELF. I THOUGHT I'D MAKE IT LOOK LIKE EITHER ALDRIN OR ARMSTRONG HAD KILLED ME, BUT NOW I SEE HOW WRONG THAT IS, AND I'M LEAVING THIS NOTE TO SET THE RECORD STRAIGHT. WELL, I'M DYING NOW, SO THAT'S ALL YOU'LL HEAR FROM ME. SINCERELY YOURS, SMEDLEY."
I GUESS THAT LETS YOU TWO OFF THE HOOK!
PHEW!
WHAT A RELIEF!
SMEDLEY WAS A REAL HEEL, BUT AT THE END, HE DID THE RIGHT THING!
THE MURDER MYSTERY CLEARED UP, COLUMBO DEPARTS, AND ALDRIN & ARMSTRONG LOAD THE GOLD INTO THEIR SPACECRAFT.
HEY, I JUST REALIZED... WE BEEN FORGETTING TO WEAR OUR HELMETS ALL THIS TIME!
WEIRD! ...I FEEL FINE!
SNYDER, I'M AFRAID YOU WENT TOO FAR THIS TIME. ROMAN PIZZA GARDEN STYLE SALAD DRESSING DOES NOT GIVE PEOPLE SYPHILIS!
BUT THERE'S ONE PAGE LEFT! WHO IS GOING TO BE THE SPONSOR?
URINECHARGE! IT'S A NEW PAY-PER-URINE SERVICE.
URINECHARGE, EH? SOUNDS LIKE AN IDEA WHOSE TIME HAS COME!

LOOKIT THIS LITTLE FELLA! HE JUST APPEARED AND BECAME MY BEST FRIEND AND NOW I'M GONNA CALL HIM GLEEPY!
HAHA, THAT'S GREAT!
FINALLY, 27 DAYS AFTER THEY LEFT EARTH, THE MOON CAPSULE IS ON ITS WAY BACK, WITH ASTRONAUTS ARMSTRONG AND ALDRIN ON BOARD. ALSO A TON OF GOLD THE ASTRONAUTS ARE HOPING TO KEEP, AND THEIR NEW ODDBALL SPACE PAL GLEEPY. THIS IS WALTER CRONKITE, AND THIS HAS BEEN THE NEWS AS THEY TOLD IT TO ME.
THE SPACE ROCKET IS RE-ENTERING EARTH'S ATMOSPHERE WHEN...
GLEEPY, MY FACE! NO....AAAAAGH!
NEIL! NEIL!
WE WILL CONQUER THE EARTH
THE ALIEN HAS MERGED WITH ARMSTRONG!
WE'VE MADE YOU INTO A ROBOT, ALDRIN
I'LL HUNT DOWN MY FORMER TEAMMATE FOR YOU. LET THE GAMES BEGIN!
HALF-ALIEN ARMSTRONG SUCCEEDS IN DISAPPEARING, BUT MEANWHILE ALDRIN HAS PUT HIS OWN PLANS INTO ACTION...
THE SON-OF-A-BITCH!
GASP!
The Noo Yoik Times
"We're Fulla News"
25 Cents
HALF-ROBOT ALDRIN USES MOON GOLD TO OPEN CASINO IN MACAU
They say dreams can come true when you go to the Moon, and for one young astronaut that saying seems to have come true. Buzz "Tingle" Aldrin has used the gold he found on the Moon has enabled him to open a casino in
MACAU
I ONLY FOLLOW ONE ESSENTIAL RULE...
THE LUCKY astronaut
...ALWAYS GIVE A SUCKER AN EVEN BREAK!
YES SIR, MISTER HALF-ROBOT BUZZ ALDRIN!
THE END?

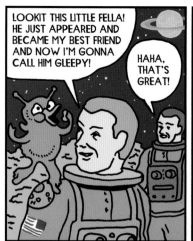

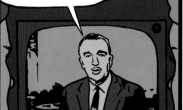

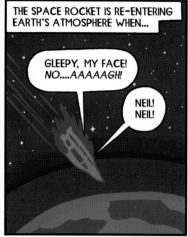

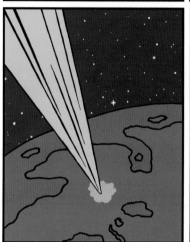

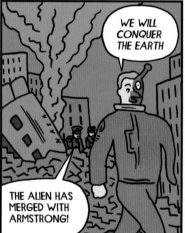

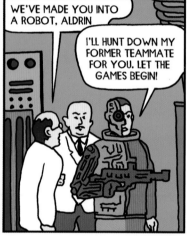

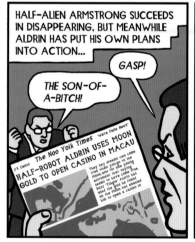

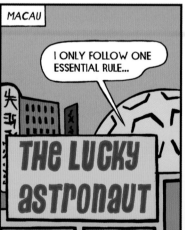

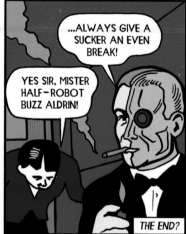

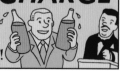

TINY ANIMALS
TO PUT IN YOUR PANTS

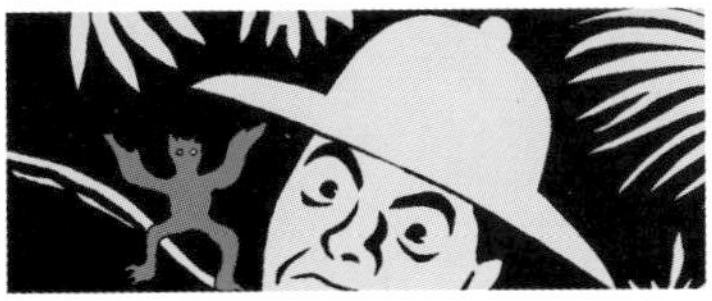

We don't know what these tiny animals are, but we found a LOAD of them in the Amazon, and we'll send you a bunch so you can put 'em down your pants.

Here's a satisfied customer:

"What, those little pants animal things? Sure, they felt great wiggling down there. Then after a while they stopped wiggling and I threw them away."

Send $5 to Pants Animals, Box 35, Ansonia NY

BAG OF HUMAN FINGERS

Don't ask us where they came from, but this bag of genuine fingers could come in quite "handy."

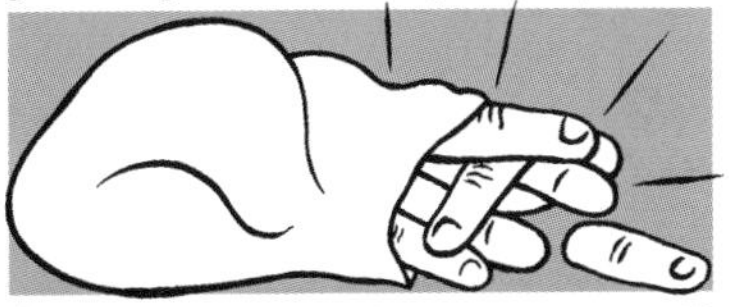

Send $5 to Finger Bag Offer, Box 35, Ansonia, NY

PEE MONKEYS

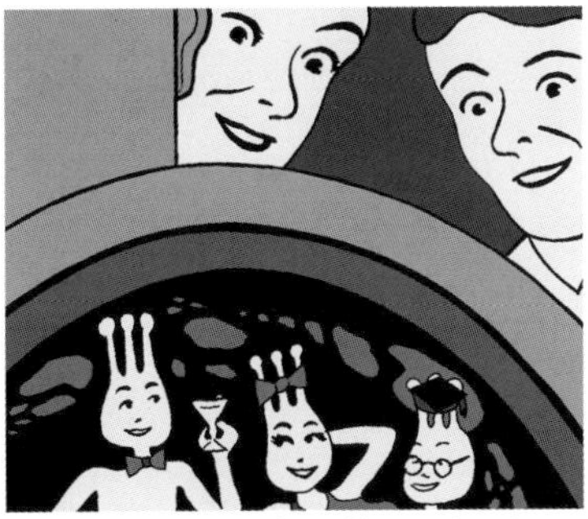

You'd swear they were living like people right up until the moment you flush the toilet! Send $6 to Pee Monkeys, Box 35, Ansonia, NY

MAGIC JEWEL TOADS

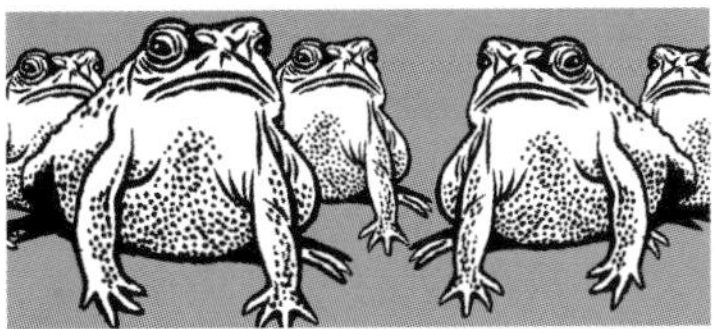

One of these toads has a magic jewel in his head... or does he? You'll have to work hard to find out! *$4 to Toads, Box 35, Ansonia, NY*

BANANA SKINS

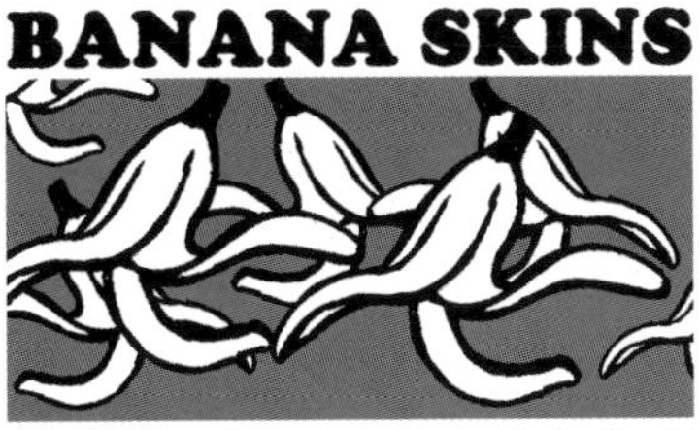

The fruit peel of 1000 uses. Invaluable for slips & pratfalls of all kinds. Ten dollars gets you 1500. *Write to: Banana Skins, Box 35, Ansonia, NY*

MEN!

HAVING TROUBLE KEEPING TRACK OF YOUR TESTICLES? THEN TRY THE NEW

NUT BUTLER

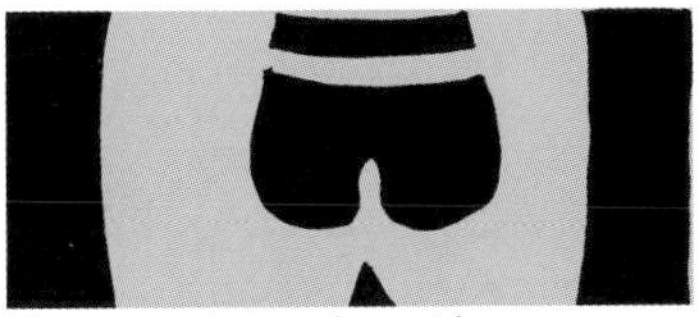

This amazing device makes testicle sortage an easy matter. "One... two... there you are, boys!" Send $12 to Nut Butler, Box 35, Ansonia, NY.

USED STAIRCASES

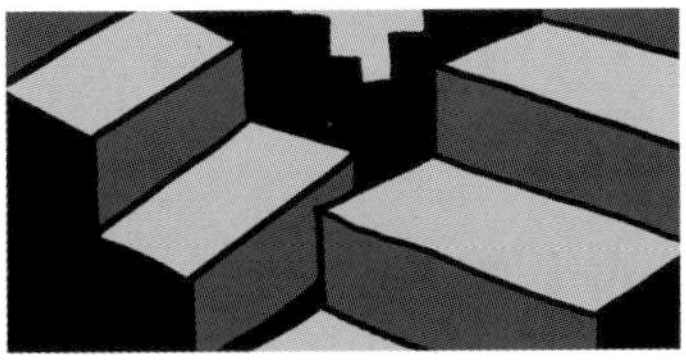

We got all kinds. Never you mind where they came from. Some w/carpets. Inquire Box 35, Ansonia NY

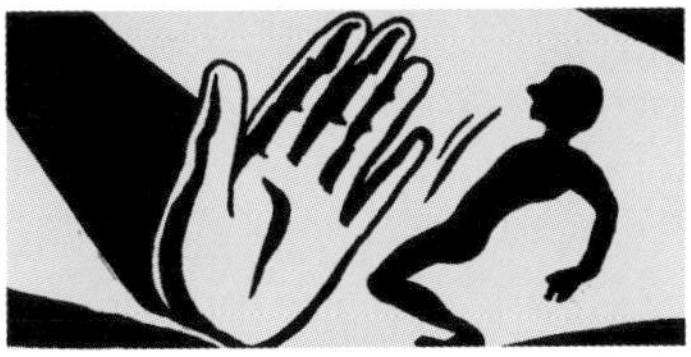

TIRED OF BEING PUSHED AROUND, TINY?

It's simple fact: a low-weight person has a tiny center of gravity, and they can be easily moved and shoved around. Is this you? Perhaps you'd enjoy being many times the size you are now. Now a Revolutionary Discovery by a reputed Doctor can lead you to never-before-dreamed-of heights of immensitude. Your circumference will increase radically and drastically. From now on if they want to push you around they'd better bring a bulldozer!

YOU CAN BE ENORMOUS

Stage one of my plan involves eating all the rich fried foods you want and then more. Never again will you leave the table hungry, because you will never leave the table again. You will simply sit there, eating and eating. Gradually you will introduce metals into your diet, both regular & "heavy," and compounds designed to help encourage possible height growth. During stage two other structural elements will be introduced to enable unimagined size growth. Concrete, wood and natural stone will be used to shore up and reinforce your bulk. In stage three you will be encouraged to commence gravity production, and develop your own atmosphere before being launched into space as a human satellite.

To get started, send a self-addressed stamped envelope to BULK GROWTH CORP, Box 35, Ansonia, NY. Do it today— don't delay!

FAIRY-TALE FOODS

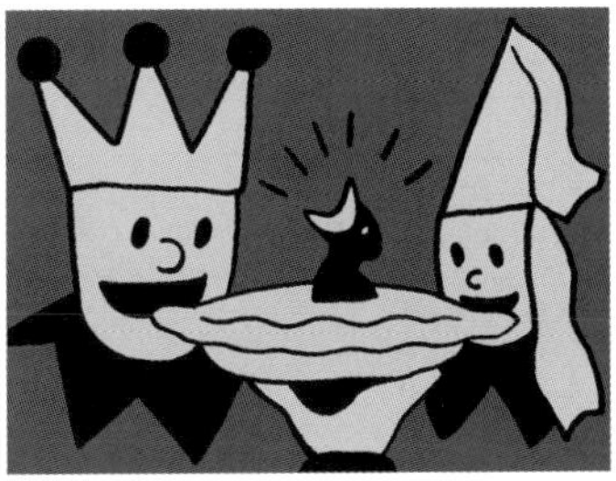

Canned Jack Sprats
Mashed Humpty Dumpty
Mother Goose Spread

CATALOGUE AVAILABLE ON REQUEST

Looking for that new and different handshake that will set you apart from the herd? Time to call:

HANDSHAKE SOLUTIONS

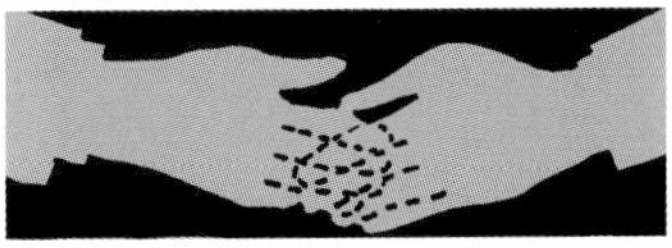

Our team of handshake designers will work day and night to fit you with a personalized handshake.

CALL 1-800 756-4535 EXTENTION 3547

THE HIDDEN SECRETS
OF PRETENDING THAT YOU HAVE TINY ANIMALS IN YOUR PANTS

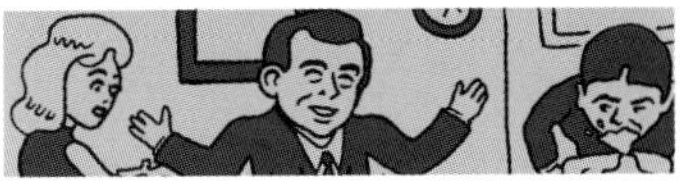

ARE YOU UNABLE TO AFFORD TINY ANIMALS TO PUT IN YOUR PANTS? OR ARE YOU CONCERNED ABOUT THE INJURIES THEIR TINY CLAWS AND PAWS MIGHT CAUSE? BUT DO YOU STILL WANT TO GIVE, IN PUBLIC, THE APPEARANCE OF HAVING ANIMALS IN YOUR PANTS NONETHELESS? PERHAPS YOUR PROMOTION DEPENDS ON IT. OR MAYBE YOUR MARRIAGE. SEND $4.95 TO PRETANTIMALS, BOX 35, ANSONIA NEW YORK

BOX OF GOO

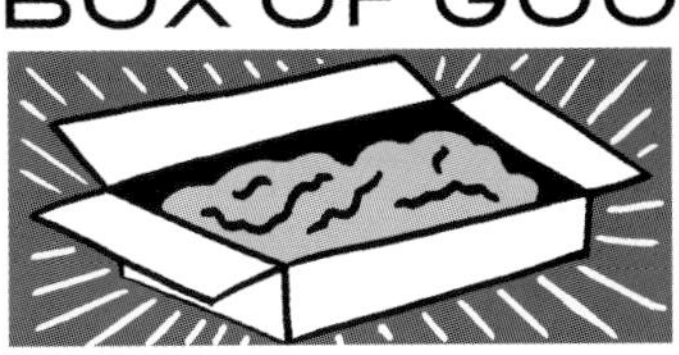

SEND $3 TO "GOO," BOX 35, ANSONIA NY

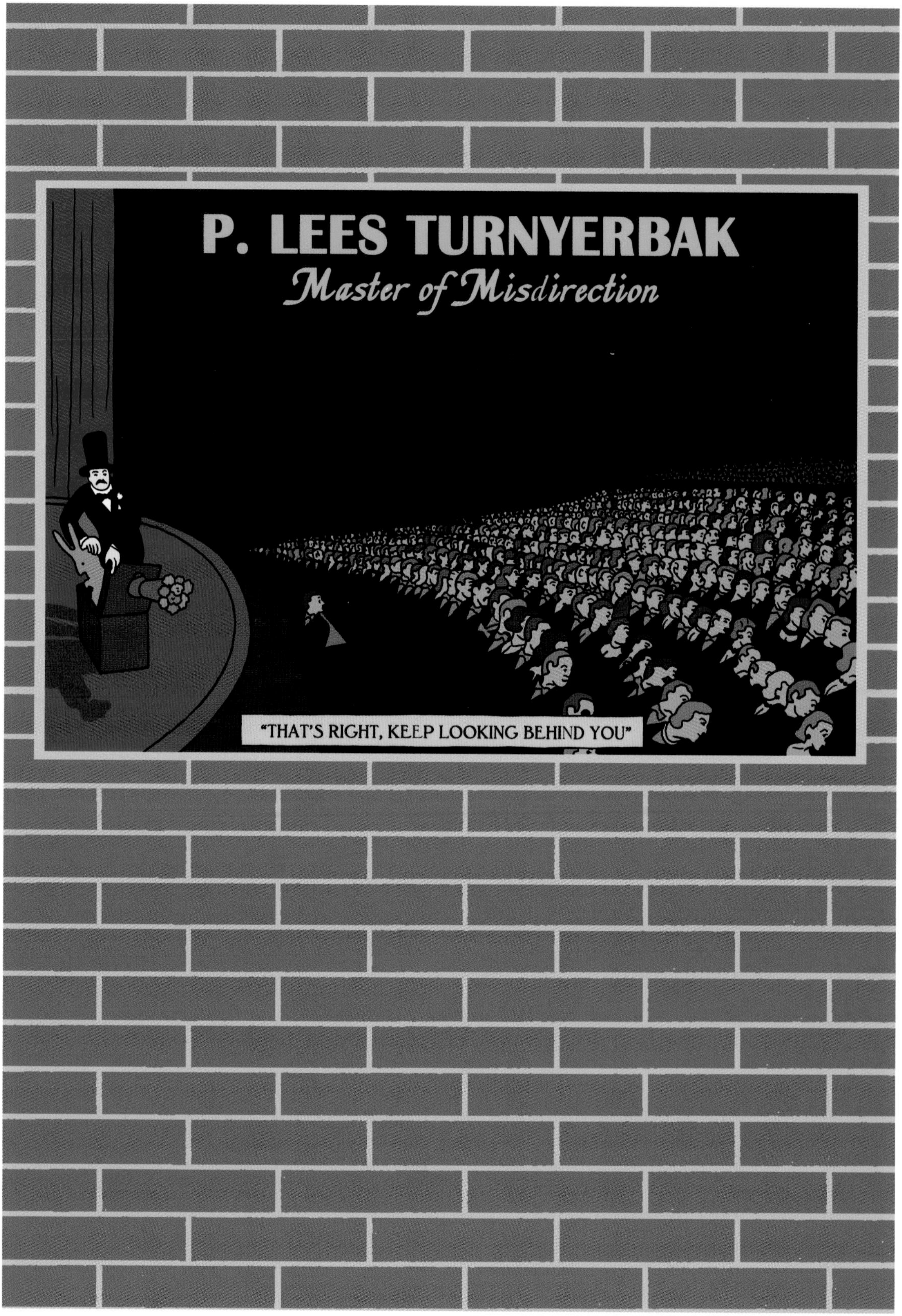
P. LEES TURNYERBAK
Master of Misdirection
"THAT'S RIGHT, KEEP LOOKING BEHIND YOU"

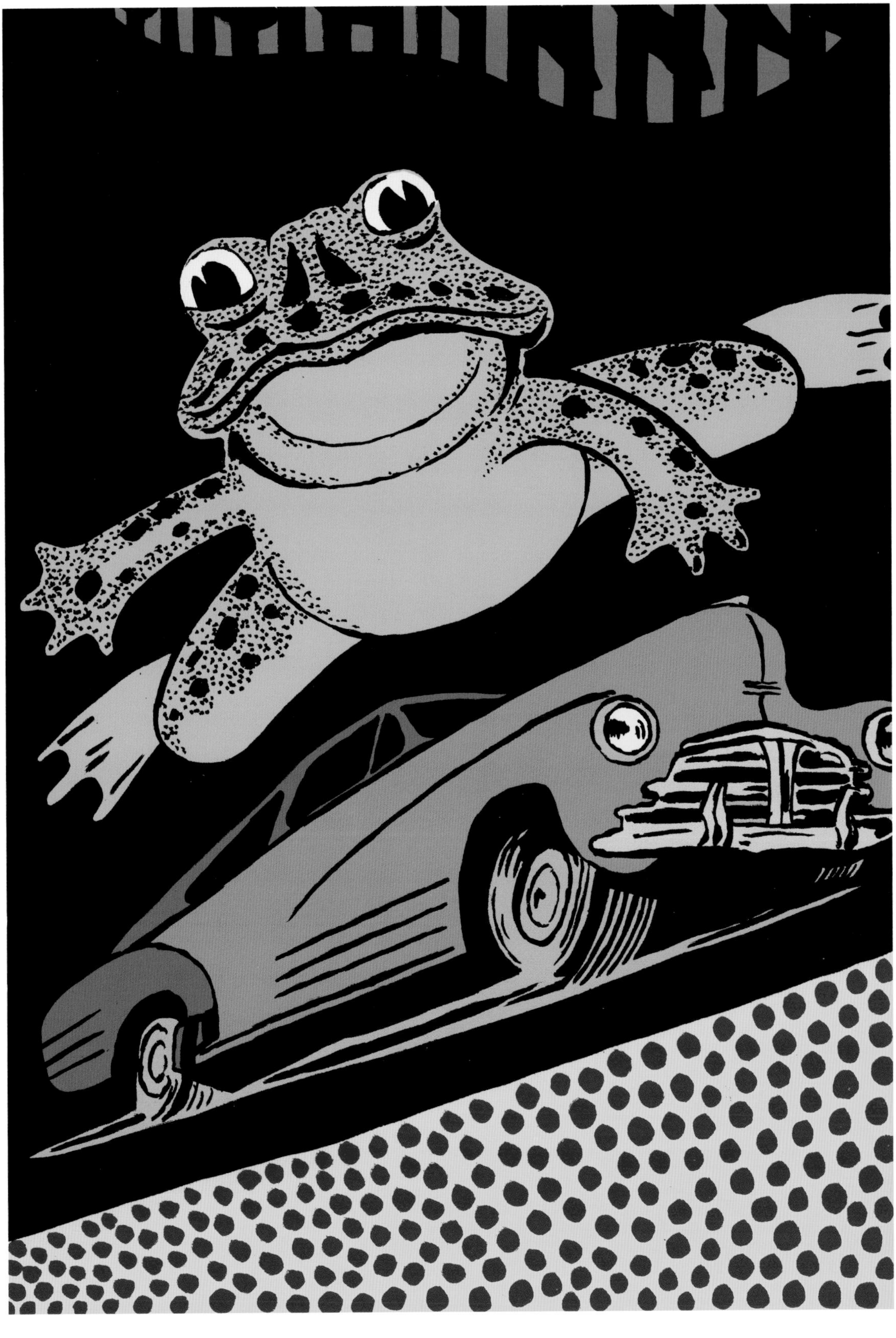

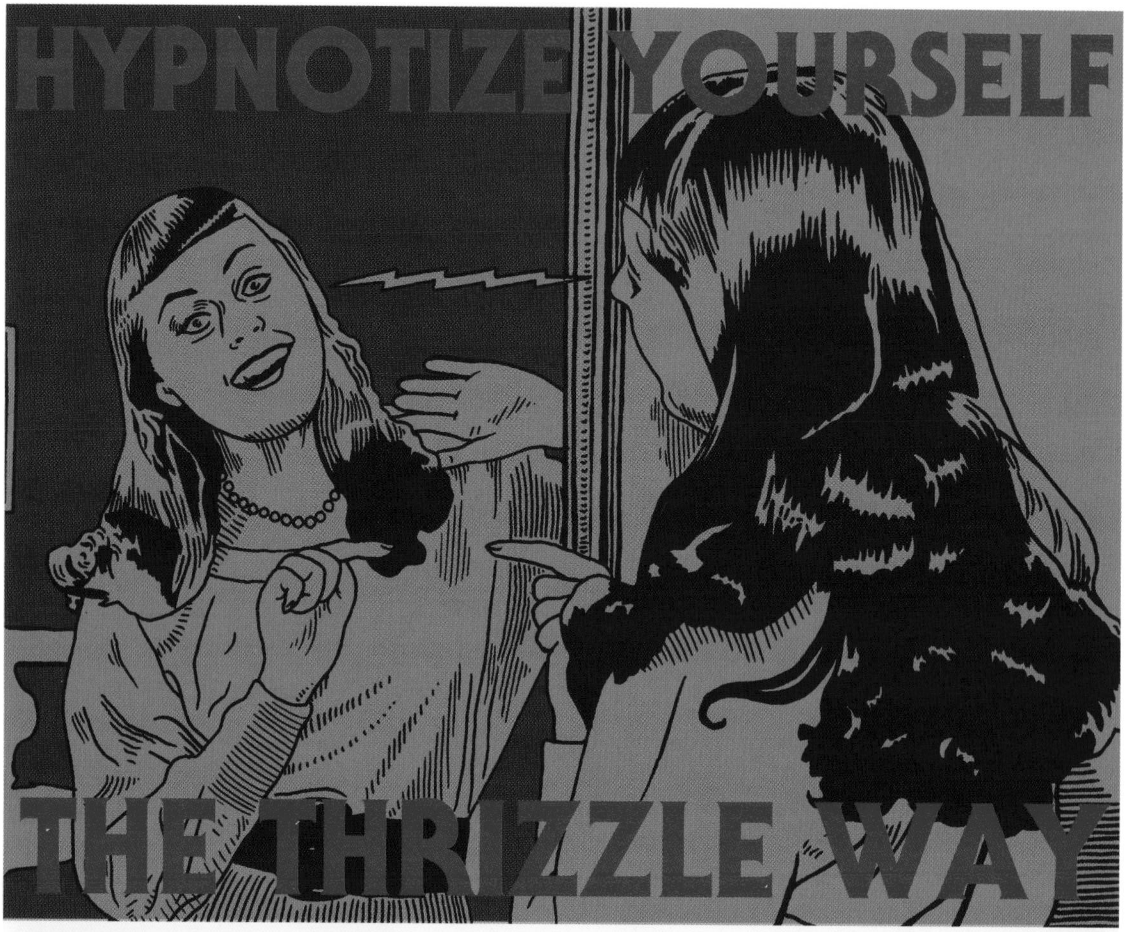
HYPNOTIZE YOURSELF
THE THRIZZLE WAY

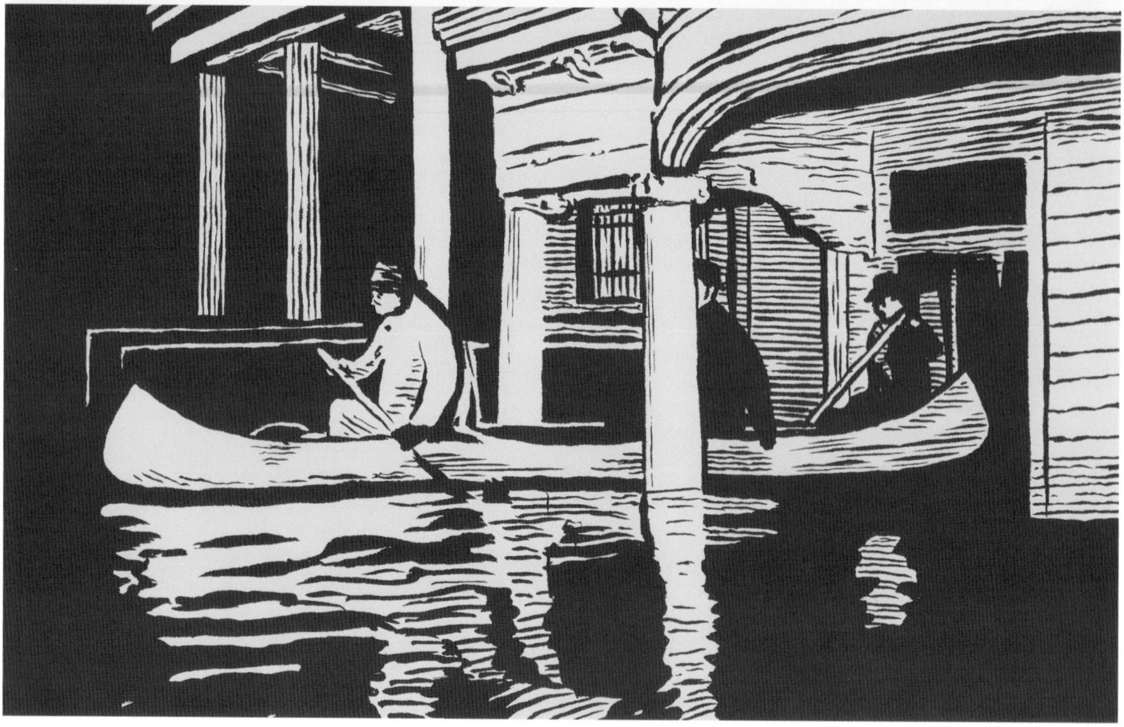

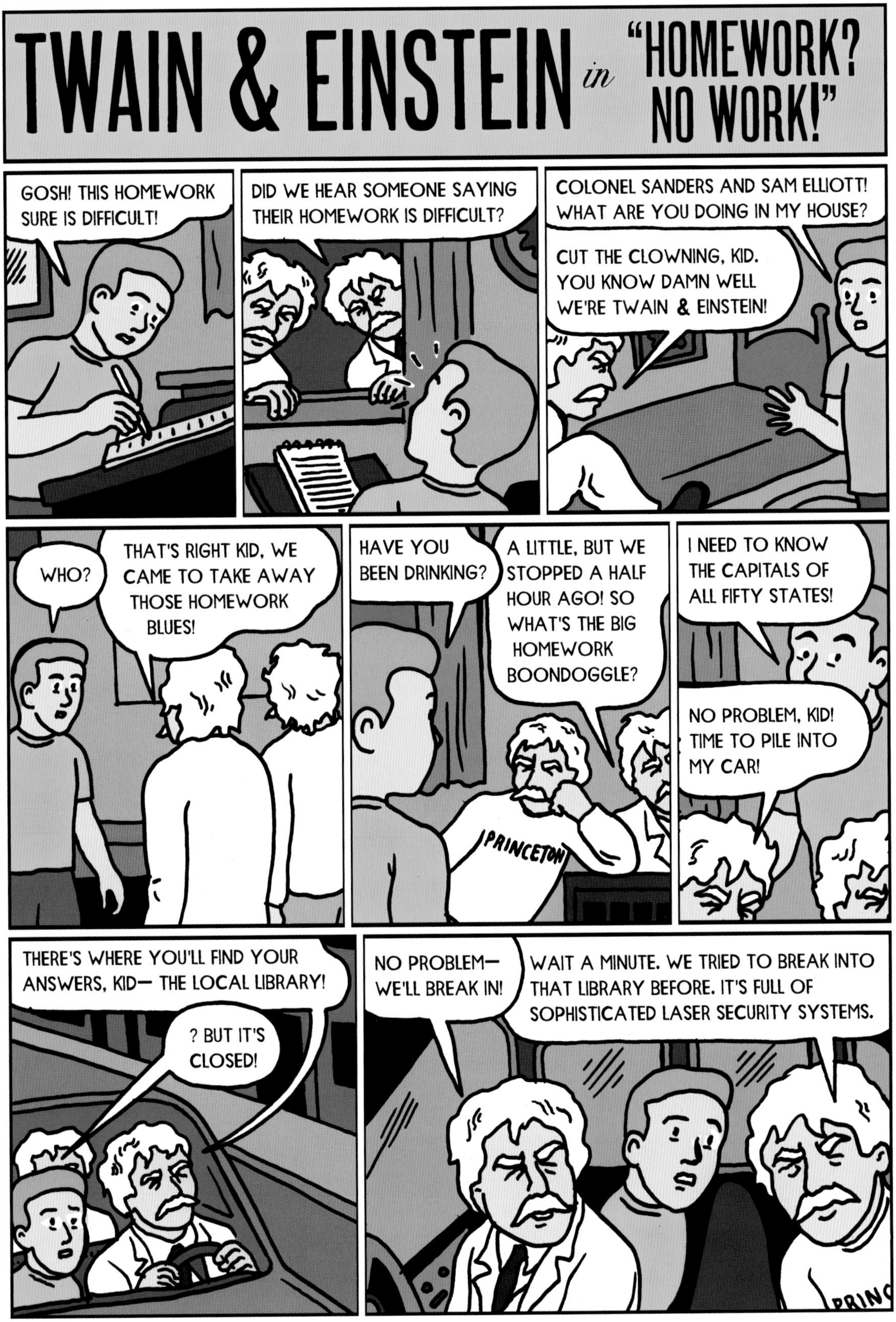
TWAIN & EINSTEIN in "HOMEWORK? NO WORK!"
GOSH! THIS HOMEWORK SURE IS DIFFICULT!
DID WE HEAR SOMEONE SAYING THEIR HOMEWORK IS DIFFICULT?
COLONEL SANDERS AND SAM ELLIOTT! WHAT ARE YOU DOING IN MY HOUSE?
CUT THE CLOWNING, KID. YOU KNOW DAMN WELL WE'RE TWAIN & EINSTEIN!
WHO?
THAT'S RIGHT KID, WE CAME TO TAKE AWAY THOSE HOMEWORK BLUES!
HAVE YOU BEEN DRINKING?
A LITTLE, BUT WE STOPPED A HALF HOUR AGO! SO WHAT'S THE BIG HOMEWORK BOONDOGGLE?
PRINCETON
I NEED TO KNOW THE CAPITALS OF ALL FIFTY STATES!
NO PROBLEM, KID! TIME TO PILE INTO MY CAR!
THERE'S WHERE YOU'LL FIND YOUR ANSWERS, KID— THE LOCAL LIBRARY!
? BUT IT'S CLOSED!
NO PROBLEM— WE'LL BREAK IN!
WAIT A MINUTE. WE TRIED TO BREAK INTO THAT LIBRARY BEFORE. IT'S FULL OF SOPHISTICATED LASER SECURITY SYSTEMS.

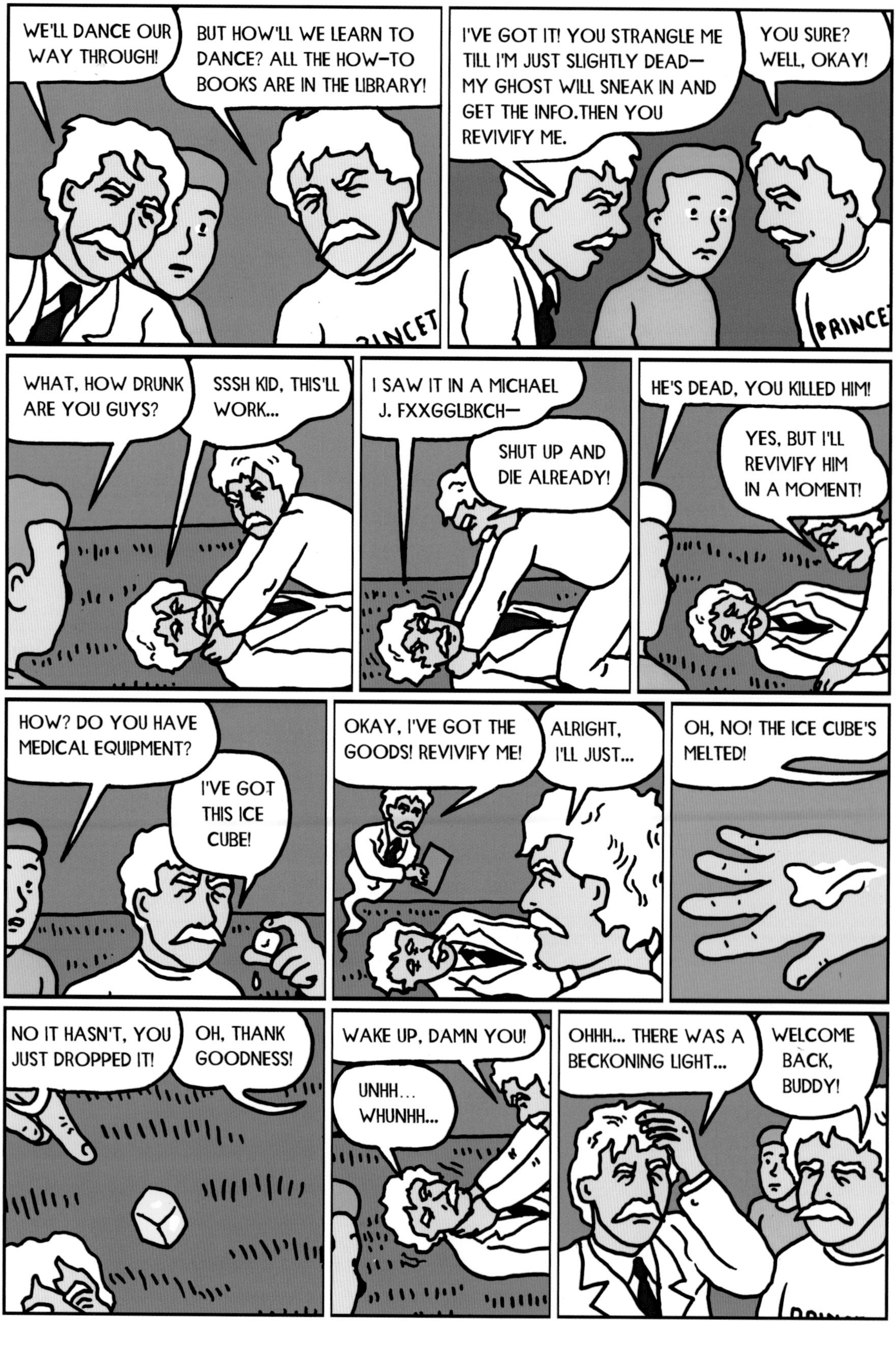
WE'LL DANCE OUR WAY THROUGH!
BUT HOW'LL WE LEARN TO DANCE? ALL THE HOW-TO BOOKS ARE IN THE LIBRARY!
PRINCET
I'VE GOT IT! YOU STRANGLE ME TILL I'M JUST SLIGHTLY DEAD— MY GHOST WILL SNEAK IN AND GET THE INFO.THEN YOU REVIVIFY ME.
YOU SURE? WELL, OKAY!
PRINCET
WHAT, HOW DRUNK ARE YOU GUYS?
SSSH KID, THIS'LL WORK...
I SAW IT IN A MICHAEL J. FXXGGLBKCH—
SHUT UP AND DIE ALREADY!
HE'S DEAD, YOU KILLED HIM!
YES, BUT I'LL REVIVIFY HIM IN A MOMENT!
HOW? DO YOU HAVE MEDICAL EQUIPMENT?
I'VE GOT THIS ICE CUBE!
OKAY, I'VE GOT THE GOODS! REVIVIFY ME!
ALRIGHT, I'LL JUST...
OH, NO! THE ICE CUBE'S MELTED!
NO IT HASN'T, YOU JUST DROPPED IT!
OH, THANK GOODNESS!
WAKE UP, DAMN YOU!
UNHH... WHUNHH...
OHHH... THERE WAS A BECKONING LIGHT...
WELCOME BACK, BUDDY!

OKAY, SO HERE ARE THE FILES ON HOW TO DANCE OUR WAY THROUGH A LASER SYSTEM!
GREAT, LET'S GET STUDYING!
PRIVATE
OR WE COULD GO TRY THAT STRANGLING THING ON EACH OTHER OUTSIDE THE YWCA!
HEY KID, WOULD YOU MIND WALKING HOME?
!
SOON—
OKAY, LET'S STRANGLE EACH OTHER!
HNNNGGHH!
NNNGGGHH!
IT'S NO USE! WHENEVER YOU GET CLOSE TO SUCCEEDING MY GRIP WEAKENS, AND VICE VERSA!
BAH— WE CAN'T BECOME GHOSTS!
WHY DON'T WE JUST PRETEND?
?
WOOOOOHH! WE'RE GHOSTS!
OUR RESTLESS SPIRITS SEEK THE PLACATION OF NUDITY! AAAHHHH!!
AND—
FRANKLY, I'M SADDENED BY THIS TYPE OF BEHAVIOR. A GREAT WRITER— SOME SAY THE GREATEST THIS COUNTRY HAS EVER PRODUCED— AND A PHYSICIST WHO TOOK WHAT WE KNEW ABOUT THE UNIVERSE AND SET IT UPSIDE DOWN. YET HERE YOU ARE BEHAVING LIKE A COUPLE OF DUMB COLLEGE KIDS. NOW WHAT DO YOU HAVE TO SAY FOR YOURSELVES?
WE'RE ACTUALLY COLONEL SANDERS AND SAM ELLIOTT

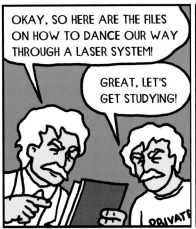

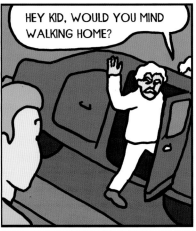

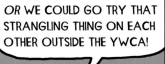

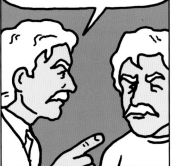

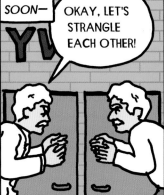

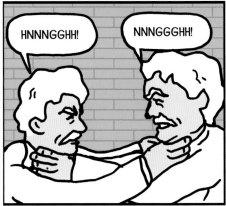

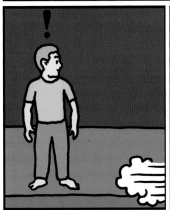

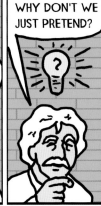

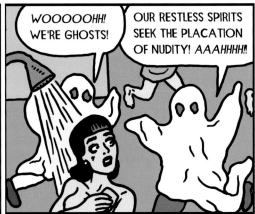

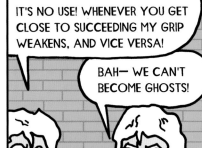

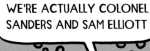

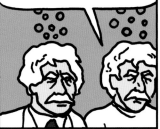

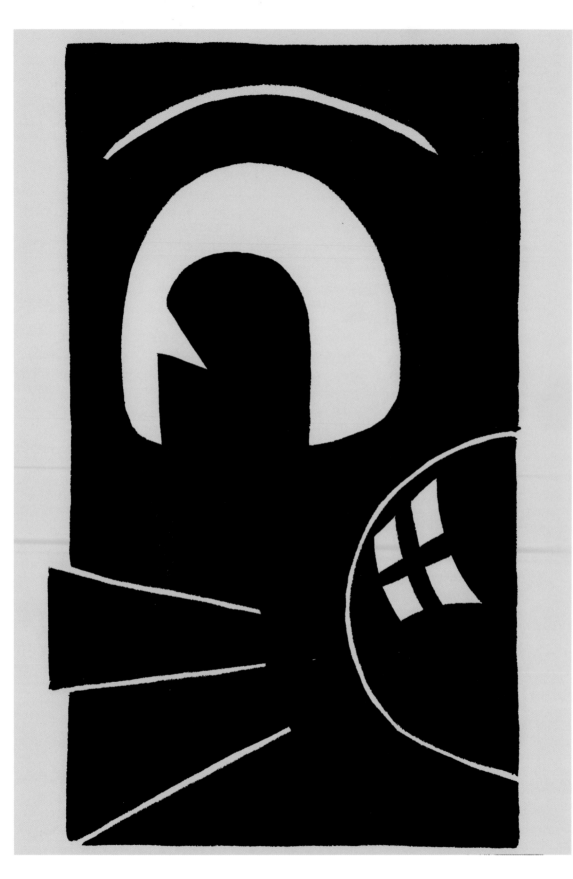